THE

50 GREATEST PLAYERS

IN

PHILADELPHIA EAGLES

HISTORY

ROBERT W. COHEN

LYONS
PRESS

Guilford, Connecticut

An imprint of The Rowman & Littlefield Publishing Group, Inc.
4501 Forbes Blvd., Ste. 200
Lanham, MD 20706
www.rowman.com

Distributed by NATIONAL BOOK NETWORK

British Library Cataloguing in Publication Information available

Library of Congress Cataloging-in-Publication Data

Names: Cohen, Robert W., author.
Title: The 50 greatest players in Philadelphia Eagles history / Robert W. Cohen.
Other titles: Fifty greatest players in Philadelphia Eagles history
Description: Guilford, Connecticut : Lyons Press, [2019] | Includes bibliographical references.
Identifiers: LCCN 2019014593 (print) | LCCN 2019021883 (ebook) | ISBN 9781493038206 (e-book) | ISBN 9781493038190 (hardback : alk. paper)
Subjects: LCSH: Philadelphia Eagles (Football team)—History. | Philadelphia Eagles (Football team)—Biography. | Football players—Pennsylvania—Philadelphia—Biography. | Football players—Rating of—United States.
Classification: LCC GV956.P44 (ebook) | LCC GV956.P44 C64 2019 (print) | DDC
796.332/640974811—dc23
LC record available at https://lccn.loc.gov/2019014593

This book is dedicated to my beloved Smoky,
who passed away during its writing.

— CONTENTS —

— ACKNOWLEDGMENTS —

I wish to thank Troy Kinunen of MEARSonlineauctions.com, Kate of RMYauctions.com, Richard Albersheim of AlbersheimsStore.com, Pristine Auction.com, SportsMemorabilia.com, BoxingTreasures.com, FootballCard Gallery.com, DynastySports.com, MainlineAutographs.com, Autographs Madeasy, The Philadelphia Connection Store, Poppel Sports, George A. Kitrinos, Keith Allison, Darrin Schieber, Matt Bresee, Kevin Burkett, Matthew Straubmuller, Andrei Snitko, Jeffrey Beall, Kevin Doohan, Donna T. Jeffries, Keith Lovett, Luis Antonio Rodriguez Ochoa, Scott Miller, Eliza Devroe, and Diana Quinlan, each of whom generously contributed to the photographic content of this work.

— INTRODUCTION —

THE EAGLE LEGACY

The Philadelphia Eagles came into being in 1933, two years after the city's first NFL team, the Frankford Yellow Jackets, ceased operations after going bankrupt. Granted an expansion franchise by the league office in exchange for an entry fee of $2,500, a syndicate headed by former University of Pennsylvania teammates Lud Wray and Bert Bell inherited the NFL rights to the Philadelphia area, after which it assembled an almost entirely new team, retaining the services of only one member of the 1931 Yellow Jackets. Drawing inspiration from the "blue eagle," which served as the insignia of President Franklin D. Roosevelt's National Recovery Act, Bell and Wray named their new franchise the Philadelphia Eagles, with Bell taking on the roles of president and general manager and Wray assuming head-coaching duties.

Taking up residence in the NFL's Eastern Division, which they shared with the New York Giants, Brooklyn Dodgers, Boston Redskins, and Pittsburgh Pirates (who eventually became known as the Steelers), the Eagles experienced very little success their first three seasons under Wray while playing their home games at Philadelphia's Baker Bowl, compiling an overall record of just 9-21-1 from 1933 to 1935. Continuing to struggle after they moved into Philadelphia Municipal Stadium and Bell replaced Wray at the helm in 1936, the Eagles finished at, or near, the bottom of the division standings in each of the next five seasons, posting more than two victories just once during that time.

The Eagles remained cellar dwellers after they changed their home venue to Connie Mack Stadium in 1940, compiling a record of just 1-10 their first year there. However, things finally began to turn around for them shortly after a complicated change in ownership occurred prior to the start of the ensuing campaign. After Wray sold his half-interest in the team to Art Rooney, who had just sold the Pittsburgh Steelers to Alexis Thompson, Bell/Rooney and Thompson swapped franchises, but not teams. Bell/Rooney's entire Eagles corporate organization, including most of the players, moved to Pittsburgh, while Thompson's Steelers moved to Philadelphia, leaving only the team nicknames in their original cities. After assuming ownership of the revamped Eagles, Thompson hired former MLB outfielder, pro football player, and college football coach Earle "Greasy" Neale to guide his team from the sidelines. Although the Eagles won a total of only four games their first two years under Neale, they posted a winning mark in each of the next seven seasons, capturing their first division title in 1947, before winning the NFL championship in both 1948 and 1949.

The Eagle teams of the late-1940s proved to be the finest in all of football, appearing in three consecutive NFL title games. After dropping a 28–21 decision to the Chicago Cardinals in the 1947 title tilt, the Eagles avenged that loss the following year by claiming their first league championship with a 7–0 victory over the Cardinals in a contest played in a blinding snowstorm. Returning to the championship game once again in 1949, the Eagles capped off a brilliant 11-1 campaign in which they outscored their opponents by a combined margin of 364–134 by shutting out the Los Angeles Rams by a score of 14–0. Although receiver Pete Pihos and two-way linemen Al Wistert, Vic Sears, and Frank "Bucko" Kilroy all starred for the Eagles during their period of dominance, running back Steve Van Buren established himself as the team's most recognizable figure and first truly great player, leading the NFL in rushing four times between 1945 and 1949.

The 1949 campaign also marked the end of the Alexis Thompson era in Philadelphia, with the Eagles' owner selling his team to a syndicate of 100 buyers known as the "Happy Hundred" that included noted Philadelphia businessman James P. Clark and Leonard Tose, whose name eventually became quite familiar to Eagles fans. More changes followed, with Greasy Neale announcing his retirement after the Eagles finished just 6-6 in 1950, leading to a revolving door of head coaches in the "City of Brotherly Love" over the course of the next several seasons. After new head man Bo McMillin retired due to terminal stomach cancer just two games into the 1951 campaign, assistant coach Wayne Millner assumed control of the team for the rest of the year. Former Wichita State University head coach Jim Trimble replaced Millner at the helm in 1952, leading the Eagles to an overall record of 25-20-3 the next four seasons, before being relieved of his duties following the conclusion of the 1955 campaign. Hugh Devore subsequently led the Eagles to an underwhelming mark of 7-16-1 the next two years, before being replaced by former college and San Francisco 49ers head coach Buck Shaw in 1958, the same year the Eagles began playing their home games at Franklin Field—a 60,658-seat stadium located at the eastern edge of the University of Pennsylvania's campus that originally opened in 1895.

Although the Eagles compiled a winning record just four times during the 1950s, they featured several outstanding players during that time. Pete Pihos remained one of the best receivers in the game, while fellow receivers Pete Retzlaff and Tommy McDonald also gradually emerged as top threats on offense. Bobby Walston proved to be one of the league's most reliable receivers and placekickers. And Chuck Bednarik, who first arrived in Philadelphia in 1949, starred on both sides of the ball for the Eagles throughout the decade, establishing himself as one of the greatest and most beloved players in franchise history.

After going just 2-9-1 in Buck Shaw's first year at the helm, the Eagles improved dramatically in 1959, compiling a mark of 7-5 that earned them a second-place finish in the NFL's Eastern Division, which they shared at the time with the New York Giants, Cleveland Browns, Pittsburgh Steelers, Washington Redskins, and Chicago Cardinals. The Eagles surprised everyone by emerging as the class of the league the following year, concluding the 1960 campaign with a regular-season record of 10-2, before winning their first NFL title in more than a decade by earning a hard-fought 17–13 victory over Vince Lombardi's Green Bay Packers in the NFL championship game. Led by Hall of Fame quarterback Norm Van Brocklin, Pro Bowl receivers Retzlaff and McDonald, and the incomparable Bednarik, who sealed Philadelphia's win over Green Bay with a game-saving tackle of running back Jim Taylor in the closing moments, the 1960 Eagles featured several excellent players. Yet, they reached the pinnacle of their sport largely because of their grit and determination, which enabled them to overcome teams that possessed even more talent.

With Buck Shaw choosing to announce his retirement following the conclusion of the 1960 campaign, ownership elected to replace him with former assistant coach Nick Skorich, who led a strong Eagles team that featured Bednarik and talented young players such as quarterback Sonny Jurgensen, linebacker Maxie Baughan, and running back/kickoff returner Timmy Brown to a 10-4 record and a close second-place finish in the NFL East his first year in charge. However, bad management, poor decision-making, and a lack of leadership subsequently caused the Eagles to enter in to an extended period of mediocrity that lasted 16 years. After the Eagles posted a total of only five victories in 1962 and 1963, Skorich was relieved of his duties by new team owner Jerry Wolman, a 36-year-old millionaire Washington developer who purchased the club from the 65 shareholders who remained from the original "Happy Hundred." Wolman immediately replaced Skorich with former Cardinals and Washington Redskins head coach Joe Kuharich, who spent the next five years running the Eagles into the ground, although they managed to win nine games under him in 1966. In addition to trading Jurgensen to Washington for journeyman signal-caller Norm Snead in 1964, Kuharich made poor use of the NFL Draft, selecting only two players (Bob Brown and Ben Hawkins) who ended up making much of an impact in Philadelphia. After the Eagles finished just 2-12 in 1968, Kuharich received his walking papers from new owner Leonard Tose, the self-made trucking millionaire who purchased the team from Wolman at season's end.

Unfortunately, the change in ownership did little to alter the fortunes of the Eagles, who failed to post a winning record in any of the next seven seasons, during which time they moved into newly built Veterans Stadium. Completed by the start of the 1971 campaign and located at the northeast corner of Broad Street and Pattison Avenue, Veterans Stadium, which seated 65,358 patrons for football and 56,371 for baseball, ended up serving as home to both the Eagles and Phillies for the next 32 years. Yet, despite their new surroundings and the outstanding performances of talented players such as wide receiver Harold Carmichael, safeties Bill Bradley and Randy Logan, and perennial All-Pro linebacker Bill Bergey, the Eagles continued to struggle on the field, compiling an overall record of just 31-62-5 from 1969 to 1975, as Jerry Williams (1969–1971), Ed Khayat (1971–1972), and Mike McCormack (1973–1975) all took turns coaching the team.

Displeased with the Eagles' 4-10 finish in 1975, Leonard Tose fired McCormack and replaced him with former UCLA head coach Dick Vermeil, who led the Bruins to a 9-2-1 record and a victory over number one ranked Ohio State in the Rose Bowl the previous season. Although the Eagles initially failed to show much improvement under the energetic and upbeat Vermeil, winning a total of only nine games his first two years in charge, they embraced his enthusiastic attitude, which, coupled with the additions of quarterback Ron Jaworski and running back Wilbert Montgomery, the continued outstanding play of Bergey and Carmichael, and one of the league's hardest-hitting defenses, helped them advance to the playoffs as a wild card in 1978. After earning another wild card berth the following year, the Eagles claimed their first division title in 20 seasons in 1980 by compiling a record of 12-4. They subsequently posted victories over the

Minnesota Vikings (31–16) and Dallas Cowboys (20–7) in the playoffs, before losing to the Oakland Raiders by a score of 27–10 in Super Bowl XV.

The Eagles appeared to be headed for another NFC title in 1981, winning their first six games, before losing six of their next 10 contests and ultimately suffering an unexpected 27–21 defeat at the hands of the New York Giants in the wild card round of the playoffs. They then suffered through a dismal strike-shortened 1982 campaign, finishing last in the division with a record of 3-6, which prompted Vermeil to announce his resignation, citing "burnout" as the cause of his departure. The Eagles continued to struggle under former defensive coordinator Marion Campbell the next three years, posting an overall mark of just 18-29-1 from 1983 to 1985, before new team owner, Norman Braman, the billionaire car dealer who purchased the club from Leonard Tose in April 1985, replaced him with Buddy Ryan, who helped build the dominant Chicago Bears defense of the 1980s. After compiling a losing record under Ryan in each of the next two seasons, the Eagles, led by star quarterback Randall Cunningham and a smothering defense that included Clyde Simmons, Jerome Brown, and the great Reggie White up front, Seth Joyner and Byron Evans at linebacker, and Eric Allen, Andre Waters, and Wes Hopkins in the secondary, advanced to the playoffs three straight times. But, with the outspoken Ryan failing to lead them to a single postseason victory despite his tough talk and bold predictions, Braman decided to replace him with offensive coordinator Rick Kotite following the conclusion of the 1990 campaign.

The Eagles initially performed well under Kotite, compiling a record of 10-6 in 1991, before making the playoffs as a wild card the following year by going 11-5. However, the loss of Jerome Brown, who died tragically in a high-speed automobile crash on June 25, 1992, and the free agent departure of Reggie White prior to the start of the 1993 campaign ultimately proved to be too much to overcome, causing the Eagles to post an overall mark of just 15-17 from 1993 to 1994, and prompting Braman to sell the team to movie producer and current owner Jeffrey Lurie, who wasted no time in relieving Kotite of his duties.

Following the departure of Kotite, former San Francisco 49ers defensive coordinator Ray Rhodes assumed control of the Eagles, leading them to a 10-6 finish and a playoff berth his first year in charge. However, after defeating the Detroit Lions by a score of 58–37 in the NFC wild card game, the Eagles suffered a 30–11 defeat at the hands of the arch-rival Dallas Cowboys in the divisional round of the postseason tournament the following week. Returning to the playoffs in 1996, the Eagles failed to advance beyond the first round, losing the wild card game to the 49ers by a score of

14–0. Rhodes remained in Philadelphia two more years, losing his job after the Eagles won a total of only nine games in 1997 and 1998.

After firing Rhodes, Lurie replaced him with former Packers assistant coach Andy Reid, who spent the previous seven seasons in Green Bay developing the skills of future Hall of Fame QB Brett Favre. Making the drafting of quarterback Donovan McNabb with the second overall pick of the 1999 NFL Draft one of his first moves, Reid turned the Eagles into perennial contenders before long, leading them to five straight playoff appearances, four consecutive division titles, and one trip to the Super Bowl between 2000 and 2004. After being eliminated by the Giants in the divisional round of the postseason tournament in 2000, the Eagles appeared in four straight conference championship games, losing to the St. Louis Rams in 2001, the Tampa Bay Buccaneers in 2002, and the Carolina Panthers in 2003, before capturing their second NFC title by recording a 27–10 victory over the Atlanta Falcons in the 2004 conference championship game. However, they subsequently came up just short against New England in Super Bowl XXXIX, losing to the Patriots by a score of 24–21.

Over the course of those five seasons, the Eagles also christened Lincoln Financial Field as their new home. Located in South Philadelphia, on Pattison Avenue, between 11th and South Darien Streets, Lincoln Financial, which has a seating capacity of 69,176, officially opened to the public on August 3, 2003. It has since hosted several notable events, including three divisional round playoff games and three NFC championship games.

Despite making the playoffs four more times under Reid from 2005 to 2012, the Eagles failed to sustain the same level of excellence, compiling an overall record during that time of 66-61-1, and advancing beyond the first round of the postseason tournament just twice. A 4-12 finish in 2012 sealed Reid's fate, with Lurie choosing to replace him with former Oregon head coach Chip Kelly at season's end. Reid left Philadelphia having led the Eagles to an overall record of 130-93-1 over 14 seasons, making him the longest-tenured and winningest coach in franchise history. In addition to McNabb, other players that excelled for the Eagles under Reid include running back LeSean McCoy, wide receiver DeSean Jackson, running back/punt returner Brian Westbrook, defensive end Trent Cole, linebacker Jeremiah Trotter, and defensive backs Troy Vincent and Brian Dawkins.

The Eagles performed well their first two seasons under Kelly, posting back-to-back 10-6 records and capturing the division title in 2013, before losing to the New Orleans Saints by a score of 26–24 in the opening round of the playoffs. However, after they went just 7-9 in 2015, Kelly received his pink slip from Lurie, who subsequently hired Kansas City Chiefs offensive coordinator Doug Pederson to be his replacement. After posting an identical 7-9 mark their first year under Pederson, the Eagles, led by second-year quarterback Carson Wentz and one of the league's stingiest defenses, finished a conference-best 13-3 in 2017. Nevertheless, with Wentz sidelined by a late-season injury, most pundits considered them a longshot to win the NFC title heading into the playoffs. Displaying tremendous resolve, the Eagles went on to defeat the Atlanta Falcons by a score of 15–10 in the divisional round of the postseason tournament, before claiming the conference championship with a lopsided 38–7 victory over the Minnesota Vikings in the NFC title game. With backup quarterback Nick Foles performing exceptionally well behind center, the Eagles then recorded a 41–33 victory over the New England Patriots in Super Bowl LII, giving them their fourth league championship.

Besieged by injuries, and perhaps suffering from a "Super Bowl hangover," the Eagles got off to a slow start in 2018, losing six of their first 10 games, before rebounding to win five of their final six contests, thereby sneaking into the playoffs as a wild card. Displaying their championship mettle, the Eagles then posted a heart-stopping 16–15 victory over the favored Chicago Bears in the first round of the postseason tournament. However, they subsequently suffered a 20–14 defeat at the hands of the New Orleans Saints in their divisional round playoff matchup, ending their dreams of repeating as NFL champions. Nevertheless, with a defense anchored by All-Pro tackle Fletcher Cox and an offense led by Wentz, Pro Bowl tight end Zach Ertz, and other standout performers such as receiver Nelson Agholor and linemen Jason Kelce and Lane Johnson, the Eagles figure to be perennial contenders for conference championship honors in the years ahead. Their next NFC title will be their fourth. They have also won 14 division titles, four NFL championships, and one Super Bowl. Featuring a plethora of exceptional performers through the years, the Eagles have inducted 34 players into their Hall of Fame, nine of whom have had their numbers retired by the team. Meanwhile, 17 members of the Pro Football Hall of Fame spent at least one full season in Philadelphia, with 10 of those men wearing an Eagles uniform during many of their peak seasons.

FACTORS USED TO DETERMINE RANKINGS

It should come as no surprise that selecting the 50 greatest players ever to perform for a team with the rich history of the Eagles presented quite a challenge. Even after narrowing the field down to a mere 50 men, I still needed to devise a method of ranking the elite players that remained.

Certainly, the names of Reggie White, Chuck Bednarik, Steve Van Buren, Clyde Simmons, Brian Dawkins, and Donovan McNabb would appear at, or near, the top of virtually everyone's list, although the order might vary somewhat from one person to the next. Several other outstanding performers have gained general recognition through the years as being among the greatest players ever to wear an Eagles uniform. Bill Bergey, Wilbert Montgomery, Randall Cunningham, and Seth Joyner head the list of other Eagles icons. But, how does one compare players who lined up on opposite sides of the ball with any degree of certainty? Furthermore, how does one differentiate between the pass-rushing and run-stopping skills of linemen such as Reggie White and Clyde Simmons and the ball-hawking skills of defensive backs such as Brian Dawkins and Bill Bradley? And, on the offensive end, how can a direct correlation be made between the contributions made by standout lineman Jason Peters and skill position players such as Steve Van Buren and Pete Retzlaff? And then there is the great Chuck Bednarik, who starred on both sides of the ball for the Eagles for more than a decade. After initially deciding whom to include on my list, I then needed to determine what criteria I should use to formulate my final rankings.

The first thing I decided to examine was the level of dominance a player attained during his time with the Eagles. How often did he lead the NFL in a major statistical category? Did he ever capture league MVP honors? How many times did he earn a trip to the Pro Bowl or a spot on the All-Pro Team?

I also chose to assess the level of statistical compilation a player achieved while wearing an Eagles uniform. I reviewed where he ranks among the team's all-time leaders in those statistical categories most pertinent to his position. Of course, even the method of using statistics as a measuring stick has its inherent flaws. Although the level of success a team experiences rushing and passing the ball is impacted greatly by the performance of its offensive line, there really is no way to quantifiably measure the level of play reached by each individual offensive lineman. Conversely, the play of the offensive line affects tremendously the statistics compiled by a team's quarterback and running backs. Furthermore, the NFL did not keep an official record of defensive numbers such as tackles and quarterback sacks until the 1980s (although the Eagles kept their own records prior to that). In addition, when examining the statistics compiled by offensive players, the era during which a quarterback, running back, or wide receiver competed must be factored into the equation.

To illustrate my last point, rules changes instituted by the league office have opened up the game considerably over the course of the last two decades. Quarterbacks are accorded far more protection than ever before, and officials have also been instructed to limit the amount of contact defensive backs are allowed to make with wide receivers. As a result, the game has experienced an offensive explosion, with quarterbacks and receivers posting numbers players from prior generations rarely even approached. That being the case, one must place the numbers Donovan McNabb compiled during his career in their proper context when comparing him to other top Eagles quarterbacks such as Randall Cunningham and Ron Jaworski. Similarly, the statistics posted by DeSean Jackson must be viewed in moderation when comparing him to previous Eagles wideouts Tommy McDonald and Pete Pihos.

Other important factors I needed to consider were the overall contributions a player made to the success of the team, the degree to which he improved the fortunes of the club during his time in Philadelphia, and the manner in which he impacted the team, both on and off the field. While the number of championships and division titles the Eagles won during a player's years with the team certainly factored into the equation, I chose not to deny a top performer his rightful place on the list if his years in Philadelphia happened to coincide with a lack of overall success by the club. As a result, the names of players such as Timmy Brown and Bill Bradley will appear in these rankings.

One other thing I should mention is that I only considered a player's performance while playing for the Eagles when formulating my rankings. That being the case, the name of Hall of Fame quarterback Norm Van Brocklin, who had most of his finest seasons for the Los Angeles Rams, may appear lower on this list than one might expect. Meanwhile, the names of other standout performers such as Sonny Jurgensen and Terrell Owens are nowhere to be found.

Having established the guidelines to be used throughout this book, the time has come to reveal the 50 greatest players in Eagles history, starting with number 1 and working our way down to number 50.

1

― REGGIE WHITE ―

Reggie White received stiff competition from Chuck Bednarik and Steve Van Buren for the number one spot in these rankings, with Bednarik's exceptional two-way play for more than a decade making him a particularly strong contender. Nevertheless, the level of dominance that White displayed during his eight seasons in Philadelphia enabled him to finish just ahead of his two closest rivals for the top spot on this list. Considered by many football experts to be the greatest defensive end in the history of the game, White earned more individual accolades over the course of his 15-year NFL career than any other player ever to man the position. Having most of his finest seasons for the Eagles from 1985 to 1992, White gained Pro Bowl and All-Pro recognition seven times each as a member of the team, with his extraordinary play in 1987 earning him NFL Defensive Player of the Year honors for the first of two times. The franchise's all-time leader in sacks, White brought down opposing quarterbacks behind the line of scrimmage more than 10 times in each of his eight seasons with the Eagles, ending his time in Philadelphia with 124 sacks in only 121 games. An outstanding run-defender as well, White also recorded more than 100 tackles five times, with his 794 solo stops placing him fifth in team annals. White's brilliant play helped the Eagles capture one division title and advance to the playoffs four times, prompting the team to eventually induct him into its Hall of Fame and retire his #92.

Born in Chattanooga, Tennessee, on December 19, 1961, Reginald Howard White spent his early years being raised by his unwed mother, before being placed with his grandmother, Mildred Dodd, after he turned eight years of age. Inspired by the ministers and teachers he met at the local Baptist church he attended regularly, White, according to his mother, announced at the age of 12 that he wanted to be two things: a football player and a minister. Reflecting back on his youth, White told *Sports Illustrated*, "When I was a child, I was always bigger than the other kids.

Kids used to call me Bigfoot or Land of the Giant. They'd tease me and run away. Around seventh grade, I found something I was good at. I could play football, and I could use my size and achieve success by playing within the rules. I remember telling my mother that someday I would be a professional football player and I'd take care of her for the rest of her life."

After lettering in football, basketball, and track and field at Howard

High School, White, who became an ordained minister at the age of 17, accepted an athletic scholarship from the University of Tennessee. Acquiring the nickname "The Minister of Defense" while in college, White set school records for most sacks in a career (32) and in a season (15). Performing particularly well as a senior in 1983, White recorded 100 tackles (72 solo), nine tackles for loss, and 15 sacks, en route to earning SEC Player of the Year and consensus All-America honors.

Subsequently selected by the Memphis Showboats in the 1984 USFL Territorial Draft, and by the Philadelphia Eagles with the fourth overall pick of the 1984 NFL Supplemental Draft, White chose to remain close to home and signed a five-year deal with Memphis. However, after registering a total of 23½ sacks in his two years with the Showboats, White signed with the Eagles when the USFL folded in 1985.

Many people consider Reggie White to be the greatest defensive end ever to play the game.
Courtesy of George A. Kitrinos

Thrilled that a player of White's ability became available to his team, Eagles owner Norman Braman stated at the news conference announcing his signing, "From the very outset, Marion [Campbell] has been mentioning Reggie White—'Try to get him, try to get him'—and I tell you that, through a long and very difficult process, I am pleased to announce that Sara [White's wife] and Reggie White are part of the Philadelphia Eagles family. He'll be one of the great anchors of an already formidable defense. . . . It's very rare that a player of Reggie's quality comes along. Reggie has been described as a franchise player, and we'll look on him in that manner. We were very lucky to get him."

White, in turn, told the assembled media, "I am glad to be here. This was always my dream as a kid. I have always wanted to be an NFL player and today I have the opportunity."

Joining the Eagles three weeks into the 1985 campaign, White ended up recording 100 tackles and tying for the team lead with 13 sacks, with his exceptional play at left defensive end earning him NFL Defensive Rookie of the Year honors. He followed that up with another outstanding season, gaining Pro Bowl and All-Pro recognition for the first of 13 straight times by registering 98 tackles and 18 sacks, which placed him third in the league rankings. Performing even better during the strike-shortened 1987 campaign, White earned NFL Defensive Player of the Year honors by recording a franchise record and league-leading 21 sacks in just 12 games. Turning in another virtuoso performance the following year, White led the Eagles to the NFC East title by recording 133 tackles and a league-high 18 sacks.

Virtually impossible to block one-on-one due to his size, strength, and quickness, the 6'5", 291-pound White typically found himself being engaged by multiple blockers. But, no matter how opposing teams tried to slow him down, White invariably forced them to alter their approach by creating havoc in the offensive backfield. In discussing how he prepared himself mentally to play against White, longtime New York Giants quarterback Phil Simms offered, "You didn't worry about going over your game plan. I truly would sit on my stool in the locker room going, 'OK now. Hang in there. Alright. You know, hang in there. It's going to be rough. Just, you know, come on, hang.' You had to give yourself a pep talk to be tough enough to endure what was going to happen, because it always did happen."

Simms then added, "He was the greatest, he was the most talented person I ever played against in the league, and you know I'm putting some unbelievable players in that category."

Eagles head coach Buddy Ryan, who built his defense around White after he assumed control of the team in 1986, agreed with Simms's assessment, once calling his best player "the perfect defensive lineman . . . probably the most gifted defensive athlete I've ever been around."

Meanwhile, Eagles linebacker Seth Joyner said of his longtime teammate, "He was the most dominant player I have ever seen. Size, strength, speed. He could run as fast as most linebackers."

Although White built much of his reputation on his ability to sack opposing quarterbacks, he also excelled against the run, revealing the pride he took in that aspect of his game when he told *Sports Illustrated,* "In high school and college, you're taught to hit the ground on a double team. Here, you're expected to take it on. I get double-teamed on every play, so

I expect it. Sacks are great, and they get you elected to the Pro Bowl. But I've always felt that a great defensive lineman has to play the run and pass equally well. . . . The so-called men of the game pride themselves on being complete players."

An outstanding team leader as well, White used his engaging personality to bring humor to the locker room. Meanwhile, he served as a spiritual and emotional leader to his teammates, none of whom ever recalled hearing him curse or seeing him fight.

Yet, as much as White gave of himself to the Eagles, he also contributed significantly to the community, spending much of his free time preaching on street corners in Philadelphia's troubled inner-city neighborhoods, donating money to dozens of Christian outreach organizations, and speaking as a member of the Fellowship of Christian Athletes. When asked about his philanthropic endeavors, White told *Sports Illustrated*, "I believe that I've been blessed with physical ability in order to gain a platform to preach the gospel. A lot of people look at athletes as role models, and to be successful as an athlete, I've got to do what I do, hard but fair . . . I try to live a certain way, and maybe that'll have some kind of effect. I think God has allowed me to have an impact on a few people's lives."

White continued to excel on the playing field for the Eagles for four more years, averaging 13½ sacks and 97 tackles from 1989 to 1992, while also forcing 12 fumbles and recovering six others. Nevertheless, bad feelings gradually developed between him and team owner Norman Braman, with Eagles historian and noted columnist Ray Didinger writing, "They split on so many issues—the 1987 players' strike, the 1990 firing of head coach Buddy Ryan, the 1992 loss of free agent Keith Jackson—that, in the end, they had nothing to build on. There was no trust, no goodwill to serve as the foundation for constructive talks."

Things finally came to a head when White became a free agent following the conclusion of the 1992 campaign. Upset that Braman failed to make him an offer during the early stages of his free agency, and disappointed that head coach Rich Kotite hadn't contacted him, White stated during a conference call with Philadelphia writers from his agent's office, "It's somewhat discouraging. In some ways, I've gotten my hopes up and then they've torn it down. I believe I can get money anywhere, but I'm looking for a team that makes a commitment to winning. I have nothing personal against Norman, but I think Norman is so business-minded that he can't see the important things needed."

White then added, "I'm sort of getting fed up with Mr. Braman bringing up things he did for me. I can't handle negotiations that way."

White also expressed his dissatisfaction with team ownership for lobbying with the league for a high draft pick if he left, suggesting, "It looks like they're trying to cover their tails. It's like they're preparing to lose me, instead of trying to keep me."

White ultimately elected to sign a four-year, $17 million deal with the Packers, later claiming that God told him to go to Green Bay. After signing with the Packers, White told the *Philadelphia Daily News* that his relationship with Braman "had deteriorated to a point where he was probably glad to see me go."

White recorded more sacks than anyone else in franchise history.
Courtesy of George A. Kitrinos

In addition to recording 124 sacks and 794 solo tackles during his time in Philadelphia, White forced 18 fumbles, recovered 11 others, intercepted two passes, and scored two touchdowns on defense.

White ended up spending six seasons in Green Bay, making a huge impact on the Packers and the city as a whole during that time. Recording 68½ sacks and 301 tackles over the course of those six seasons, White earned Pro Bowl and All-Pro honors each year, gained recognition as NFL Defensive Player of the Year for the second time in his career in 1998, and led the Packers to six straight playoff appearances, three division titles, two NFC championships, and one Super Bowl victory. Furthermore, White helped change the perception that many players in the league had of Green Bay, as team president Bob Harlan noted when he said, "Everyone thought the last place he would sign was Green Bay, and it was monumental because, not only did he sign, but he recruited for Green Bay and got guys like Sean Jones to come here. He sent a message to the rest of the NFL that Green Bay was a great place to play."

Choosing to announce his retirement following the conclusion of the 1998 campaign, White subsequently remained away from the game for one year, before electing to come out of retirement and sign with the Carolina

Panthers, for whom he recorded 5½ sacks in 2000. Retiring for good at season's end, White concluded his NFL career with 198 sacks, which leaves him second only to Bruce Smith in league history. However, his 23½ sacks as a member of the USFL's Memphis Showboats gives him a total of 221½ sacks as a professional, making him pro football's all-time sacks leader. White also recorded more than 1,100 tackles, intercepted three passes, forced 33 fumbles, and recovered 20 others, two of which he returned for touchdowns. In addition to being elected to the Pro Football Hall of Fame the first time his name appeared on the ballot, White received the additional distinctions of being named to the NFL's 75th Anniversary All-Time Team and being accorded a number 22 ranking on the *Sporting News'* 1999 list of the 100 Greatest Players in NFL History.

Unfortunately, White did not live long after his playing career ended, succumbing to cardiac arrhythmia on the morning of December 26, 2004, just one week after he celebrated his 43rd birthday. The Medical Examiner's Office subsequently speculated that the pulmonary sarcoidosis and sleep apnea from which White had suffered for years likely caused his death.

Upon learning of his passing, NFL commissioner Paul Tagliabue said, "Reggie White was a gentle warrior who will be remembered as one of the greatest defensive players in NFL history. Equally impressive as his achievements on the field was the positive impact that he made off the field and the way he served as a positive influence on so many young people."

Former Packers coach Mike Holmgren paid tribute to White by stating, "First of all, he was just a wonderful player. Then, as a person, he was just the best. He was one of the leaders, along with Brett Favre, of our football team in Green Bay. I'm a better person for having been around Reggie White."

Johnny Majors, who coached White at the University of Tennessee, commented, "He was one of the greatest players who ever put on a uniform at his position. I once referred to him as the Tony Dorsett of defensive linemen. There's never been a better one."

Brett Favre expressed his admiration for his former teammate by saying, "I had the utmost respect for Reggie White as a player. He may have been the best player I've ever seen, and he certainly was the best I've ever played with or against."

In assessing his playing career, White once said, "The thing that I know, and everyone else knows, is that no one can ever take my accomplishments away. My goal as a football player was to be the best to ever play my position. I believe I've reached my goal." You will not find any disagreement with that statement here.

EAGLES CAREER HIGHLIGHTS

Best Season

White performed magnificently for the Eagles in 1988, earning First-Team All-Pro honors by recording a league-leading 18 sacks and a career-high 133 solo tackles. However, he proved to be even more dominant during the strike-shortened 1987 campaign, when, despite playing in only 12 games, he registered a league-leading and career-best 21 sacks, recorded 76 solo tackles and four forced fumbles, and scored one touchdown, with his brilliant play gaining him recognition as the NFL Defensive Player of the Year.

Memorable Moments/Greatest Performances

Although the Eagles lost in overtime to the Giants by a score of 16–10 on September 29, 1985, White recorded his first 2½ sacks as a member of the team during the contest.

White led a defensive onslaught against Neil Lomax on November 17, 1985, registering three of the seven sacks the Eagles recorded against the St. Louis quarterback during a 24–14 win over the Cardinals.

White excelled during a 13–10 loss to the Cardinals on November 2, 1986, getting to St. Louis quarterbacks a total of four times.

White had another big game four weeks later, sacking Jim Plunkett four times during a 33–27 overtime win over the Los Angeles Raiders on November 30, 1986.

White earned NFC Defensive Player of the Week honors for the first time by sacking Steve Pelluer three times during a 23–21 victory over the Dallas Cowboys on December 14, 1986.

Although the Eagles suffered a 34–24 defeat at the hands of the Washington Redskins in the opening game of the 1987 regular season, White scored the first points of his career during the contest when he returned a fumble 70 yards for a touchdown.

White once again starred in defeat on September 25, 1988, recording four sacks during a 23–21 loss to the Minnesota Vikings.

White contributed to a 28–14 victory over the Redskins on November 12, 1990, by recording two sacks and the first of his three career interceptions, which he subsequently returned 33 yards.

White led the Eagles to a convincing 20–3 win over Green Bay in the 1991 regular-season opener by sacking Packers quarterback Don Majkowski three times, with his outstanding play earning him NFC Defensive Player of the Week honors.

White scored the last of his two career touchdowns during a 31–14 victory over the Cardinals on September 13, 1992, when he returned a recovered fumble 37 yards for a TD.

White turned in his last dominant performance as a member of the Eagles on November 22, 1992, when he recorded 3½ sacks during a 47–34 win over the New York Giants.

Notable Achievements

- Scored two career touchdowns.
- Finished in double digits in sacks eight straight times, recording 21 sacks once and 18 sacks twice.
- Recorded more than 100 tackles five times.
- Led Eagles in sacks six times and tackles once.
- Led NFL in sacks twice.
- Finished second in NFL with 15 sacks in 1991.
- Finished third in NFL with 18 sacks in 1986.
- Holds Eagles career record for most sacks (124).
- Holds Eagles single-season record for most sacks (21 in 1987).
- Ranks among Eagles career leaders with 794 solo tackles (5th) and 18 forced fumbles (4th).
- Ranks second in NFL history with 198 career sacks.
- 1988 division champion.
- Three-time NFC Defensive Player of the Week.
- 1985 NFL Defensive Rookie of the Year.
- 1987 NFL Defensive Player of the Year.
- Two-time NFC Defensive Player of the Year (1987 and 1991).
- Seven-time Pro Bowl selection (1986, 1987, 1988, 1989, 1990, 1991, and 1992).
- Six-time First-Team All-Pro selection (1986, 1987, 1988, 1989, 1990, and 1991).
- 1992 Second-Team All-Pro selection.
- Seven-time First-Team All-Conference selection (1986, 1987, 1988, 1989, 1990, 1991, and 1992).
- NFL 1980s All-Decade Team.
- NFL 1990s All-Decade Team.
- Pro Football Reference All-1990s First Team.
- Named to NFL's 75th Anniversary Team in 1994.

- Named to Eagles 75th Anniversary Team in 2007.
- Inducted into Philadelphia Eagles Hall of Fame in 2005.
- #92 retired by Eagles.
- Named to *Sporting News* All-Century Team in 1999.
- Number 22 on the *Sporting News'* 1999 list of the 100 Greatest Players in NFL History.
- Number seven on the NFL Network's 2010 list of the NFL's 100 Greatest Players.
- Elected to Pro Football Hall of Fame in 2006.

2

— CHUCK BEDNARIK —

Having fallen just short of earning the top spot on this list, Chuck Bednarik lays claim to the number two position, edging out Steve Van Buren for that distinction. The last of the NFL's "Sixty-Minute Men," Bednarik spent most of his 14 seasons in Philadelphia starring on both sides of the ball for the Eagles, excelling at center on offense and linebacker on defense. Once described as "75 percent animal and 25 percent human being" by teammate Al Wistert, who also figures prominently in our rankings, Bednarik proved to be an enormous presence on the field and in the locker room his entire time in Philly, intimidating the opposition with his intense and physical style of play, while also providing leadership to his teammates. An eight-time Pro Bowl selection and nine-time All-Pro, "Concrete Charlie," as he came to be known, helped lead the Eagles to two NFL championships, with his brilliant play also earning him many other individual honors following the conclusion of his playing career, including a spot on the NFL's 75th Anniversary Team, a number 54 ranking on the *Sporting News'* 1999 list of the 100 Greatest Players in NFL History, the retirement of his #60 by the Eagles, and induction into the Pro Football Hall of Fame.

Born in Bethlehem, Pennsylvania, on May 1, 1925, to Slovakian parents who emigrated to the United States five years earlier, Charles Philip Bednarik Jr. attended Bethlehem's Liberty Catholic High School, where he starred on the gridiron as a two-way lineman. Choosing to enlist in the US Army Air Force before finishing his senior year, Bednarik served his country during World War II as a waist-gunner aboard a B-24, flying 30 combat missions over Europe, for which he earned the Air Medal with five Oak Leaf Clusters, the European–African–Middle Eastern Campaign Medal, and five Battle Stars. Returning home following his discharge from the military, Bednarik enrolled at the University of Pennsylvania, where he spent three years starring at center and linebacker for the Quakers, earning All-America honors three times, winning the

Maxwell Award as the Top College Player as a senior in 1948, and finishing third in the Heisman Trophy voting that same year.

Subsequently selected by the Eagles with the first overall pick of the 1949 NFL Draft, Bednarik began his pro career in fine fashion, starting at center for Philadelphia's 1949 NFL championship team. The following year, he became one of a vanishing breed, beginning a string of eight straight seasons in which he played both offense and defense. Establishing himself during that time as arguably the league's finest player at both center and linebacker, Bednarik gained Pro Bowl recognition seven times and All-Pro honors in each of those eight seasons.

Although Bednarik became known for his bone-jarring hits on defense, he proved to be equally effective on the offensive side of the ball, using his burly 6'3", 235-pound frame and superb technique to provide outstanding protection for his quarterback and create holes at the line of scrimmage for Eagles running backs. A bulldozing blocker, Bednarik drew praise from George Allen in the latter's 1982 book *Pro Football's 100 Greatest Players*, with the legendary coach writing, "Chuck Bednarik not only was the best linebacker I ever saw, but he also was the best offensive center of the past 30 years, and he would have ranked right up there with Mel Hein and Bulldog Turner among the offensive linemen had I chosen to put him on that list. He was the surest, strongest snapper I've ever seen and an absolutely brutal and unbeatable blocker."

Longtime Eagles teammate Frank "Bucko" Kilroy stated, "Most people think of Bednarik as a linebacker, and he was a great linebacker, not taking anything away from Chuck. But a lot of people forget that he was far and away the best offensive center in pro football. He might have been one of the great offensive centers of all time."

In speaking of Bednarik, former Eagles coach Nick Skorich said, "This guy was a football athlete. He was a very strong blocker at center and quick as a cat off the ball."

Chuck Bednarik spent most of his career starring on both sides of the ball for the Eagles.
Courtesy of RMYAuctions.com

Yet, Bednarik, who acquired his nickname "Concrete Charlie" due to both his toughness and his part-time job of selling concrete during the offseason, built his reputation largely on his hard-hitting defensive style of play, with his most memorable hit coming at the expense of New York Giants star running back Frank Gifford, whom he forced into temporary retirement. Revealing the mentality with which he approached playing linebacker, Bednarik stated, "A linebacker is an animal. He's like a tiger or a lion that goes after prey. He wants to eat him. He wants to kick the shit out of him. That's a linebacker."

Capable of stopping an enemy runner in his tracks, Bednarik, said Cleveland Browns great Jim Brown long after the playing careers of both men ended, "was as great as any linebacker who ever lived. I don't know how old he is, but I'll bet nobody can kick his butt today." Brown then added, "He was a pure gladiator and a great football player."

In discussing his former teammate, Eagles defensive back Tom Brookshier said, "Dick Butkus was the one who manhandled people. Chuck just snapped them down like rag dolls." But Brookshier also suggested that Bednarik depended on more than just brute force to stifle opposing offenses when he stated, "He had such a sense for the game. You could do all that shifting and put all those men in motion, and Chuck still went right where the ball was."

Agreeing with Brookshier's assessment, Maxie Baughan said of his fellow Eagles linebacker, "He was probably the most instinctive football player I've ever seen."

After spending the previous eight seasons playing both offense and defense, Bednarik manned the center position almost exclusively from 1958 to 1961, although he found himself doing double-duty once again in 1960 following an injury to starting left-outside linebacker Bob Pellegrini. Looking back at the way the 1960 campaign unfolded, Bednarik recalled, "I was going to play center, which is the easiest position from a physical standpoint. It's not like linebacker, where somebody is coming at you from an angle, hitting you on every play. I was 35, but I thought I could play maybe three or four more years at center. A guy like [Oakland center] Jim Otto was still playing at 40. So, I was playing center and doing okay, then, boom, Bob Pellegrini gets hurt in Cleveland and everything changes."

Spending the final two months of the season excelling on both sides of the ball for the Eagles, Bednarik helped lead them to the NFL title, with Maxie Baughan later expressing his admiration for his teammate by saying, "I remember looking up and seeing Chuck in the (defensive) huddle. I was surprised, but then I realized, 'That's Chuck Bednarik.' You never doubt what he can do. I played the right side and Chuck played the left. Chuck Weber was in the middle, and he made the calls. Instinct is a wonderful thing, and Bednarik had it. He could read a play and get to the football and, when he did, it was one heckuva collision. Frank Gifford can tell you all about that."

"Concrete Charlie" missed just three games in 14 seasons.
Courtesy of Richard Albersheim of Albersheims .com

Bednarik, who earned Pro Bowl and All-Pro honors for the final time in 1960, spent two more seasons in Philadelphia, playing center exclusively in 1961, before starting at middle linebacker his final year in the league. Revealing what continued to drive him during the latter stages of his career, Bednarik stated during a 1961 interview, "I just want to play, that's all. I guess you can call it desire. That's the biggest asset I have. When I go out there, I want to be the greatest football player who ever lived. I realize I won't ever be, of course, but that's the attitude I play with."

Finally choosing to announce his retirement following the conclusion of the 1962 campaign, Bednarik ended his career with 20 interceptions, which he returned for a total of 268 yards and one touchdown. He also recorded a franchise-record 21 fumble recoveries and missed just three games in 14 seasons.

After spending more than a decade away from the game following his retirement, Bednarik returned to the football field to serve as an associate coach for Dick Vermeil when the latter became head coach of the Eagles in 1976. He also served as an analyst on the HBO program *Inside the NFL* for its inaugural season in 1977-78.

Continuing to be lauded for his exceptional play long after he retired, Bednarik drew praise from Arizona State head football coach Frank Kush, who stated, "Chuck Bednarik, to me, is the epitome of what the game of football is all about. I'm talking about the discipline, I'm talking about the toughness, I'm talking about the focus, I'm talking about the intensity. He will go down in history as probably one of the toughest individuals that ever played football."

In speaking of Bednarik, longtime Philadelphia sportswriter, author, and radio personality Ray Didinger said, "It was almost as if he was some sort of creation that had come to life and stepped out of a display case in Canton. It was almost as if everything about him—the way he looked, the way he walked, the way he spoke, the way he played, more than anything—was the embodiment of everything you associate with pro football."

Didinger then added, "He was a guy who could dominate a game without ever touching the ball, and there aren't a lot of guys you can say that about. . . . There were players in the league that were afraid of Bednarik. It takes a very unusual sort of guy to make other pro players wary."

Bednarik, who gained induction into the Pro Football Hall of Fame in 1967, received the additional distinction of being voted "The Greatest Center of All-Time" by a panel of sportswriters, coaches, and Hall of Fame players two years later.

Displaying a penchant for clinging to the past as the years rolled on, Bednarik became an outspoken critic of modern players, who he described as "pussyfooters" who "suck air after five plays" and "couldn't tackle my wife Emma." Especially critical of Deion Sanders, who became in 1996 the first NFL player to assume a two-way role since he retired in 1962, Bednarik said, "The positions I played, every play, I was making contact, not like that . . . Deion Sanders, he couldn't tackle my wife. He's back there dancing out there instead of hitting."

Bednarik continued, "Sure I'm envious of what they make these days. I see what they make compared to what I did, and it makes me nauseous. I just scan the games on TV. I know they're bigger today. Everyone goes 300 pounds. But look at 'em when they come off the field. They're sitting there taking their last breath. They gotta have oxygen after one play! Think any of them will live to be 50? So, yeah, they're bigger. Faster, too. But better? Show me."

Bednarik spent his final years residing in Coopersburg, Pennsylvania, before passing away at an assisted living center in Richland, Pennsylvania, at the age of 89, on March 21, 2015. Upon learning of his passing, Eagles chairman and CEO Jeffrey Lurie said, "The Eagles and our fans have lost a legend. Fans expect toughness, all-out effort, and a workmanlike attitude. So much of that image has its roots in the way Chuck played the game."

Although the Eagles released a statement saying that he died after a "brief illness," Bednarik's eldest daughter, Charlene Thomas, disputed that claim, stating that he had Alzheimer's disease, from which he had been suffering for years, and that football-related injuries contributed to his decline.

CAREER HIGHLIGHTS

Best Season

Bednarik had his finest season at linebacker in 1953, when he recovered four fumbles and recorded six interceptions, which he returned for a total of 116 yards and the only touchdown of his career. However, Bednarik contributed most to the success of the Eagles in 1960, serving as a pillar of strength on both sides of the ball throughout their unexpected championship run, during which time he played nearly 60 minutes every game.

Memorable Moments/Greatest Performances

Bednarik and his offensive line–mates helped lead the way for Eagles running backs to gain a season-high total of 307 yards on the ground during a 35–21 win over the Washington Redskins on December 2, 1951.

Bednarik scored his only career touchdown on November 15, 1953, when he punctuated a 45–14 blowout of the Baltimore Colts by returning an interception 26 yards for the game's final score.

Bednarik anchored a Philadelphia defense that limited the Cardinals to just 49 yards of total offense and sacked Chicago quarterbacks seven times, in leading the Eagles to a lopsided 27–3 victory over their overmatched opponents on December 4, 1955.

Bednarik picked off two passes in one game for the only time in his career during a 35–24 win over the Pittsburgh Steelers on December 3, 1961.

Bednarik created the two most indelible images of himself in the minds of football fans in 1960, with perhaps his most memorable moment taking place during the Eagles' 17–10 victory over the New York Giants at Yankee Stadium on November 20. With the two teams battling for first place in the Eastern Division, the Eagles found themselves clinging to a seven-point lead with the Giants in possession of the ball near midfield with less than two minutes remaining in the final period. Giants quarterback George Shaw threw a short pass over the middle to star running back Frank Gifford, who, after making the reception, headed upfield. However, before Gifford got very far, Bednarik delivered a devastating forearm blow to his neck and shoulders that knocked him to the turf, separating him from the ball in the process. As Gifford lay unconscious, Chuck Weber recovered the loose pigskin for the Eagles at their own 30-yard line, sealing the victory for Philadelphia. With Bednarik thrilled over the sudden turn of events, photographers subsequently pictured him celebrating as he stood over Gifford. However, Bednarik always maintained that he never meant to taunt his victim, claiming, "I wasn't gloating over him. I didn't even know he was there. My eyes were closed, and I yelled, 'This f—king game is over.' If he doesn't fumble, they beat us, and the Eagles would not have won the championship. . . . It was the most important play and tackle in my life. They were from the big city. The glamor boys. The guys who got written up in all the magazines. But I thought we were the better team."

Speaking of the hit on Gifford, who, after being carted off the field on a stretcher, sat out the next 18 months before finally returning to action, Eagles defensive back Tom Brookshier commented, "He caught him as flush as you could catch him. Giff never saw him coming. It was amazing . . . I played football a long time, but I never heard anything like that collision. It wasn't the usual thud. This was a loud crack, like an axe splitting a piece of wood. I saw Frank on the ground, and he looked like a corpse. I thought he was dead." Meanwhile, Giants linebacker Sam Huff stated, "I was one of the first guys who went by him. I really thought he was dead. His eyes rolled back into his head. He was really unconscious. It was a great hit. I've hit some guys like that, but not that good. That's the kind of hit linebackers dream about."

Bednarik also created a permanent place for himself in football lore by playing on both offense and defense for much of the 1960 campaign, manning the center position whenever the Eagles gained possession of the ball, while also doing a superb job from his linebacker post on defense. In the process, the 35-year-old Bednarik, who also snapped on punts, extra points, and field goals, established himself as the NFL's last full-time two-way player. Looking back at his amazing achievement, Bednarik said, "It was 20 years before it dawned on me what I did. I took it for granted. They told me to play, so I played. But, as I got older, I thought about it. I said, 'Do you know what the hell you did?' No one will ever do it again, certainly not at the professional level. You don't even see two-way players in college anymore . . . I was the end of an era."

Making a lasting impression on rookie Eagles linebacker Maxie Baughan with his exceptional display of endurance, Bednarik, who played 58 minutes in the NFL championship game and secured the victory for the Eagles with a game-saving tackle of Green Bay running back Jim Taylor deep inside Philadelphia territory in the closing seconds, drew praise from his former teammate, who stated, "I was in awe of Chuck. We would come on the field and Chuck would be waiting for us. He'd say, 'Let's go . . . let's get together.' If he was tired, he never let it show."

Notable Achievements

- Scored one defensive touchdown during career.
- Recorded six interceptions and 116 interception-return yards in 1953.
- Missed just three games in 14 seasons.
- Holds Eagles career records for most fumble recoveries (21) and most seasons played (14).
- Ranks fifth in Eagles history in games played (169).
- Two-time Eastern Division champion (1949 and 1960).
- Two-time NFL champion (1949 and 1960).
- Eight-time Pro Bowl selection (1950, 1951, 1952, 1953, 1954, 1956, 1957, and 1960).
- Six-time First-Team All-Pro selection (1950, 1951, 1952, 1953, 1954, and 1960).
- Three-time Second-Team All-Pro selection (1955, 1956, and 1957).
- NFL 1950s All-Decade Team.
- Pro Football Reference All-1950s First Team.
- Named to NFL's 75th Anniversary Team in 1994.
- Named to Eagles 75th Anniversary Team in 2007.
- Inducted into Philadelphia Eagles Hall of Fame in 1987.
- #60 retired by Eagles.
- Number 54 on the *Sporting News'* 1999 list of the 100 Greatest Players in NFL History.
- Number 35 on the NFL Network's 2010 list of the NFL's 100 Greatest Players.
- Elected to Pro Football Hall of Fame in 1967.

3

STEVE VAN BUREN

The first player to lead the NFL in rushing three straight times, Steve Van Buren established himself as the premier rusher of his era and the greatest running back in Eagles history during his time in Philadelphia, which lasted from 1944 to 1951. Turning the Eagles into playoff contenders as soon as he joined them, Van Buren proved to be the driving force behind their first two NFL championships, elevating the level of play of everyone around him with his superb running and quiet leadership. Rushing for more than 1,000 yards twice and at least 10 touchdowns four times, Van Buren led the league in each of those categories on four separate occasions, while also topping the circuit in yards from scrimmage twice and points scored, all-purpose yards, punt-return average, and kickoff-return average once each. The franchise's all-time leader in rushing touchdowns, Van Buren continues to rank extremely high in team annals in several other categories as well, even though it has now been nearly 70 years since he played his last game for the Eagles. In all, Van Buren, who retired as the NFL's all-time leading rusher, gained All-Pro recognition a total of five times, before earning the additional distinctions of being named to the NFL's 75th Anniversary Team, the Eagles Hall of Fame, the *Sporting News'* 1999 list of the 100 Greatest Players in NFL History, the NFL Network's 2010 list of the NFL's 100 Greatest Players, and the Pro Football Hall of Fame following the conclusion of his playing career.

Born in the port city of La Ceiba, Honduras, to an American father and a mother believed to be of Honduran descent on December 28, 1920, Stephen W. Van Buren became an orphan at the age of 10 after losing his mother following the earlier passing of his father. Sent to live with his grandparents in New Orleans, young Stephen developed his love for football shortly thereafter, recalling years later, "My first year at Warren Easton High School in New Orleans, I used to watch the other boys play football. It seemed like a good game, so I went out for the team. But I only weighed 125 pounds, and all the coach would let me do was run up and down the field—not play or scrimmage. When it came to actually playing football, he told me to forget it. He was afraid I would get hurt."

However, after dropping out of school and going to work in an iron foundry, Van Buren spent the next two years adding several inches in height and more than 30 pounds of bulk to his frame, making him nearly six feet tall and 155 pounds by the time he decided to return to school. Making the football team as an end in his senior year, Van Buren later credited his time in the foundry to his physical maturation, stating, "The foundry work was hard, but I liked it, and it built me up."

Performing well in his one year of high school ball, Van Buren earned an athletic scholarship to Louisiana State University, where, after filling out to 210 pounds, he spent his first few seasons blocking for star tailback Alvin Dark, before emerging as one of college football's top running backs as a senior, when he finished second in the nation with 847 yards rushing, while ranking first in scoring with 98 points. Reflecting back on Van Buren's brilliant play in his senior year, LSU head coach Bernie Moore said, "He was probably the greatest running back in Southern Conference history, and I used him as a blocking back until his last year. The folks in Baton Rouge never let me forget that."

Granted a Class IV-F exemption from the Army due to an eye defect, Van Buren entered the 1944 NFL Draft, where the Eagles selected him in the first round, with the fifth overall pick. Making an immediate impact upon his arrival in Philadelphia, Van Buren helped the Eagles post a record of 7-1-2 in 1944 that earned them a close second-place finish in the NFL's Eastern Division. Performing exceptionally well as a rookie, Van Buren ranked among the league leaders with 444 yards rushing, five rushing touchdowns, seven total touchdowns, and 987 all-purpose yards. He also scored two touchdowns on special teams, topped the circuit with

Steve Van Buren led the Eagles to their first two NFL championships.
Courtesy of RMYAuctions.com

averages of 5.6 yards per carry and 15.3 yards per punt return, and recorded five interceptions from his left-halfback position on defense, which he manned until 1948, with his outstanding all-around play gaining him First-Team All-Pro recognition.

Performing even better in 1945, Van Buren once again earned First-Team All-Pro honors by leading the NFL with 832 yards rushing, 1,478 all-purpose yards, 15 rushing touchdowns, 18 total touchdowns, 110 points scored, and an average of 28.7 yards per kickoff return, while also placing near the top of the league rankings with 955 yards from scrimmage, 527 kickoff and punt-return yards, and a rushing average of 5.8 yards per carry. Despite being plagued by injuries that limited him to just nine games the following year, Van Buren managed to rank among the league leaders with 529 yards rushing, 604 yards from scrimmage, 1,012 all-purpose yards, five rushing touchdowns, six total touchdowns, and an average of 4.6 yards per carry, with his solid play gaining him unofficial All-Pro recognition from the UPI and the *New York Daily News*. Fully healthy by the start of the 1947 campaign, Van Buren began an exceptional three-year run during which he clearly established himself as the finest running back in the game, posting the following numbers during that time:

YEAR	RUSH YD	YD FROM SCRIMMAGE	ALL-PURPOSE YD	TD
1947	**1,008**	**1,087**	1,465	**14***
1948	**945**	**1,041**	1,365	10
1949	**1,146**	1,234	1,522	12

* Please note that any numbers printed in bold throughout this book indicate that the player led the NFL in that statistical category that year.

In addition to leading the NFL in rushing all three years, Van Buren topped the circuit in rushing attempts and rushing touchdowns each season. He also finished at, or near, the top of the league rankings in rushing average, points scored, yards from scrimmage, and all-purpose yards all three years, with his tremendous all-around play earning him three consecutive First-Team All-Pro nominations. More importantly, the Eagles won the Eastern Division title each season and captured the NFL championship in both 1948 and 1949, with Van Buren serving as the central figure in both title games, scoring the game's only touchdown on a 5-yard run in 1948, before gaining 196 yards on the ground during a 14–0 victory over the Los Angeles Rams the following year.

Nicknamed "Wham-Bam" and "Supersonic Steve" for his quick and punishing running style, the 6-foot, 200-pound Van Buren earned the respect of teammates and opponents alike with his superb running ability and aggressive style of play, with longtime teammate Russ Craft stating, "When Steve carried the ball, he struck fear in the heart of the defense. He leaned forward so much and ran so hard, you could actually see the dirt fly off his cleats. When he hit the line, he looked like a bulldozer going through a picket fence."

Van Buren led the league in rushing three straight times.
Courtesy of PristineAuctions.com

After calling Van Buren "the best halfback in modern times," former Eagles head coach Greasy Neale went on to say, "Red Grange had the same ability to sidestep, but he never had Van Buren's power to go with it. He was better than Grange because Grange needed a blocker. Van Buren didn't. He could run away from tacklers like Grange, or over them like Bronko Nagurski."

Former Eagles teammate George Savitsky agreed with Neale's assessment, proclaiming, "Steve was the best runner in the game. He could run away from people but liked running over them better."

When asked about his aggressive mindset, Van Buren responded, "The object of the game then, as it is now, was to beat the hell out of the opposing team."

Although Van Buren's physical style of play caused him to lose some of his speed after his first few years in the league, he remained an elite runner, retaining his quickness and power, while using his experience to his advantage. Learning how to make better use of his blocking, Van Buren demonstrated more patience as a runner, waiting for a hole to develop, and then exploding through it. He also occasionally gave ground to his opponent as a way of setting up his blocking and finding additional running room.

Nevertheless, the physical nature of Van Buren's game began to take its toll on him by 1950. Limping through the year with sore ribs, a broken toe, and bone spurs, he sat out two contests and split running chores with Frank Ziegler, limiting him to just 629 yards and four touchdowns. Van Buren subsequently suffered an injury to his knee during training camp in 1951 that relegated him to part-time duty, allowing him to gain only 327 yards on the ground, although he still managed to score six touchdowns. Choosing to announce his retirement at season's end, Van Buren concluded his playing career with 5,860 yards rushing, 6,383 yards from scrimmage, 8,958 all-purpose yards, 69 rushing touchdowns, 77 total touchdowns, and 464 points scored, all of which continue to place him among the franchise's all-time leaders. He also averaged 4.4 yards per carry and recorded nine interceptions over the course of his career. In addition to retiring as the NFL's all-time leading rusher, Van Buren held league marks for most rushing attempts (1,320), rushing touchdowns, and rushing yards in a championship game (196) at the time of his retirement.

Looking back on Van Buren's career, Allie Sherman, who spent several years coaching the New York Giants, described his former teammate as "the Jim Brown of his time—a player who had speed, size, strength, toughness, and quickness." Sherman then added, "People don't appreciate what Steve Van Buren did."

Named the greatest player in franchise history at a 25th anniversary celebration in 1957, Van Buren received the additional honors of having his #15 retired by the Eagles in 1951, being inducted into the Pro Football Hall of Fame in 1965, being named to the NFL's 75th Anniversary All-Time Team in 1994, and being named to the Eagles 75th Anniversary Team as the starting running back in 2007.

Following his playing days, Van Buren remained in the Philadelphia area with his wife and three daughters, briefly coaching and scouting for the Eagles, before running an antiques shop with his son-in-law. He also owned and operated a used-car lot and a dance hall at different times. After developing Alzheimer's disease some 10 years earlier, Van Buren died of pneumonia at the age of 91 on August 23, 2012.

Upon learning of his passing, Eagles chairman and CEO Jeffrey Lurie said, "On the field and off, as a player, a leader, and a man, Steve Van Buren embodied the finest characteristics of our city and our sport. He was a friend and an inspiration to generations of fans, and the model of what an Eagle should be."

Eagles head coach Andy Reid also paid tribute to the former Eagles great, stating, "Watch those old films and you know that Steve Van Buren was something special. He was special in person too, humble about his own accomplishments and encouraging to others. His memory will be with Eagles fans for as long as this team takes the field."

CAREER HIGHLIGHTS

Best Season

Van Buren performed brilliantly for the Eagles from 1947 to 1949, gaining more than 1,000 yards on the ground in two of those three seasons and leading the league in yards rushing and rushing touchdowns all three years. However, he had his finest all-around season in 1945, when he led the NFL with 832 yards rushing, 1,478 all-purpose yards, 15 rushing touchdowns, 18 total touchdowns, a career-high 110 points scored, and an average of 28.7 yards per kickoff return, earning in the process consensus First-Team All-Pro honors.

Memorable Moments/Greatest Performances

Van Buren scored his first career touchdown on a 55-yard punt return during a 38–0 thrashing of the Boston Yanks on October 22, 1944.

Van Buren went over 100 yards rushing for the first time as a pro two weeks later, when he carried the ball 12 times for 129 yards and two touchdowns during a 21–7 win over the Brooklyn Tigers on November 5, 1944, with his TD runs covering 44 and 70 yards.

Van Buren scored his second touchdown on special teams the following week, returning a kickoff 97 yards for a TD during a 21–21 tie with the Giants on November 12, 1944.

Van Buren helped the Eagles begin the 1945 season on a winning note, scoring a pair of touchdowns on a 47-yard run and a 33-yard pass reception during a 21–6 victory over the Chicago Cardinals in the regular-season opener.

Van Buren starred in defeat on October 14, 1945, recording touchdown runs of 69 and 26 yards during a 28–24 loss to the Detroit Lions.

Van Buren led the Eagles to a 38–17 win over the Giants on November 11, 1945, by rushing for 129 yards and two touchdowns, the longest of which covered 22 yards.

Although the Eagles suffered a 28–21 defeat in their rematch with the Giants three weeks later, Van Buren had a big game, rushing for 100 yards and scoring three touchdowns, which came on a pair of 4-yard runs and a 98-yard kickoff return.

Van Buren again gained 100 yards on the ground and scored three touchdowns during Philadelphia's lopsided 35–7 victory over the Boston Yanks in the 1945 regular-season finale, scoring his TDs on runs of 29, 7, and 8 yards.

Van Buren proved to be a thorn in the side of the Yanks once again in the final game of the 1946 regular season, returning a punt 50 yards for a touchdown during a 40–14 Eagles win.

Van Buren continued to excel on special teams in the 1947 regular-season opener, returning a kickoff 95 yards for a touchdown during a 45–42 victory over the Washington Redskins.

Van Buren led the Eagles to another win over Washington on November 2, 1947, carrying the ball 17 times for 138 yards and two touchdowns during a 38–14 victory.

Van Buren provided most of the offensive firepower during a 28–14 win over the Packers in the 1947 regular-season finale, scoring three touchdowns, with the longest of those coming on a 38-yard scamper.

Van Buren shouldered much of the offensive burden when the Eagles defeated the Giants by a score of 35–14 on November 7, 1948, carrying the ball 25 times for 143 yards and two TDs, which came on a pair of short runs.

Van Buren contributed significantly to a 42–21 victory over the Redskins two weeks later, rushing for one touchdown and a season-high 171 yards during the contest.

Van Buren led the Eagles to a 42–0 rout of the New York Bulldogs on November 20, 1949, by rushing for 174 yards and two touchdowns.

Van Buren topped that performance the following week, toting the ball 27 times for a then–franchise record 205 yards during a 34–17 win over the Pittsburgh Steelers.

Van Buren proved to be the difference when the Eagles defeated the Chicago Cardinals by a score of 7–0 in the 1948 NFL championship game. With the two teams playing under blizzard conditions at Philadelphia's Shibe Park, Van Buren scored the game's only touchdown when he ran the ball in from 5 yards out in the fourth quarter. He finished the contest with 98 yards on 26 carries. Amazingly, Van Buren performed as well as he did after taking three trolleys and trudging 12 blocks through the snow after he found himself unable to start his car.

Van Buren again starred in the 1949 title tilt, leading the Eagles to a 14–0 victory over the Los Angeles Rams by carrying the ball 31 times for

196 yards, in a game played in a torrential California rain storm. Recalling his teammate's brilliant performance, Eagles guard Dusan Maronic said, "Steve was hell on a leash against the Rams. They couldn't stop him, but then nobody really ever stopped Steve anytime. He just ran, ran, ran. The mud and rain didn't affect him one bit. When you had a back like Steve— one you knew was going to get yardage—it was fun to block for him." Eagles end Jack Ferrante added, "With the field in the condition it was, we knew we couldn't pass that much. But Steve had a helluva day. They just couldn't stop him. He carried the ball on nearly every play and always got yardage. He didn't score, but he was the big gun for us offensively." Revealing that the Rams provided him with additional incentive during the early stages of the contest, Van Buren remembered, "Early in the game, I got knocked out of bounds near their bench. One of their guys said, 'We're gonna kill you, Steve.' It made me mad. I told (QB) Tommy Thompson, 'Give me the ball.' So, he did. He just kept giving it to me."

Notable Achievements

- Rushed for more than 1,000 yards twice.
- Rushed for at least 10 touchdowns four times.
- Surpassed 1,000 yards from scrimmage three times.
- Surpassed 1,000 all-purpose yards five times, topping 1,500 yards once.
- Averaged more than 4.5 yards per carry five times, topping 5 yards per carry twice.
- Returned two punts and three kickoffs for touchdowns during career.
- Scored more than 100 points once (110 in 1945).
- Intercepted five passes in 1944.
- Led NFL in: rushing yards four times; rushing touchdowns four times; rushing attempts four times; rushing average once; touchdowns scored twice; points scored once; yards from scrimmage twice; all-purpose yards once; punt-return average once; and kickoff-return average once.
- Finished second in NFL in: touchdowns scored once; yards from scrimmage twice; all-purpose yards three times; punt-return yards once; and kickoff-return yards once.
- Led Eagles in rushing six straight times.
- Holds Eagles career record for most rushing touchdowns (69).
- Ranks among Eagles career leaders with: 5,860 yards rushing (4th); 77 touchdowns (2nd); 464 points scored (5th); 6,383 yards from

scrimmage (10th); 8,958 all-purpose yards (6th); and 2,030 kickoff-return yards (6th).
- Retired as NFL's all-time leading rusher.
- Three-time Eastern Division champion (1947, 1948, and 1949).
- Two-time NFL champion (1948 and 1949).
- Five-time First-Team All-Pro selection (1944, 1945, 1947, 1948, and 1949).
- NFL 1940s All-Decade Team.
- Named to NFL's 75th Anniversary Team in 1994.
- Named to Eagles 75th Anniversary Team in 2007.
- Inducted into Philadelphia Eagles Hall of Fame in 1987.
- #15 retired by Eagles.
- Number 77 on the *Sporting News'* 1999 list of the 100 Greatest Players in NFL History.
- Number 58 on the NFL Network's 2010 list of the NFL's 100 Greatest Players.
- Elected to Pro Football Hall of Fame in 1965.

4

─ BRIAN DAWKINS ─

Called "the heartbeat of the defense" by then–Eagles head coach Andy Reid, Brian Dawkins proved to be the heart and soul of the Philadelphia defense for more than a decade. Spending the first 13 years of his Hall of Fame career in the City of Brotherly Love, Dawkins, who earned the nickname "Weapon X" for his ferocious and energetic style of play, recorded more interceptions and forced more fumbles than anyone else in franchise history, with his brilliant play at free safety helping the Eagles advance to the playoffs eight times, capture five division titles, and win one NFC championship. The only player in NFL history with at least 25 interceptions, 25 sacks, and 25 forced fumbles, Dawkins earned seven trips to the Pro Bowl and four All-Pro selections during his time in Philadelphia, before being further honored following the conclusion of his playing career by having his #20 retired by the Eagles, being named to the NFL 2000s All-Decade Team, and being inducted into both the Eagles and the Pro Football Hall of Fame.

Born in Jacksonville, Florida, on October 13, 1973, Brian Patrick Dawkins attended William M. Raines High School, where he earned All-State honors on the gridiron by helping to lead his team to 30 straight victories. After initially accepting a scholarship from the University of Florida, Dawkins instead enrolled at Clemson University in South Carolina when the Gators rescinded their offer to him due to his struggles in the classroom. Dawkins ended up starting for the Tigers at free safety for three seasons, recording 247 tackles and 11 interceptions during that time, with his conference-leading six picks as a senior in 1995 gaining him All-ACC and Second-Team All-America recognition.

Considered one of the top defensive backs heading into the 1996 NFL Draft, Dawkins made an extremely favorable impression on Philadelphia Eagles' director of scouting John Wooten, who later recalled, "He just took over the combine. You would've thought he was the captain of the DBs at the workout. He was ahead of everybody. He was doing everything, which is the same thing I saw at Clemson."

Impressed with Dawkins's leadership ability and varied skill set, the Eagles made him the 61st overall pick of that year's draft when they selected him in the second round. Performing well his first year in the league, Dawkins earned a spot on the NFL All-Rookie Team by picking off three passes, recording 74 tackles, recovering two fumbles, and registering one sack. He followed that up with another solid season, once again recording 74 tackles and three interceptions, one of which he returned 64 yards for the first touchdown of his career.

Yet, even though Dawkins quickly established himself as a top defender following his arrival in Philadelphia, he soon found himself succumbing to the pressures of being a professional athlete in a large media market. Further burdened by the demands being placed on him by friends and family members, as well as the seriousness of being a new husband and father, Dawkins went into a deep depression, turned to drinking, and contemplated suicide, revealing years later, "Overall, I didn't have any outlets, and so I began to drink a little more than I needed to, and that quickly spiraled down into depression. I went through a real dark, deep depression. Alcohol was a tremendous crutch. There were times I didn't even want to be around my family, didn't want to be around my son. I just wanted to be in a dark room by myself with nobody. My faith back then wasn't that strong, so I listened to the other voice in my head, and that's where suicidal thoughts came in, and then actually planning how I would go about it in such a way that (my wife) Connie and my son would get the money from my insurance policy."

Relying heavily on his belief in God and his friendship with then–Eagles defensive coordinator, Emmitt Thomas, who

Brian Dawkins proved to be the heart and soul of the Eagles defense for more than a decade.
Courtesy of PristineAuction.com

convinced him to seek the help he needed, Dawkins eventually overcame his demons, stating, "Emmitt got me to recognize what I could do. I didn't see myself the way he saw me."

With his personal life back in order, Dawkins reached his full potential as a player following the hiring of Jim Johnson as the team's new defensive coordinator in 1999. Forming a special bond with Johnson, who served as both his coach and confidant, Dawkins emerged as arguably the finest safety in all of football, earning seven Pro Bowl nominations and four First-Team All-Pro selections between 1999 and 2006. Named the Eagles' Most Valuable Defensive Player in five of those eight seasons, Dawkins recorded four interceptions four times and registered more than 90 tackles twice, with his stellar play helping the Eagles win four consecutive division titles and one NFC championship from 2001 to 2004.

Establishing himself during that time as the Eagles' unquestioned leader on defense, Dawkins, who remained quiet and mild-mannered off the field, played the game with great intensity, often firing up his teammates with emotional pregame speeches. In discussing the manner with which he expressed himself once he took the playing field, Dawkins said, "I played with a chip on my shoulder. I wanted to have a good time. I danced, I celebrated after plays, I celebrated with my teammates . . . I played with what I feel was a genuine heart. I put things on myself, never my teammates. I had to be that rock. I was never afraid to show it on a football field, to show my emotions, and to play with a passion and give everything I could give."

Dawkins, who, after entering the league at 190 pounds, gradually added 20 more pounds of muscle onto his frame, also became known for the physicality of his game, with the *Sporting News* identifying him as the NFL's hardest hitter in 2004. Providing credence to that publication's selection, teammate Jeremiah Trotter told Marcus Hayes of the *Philadelphia Daily News*, "Dawk is the hardest hitter on the team. He hits like a linebacker. He hurts people. He's knocked them out. He's knocked himself out. Shoot, he's knocked us out."

Opposing quarterback Kerry Collins stated, "When you play the Eagles, the first thing you have to do is find number 20. They have an aggressive scheme and good players, but it all revolves around Dawkins. You have to be aware of where he is at all times because he can do so many things. He's always a threat to make the big play."

Commenting on the totality of Dawkins' game, Jim Johnson said, "If I'm going to build a football team, Brian Dawkins is my free safety. Brian could play strong safety, corner, free safety and not miss a beat. He is in the

Jerry Rice mold in terms of self-sacrifice. He practices as hard as he plays. He has no regard for his body."

Helping to redefine the safety position with his unique skill set, Dawkins, who referred to himself as a "free-lance safety," stated during a 2002 interview with *Pro Football Weekly*, "Most people don't think of the safety as an important part of the defense. It's like the safety is the last line of defense, and that's it. I want to redefine the safety position as one to be reckoned with."

Claiming that Dawkins achieved his desired goal, lifelong Eagles fan and Hall of Fame writer Ray Didinger noted, "Before Brian, the safety was not a very important player in the NFL. But that changed with Andy Reid and Jim Johnson. They built the defense around Dawkins' skills. Other teams saw that, and you started to see guys like Ed Reed and Troy Polamalu come in. These guys were football descendants of Brian Dawkins. . . . Safeties have now become marquee players on the defense, and he started it. He made a great impact around the league."

Dawkins remained in Philadelphia through the end of 2008, signing with the Denver Broncos as a free agent the following offseason when the Eagles didn't come close to matching the contract Denver offered him. Dawkins left the Eagles with career totals of 34 interceptions, 515 interception-return yards, 898 tackles (707 solo), 21 sacks, 32 forced fumbles, 16 fumble recoveries, and four

Dawkins helped redefine the safety position during his time in Philadelphia.
Courtesy of SportsMemorabilia.com

touchdowns, with his 34 picks and 21 sacks making him one of only five players in NFL history to top the 20-mark in both categories. Dawkins also appeared in 183 games as a member of the Eagles, the second-highest total in franchise history.

Expressing his love for the city of Philadelphia following his arrival in Denver, Dawkins said during an interview, "I was born and raised in Philadelphia, as far as being a professional athlete. Philadelphia is where everything happened for me. When you have played for an organization and given all the things that you have given, there's a relationship formed there along the way . . . I've become close to many fans there, and there is a love for the city and a love for the team that will never leave. I definitely enjoyed my time in Philadelphia, and it toughened my skin."

Dawkins then added, "The thing I learned growing up in Philadelphia is that no matter what it is, you go forward. It's just like the times when Donovan (McNabb) was hurt. No matter who was in there, we would rally around him."

Admitting during a 2014 interview that he made a mistake by letting Dawkins sign with the Broncos, then–Eagles GM Howie Roseman said, "When you look around the league, it's hard to find safeties who can cover, who can blitz, who can play the run. I mean, he was an unbelievable player and I think the more we get away from him, and we knew what a great player he was when he was here, but the more you get away from him, you find out how special he really was. He's probably a once-in-a-lifetime kind of player."

Dawkins ended up spending three seasons in Denver, earning two more Pro Bowl selections and one more All-Pro nomination, before announcing his retirement following the conclusion of the 2011 campaign with career totals of 37 interceptions, 1,131 tackles, 26 sacks, 36 forced fumbles, 19 fumble recoveries, and four touchdowns. Five days after he announced his retirement, Dawkins signed a one-day contract with the Eagles, enabling him to officially retire as a member of the team. The Eagles subsequently retired his #20 during a special ceremony held at halftime of their September 30 meeting with the New York Giants.

Remaining close to the game following his playing career, Dawkins joined the ESPN staff as an NFL studio analyst in 2012, before returning to the Eagles in 2016 as the team's football operations executive. After fulfilling that role for two years, Dawkins handed in his resignation on May 22, 2018, stating that he wished to pursue other opportunities.

Looking back on Dawkins's time in Philadelphia, Ray Didinger said, "He is the best safety in franchise history. He is probably the best defensive back in franchise history. Even when he was just a kid, you could see that he had great quickness when the ball was in the air. He was able to close in on a ball so quickly, from point A to point B."

Didinger continued, "His ability to blitz from the safety position was something else that made him stand out. Blitzing is very much a timing thing. Some guys can just anticipate and have a great sense of when to take off. Dawkins had that. Ray Rhodes and Emmitt Thomas were a little distrustful of young players. But, when Andy Reid came in and brought in Jim Johnson, he saw that they had a uniquely talented player."

One of the most beloved players in franchise history, Dawkins says that he developed a special bond with the fans of Philadelphia, stating, "I love the Eagles fans. Yeah, they're crazy, they're twisted in some ways, but I love them. They're as tough as I am. There's a lot of parts of me that are twisted in a lot of different ways. That's why I did some of the crazy stuff on the field. So, we fit. Like hand in glove, we fit."

EAGLES CAREER HIGHLIGHTS

Best Season

Dawkins played some of the best ball of his career for the Eagles from 2004 to 2006, totaling 11 interceptions, 239 tackles, 11 forced fumbles, and 7½ sacks during that time, en route to earning three straight trips to the Pro Bowl and two First-Team All-Pro selections. He also performed extremely well in 2001, gaining First-Team All-Pro recognition by picking off two passes, registering 68 tackles, and scoring one touchdown. Nevertheless, the 1999 campaign would have to be considered Dawkins's finest all-around season, since, in addition to recording 78 tackles and 1½ sacks, he forced six fumbles, recovered two others, and intercepted four passes, which he returned for a career-high 127 yards and one touchdown.

Memorable Moments/Greatest Performances

Dawkins recorded the first interception of his career during a 33–18 win over the Atlanta Falcons on September 22, 1996.

Although the Eagles lost to the Giants by a score of 31–21 on December 7, 1997, Dawkins scored his first career touchdown when he picked off a Danny Kanell pass on New York's opening drive of the second half and returned the ball 64 yards for a TD.

Dawkins lit the scoreboard again during a 16–13 loss to the Miami Dolphins on October 24, 1999, when he intercepted a Damon Huard pass and returned the ball 67 yards for a touchdown.

Dawkins contributed to a lopsided 34–9 victory over the Arizona Cardinals on November 19, 2000, by recording two of the eight sacks the Eagles registered on the day.

In addition to making eight tackles, breaking up two passes, and forcing a fumble during a 24–14 win over San Diego on December 9, 2001, Dawkins crossed the opponent's goal line for the third time in his career when he returned a fumble 49 yards for a touchdown.

Dawkins followed that up with a strong outing against Washington on December 16, 2001, picking off two passes during a 20–6 Eagles win.

Dawkins turned in a tremendous all-around effort during a 35–17 victory over the Houston Texans on September 29, 2002, earning NFC Defensive Player of the Week honors by becoming the first player in NFL history to intercept a pass, record a sack, recover a fumble, and catch a touchdown pass in the same game, with his 57-yard connection with Brian Mitchell following a fake punt proving to be the only offensive TD of his career.

Dawkins made an enormous impact in the 2004 NFC championship game, helping to lead the Eagles to a decisive 27–10 victory over the Atlanta Falcons by intercepting a pass, deflecting two others, and delivering a devastating hit to Atlanta tight end Alge Crumpler during the early stages of the contest that set the tone for the entire game.

Dawkins had a huge game against the Giants on December 17, 2006, recording an interception and 13 tackles during the Eagles' 36–22 win over their Eastern Division rivals, with his outstanding play once again gaining him recognition as the NFC Defensive Player of the Week.

Dawkins earned that distinction for the third and final time by recording seven tackles, one sack, one forced fumble, and one fumble recovery during a 15–6 win over the Steelers on September 21, 2008, with his strip-sack of Pittsburgh quarterback Ben Roethlisberger and subsequent fumble recovery late in the fourth quarter sealing the victory for the Eagles.

After battling a terrible ear infection all week leading up to the final game of the 2008 regular season, Dawkins turned in a memorable performance during a lopsided 44–6 victory over the Dallas Cowboys that clinched a playoff berth for the Eagles, recording five tackles, one sack, and two forced fumbles, both of which the Eagles subsequently returned for touchdowns.

Before departing for Denver, Dawkins helped the Eagles record a 23–11 win over the Giants in the divisional round of the 2008 playoffs by making a game-high eight solo tackles (10 total).

Notable Achievements

- Scored three defensive touchdowns during career and caught one TD pass.
- Amassed more than 100 interception-return yards once (127 in 1999).
- Recorded more than 90 tackles twice.
- Holds Eagles career records for most interceptions (34) and most forced fumbles (32).
- Ranks among Eagles career leaders with: 515 interception-return yards (2nd); 16 fumble recoveries (3rd); 898 tackles (6th); and 183 games played (2nd).
- Member of 20/20 club (20 sacks and 20 interceptions).
- First player in NFL history to record a sack, an interception, a fumble recovery, and a touchdown reception in a single game.
- First player in NFL history to record at least 30 career interceptions and 30 forced fumbles.
- Five-time division champion (2001, 2002, 2003, 2004, and 2006).
- 2004 NFC champion.
- Member of 1996 NFL All-Rookie Team.
- 2008 "Whizzer" White NFL Man of the Year.
- Three-time NFC Defensive Player of the Week.
- December 2006 NFC Defensive Player of the Month.
- Five-time Eagles Defensive MVP (1999, 2002, 2004, 2005, and 2006).
- Seven-time Pro Bowl selection (1999, 2001, 2002, 2004, 2005, 2006, and 2008).
- Four-time First-Team All-Pro selection (2001, 2002, 2004, and 2006).
- Three-time First-Team All-Conference selection (1999, 2001, and 2004).
- NFL 2000s All-Decade Team.
- Pro Football Reference All-2000s First Team.
- Named to Eagles 75th Anniversary Team in 2007.
- #20 retired by Eagles.
- Inducted into Philadelphia Eagles Hall of Fame in 2012.
- Elected to Pro Football Hall of Fame in 2018.

5

PETE PIHOS

Arguably the finest receiver of his era, Pete Pihos starred for the Eagles from 1947 to 1955, helping lead them to three division titles and two NFL championships. An exceptional pass-catcher, powerful runner, and outstanding blocker, Pihos excelled in all phases of the game, also performing well on the defensive side of the ball his first few years in the league, before playing almost exclusively on offense after the NFL instituted a platoon system during the 1950s. Catching more than 60 passes three times and amassing more than 1,000 receiving yards once, Pihos annually ranked among the league leaders in both categories, topping the circuit in receptions three times and receiving yards twice. Nearly 65 years after he played his last game for the Eagles, Pihos continues to rank among the franchise's all-time leaders in every major pass-receiving category, making him, aside from Steve Van Buren, the most dominant offensive player in team annals. In all, Pihos earned six Pro Bowl selections and six All-Pro nominations during his time in Philadelphia, with his outstanding play also earning him a spot on the Eagles 75th Anniversary Team and a place in the Pro Football Hall of Fame.

Born to Greek immigrant parents in Orlando, Florida, on October 22, 1923, Peter Louis Pihos starred in football and basketball while attending Orlando High School, before moving with his mother and siblings to Chicago, Illinois, shortly after police discovered his father murdered at the all-night restaurant he operated. After graduating from Austin High School, Pihos enrolled at Indiana University, where he earned All-America honors at two different positions, while also taking time out to serve his country during World War II. After gaining consensus First-Team All-America recognition as a two-way end in his junior year of 1943, Pihos spent the next 14 months serving in the 35th Infantry Division under General George S. Patton, during which time he received five combat medals and a battlefield commission, took part in the Normandy invasion, and survived the bloody Battle of the Bulge. Granted a furlough to return to Indiana University in

Pete Pihos led the NFL in receptions three times and receiving yards twice.
Courtesy of RMYAuctions.com

September 1945, Pihos spent his final two years of college starring for the Hoosiers at fullback, once again earning All-America honors, and ending his college career as the school's all-time leading scorer, with 138 points to his credit. Commenting on Pihos's exceptional play at the collegiate level, Indiana's head football coach, Bo McMillin, called him "the greatest all-around football player our team has known in my time at Indiana."

Pihos performed so well at Indiana that the Eagles selected him in the fifth round of the 1945 NFL Draft, with the 41st overall pick, even though he had yet to complete his military service or college education, with Philadelphia head coach Greasy Neale stating at the time, "I can wait for a player like Pihos." After signing with the Eagles in February 1947, Pihos joined them later that year, establishing himself as a two-way starter immediately upon his arrival in the City of Brotherly Love. Playing end on both sides of the ball, Pihos had a solid rookie season, leading the team with 23 receptions and 382 receiving yards, while also scoring seven touchdowns and recovering one fumble on defense. Improving upon those numbers the following year, Pihos helped lead the Eagles to their first NFL title by finishing second in the league with 46 receptions, 766 receiving yards, and 11 touchdowns, earning in the process Second-Team All-Pro honors. Pihos also proved to be a major contributor to Philadelphia's 1949 NFL championship team, gaining First-Team All-Pro recognition by catching 34 passes, amassing 484 receiving yards, and scoring four touchdowns.

Continuing to perform well in 1950, Pihos began a string of six straight seasons in which he earned Pro Bowl honors by making 38 receptions for 447 yards and six touchdowns, before catching 35 passes, accumulating 536 receiving yards, scoring five touchdowns, and recording the only two interceptions of his career in 1951. Pressed into extensive action on defense the following year, Pihos recovered four fumbles, en route to earning First-Team All-Pro honors as a defensive end, although he made just 12 receptions for 219 yards and one touchdown on the offensive side of the ball. Not willing to take a pay cut and hoping to regain his earlier form on offense in 1953, Pihos trained heavily during the subsequent offseason, enabling him to compile the most impressive numbers of his career over the course of the next three seasons:

YEAR	REC	REC YD	TD REC
1953	63	1,049	10
1954	60	872	10
1955	62	864	7

Placing in the league's top five in every major pass-receiving category all three years, Pihos earned three straight First-Team All-Pro nominations, with his league-leading 63 catches, 1,049 receiving yards, and 10 TD receptions in the first of those campaigns making him just the third player in NFL history to capture the "triple crown" of receiving. Pihos's 1,049 receiving yards in 1953 also made him the first Eagles player to surpass the magical 1,000-yard mark in a season.

Although the 6'1", 210-pound Pihos lacked great speed, he had soft hands, clever moves, and outstanding strength that made him extremely difficult to bring down in the open field, with Eagles head coach Greasy Neale noting, "When he gets his hands on a ball, there isn't much the defense can do. He just runs over people."

In discussing his longtime teammate, Eagles defensive back Russ Craft stated, "Pete could do everything. He had those big paws and he could catch the ball in a crowd better than any receiver I've seen. Because he was a fullback in college, he knew how to run with the ball once he had it. He wasn't the fastest guy, but he was so strong he'd just knock people over in the open field."

Vince McNally, who served as Eagles GM from 1949 to 1964, added, "Pete was the greatest third-down receiver I've ever seen. He was also a great blocker. But greatest of all his assets was the fact that every week he came to play."

Pihos did indeed come to play every week, as, over the course of nine NFL seasons, he missed just one game, appearing in 107 out of a possible 108 regular-season contests. Starting many of those games on both sides of the ball, Pihos later said, "Back in '47, '48, and through to '52, it was offense and defense. All of us played two ways. On defense, I just kept up with it. It was not like it was as tough playing on the end. Back then, you had only 33 players."

Hailed as "the first great tight end" by legendary coach George Allen in his book *Pro Football's 100 Greatest Players*, Pihos technically did not play the tight end position, with offenses of the day featuring four backs and two ends (or wide receivers). But

Pihos earned Pro Bowl and All-Pro honors six times each.
Courtesy of RMYAuctions.com

the message that Allen intended to convey was that Pihos played very much like a modern tight end, proving to be both an excellent receiver and a tough, physical blocker at the line of scrimmage. Elaborating further on Pihos's skill set, Allen wrote, "Pihos was no giant, but he was big enough. He was no sprinter, but he was fast enough. He was extremely tough and durable, and he seemed to me an exceptionally smart player. He never gave an opponent anything."

Shocking the Eagles by announcing his retirement at only 32 years of age after having led the league in receptions for the third straight season in 1955, Pihos explained his decision to the media by saying, "It wasn't my age that made me quit. I've always kept in top condition, and I never smoke or drank. I know I have a couple years of football left, but I've reached that stage in life when a man cannot serve two masters. I think I've found myself in the business world. I can no longer afford to give five months to football. And I can no longer be a stranger to my family. Just the other day, my little girl asked me, 'Daddy, when are you going to stay home?'"

Many years later, Pihos revealed during a 1981 interview with the *Philadelphia Bulletin* that a chance encounter with baseball great Joe DiMaggio also influenced his decision to retire, telling that newspaper, "I ran into Joe once in Atlantic City. He said, 'Pete, when you retire, make sure you retire on top. Things will be better for you. Don't retire as a has-been.' I always remembered that. I could've played longer, but I chose to retire on top."

Pihos ended his career with 373 receptions, 5,619 receiving yards, and 61 TD catches, all of which continue to place him among the top five players in franchise history. Meanwhile, Pihos's six Pro Bowl selections represent the fifth highest total in team annals, with only Chuck Bednarik, Reggie White, Brian Dawkins, and Jason Peters garnering more nominations.

Following his playing days, Pihos served as head football coach at National Agricultural College from 1956 to 1958, before assuming the same position with Tulane University from 1959 to 1960 and Richmond of the Atlantic Coast Football League from 1964 to 1965. After leaving football, Pihos embarked on a successful business career, serving as vice president of Regal Home Improvement Co. in Richmond, Virginia, for much of the 1970s, and, later, as VP of Franklin National Life Insurance Co. in Fort Wayne, Indiana.

Maintaining a warm place in his heart for the game of football long after he retired, Pihos continued to watch the NFL on television for many years, although he found himself becoming increasingly frustrated with the number of dropped passes he witnessed each week. Expressing his frustration during a 1999 interview with NFL Films, Pihos stated, "I never dropped a pass, period. A few might have gone over my head or something like that, but, if the ball hit my hands, it was caught. If you can't catch the ball, you shouldn't be out there."

Diagnosed with Alzheimer's disease just two years later, Pihos spent his final years residing at the Grace Healthcare nursing home in Winston-Salem, North Carolina, before passing away at the age of 87, on August 16, 2011. Pihos's neurologist subsequently attributed his condition to the many blows he sustained to his head during his playing career.

CAREER HIGHLIGHTS

Best Season

Pihos posted the most prolific numbers of his career in 1953, when he earned First-Team All-Pro honors for the second of four straight times by leading the NFL with 63 receptions, 1,049 receiving yards, and 10 TD catches, while also ranking among the league leaders in yards from scrimmage, touchdowns, and points scored.

Memorable Moments/Greatest Performances

Pihos made an immediate impact upon his arrival in Philadelphia, collaborating with quarterback Tommy Thompson on scoring plays that covered 19 and 21 yards during a 45–42 win over the Washington Redskins in the opening game of his rookie campaign of 1947.

Pihos had another big day against Washington on November 2, 1947, returning a blocked punt 26 yards for a touchdown, and scoring another TD on a 10-yard pass from Tommy Thompson, in helping the Eagles defeat the Redskins by a score of 38–14.

Pihos concluded the 1947 season with a strong effort against Green Bay, topping 100 receiving yards for the first time in his career by making four receptions for 108 yards during a 28–14 victory.

Pihos helped the Eagles forge a 28–28 tie with the Los Angeles Rams on October 3, 1948, by making TD grabs of 40 and 36 yards.

Pihos torched New York's defensive secondary for five catches, 128 receiving yards, and two touchdowns during a 35–14 win over the Giants on November 7, 1948, with his scoring plays covering 26 and 34 yards.

Although Pihos made just one reception in the 1949 NFL championship game, it proved to be a big one, as he scored the game's first points in the second quarter when he hauled in a 31-yard TD pass from Tommy Thompson. The Eagles went on to win the contest by a score of 14–0.

Pihos scored the only defensive touchdown of his career on November 16, 1952, when he helped the Eagles record a 10–7 victory over the Chicago Cardinals by returning a fumble 12 yards for a TD early in the second quarter.

Pihos led a 56–17 rout of the Cardinals on October 25, 1953, by making eight receptions for 156 yards and one touchdown.

Pihos turned in another outstanding effort during a 30–7 win over the Giants two weeks later, catching seven passes for 145 yards and two touchdowns, the longest of which covered 32 yards.

Pihos followed that up with another strong outing on November 15, 1953, making seven receptions for 118 yards and one touchdown during a 45–14 blowout of the Baltimore Colts. Pihos scored his TD in the second quarter, when he collaborated with Bobby Thomason on a 56-yard pass play.

Pihos made his lone catch against Pittsburgh on October 9, 1954, a big one, giving the Eagles a 24–22 victory when he hauled in a 13-yard TD pass from Adrian Burk late in the fourth quarter.

The combination of Pihos and Burk proved to be lethal to the Washington Redskins the following week, with Pihos making nine receptions for 132 yards and three touchdowns during a 49–21 Eagles win.

Pihos turned in two of his finest performances in the final two games of his career, making 10 receptions for 127 yards and one touchdown during a 27–3 victory over the Chicago Cardinals on December 4, 1955, before catching 11 passes for 114 yards during a 17–10 loss to the Bears one week later.

Notable Achievements

- Surpassed 60 receptions three times.
- Topped 1,000 receiving yards once (1,049 in 1953).
- Made at least 10 touchdown receptions three times.
- Scored one defensive touchdown during career.
- Returned one blocked punt for a touchdown during career.
- Missed just one game in nine seasons.
- Led NFL in: receptions three times; receiving yards twice; and touchdown receptions once.
- Finished second in NFL in: receptions once; receiving yards once; touchdown receptions once; and touchdowns scored twice.

- Led Eagles in receptions eight times and receiving yards six times.
- Ranks among Eagles career leaders with: 373 receptions (5th); 5,619 receiving yards (5th); 61 touchdown receptions (tied-3rd); 63 touchdowns scored (5th); and 378 points scored (11th).
- Three-time Eastern Division champion (1947, 1948, and 1949).
- Two-time NFL champion (1948 and 1949).
- Six-time Pro Bowl selection (1950, 1951, 1952, 1953, 1954, and 1955).
- Five-time First-Team All-Pro selection (1949, 1952, 1953, 1954, and 1955).
- 1948 Second-Team All-Pro selection.
- NFL 1940s All-Decade Team.
- Pro Football Reference All-1950s Second Team.
- Named to Eagles 75th Anniversary Team in 2007.
- Inducted into Philadelphia Eagles Hall of Fame in 1987.
- Elected to Pro Football Hall of Fame in 1970.

6

— CLYDE SIMMONS —

A lthough Clyde Simmons spent virtually his entire time in Philadelphia being overshadowed by the incomparable Reggie White, he, too, established a legacy of greatness during his eight years in the City of Brotherly Love. Manning the right defensive end position for the Eagles from 1986 to 1993, Simmons recorded at least 13 sacks in a season three times, with his 76 sacks as a member of the team representing the third-highest figure in franchise history. An exceptional run-defender as well, Simmons surpassed 100 tackles in six different seasons, with his total of 720 solo stops also placing him extremely high in team annals. Simmons's brilliant all-around play helped the Eagles advance to the playoffs four times, earning him in the process two trips to the Pro Bowl, two All-Pro selections, a pair of All-NFC nominations, a spot on the Eagles 75th Anniversary Team, and eventual induction into the Eagles Hall of Fame.

Born in Lanes, South Carolina, on August 4, 1964, Clyde Simmons Jr. spent much of his youth living in North Carolina, where he attended New Hanover High School. After starring on the gridiron at New Hanover, Simmons enrolled at nearby West Carolina University, a public university located in Cullowhee, North Carolina, that is part of the University of North Carolina system.

Excelling as a defensive lineman in his four years at WCU, Simmons began garnering the attention of pro scouts during his junior year. However, his small-college background and lanky 6'6", 235-pound frame ultimately caused him to slip to the ninth round of the 1986 NFL Draft, where the Eagles selected him with the 233rd overall pick. In explaining his decision to draft Simmons, Eagles head coach Buddy Ryan, who discovered him while studying film of many of the nation's graduating seniors, later said, "We knew we weren't gonna draft a lineman high, so we were looking for a guy we might be able to get late. I was looking for a guy with some tools. I saw Clyde's speed and knew we had something."

Clyde Simmons spent most of his time in Philadelphia playing in the shadow of the great Reggie White.
Courtesy of SportsMemorabilia.com

Seth Joyner, who the Eagles selected one round earlier in that year's draft, discussed his initial impression of Simmons, stating, "When we reported to camp, I weighed more than Clyde. I was 250 pounds and he was 235. He was tall and skinny and real quiet. He was one of the nicest guys you'll ever meet, but, on the field, he was intense. We had that in common. We bonded right away."

Playing mostly on special teams as a rookie, Simmons saw very little action on the defensive side of the ball, recording just two sacks and three tackles his first year in the league. But, determined to become a more integral part of the team the following year, Simmons spent a considerable amount of time in the weight room, adding more than 20 pounds of bulk onto his frame. Weighing close to 260 pounds by the start of his second season, Simmons earned a starting job, after which he went on to start every game in each of the next seven seasons, eventually bulking up to more than 280 pounds during that time.

Performing well for the Eagles in 1987 and 1988, Simmons recorded 14 sacks and 164 tackles over the course of those two seasons, before having his breakout year in 1989, when he ranked among the league leaders with 15½ sacks and 135 solo tackles. Commenting on his teammate's improvement, Reggie White said, "Clyde is on par with anybody in the league, he's come that far. The first time I saw him, he was this tall, skinny kid. Now, he's bulked up, and that made the difference in his game."

Yet, despite Simmons's superb play, he failed to gain either Pro Bowl or All-Pro recognition, prompting Eagles defensive coordinator Bud Carson to suggest, "It's a shame. Clyde should be an All-Pro, but he's a victim of playing on the same line with Reggie White. He's the smartest defensive end I've ever been around. You don't fool him. You run a bootleg to his side and you earn it because he's not going to make a mistake."

After undergoing surgery to repair his Achilles tendon prior to the start of the 1990 season, Simmons posted somewhat less impressive numbers, concluding the campaign with "only" 7½ sacks and 109 tackles. However, he returned to top form the following year, earning Pro Bowl and First-Team All Pro honors for the first of two straight times by finishing sixth in the NFL with 13 sacks, while also recording 115 tackles. Posting exceptional numbers once again in 1992, Simmons made 96 solo stops and led the league with 19 sacks.

Simmons ranks third in franchise history in sacks.
Courtesy of George A. Kitrinos

Although Simmons's gangly build made him appear somewhat awkward at times, he possessed outstanding athletic ability, with the combination of his quickness, speed, and strength making him extremely difficult for opposing offensive tackles to block. Simmons's long arms added to his effectiveness, allowing him to get his hands on his opponents quickly and ward them off at the line of scrimmage.

Simmons spent one more year in Philadelphia, recording five sacks and 98 solo tackles in 1993, before signing with the Arizona Cardinals as a free agent at season's end. In addition to the 76 sacks and 720 solo tackles that Simmons made as a member of the Eagles, he forced 12 fumbles, recovered 10 others, recorded one safety, intercepted two passes, and scored four touchdowns. Particularly dominant from 1988 to 1992, Simmons ranked second in the NFL with 63 sacks over that five-year period, with only teammate Reggie White (72) recording more.

Simmons remained in Arizona for two years, recording 17 sacks and 99 tackles for the Cardinals from 1994 to 1995, before spending the next two seasons with the Jacksonville Jaguars, for whom he totaled 16 sacks and 78 tackles. From Jacksonville, Simmons moved on to Cincinnati, where he spent one season with the Bengals. He then joined the Chicago Bears, with whom he spent his final two seasons serving as a part-time player, before announcing his retirement following the conclusion of the 2000 campaign. Simmons ended his career with a total of 121½ quarterback sacks, which placed him 11th in NFL history at the time of his retirement. He also recorded 966 tackles, 25 forced fumbles, and 14 fumble recoveries, intercepted three passes, and scored five touchdowns.

Following his playing days, Simmons briefly worked for a mortgage company and spent some time as a probation officer, before returning to the NFL as the assistant defensive line coach for the St. Louis/Los Angeles Rams. After spending five seasons helping to develop the pass-rushing and run-stopping skills of All-Pro linemen Aaron Donald and Robert Quinn, Simmons accepted the position of defensive line coach of the Cleveland Browns in 2017.

Inducted into the Eagles Hall of Fame in 2018, Simmons drew praise from team chairman and CEO Jeffrey Lurie, who, upon making the announcement of the former defensive end's impending enshrinement, stated, "Clyde Simmons was one of the most feared pass rushers ever to play in Philadelphia, but he was also ferocious against the run and made his presence felt each and every week in the trenches. He was a pillar on one of the best defenses in NFL history and an integral part of the team's success for many years. Clyde's explosive and aggressive style of play resonated with our fans and allowed him to become a dominant defensive lineman over the course of his career."

EAGLES CAREER HIGHLIGHTS

Best Season

Simmons had a tremendous all-around year in 1989, earning Eagles Defensive MVP honors by recording a career-best 135 solo tackles and a team-leading 15½ sacks, while also forcing three fumbles and intercepting a pass, which he returned for a touchdown. He also performed exceptionally well in 1991, gaining Pro Bowl and First-Team All-Pro recognition for the first of two straight times by registering 13 sacks, 115 solo tackles, two forced fumbles, and three fumble recoveries. Nevertheless, the ensuing campaign would have to be considered the most dominant of Simmons's career. In addition to making 96 tackles in 1992, Simmons led the NFL with 19 sacks, which represents the second-highest single-season total in franchise history.

Memorable Moments/Greatest Performances

Simmons recorded the first sack of his career when he brought down Neil Lomax behind the line of scrimmage during a 10–10 tie with the St. Louis Cardinals on December 7, 1986.

Simmons earned NFC Defensive Player of the Week honors for his performance during a 32–23 victory over the Houston Oilers on October 2, 1988, sacking quarterback Cody Carlson twice and applying constant pressure to him throughout the contest.

Simmons gave the Eagles a 23–17 overtime victory over New York on November 20, 1988, when, after the Giants blocked a field goal attempt by Luis Zendejas, he scooped up the loose football at the New York 15-yard line and ran it in for the game-winning touchdown.

Simmons had a huge game against the Denver Broncos on October 29, 1989, recording 3½ sacks of John Elway during a 28–24 Eagles win.

Continuing to be a thorn in the side of the Giants, Simmons made a key play during the Eagles' 24–7 victory over New York on December 3, 1989, when he picked off a Phil Simms pass, which he subsequently returned 60 yards for the second touchdown of his career.

Simmons lit the scoreboard again during a 28–14 win over Washington on November 12, 1990, when he recovered a fumble, which he returned 18 yards for a touchdown.

Simmons had the greatest day of his career on September 15, 1991, when he earned NFC Defensive Player of the Week honors by recording a franchise-record 4½ sacks during a 24–0 thrashing of the Dallas Cowboys.

Simmons contributed to a 34–14 victory over the Phoenix Cardinals on November 24, 1991, by scoring his fourth career touchdown when he recovered a fumble in the end zone.

Simmons turned in a pair of dominant performances in 1992, sacking Chris Chandler three times during a 31–14 win over the Cardinals on September 13, before getting to New York quarterbacks three times during a 47–34 victory over the Giants on November 22.

Notable Achievements

- Scored four touchdowns.
- Finished in double digits in sacks three times.
- Recorded more than 100 tackles six times.
- Led NFL with 19 sacks in 1992.
- Led Eagles in sacks twice.

- Holds Eagles official record for most sacks in one game (4½ vs. Dallas on September 15, 1991).
- Ranks among Eagles career leaders with 76 sacks (3rd) and 720 solo tackles (7th).
- 1988 division champion.
- Three-time NFC Defensive Player of the Week.
- 1989 Eagles Defensive MVP.
- Two-time Pro Bowl selection (1991 and 1992).
- Two-time First-Team All-Pro selection (1991 and 1992).
- 1991 First-Team All-Conference selection.
- 1989 Second-Team All-Conference selection.
- Named to Eagles 75th Anniversary Team in 2007.
- Inducted into Philadelphia Eagles Hall of Fame in 2018.

7

AL WISTERT

One of the finest two-way players yet to be inducted into the Pro Football Hall of Fame, Al Wistert spent his entire nine-year NFL career in Philadelphia, helping to lead the Eagles to three division titles and two league championships. Excelling at tackle on both sides of the ball for the Eagles from 1943 to 1951, Wistert proved to be a dominant blocker on offense and a tremendous force on defense, with his superb all-around play earning him First-Team All-League recognition more times (24) by the various selection committees than any other NFL tackle who played during either the 1930s or the 1940s. A consensus First-Team All-Pro four straight times, Wistert made All-Pro on six separate occasions, en route to earning a spot on the NFL 1940s All-Decade Team. Inducted into the Eagles Hall of Fame in 2009, Wistert also holds the distinction of being the first player in franchise history to have his number retired by the team.

Born to Lithuanian parents in Chicago, Illinois, on December 28, 1920, Albert Alexander Wistert grew up mostly without his father, a Spanish-American War veteran who lost his life in the line of duty while working for the Chicago Police Department in 1927. After graduating from Foreman High School, Wistert enrolled at the University of Michigan, where, after playing baseball and basketball as a freshman, he spent his final three years starring as a two-way lineman on the gridiron, earning consensus All-America and team MVP honors as a senior in 1942.

Having led the Wolverines to an overall record of 20-5-1 in his three years of varsity play, Wistert entered the 1943 NFL Draft, where the Eagles selected him in the fifth round, with the 32nd overall pick. Classified as unfit for duty due to a wrist injury he suffered while in college, Wistert joined the Eagles rather than the US military, after which he encountered a considerable amount of resentment from several of the team's veteran players for having signed a contract worth the then-princely sum of $3,800. Before long, though, Wistert won over his new teammates with his exceptional play on both sides of the ball, which helped the Eagles post their first

Al Wistert is the first Eagles player to have his number retired by the team.
Courtesy of MEARSOnlineAuctions.com

winning record in franchise history—a mark of 5-4-1 in 1943 that earned
them a third-place finish in the NFL's Eastern Division. Continuing to
excel at tackle on both offense and defense, Wistert subsequently gained
consensus First-Team All-Pro recognition in each of the next four seasons,
a period during which the Eagles finished second in the division three times
and advanced to the NFL title game the other year.

Described as a game-changing tackle on defense despite his smallish
6'1", 214-pound frame, Wistert became known for his speed, strength, and
tenacity, with Hall of Fame coach George Allen calling him one of the 10

best defensive linemen in NFL history in his 1982 book *Pro Football's 100 Greatest Players*. In discussing Wistert, Allen wrote, "Wistert seemed to be born with perfect balance. He always played in perfect position and seldom was off his feet. He was a superb pursuit man and seemed somehow to get in on every play. He was a sure tackler. He maybe was best against the run, but he was among the good early pass rushers."

Equally effective on offense, Wistert typically controlled the line of scrimmage from his right tackle position, using his quickness, strength, and superb technique to open huge holes for running backs Steve Van Buren and Josh Pritchard, who said of his former teammate, "He was always first down the field on kickoffs and punts. He was very fast pulling out of the line on offense. He was an excellent downfield blocker. He did it all. Al was the greatest offensive tackle I have ever seen or played with."

A tremendous trap blocker, Wistert drew praise for his work up front in *Total Football: The Official Encyclopedia of the National Football League*, which claimed, "During the 1940s, the surest gain in the NFL was the Eagles' Steve Van Buren off right tackle. Van Buren was a phenomenal runner, but it was Wistert's key blocks at the line of scrimmage that sprang Van Buren into the opponent's secondary."

In addressing Wistert's blocking ability in *Pro Football's 100 Greatest Players*, George Allen wrote, "He was as fine a blocker as you could want. He didn't have the size to overpower people on the pass block, but he was a master of every kind of block."

Considered the Eagles' best offensive lineman even though he played alongside fellow All-Pros Bucko Kilroy and Vic Sears, Wistert, wrote Bob Carroll in his 1988 book *The Hidden Game of Football*, "was the top lineman, among several outstanding guards and tackles, on one of the NFL's dynasties, the post-war Eagles."

Nicknamed "The Ox" for his strength and endurance, Wistert rarely took himself out of games,

Wistert earned consensus First-Team All-Pro honors four straight times. Courtesy of PristineAuction.com

frequently playing all 60 minutes. An outstanding team leader as well, Wistert served as captain of the Eagles his final five seasons in Philadelphia, helping lead them to back-to-back NFL titles in 1948 and 1949, earning in the process two more All-Pro selections. Displaying his exceptional leadership ability after the Eagles defeated Pittsburgh to win the Eastern Division title in 1947, Wistert stated during a postgame interview, "Want to know where the game was won? It was won yesterday in Philadelphia, where every man gave a short speech, telling how he thought the game could be won. We knew right then that we wouldn't be beaten."

Although Wistert remained an extremely effective player throughout his entire career, he elected to announce his retirement following the conclusion of the 1951 campaign, later stating that he based his decision on his somewhat diminishing skills. The Eagles retired his #70 one year later, making him the first player to be so honored. Following his playing days, Wistert spent the next 40 years selling life insurance in California and Grand Pass, Oregon. He also briefly coached football at Riverside High School in Riverside Township, New Jersey. Wistert lived until the ripe old age of 95, passing away on March 5, 2016, while residing in an assisted-living facility in Grand Pass.

Looking back at his playing career some 10 years earlier, Wistert, who still began each day by doing 50 sit-ups and 50 jumping jacks well into his 80s, said of his size, "It was always a problem. Each guy that I played against outweighed me by 40 or 50 pounds, and that was never easy."

Wistert continued, "Playing nine years in the NFL would be a long time in any era. I didn't have a lot of injuries, though. I usually played 60 minutes and didn't come out of the game. But I managed to survive it. I guess I was pretty tough." He then added, "I played the game to the hilt. I gave it everything I had on that football field. That's the only way I knew how to play the game."

CAREER HIGHLIGHTS

Best Season

Wistert proved to be the NFL's most dominant two-way lineman for much of the 1940s, earning four First-Team All-Pro selections and two First-Team All-NFL/AAFC nominations between 1944 and 1949. Turning in arguably his finest performance in 1945, Wistert earned consensus First-Team

All-Pro honors by helping the Eagles finish first in the league in points scored (272) and second in points allowed (133).

Memorable Moments/Greatest Performances

Wistert led the Eagles to a 28–7 victory over the Boston Yanks in the 1944 regular-season opener by anchoring a defense that allowed just 8 yards rushing and 66 yards of total offense.

Wistert and his defensive mates turned in a similarly dominant effort later in the year, when, during a 34–0 manhandling of the Brooklyn Tigers on December 3, 1944, they surrendered only 13 yards rushing and 29 yards of total offense to their overmatched opponents.

Excelling on the other side of the ball as well, Wistert helped the Eagles amass a season-high 437 yards of total offense during a 38–17 trouncing of the Giants on November 11, 1945, with 261 of those yards coming on the ground.

Wistert and the rest of the Eagles' offense topped that performance, though, on November 21, 1948, gaining a total of 575 yards during a convincing 42–21 victory over Washington. Dominating the Redskins at the line of scrimmage, the Eagles rushed for a total of 376 yards, with 171 of those coming from Steve Van Buren.

Wistert and his line-mates once again opened huge holes against Washington's defense on November 13, 1949, with Philadelphia running backs rushing for 256 yards during a 44–21 win that saw the Eagles post 550 yards of total offense.

Wistert delivered a key block during the 1948 NFL title game, taking out two defenders on Steve Van Buren's 5-yard touchdown run that gave the Eagles a 7–0 victory over the Chicago Cardinals.

Notable Achievements

- Three-time Eastern Division champion (1947, 1948, and 1949).
- Two-time NFL champion (1948 and 1949).
- 1950 Pro Bowl selection.
- Four-time First-Team All-Pro selection (1944, 1945, 1946, and 1947).
- Two-time First-Team All-NFL/AAFC selection (1948 and 1949).
- NFL 1940s All-Decade Team.
- Inducted into Philadelphia Eagles Hall of Fame in 2009.
- #70 retired by Eagles.

8

— DONOVAN McNABB —

His selection by the Eagles with the second overall pick of the 1999 NFL Draft greeted with derision by fans of the team in attendance at New York's Madison Square Garden, Donovan McNabb went on to become one of the most polarizing figures in Philadelphia sports history. Praised by some for the many things he accomplished during his 11 years in the City of Brotherly Love, McNabb also found himself being criticized by others for failing to lead the Eagles to an NFL championship. Yet, even though McNabb's detractors accused him of shrinking in big-game situations, the fact remains that he clearly established himself as the finest signal-caller in franchise history during his time in Philadelphia. Just the fourth NFL quarterback to amass more than 30,000 passing yards, 3,000 rushing yards, 200 touchdown passes, and 20 rushing TDs, McNabb joined Fran Tarkenton, John Elway, and Steve Young on an extremely exclusive list. Recording more victories than any other quarterback in the league from 2000 to 2004, McNabb led the Eagles to five straight playoff appearances, four consecutive division titles, and one NFC championship over the course of those five seasons, ending his time in Philadelphia with a total of five trips to the NFC title game. Along the way, McNabb set franchise records for most pass attempts, pass completions, passing yards, and touchdown passes, with his consistently excellent play earning him six Pro Bowl selections, a spot on the Eagles 75th Anniversary Team, and a place in the Eagles Hall of Fame.

Born in Chicago, Illinois, on November 25, 1976, Donovan Jamal McNabb spent his early years living on Chicago's notorious South Side, before moving with his parents some 30 minutes south, to the suburb of Dolton, at the age of eight. After using his engaging personality to ingratiate himself to his new neighbors, who initially resented the arrival of a family of African-American heritage, McNabb entered Mount Carmel High School in the fall of 1990. Starring in both football and basketball at Mount Carmel, McNabb led the school to a 25-4 record on the hardwood as a senior point guard, gaining in the process All-Area recognition from the *Chicago Sun-Times.* Even more impressive on the gridiron, McNabb used his strong arm and outstanding running ability to help lead his school to the Chicago Prep Bowl Championship that same year.

After being recruited by several colleges, including the University of Nebraska and Syracuse University, McNabb chose the latter because of its broadcasting journalism program. He subsequently redshirted his first year at Syracuse, before starting every game at quarterback for the Orangemen in each of the next four seasons, leading them to an overall record of 35-14 during that time. Performing brilliantly throughout his college career, McNabb earned Big East Offensive Player of the Year honors three times and serious consideration for the 1998 Heisman Trophy in his senior year after passing for 2,134 yards and tying a single-season school record by throwing 22 TD passes.

Donovan McNabb holds virtually every Eagles passing record.
Courtesy of Matt Breese

Impressed with McNabb's superb play at the collegiate level, the Eagles selected him with the second overall pick of the 1999 NFL Draft, much to the chagrin of those Eagles fans in attendance, who expressed their disappointment that their team had not selected Texas running back Ricky Williams instead by showering McNabb with boos. Attempting to hide his hurt, McNabb said during an interview conducted moments later, "All we have to do really is to get everything back to the way it used to be, get back on the winning track, then they'll believe it was the right pick."

McNabb subsequently spent the first half of his rookie campaign sitting on the bench, before finally breaking into the starting lineup in Week 10, when he led the Eagles to a 35–28 win over Washington. Although McNabb won just one of his next five starts, he finished his first NFL season with decent numbers, completing just under 50 percent of his passes for 948 yards, throwing eight touchdown passes and seven interceptions, and rushing for 313 yards.

Establishing himself as Philadelphia's full-time starting quarterback the following year, McNabb began a string of five straight seasons in which he led the Eagles into the playoffs, with the team advancing to the NFC title game in each of the last four seasons. Earning Pro Bowl honors each year, McNabb compiled the following numbers from 2000 to 2004:

YEAR	YD PASSING	TD PASSES	INTS	COMP %	QBR	YD RUSHING
2000	3,365	21	13	58.0	77.8	629
2001	3,233	25	12	57.8	84.3	482
2002	2,289	17	6	58.4	86.0	460
2003	3,216	16	11	57.5	79.6	355
2004	3,875	31	8	64.0	104.7	220

Passing for well over 3,000 yards in four of those five seasons, McNabb failed to do so only in 2002, when he sat out the last six games of the regular season after breaking his ankle against Arizona in Week 11. Using both his arm and his legs to account for nearly 75 percent of the Eagles' yards from scrimmage in 2000, McNabb earned a runner-up finish to Marshall Faulk in the league MVP voting, with former Raiders head coach and NFL analyst John Madden stating, "McNabb is as close to a one-man gang as anyone in the NFL since John Elway."

McNabb also received high praise from Brett Favre, who said, "He has a chance to be one of the best that's ever played this game. He's an awesome talent. But, more than that, he's a learner. He wants to learn, and that makes a big difference."

Reaching the zenith of his career in 2004, McNabb led the Eagles to the NFC title by becoming the first NFL quarterback to throw more than 30 touchdown passes and fewer than 10 interceptions in the same season, prompting Philadelphia head coach Andy Reid to proclaim, "We've got the top quarterback in the National Football League. He's on our football team."

Eagles tight end Chad Lewis added, "You know what we have with Donovan. We have complete confidence that he'll find a way to make a play. He's a winner. He's our leader. He's going to fight right to the end and win the game for us."

Blessed with a powerful throwing arm, the 6'2", 240-pound McNabb gradually learned how to take something off his shorter passes and elevate his longer throws, making him a far more effective passer. He also excelled at using his legs to buy time in and out of the pocket, doing a particularly good job of throwing the ball on the run. And, when he found himself unable to find any open receivers, McNabb proved to be an extremely effective runner, rushing for more than 3,000 yards and 28 touchdowns during his time in Philadelphia.

Expressing his admiration for McNabb, former Eagles signal-caller Ron Jaworski said, "He's incredibly mature and poised in the pocket. He can beat you with his arms or with his legs. It's so hard to scheme against a multi-talented, multi-purpose player like that."

McNabb also developed into an outstanding team leader and one of the Eagles' most popular players his first few years in Philadelphia, with Andy Reid saying of his quarterback, "He likes to have fun, but he's all about winning, and that rubs off on the whole team."

Yet, even as McNabb rose to elite status among NFL signal-callers, his failure to lead the Eagles to an NFL title served as fodder to his critics, who claimed that he lacked the intestinal fortitude present in most championship quarterbacks. Adding fuel to the fire, McNabb struggled at times against New England's defense in Super Bowl XXXIX, throwing three interceptions during a 24–21 loss to the Patriots, although he also passed for 357 yards and three touchdowns. Some sources even claimed that the enormity of the situation caused McNabb to become physically ill at one point during the contest. However, other reports labeled the alleged incident "a myth," suggesting that McNabb simply grew increasingly fatigued as the contest wore on.

With a sports hernia sidelining McNabb for the final seven games of the 2005 campaign, the Eagles failed to make the playoffs for the first time in six years, finishing the season with a disappointing 6-10 record. Although McNabb's 2006 season also ended prematurely after he tore the ACL in his right knee against Tennessee on November 19, the Eagles managed to win the NFC East title for the fifth time in six seasons, with McNabb passing for 2,647 yards, throwing 18 TD passes and only six interceptions, completing 57 percent of his passes, and compiling a passer rating of 95.5 before sustaining his injury.

Healthy for most of the next three seasons, McNabb led the Eagles to two more playoff appearances and another trip to the NFC championship game, which they ended up losing to the Arizona Cardinals by a score of 32–25. Performing extremely well over the course of those three seasons, McNabb threw for more than 3,000 yards each year, with his 3,916 yards through the air in 2008 representing a career-high mark. He also threw 64 touchdown passes and only 28 interceptions during that time, while completing more than 60 percent of his passes each year.

Nevertheless, with the Eagles having signed Michael Vick one year earlier, they elected to trade McNabb to the Redskins for a pair of draft picks on April 5, 2010, ending his 11-year stay in Philly. Upon completion of the deal, Andy Reid stated, "Donovan McNabb represented everything a football player could be during his 11 seasons in Philadelphia. He carried this organization to new heights and set a high standard of excellence, both on and off the field."

McNabb led the Eagles to five straight playoff appearances and a total of five trips to the NFC title game.
Courtesy of Kevin Burkett

In addition to setting franchise records for most pass attempts (4,746), pass completions (2,801), passing yards (32,873), and touchdown passes (216) during his time in Philadelphia, McNabb threw 100 interceptions, completed 59 percent of his passes, compiled a passer rating of 86.5, and rushed for 3,249 yards and 28 touchdowns. Over the course of his 11 seasons in Philadelphia, McNabb led the Eagles to an overall regular-season record of 92-49-1 as a starter, with the team compiling a mark of 9-7 in postseason play with him behind center.

After learning of the trade, new Redskins head coach Mike Shanahan expressed his glee over McNabb's impending arrival by stating, "Donovan is an accomplished quarterback who has been a proven winner in the National Football League. I have long admired his competitiveness and feel he will be an outstanding addition to the Redskins and our community. He knows our division and the road map to success in the NFC East."

Washington players also lauded the move, with cornerback DeAngelo Hall saying of his team's new quarterback, "He's a proven winner in this league and I'm excited to have him as part of our football team. This instantly makes us a contender for a Super Bowl championship."

Redskins wide receiver Devin Thomas added, "He's a Hall of Fame quarterback. For one, he's a leader at the position. He has that charisma and he has that playmaker ability with his feet and with his big arm. He has that toughness from playing in the NFC East his whole career. He's everything you want. And, for a young receiver such as myself, who's ready to break out, I couldn't dream of a better quarterback."

McNabb ended up spending just one season in Washington, leading the Redskins to a disappointing 5-8 record in his 13 starts behind center, before being dealt to the Minnesota Vikings on July 27, 2011. After McNabb lost his starting job in Minnesota midway through the 2011 campaign, the Vikings released him at season's end. Unable to garner interest from any other NFL team, McNabb officially announced his retirement more than one year later, doing so after signing a one-day contract with the Eagles on July 29, 2013. Over the course of his career, McNabb passed for 37,276 yards, threw 234 touchdown passes and 117 interceptions, completed 59 percent of his passes, compiled a passer rating of 85.6, and ran for 3,459 yards, which places him sixth all-time among NFL quarterbacks. McNabb, who compiled an overall record of 98-62-1 as a starter, also posted the fourth most wins of any NFL QB during his 13 years in the league, with only Peyton Manning, Tom Brady, and Brett Favre leading their teams to more victories.

The Eagles subsequently honored McNabb by retiring his #5 jersey during halftime of their September 19, 2013, meeting with the Kansas City Chiefs, with team owner Jeffrey Lurie describing him during the ceremony as "one of the greatest players in the history of the Eagles and, certainly, the greatest quarterback in the history of the Eagles."

Former Eagles running back Brian Westbrook agreed with Lurie's assessment, stating, "Donovan is, in my opinion, the best quarterback that the franchise has ever had. Even before I got there, he was able to carry that football team on his shoulders, especially offensively, for a very long time."

Following his playing days, McNabb embarked on a career in broadcasting, joining the NFL Network as an analyst in 2012, before assuming a similar position at Fox Sports the following year. After providing color commentary alongside veteran announcer Dick Stockton for a few NFL games in 2014, McNabb resigned from Fox in 2015 to accept an analyst position with ESPN Radio. He remained in that post for almost two years, before being suspended by ESPN on December 12, 2017, amid allegations that he sent inappropriate text messages to former NFL Network employee Jami Cantor during his time at that station. Following a subsequent investigation, McNabb, who previously served two brief jail sentences for driving under the influence of alcohol, was permanently relieved of his duties.

EAGLES CAREER HIGHLIGHTS

Best Season

Although McNabb threw for a career-high 3,916 yards in 2008, he had his finest all-around season in 2004, leading the Eagles to the NFC championship by passing for 3,875 yards, throwing 31 TD passes and only eight interceptions, completing 64 percent of his passes, and posting a quarterback rating of 104.7, with his exceptional play earning him NFC Offensive Player of the Year honors.

Memorable Moments/Greatest Performances

McNabb led the Eagles to a lopsided 38–10 victory over the Atlanta Falcons on October 1, 2000, by completing 30 of 44 pass attempts for 311 yards and two touchdowns, while also rushing for 61 yards.

McNabb earned NFC Offensive Player of the Week honors for the first of five times for his performance during a 23–20 win over the Redskins on

November 26, 2000, when he passed for one touchdown, ran for another, and gained 125 yards on 11 carries.

McNabb earned that distinction again two weeks later by throwing for 390 yards and four touchdowns during a 35–24 victory over the Cleveland Browns on December 10, with the longest of his TD passes coming on a 38-yard connection with Charles Johnson.

McNabb had a huge game against Dallas on September 22, 2002, once again gaining recognition as the NFC Offensive Player of the Week by leading the Eagles to a convincing 44–13 win. In addition to running for 67 yards and one touchdown, McNabb passed for 287 yards and three TDs, the longest of which came on a 59-yard hookup with Antonio Freeman.

McNabb displayed his toughness on November 17, 2002, when, after breaking his ankle on the Eagles' first possession of the game, he went on to lead them to a 38–14 victory over the Arizona Cardinals by completing 20 of 25 pass attempts for 255 yards and four touchdowns.

McNabb gave the Eagles a dramatic 17–14 win over Green Bay on November 10, 2003, by throwing a 6-yard TD pass to Todd Pinkston with only 27 seconds remaining in regulation.

McNabb led the Eagles to a 28–10 victory over the Giants the following week by completing 24 of 30 pass attempts for 314 yards and two touchdowns, earning in the process NFC Offensive Player of the Week honors for the fourth time.

McNabb came up big for the Eagles in their 2003 divisional round playoff matchup with Green Bay, giving them a 20–17 overtime win by throwing for 248 yards and two touchdowns, while also running for 107 yards.

McNabb helped the Eagles begin the 2004 campaign on a positive note, passing for 330 yards and four touchdowns during a 31–17 victory over the Giants in the regular-season opener, with three of his TD passes going to Terrell Owens and the other to L. J. Smith.

McNabb had another big game against Detroit two weeks later, leading the Eagles to a 30–13 win by running for one score and throwing for 356 yards and two touchdowns.

McNabb continued to perform brilliantly the following week, passing for 376 yards and four touchdowns during a 34–31 overtime victory over the Cleveland Browns.

McNabb turned in a similarly impressive effort against Dallas on November 15, 2004, leading the Eagles to a convincing 49–21 win by throwing for 345 yards and four touchdowns, with three of his TD passes going to Terrell Owens and the other being a 59-yard connection with Todd Pinkston.

McNabb earned NFC Offensive Player of the Week honors for the fifth and final time by passing for a career-high 464 yards and five touchdowns during a 47–17 dismantling of the Packers on December 5, 2004. McNabb, who finished the day 32-of-43, set a new NFL record by completing 24 straight passes at one point during the contest.

McNabb had another huge game on September 18, 2005, throwing for 342 yards and five touchdowns during a 42–3 blowout of the 49ers, with his longest completion of the day being a 68-yard TD connection with Terrell Owens.

McNabb starred again two weeks later, throwing for 369 yards and three touchdowns during a 37–31 win over the Kansas City Chiefs on October 2, 2005.

McNabb led the Eagles to a 56–21 rout of the Detroit Lions on September 23, 2007, by completing 21 of 26 pass attempts for 381 yards and four touchdowns, with three of his TD passes going to Kevin Curtis and the other to Brian Westbrook.

McNabb passed for 361 yards and three TDs during a 38–3 win over the Rams in the 2008 regular-season opener, with the longest of his TD passes going 90 yards to Hank Baskett.

Although the Eagles ended up losing the 2008 NFC championship game to the Cardinals by a score of 32–25, McNabb performed heroically, bringing his team all the way back from a 24–6 deficit by throwing three second-half touchdown passes, before the Cardinals won the game with less than three minutes left in regulation on an 8-yard TD pass from Kurt Warner to Tim Hightower. McNabb finished the day with 28 completions on 47 attempts, for 375 yards.

McNabb once again starred in defeat on November 15, 2009, throwing for 450 yards and two touchdowns during a 31–23 loss to the San Diego Chargers.

Notable Achievements

- Passed for more than 3,000 yards seven times, surpassing 3,800 yards twice.
- Threw more than 20 touchdown passes five times, topping 30 TD passes once (31 in 2004).
- Completed more than 60 percent of passes four times.

- Posted touchdown-to-interception ratio of better than 2–1 seven times.
- Posted quarterback rating above 90.0 three times, finishing with mark of 104.7 in 2004.
- Rushed for more than 300 yards five times, topping 600 yards once (629 in 2000).
- Rushed for 28 touchdowns.
- Averaged more than 5 yards per carry seven times, posting mark of 7.3 twice.
- Finished third in NFL with 31 touchdown passes in 2004.
- Holds Eagles career records for most: pass attempts (4,746); pass completions (2,801); passing yards (32,873); and touchdown passes (216).
- Ranks fourth in Eagles history with quarterback rating of 86.5 (minimum 500 attempts).
- Holds Eagles single-season record for most yards passing (3,916 in 2008).
- Five-time division champion (2001, 2002, 2003, 2004, and 2006).
- 2004 NFC champion.
- Five-time NFC Offensive Player of the Week.
- September 2005 NFC Offensive Player of the Month.
- 2004 NFC Offensive Player of the Year.
- Six-time Pro Bowl selection (2000, 2001, 2002, 2003, 2004, and 2009).
- Named to Eagles 75th Anniversary Team in 2007.
- Inducted into Philadelphia Eagles Hall of Fame in 2013.
- #5 retired by Eagles.

9

PETE RETZLAFF

A versatile player who started at three different positions for the Eagles during his time in Philadelphia, Pete Retzlaff began his 11-year NFL career as a running back, before moving to wide receiver and, later, tight end, where he made his greatest overall impact. Joining Hall of Fame tight ends Mike Ditka and John Mackey in helping to redefine the position, Retzlaff spent his final four seasons at that post, earning three trips to the Pro Bowl and two All-Pro selections during that time. In all, Retzlaff, who continues to rank among the Eagles' all-time leaders in several offensive categories more than 50 years after he retired, gained Pro Bowl recognition five times and made All-Pro on three separate occasions, with his outstanding play also earning him NFL Player of the Year honors in 1965 and a place in the Eagles Hall of Fame. Retzlaff accomplished all he did even though he entered the NFL three years later than he should have after failing to catch a single pass in college.

Born in Ellendale, North Dakota, on August 21, 1931, Palmer Edward Retzlaff attended Ellendale High School, where he starred on the gridiron as a running back, prompting South Dakota State University to offer him a football scholarship. An outstanding all-around athlete, Retzlaff set 16 school records in track and football while at SDSU, excelling in track and field in the shotput and discus throw, while also earning Little All-America honors as a fullback by rushing for 1,016 yards in his senior year of 1952.

Selected by the Detroit Lions in the 22nd round of the 1953 NFL Draft, with the 266th overall pick, Retzlaff failed to earn a spot on the roster of the defending NFL champions, prompting him to return to SDSU, where he spent the next year working on the school's athletic staff. Entering the military in 1954, Retzlaff spent the next two years serving in the Army as a first lieutenant, before giving football another try when he returned to the States in 1956. Failing to make much of an impression on the Lions once again, Retzlaff found himself headed to Philadelphia when the Eagles acquired him from Detroit for the $100 waiver fee.

Initially employed by the Eagles as a reserve blocking back, the 6'1", 210-pound Retzlaff accomplished very little his first two seasons in Philadelphia, gaining no yardage on the ground and making a total of just 22 receptions for 279 yards and no touchdowns. But the 27-year-old former Little All-American received his big break when the Eagles acquired future Hall of Fame quarterback Norm Van Brocklin prior to the start of the 1958 campaign. Taking note of Retzlaff's speed, soft hands, and excellent route-running, which he said reminded him of former Los Angeles Rams

Pete Retzlaff starred at three different positions for the Eagles during his time in Philadelphia.
Courtesy of BoxingTreasures.com

teammate Elroy "Crazy Legs" Hirsch, Van Brocklin suggested that the coaches try him at split end. With Eagles cornerback Tom Brookshier claiming that he couldn't cover Retzlaff in practice, the coaching staff acquiesced to Van Brocklin's wishes, after which the quarterback set about teaching his new receiver how to properly catch the football. Working extremely hard with Retzlaff, Van Brocklin taught him to reach for the ball with his hands, rather than allowing it to travel all the way into his body. Learning his lessons well, Retzlaff rapidly developed into one of the league's top wideouts, earning Pro Bowl and Second-Team All-Pro honors in 1958 by leading the NFL with 56 receptions, while also finishing fifth in the league with 766 receiving yards.

Plagued by injuries throughout much of the ensuing campaign, Retzlaff made just 34 receptions for 595 yards and one touchdown. However, he returned to top form in 1960, helping the Eagles win the NFL championship by leading the team with 46 receptions and 826 receiving yards. Retzlaff followed that up with two more solid seasons, totaling 80 receptions, 1,353 receiving yards, and 11 touchdowns from 1961 to 1962, despite being limited by a broken arm to only eight games in the second of those campaigns. Still, the best had yet to come.

With Philadelphia head coach Nick Skorich wishing to make better use of Retzlaff's blocking ability, he moved him to tight end prior to the start of the 1963 campaign. Although Retzlaff subsequently never developed into anything more than an average blocking tight end, he established himself as arguably the finest receiver at that position in all of football over the course of the next four seasons, compiling the following numbers during that time:

YEAR	REC	REC YD	TD REC
1963	57	895	4
1964	51	855	8
1965	66	1,190	10
1966	40	653	6

On the receiving end of passes thrown by King Hill, Sonny Jurgensen, and Norm Snead those four seasons, Retzlaff ranked among the league leaders in receptions and receiving yards in each of the first three seasons, earning in the process three straight trips to the Pro Bowl and two All-Pro nominations. Retzlaff also gained recognition as the NFL Player of the Year in 1965 by finishing second in the league in receiving yards, while placing third in receptions and TD catches. Hailing Retzlaff's 1965 campaign as "arguably the best season a tight end ever had," Hall of Fame wide receiver Raymond Berry later admitted that he studied film of Retzlaff's precise route-running that year so that he might perfect his own legendary skills.

In discussing that aspect of Retzlaff's game, Tom Brookshier stated, "Pete was a great technician. When you watched Pete on the field, it was like watching the diagram in the playbook come to life. He worked for hours on running patterns, getting every step exactly right. He was so disciplined in his routes, that's why quarterbacks loved to throw to him."

Expressing his admiration for Retzlaff, Dallas Cowboys perennial All-Pro defensive back Mel Renfro recalled, "I was a young guy just coming into the league, and Pete was the guy, the receiver in those days. He was a great route runner, more like a wide receiver than a tight end. Many times, I had to grab his shirt as he ran by me. He was a quiet guy, never brought attention to himself, but a very tough competitor."

Meanwhile, former Eagles teammate Maxie Baughan discussed how Retzlaff helped to change the position of tight end in the NFL, saying, "Pete was one of the first tight ends with enough versatility to be a receiver as well as a blocker. He changed the game because defenses had to alter their coverages to guard him."

Providing an excellent description of Retzlaff, *Philadelphia Bulletin* columnist Sandy Grady once wrote, "The mind's lens sees Retzlaff crouching, then fighting out of the linebacker's grasp, then the No. 44 shirt tilting downfield, shoulders bulldog low. There is a head bob, a foot planted to the outside, freezing a cornerback for an instant, and Pete careening into the middle snatching a ball in the mob's flurry, then knocking down people like bowling pins."

Retzlaff earned NFL Player of the Year honors in 1965.
Courtesy of MEARSOnlineAuctions.com

Although Retzlaff performed brilliantly in 1965, the season ended up taking a huge toll on him since he played the entire year in pain. Suffering from a heel injury that often prevented him from taking part in practice, Retzlaff found himself able to play on Sundays only after he received multiple injections of painkillers before he took the playing field. After contemplating retirement during the subsequent offseason, Retzlaff decided to return for one more year, with his 40 receptions and 653 receiving yards representing his lowest totals since he moved to the tight end position in 1963. Announcing his retirement following the conclusion of the campaign, Retzlaff ended his career with 452 receptions, 7,412 receiving yards, and 47 TD catches, with the first two figures placing him second in franchise history.

After retiring as an active player, Retzlaff, who served as president of the NFL Players Association from 1962 to 1964, held the position of Eagles' vice president and general manager from 1969 to 1972, before spending the next two years working as a color analyst for NFL coverage on CBS television. He also later worked as a sportscaster on several local radio and television stations, before getting involved in investing and land acquisition. Now 87 years old, Retzlaff currently lives with his wife, Patty, on a farm just outside of Gilbertsville, Pennsylvania, where they raised their four children. Looking back on his life, Retzlaff says, "Things have worked out pretty good. I can't complain. There are always going to be bumps along the way, but sometimes the bumps help you. You learn from them. Coming to Philadelphia is probably about the best thing that could've happened to us. It led to a lot of really good things."

CAREER HIGHLIGHTS

Best Season

Retzlaff played his best ball for the Eagles after he moved to the tight end position during the latter stages of his career, having his finest season in 1965, when he earned NFL Player of the Year honors and his lone First-Team All-Pro selection by placing near the top of the league rankings with 66 receptions, 1,190 receiving yards, and 10 touchdown catches, establishing in the process career-high marks in all three categories.

Memorable Moments/Greatest Performances

Although the Eagles lost a 38–35 shootout with the Packers on October 26, 1958, Retzlaff amassed more than 100 receiving yards for the first time in his career, making six receptions for 121 yards, with his longest gain of the day being a 49-yard connection with Norm Van Brocklin.

Retzlaff scored just one touchdown in 1959, which came on a 40-yard hookup with Van Brocklin on November 15 that contributed to a 27–17 victory over the Chicago Cardinals. He finished the game with five catches for 137 yards and that one TD.

Retzlaff continued to be a thorn in the side of the Cardinals after they moved to St. Louis the following year, making seven receptions for 132 yards and two touchdowns during a 31–27 Eagles win on October 9, 1960.

Although Retzlaff made just one reception against Green Bay in the 1960 NFL Championship Game, it proved to be a big one, with his 41-yard grab helping to set up an Eagles field goal that contributed to their 17–13 victory.

Retzlaff helped lead the Eagles to a 27–24 win over the Washington Redskins on October 29, 1961, by making seven receptions for 125 yards and two touchdowns, which came on hookups of 44 and 11 yards with Sonny Jurgensen.

Retzlaff again starred against Washington on December 2, 1962, catching eight passes for 135 yards and one touchdown during a 37–14 victory.

Retzlaff helped key a 17–14 win over the Dallas Cowboys on November 15, 1964, by making three catches for 90 yards and two touchdowns, with his 38-yard TD grab in the fourth quarter providing the margin of victory.

Although the Eagles lost their November 7, 1965, meeting with the Cleveland Browns by a score of 38–34, Retzlaff had a big game, making seven receptions for 151 yards and three touchdowns, the longest of which covered 39 yards.

Retzlaff contributed to a 21–14 win over the Washington Redskins on November 14, 1965, by making seven catches for a career-high 204 yards.

Retzlaff had another big day two weeks later, making nine receptions for 148 yards and three touchdowns during a 28–24 victory over the Cardinals on November 28, 1965.

Retzlaff surpassed 100 receiving yards for the final time in his career on September 25, 1966, when he made five catches for 120 yards and one touchdown during a 35–17 win over the Giants.

Notable Achievements

- Surpassed 50 receptions five times.
- Topped 1,000 receiving yards once (1,190 in 1965).
- Made 10 touchdown receptions in 1965.
- Led NFL with 56 receptions in 1958.
- Finished second in NFL with 1,190 receiving yards in 1965.
- Finished third in NFL with 66 receptions and 10 touchdown receptions in 1965.
- Ranks among Eagles career leaders with: 452 receptions (2nd); 7,412 receiving yards (2nd); 47 touchdown receptions (5th); 47 touchdowns scored (10th); and 7,408 yards from scrimmage (5th).
- 1960 Eastern Division champion.
- 1960 NFL champion.
- 1965 Bert Bell Award winner as NFL Player of the Year.
- 1965 Wanamaker Award winner as the Outstanding Athlete in Philadelphia.
- Five-time Pro Bowl selection (1958, 1960, 1963, 1964, and 1965).
- 1965 First-Team All-Pro selection.
- Two-time Second-Team All-Pro selection (1958 and 1964).
- Four-time First-Team All-Conference selection (1958, 1963, 1964, and 1965).
- Inducted into Philadelphia Eagles Hall of Fame in 1989.
- #44 retired by Eagles.

10

— BILL BERGEY —

lready recognized as one of the NFL's top middle linebackers by the time he arrived in Philadelphia, Bill Bergey previously spent five seasons starring at that post for the Cincinnati Bengals, before being dealt to the Eagles for three high draft picks prior to the start of the 1974 campaign. Continuing to perform at an elite level after he arrived in the City of Brotherly Love, Bergey led the Eagles in tackles in six of the next seven seasons, with his strong play, fierce competitive spirit, and exceptional leadership ability helping to restore the franchise to prominence during the late-1970s. The Eagles' all-time leading tackler, Bergey earned team MVP honors three times, four trips to the Pro Bowl, five All-Pro nominations, and six All-Conference selections during his time in Philadelphia, leading the Eagles to three playoff appearances and one NFC championship in the process. And, following the conclusion of his playing career, Bergey earned the additional distinctions of being named to Pro Football Reference's All-1970s Second Team and being inducted into the Eagles Hall of Fame.

Born in South Dayton, New York, on February 9, 1945, William Earl Bergey attended South Dayton High School, where he starred in football as a fullback and linebacker. Failing to receive any scholarship offers as graduation neared, Bergey later recalled, "I played football at a Class C school. There were 47 in our graduating class. We barely had enough guys to play football. So, we never even had any films for our football games. I had my guidance director when I was a senior write to maybe eight or ten colleges, and two of them responded. One was the University of New Mexico and the other was Arkansas State University."

Bergey continued, "Now, I was from western New York, between Buffalo and Jamestown. So, I got my map out and saw where Arkansas State was closer than New Mexico, so I decided to go ahead and pursue Arkansas State."

After contacting Arkansas State coaches Bennie Ellender and Wayne Armstrong, who happened to be in New York City for a coaches' convention, Bergey received an invitation to meet them, remembering years later, "I said 'Yes.' Unbeknownst to me, from where I was in New York, it was about 425 miles away. We went to New York City. We packed up a couple of scrapbooks that I had put together and I just pleaded for any kind of scholarship help that they could give to me, because I didn't have any money at all. They gave me a partial scholarship."

Recalling his days at the university, Bergey said, "I went down to Arkansas State and red-shirted my first year. Then, I started four years in a row. I didn't start at line-

Bill Bergey helped restore the Eagles to prominence during the late 1970s. Courtesy of SportsMemorabilia.com

backer. It was kind of a platoon system that we had. I was an offensive guard and a nose guard. After a couple of plays, that whole unit would go out and another unit would come in. My junior year, they moved me to linebacker. I was standing up and could see everything. Things just started to click for me."

Bergey, who led the team in tackles three times, ended up setting school records for most fumble recoveries in a season, most tackles in a game, most tackles in a season, and most career tackles, earning in the process All–Southland Conference honors three times and First-Team College Division All-America recognition as a senior in 1968. Commenting on his performance at the collegiate level, Bergey stated, "I was a pretty good athlete. I could run real fast. I was big enough. I started out at linebacker in college around 232 or 234 (pounds). I made All-American."

Subsequently selected by the Cincinnati Bengals in the second round of the 1969 NFL Draft, with the 31st overall pick, Bergey performed extremely well his first year in the league, earning Pro Bowl and *Sporting News* NFL Defensive Rookie of the Year honors. Although Bergey failed to gain Pro Bowl recognition in any of the next four seasons, he continued to play well for the Bengals, remaining the centerpiece of one of the league's better defenses.

However, Bergey's days in Cincinnati came to an end shortly after he signed a futures contract to play with Orlando in the upstart World Football League. Recalling the events that transpired at the time, Bergey stated, "It was strictly the money. I will make no bones about it. I was making $37,500 with Paul Brown [Cincinnati's head coach]. The World Football League came along and offered me, I think it was $625,000 for three years, guaranteed, no cut, no trade. I think you can do the math on that. I was strictly in it for the cash."

Bergey continued:

> Paul Brown took me to court, stating that "It impairs the integrity of any professional athlete to play for one ball club and to be compensated by another." I had already received an $80,000 bonus from the World Football League, and that was more than twice my salary. I had one more year under Paul Brown. I had said that I would honor that one year and then I was going on to the World Football League. We had the biggest, most unbelievable court battle you can imagine in Philadelphia . . . I won the court battle. I won the appeal, and I pretty much pissed Paul Brown off, and he was not going to have anything to do with me.

But, with the WFL folding shortly thereafter and Brown seeking to rid himself of Bergey, the Bengals traded him to the Eagles for first round draft picks in 1977 and 1978, along with a second rounder in 1978. Revealing years later that he initially had concerns about joining the Eagles, Bergey said, "At first, I wasn't sure that I wanted to go to Philadelphia. I knew it was the home of the Liberty Bell and they had something called soft pretzels and losing football. Plus, Mike McCormack, the coach, had testified against me in court as a favor to Paul Brown. But Leonard Tose was very, very persistent about me coming to the Philadelphia Eagles. He honestly thought that all he needed to win the Super Bowl was a middle linebacker."

After finally agreeing to come to Philadelphia, Bergey never looked back, playing the best football of his career over the course of the next few seasons. Excelling in his first year with his new team, Bergey recorded a career-high five interceptions and led the Eagles in tackles for the first of six times, earning in the process team MVP, Pro Bowl, and First-Team All-Pro honors. Looking back at the 1974 campaign, Bergey said, "I played pretty good football my first year in Philadelphia. I was runner-up to 'Mean' Joe

Greene for Defensive Player of the Year. I made consensus All-Pro at line-backer. Everything connected in Philadelphia. I had an affair with the fans in Philadelphia, and it worked out very, very nicely."

Although the Eagles struggled on the field in each of the next three seasons, compiling an overall record of just 13-29 from 1975 to 1977, Bergey continued to perform at an extremely high level, earning two more trips to the Pro Bowl and three more All-Pro nominations, with his 233 tackles in 1976 setting a single-season franchise record that still stands. Meanwhile, despite their poor record, the Eagles gradually put together one of the league's more formidable defenses, with Bergey's intensity and physical style of play rubbing off on his teammates.

Almost maniacal in the level of intensity he displayed on the playing field, the 6'3", 245-pound Bergey proved to be one of the NFL's surest tacklers and hardest hitters over the course of his career, with Walt Michaels, who served as Eagles defensive coordinator from 1973 to 1975, once saying, "Bill reminds me of Rocky Marciano. He knows how to gather himself.

Some boxers are always on their toes, never in balance to deliver a blow. Bill delivers with his whole body. He explodes. Boom! You can't teach that. A guy has it or he doesn't."

Bergey had another big year in 1978, earning the last of his five Pro Bowl selections and helping the Eagles advance to the playoffs as a wild card by recording 167 tackles, 5½ sacks, four interceptions, four fumble recoveries, and two forced fumbles. However, he suffered a serious knee injury the following year that limited him to just three games, ending in the process his string of 89 consecutive starts. Although Bergey returned to action in 1980, leading the Eagles to

Bergey recorded more tackles than anyone else in franchise history.
Courtesy of SportsMemorabilia.com

the NFC title with his strong play at middle linebacker, he failed to reach the same level of excellence, stating years later, "If I was at one time a 100 percent football player, after my knee injury, I don't think I got past 65 percent. When I was on top of my game, I could diagnose a play and get to a spot to almost wait for a ball carrier. After the knee injury, I could still diagnose a play, but, by the time I could get to that spot, the ball carrier was gone."

Bergey added, "Nobody had to tell me that it was my time. I would always be up in the 200s, as far as tackles go. I think that the year we went to the Super Bowl, I played in every game and played on every play. I think that I was around 135 tackles. It was just dreadful. I used to watch film, and I would remember, 'Gosh, I used to be able to make that play, and it was so easy to make that play.' I just couldn't make it anymore. That's when it was time for me to hang up the old strap."

Choosing to announce his retirement after the Eagles lost Super Bowl XV to the Oakland Raiders by a score of 27–10, Bergey ended his career with 27 interceptions, 397 interception-return yards, and 21 fumble recoveries. During his time in Philadelphia, he picked off 18 passes, amassed 234 interception-return yards, recovered 15 fumbles, and recorded nearly 1,200 tackles, which remains the highest total in franchise history.

Since retiring as an active player, Bergey has remained close to the Eagles, first serving as a color commentator on the team's radio broadcasts from 1982 to 1983, before eventually doing pregame and postgame radio and television commentary for the team during the season. He also spent many years in the hospitality business, owning a few hotels and restaurants in the Philadelphia area.

Looking back at his playing career, Bergey said, "Personally, I think the thing that makes me the proudest is I know that I left everything on the field. I played as hard as I could all the time. I wasn't one of those players that takes plays off, or anything like that. I've had an awful lot of pats on the back and a lot of awards, and all of that, but, just knowing that I gave everything I had on every play, that's pretty rewarding."

Meanwhile, in expressing his fondness for the fans of Philadelphia, Bergey stated, "All the fans want is a winner, and to see effort from the players. They are no different from any other fans. We're just a little bit louder. There are just wonderful people in this area. I could have settled anywhere after my career ended. But I love Philadelphia. To this day, staying in Philadelphia was the best thing I've ever done."

EAGLES CAREER HIGHLIGHTS

Best Season

Bergey performed brilliantly for the Eagles from 1975 to 1978, making First-Team All-Pro in the first of those campaigns and Second-Team All-Pro the other three years. After recording three interceptions and a league-leading six fumble recoveries in 1975, Bergey made a franchise-record 233 tackles the following year. He also recovered four fumbles and picked off four passes in 1978, amassing a career-high 70 interception-return yards in the process. Nevertheless, Bergey made his greatest overall impact on the Eagles his first year in Philadelphia, when he provided leadership to a defense that improved markedly as the season progressed. In addition to leading the team in tackles and interceptions, Bergey brought a new level of intensity to the Eagles in 1974, helping them reach the .500-mark for the first time in eight years, with his stellar play earning him First-Team All-Pro honors and a runner-up finish to Pittsburgh's "Mean" Joe Greene in the NFL Defensive Player of the Year voting.

Memorable Moments/Greatest Performances

Bergey recorded his first interception as a member of the Eagles during a 13–7 win over the San Diego Chargers on October 6, 1974.

Bergey led the Eagles to a 20–7 victory over the Giants on December 8, 1974, by intercepting a pass and anchoring a defense that limited New York to just 35 yards rushing.

Bergey contributed to a 27–17 win over the San Francisco 49ers on November 30, 1975, by picking off two passes.

Bergey proved to be the driving force behind a 26–3 victory over the Washington Redskins in the 1975 regular-season finale, intercepting a pass and leading a defense that recorded a season-high eight turnovers.

Although the Eagles ended up losing their December 3, 1978, matchup with the Minnesota Vikings by a score of 28–27, Bergey helped set up one of his team's touchdowns by intercepting a Fran Tarkenton pass and returning the ball 50 yards, for what proved to be his longest return as a member of the Eagles.

Notable Achievements

- Intercepted five passes in 1974.
- Led NFL with six fumble recoveries in 1975.
- Led Eagles in tackles six times and interceptions once.
- Holds Eagles record for most career tackles, with nearly 1,200 "unofficial" stops.
- Holds Eagles single-season record for most tackles (233 in 1976).
- 1980 NFC champion.
- Finished second in 1974 NFL Defensive Player of the Year voting.
- Three-time Eagles MVP (1974, 1976, and 1977).
- Four-time Pro Bowl selection (1974, 1976, 1977, and 1978).
- Two-time First-Team All-Pro selection (1974 and 1975).
- Three-time Second-Team All-Pro selection (1976, 1977, and 1978).
- Five-time First-Team All-Conference selection (1974, 1975, 1976, 1977, and 1978).
- 1980 Second-Team All-Conference selection.
- Pro Football Reference All-1970s Second Team.
- Inducted into Philadelphia Eagles Hall of Fame in 1988.

11
TOMMY McDONALD

The smallest player in the Pro Football Hall of Fame, Tommy McDonald stood just 5'9" and weighed only 178 pounds. Nevertheless, McDonald established himself as one of the league's most dangerous wideouts over the course of his 12-year NFL career, ranking among the circuit leaders in receptions five times, receiving yards six times, and touchdown catches on seven separate occasions. Spending most of his peak seasons with the Eagles from 1957 to 1963, McDonald surpassed 1,000 receiving yards twice, scored at least 10 touchdowns four times, and averaged more than 20 yards per reception three times as a member of the team, with his seven-year average of 19.2 yards per catch representing the highest figure in franchise history. Also ranking among the team's all-time leaders in receiving yards, touchdown receptions, touchdowns scored, and points scored, McDonald, who proved to be a key figure in the Eagles' successful run to the NFL championship in 1960, earned five trips to the Pro Bowl, two All-Pro nominations, and three All-Conference selections during his time in Philadelphia, with his exceptional play also landing him a spot on the Eagles 75th Anniversary Team and gaining him induction into the team's Hall of Fame following the conclusion of his playing career.

Born in Roy, New Mexico, on July 26, 1934, Thomas Franklin McDonald attended Roy High School as a freshman, before transferring to Highland High School after moving with his family about 120 miles south to the city of Albuquerque prior to the start of his sophomore year. Looking back at how relocating to Albuquerque affected his life, McDonald said, "My biggest break was moving to Albuquerque for my last two years in high school. Roy was such a small town. If our family had stayed in Roy, I would never have been noticed or discovered. . . . Moving to Albuquerque was a blessing from the big guy upstairs. I had a chance for people to see my God-given talent once I got to Albuquerque."

Developing into a three-sport star at Highland High, McDonald excelled in football, basketball, and track, scoring 157 points and

Tommy McDonald starred for the Eagles at wideout for seven seasons.
Courtesy of BoxingTreasures.com

averaging more than 20 yards per carry as a running back in his senior year, while also setting the city scoring record in basketball and winning five gold medals in the state track meet as a sprinter and hurdler. Making an extremely favorable impression on college scouts with his outstanding athletic achievements, McDonald received scholarship offers from several major universities, including SMU, Texas, and TCU, before ultimately choosing to enroll at the University of Oklahoma. Concentrating primarily on football while at Oklahoma, McDonald spent three years starring at running back for head coach Bud Wilkinson, never tasting defeat during that time, with the Sooners posting 31 of their NCAA Division I record 47 consecutive victories over the course of those three seasons. Performing especially well as a senior in 1956, McDonald earned All-America honors for the second straight time, finished third in the Heisman Trophy voting, and won the Maxwell Award as college football's player of the year.

Yet, despite his exceptional play at the collegiate level, McDonald's size caused him to slip to the third round of the 1957 NFL Draft, where the Eagles finally selected him with the 31st overall pick. Used primarily on punt and kickoff returns his first year in the league while transitioning to wide receiver, McDonald saw very little action on offense, making just nine receptions for 228 yards and three touchdowns, although he did manage to rank among the NFL leaders with 431 total return yards. But, following the offseason acquisition of Hall of Fame quarterback Norm Van Brocklin, who helped him develop his pass-receiving skills, McDonald emerged as one of the Eagles' top offensive threats in 1958, earning Pro Bowl honors for the first of five straight times by making 29 receptions, amassing 603 receiving yards, and leading the league with nine TD catches. Improving upon those totals in 1959, McDonald began an outstanding four-year run during which he posted the following numbers:

YEAR	REC	REC YD	TD RECS
1959	47	846	10
1960	39	801	13
1961	64	**1,144**	**13**
1962	58	1,146	10

McDonald finished in the league's top five in receptions in three of those four seasons, placing as high as second in 1959. He also ranked among the league leaders in receiving yards and touchdown receptions all four years, topping the circuit in both categories in 1961, and finishing second in TD catches two other times. In addition to earning Pro Bowl honors all four years, McDonald gained All-Pro recognition from at least one news wire service each season.

A sure-handed receiver with elusive speed, McDonald ran with the ball exceptionally well after making the catch, with his ability to avoid defenders in the open field making him a true game-breaker. Catching at least one pass in 93 consecutive games at one point during his career, McDonald made a total of 84 TD grabs, with 66 of those coming as a member of the Eagles.

Known for his outstanding hands even though he lost the tip of his left thumb in a motorbike accident as a teenager, McDonald appeared on the cover of a 1962 issue of *Sports Illustrated*, with the headline reading, "Football's Best Hands." Taking great pride in his ability to catch the football, McDonald sandpapered his fingertips before every game, claiming that doing so made them more sensitive and helped him feel the ball better. He also scraped his fingers on the brick wall at Franklin Field before home games to achieve the same effect, saying years later, "The receivers today all wear gloves, even when they're playing indoors. I'd never wear gloves. I want to feel the ball. I want to feel every pebble on the leather."

Commenting on McDonald's ability to make even the most difficult of catches, Cardinals safety Jerry Norton claimed, "The best thing you can do after you knock McDonald down is to sit on him and pin his arms to the ground. Even then, he's liable to catch the ball between his feet."

Also renowned for his toughness and ability to perform well under pressure, McDonald drew praise from former teammate Norm Van Brocklin, who said, "I played with a lot of great receivers, including Elroy Hirsch and Tom Fears with the Rams. But, if I had to pick one guy to throw the ball to with the game on the line, I'd pick McDonald. I know somehow the little bugger would get open and he'd catch the football."

Expressing his admiration for McDonald, New York Giants head coach Allie Sherman stated, "I don't think I ever saw McDonald play a bad game. He scared the hell out of me. He might only catch four balls in a game, but two of them would be big plays that usually swung the balance. He had what I call a great sense of pace. He would shift gears on a defender, turn him around, and get open anytime he wanted. He was like Fred Biletnikoff and Steve Largent, only more explosive."

Sherman continued, "We had a defensive back named Erich Barnes who was 6-3, about 200 pounds and very good at 'man' coverage. But he had a heckuva time with McDonald. Erich could wear down other receivers, but he couldn't do that to McDonald. Tommy was too tough, too competitive. I've never seen anyone run the post pattern better. He was fearless coming across the middle."

McDonald's resolve earned him the undying respect of Chuck Bednarik, who said of his longtime teammate, "Tommy had more guts for a little guy . . . I can't say enough about him. He would catch the ball, and he'd actually challenge guys. He'd run right at them. Big guys, linebackers, it didn't matter. That's like crashing into a wall. He'd take that big hit and he'd pop right up and flip the ball to the official as if to say, 'Look, you can't hurt me.'"

In explaining his demonstrative behavior, McDonald told Ted Maule of *Sports Illustrated*, "I don't like to let some guy on the other side think he can hurt me just because I'm small. If he gives me his best lick and doesn't cave me in, he gets a little discouraged. I just get a kick out of proving there's a place for a runt in pro football. I got so tired, my whole life, hearing, 'You're too small.' All that did was make me try that much harder."

Vince Lombardi was another who greatly admired the diminutive receiver, stating on one occasion, "If I had 11 Tommy McDonalds on my team, I'd win a championship every year."

Nevertheless, with McDonald posting somewhat less impressive numbers in 1963, concluding the campaign with 41 receptions, 731 receiving yards, and eight TD catches, the Eagles elected to trade him to the Dallas Cowboys for all-purpose kicker Sam Baker, defensive tackle John Meyers, and offensive lineman Lynn Hoyem on March 20, 1964, ending his seven-year stint in Philadelphia. Over the course of those seven seasons, McDonald caught 287 passes, amassed 5,499 receiving yards, and made 66 touchdown receptions, with the last figure representing the second-highest total in franchise history.

McDonald subsequently spent just one season in Dallas, making 46 receptions for 612 yards and two touchdowns for the Cowboys in 1964, before

McDonald holds the Eagles career record for most yards per pass reception.
Courtesy of Bill Daniels

being dealt to the Los Angeles Rams prior to the start of the 1965 campaign. After earning his sixth trip to the Pro Bowl by ranking among the league leaders with 67 receptions, 1,036 receiving yards, and nine TD catches in 1965, McDonald had another solid year for the Rams, after which they traded him to the Atlanta Falcons. He then spent one year in Atlanta, before closing out his career as a backup with the Cleveland Browns in 1968. Announcing his retirement at season's end, McDonald left the game ranking sixth all-time in receptions (495), fourth in receiving yards (8,410), and second in touchdown receptions (84). Extremely durable despite his smallish frame, McDonald missed just three games his first 11 years in the league.

Following his playing days, McDonald dabbled in art, owning Tommy McDonald Enterprises, which provided artists to paint portraits on commission, mostly of athletes and well-known businessmen. After spending several years suffering from dementia, McDonald passed away at the age of 84, on September 24, 2018. Upon learning of his passing, Eagles owner Jeffrey Lurie said:

> Tommy McDonald played the game with a passion and energy that was second to none. He will be remembered as one of the most exciting players ever to play his position, but what really separated him and made him so unique was the infectious personality and charisma that he brought to his everyday life. He had a genuine love for this team, for the Philadelphia community, for the fans, and, of course, his family. He was a man of character, both on and off the field, who exemplified all the qualities that we hope to represent as an organization. . . . He was a champion, a Pro Football Hall of Famer, and one of the most genuine individuals I have ever met. On behalf of the Philadelphia Eagles, I would like to express our deepest condolences to the entire McDonald family.

Echoing Lurie's sentiments, Hall of Fame president and CEO David Baker said in a prepared statement, "Tommy McDonald lived life like he played the game of football. He was charismatic, passionate and had fun. He was such a character. Heaven is a happier place today."

Meanwhile, Philadelphia sports personality Ray Didinger, who grew up idolizing McDonald before later becoming his close personal friend, paid homage to his fallen hero by saying:

> He was extraordinary. The expression one of a kind, that's kind of thrown around a lot, but that really applies to him. I've never met anyone like him in terms of his personality, his energy, his wackiness, and how that all sort of fit together in the profile of him as an athlete. It all kind of went hand in hand. They listed him at 5-11 and 185 pounds, but he was actually 5-9 and 170, which, even in that era, was a little man. And, of course, he was a wide receiver at a time when defensive backs could do anything they wanted to do to wide receivers. For Tommy, he spent

his whole career—12 years—having to fight his way off the line of scrimmage. But, if you look at what he accomplished, he was the best big play receiver of his era, for sure. It wasn't even close in terms of touchdown catches relative to the other guys in his time.

EAGLES CAREER HIGHLIGHTS

Best Season

McDonald had an outstanding all-around season for the Eagles in 1959, earning Pro Bowl honors for the second of five straight times by ranking among the league leaders with 47 receptions, 846 receiving yards, 10 TD catches, 11 touchdowns, 444 kickoff-return yards, and a career-high 1,395 all-purpose yards. He also performed extremely well in 1962, placing in the league's top five in receptions (58), receiving yards (1,146), and touchdown receptions (10). Nevertheless, McDonald posted his most impressive overall numbers as a member of the Eagles in 1961, when, in addition to finishing fourth in the NFL with 64 receptions, he topped the circuit with 1,144 receiving yards and 13 touchdown catches.

Memorable Moments/Greatest Performances

McDonald contributed to a 21–12 victory over the Washington Redskins on November 24, 1957, by scoring the first two touchdowns of his career on pass plays that covered 61 and 36 yards, with then NFL commissioner Bert Bell reportedly calling his 61-yard TD grab "one of the greatest catches I have ever seen in pro football."

McDonald made just one catch during a 27–24 win over the Giants on October 5, 1958, but it went for a 91-yard touchdown that represented the longest play of his career.

McDonald had a huge game against the Giants on October 4, 1959, helping to lead the Eagles to a convincing 49–21 victory over their Eastern Division rivals by returning a punt 81 yards for a touchdown and scoring three more times on pass plays that covered 33, 55, and 19 yards. McDonald, who finished the contest with six catches, 133 receiving yards, more than 200 all-purpose yards, and four touchdowns, hooked up with Norm Van Brocklin on his first two TD receptions, before collaborating with Sonny Jurgensen on his final score.

During a memorable 28–24 victory over the Chicago Cardinals on October 25, 1959, McDonald completed a furious second-half comeback by the Eagles that saw them overcome a 24–0 third-quarter deficit when he made a game-winning 22-yard TD reception late in the fourth quarter. He finished the game with three receptions for 122 yards and two touchdowns.

McDonald led the Eagles to a 34–14 win over Washington on December 6, 1959, by making nine receptions for 153 yards and three touchdowns, the longest of which went for 50 yards.

McDonald again made three TD receptions during a lopsided 34–7 victory over the Steelers on November 6, 1960, scoring on pass plays that covered 24, 39, and 26 yards. He finished the contest with eight catches, 141 receiving yards, and those three touchdowns.

McDonald made one of the biggest plays of the 1960 NFL Championship Game in the second quarter, when he gave the Eagles a 7–6 lead over Green Bay by hauling in a 35-yard TD pass from Norm Van Brocklin. He finished the game with three catches for 90 yards and that one touchdown.

McDonald starred in defeat on October 1, 1961, making 11 catches for 187 yards during a 30–27 loss to the St. Louis Cardinals.

McDonald gave the Eagles a 27–24 win over the Washington Redskins on October 29, 1961, when he collaborated with Sonny Jurgensen on a 41-yard scoring play during the latter stages of the fourth quarter. He finished the contest with seven receptions for 141 yards and that one TD.

The combination of McDonald and Jurgensen proved to be too much for the Dallas Cowboys to handle during a 35–13 Eagles win on November 26, 1961, with the duo hooking up five times for 131 yards and three touchdowns, which covered 46, 40, and 27 yards.

Although the New York Giants ended up clinching the Eastern Division title with a 28–24 victory over the Eagles on December 10, 1961, McDonald performed exceptionally well throughout the contest, making seven receptions for a career-high 237 yards and two touchdowns, which came on 52- and 30-yard connections with Sonny Jurgensen.

McDonald once again starred in defeat on December 16, 1962, catching four passes, amassing 162 receiving yards, and scoring three times on plays that covered 56, 60, and 40 yards during a 45–35 loss to the St. Louis Cardinals.

McDonald had another big day in the 1963 regular-season opener, making seven receptions for 179 yards and two touchdowns during a 21–21 tie with the Pittsburgh Steelers.

A few weeks later, McDonald made a season-high eight catches, amassed 139 receiving yards, and scored twice, in helping the Eagles defeat Washington by a score of 37–24 on October 13.

Notable Achievements

- Surpassed 50 receptions twice.
- Topped 1,000 receiving yards twice.
- Made at least 10 touchdown receptions four times.
- Averaged more than 20 yards per reception three times.
- Surpassed 1,000 all-purpose yards three times.
- Returned one punt for a touchdown during career.
- Led NFL in receiving yards once and touchdown receptions twice.
- Finished second in NFL in receptions twice and touchdown receptions twice.
- Finished third in NFL in receiving yards three times and touchdowns scored twice.
- Holds Eagles career record for most yards per reception (19.2).
- Ranks among Eagles career leaders with: 5,499 receiving yards (6th); 66 touchdown receptions (2nd); 67 touchdowns scored (4th); and 402 points scored (8th).
- 1960 Eastern Division champion.
- 1960 NFL champion.
- Five-time Pro Bowl selection (1958, 1959, 1960, 1961, and 1962).
- Two-time Second-Team All-Pro selection (1959 and 1962).
- Three-time First-Team All-Conference selection (1959, 1960, and 1961).
- Pro Football Reference All-1960s Second Team.
- Named to Eagles 75th Anniversary Team in 2007.
- Inducted into Philadelphia Eagles Hall of Fame in 1988.
- Elected to Pro Football Hall of Fame in 1998.

12

— RANDALL CUNNINGHAM —

In speaking of Randall Cunningham, Eagles head coach Buddy Ryan once proclaimed, "He's the best athlete to ever play the position. He's got the best arm in the league. He's the best runner and the best punter. The only thing he can't do is play basketball."

Called "The Ultimate Weapon" by *Sports Illustrated*, Cunningham had the ability to take over a football game all by himself in any number of ways, with his powerful throwing arm, quick feet, and outstanding mobility making him the NFL's first true dual-threat quarterback. Spending his first 11 years in the league with the Eagles, Cunningham threw for more than 3,000 yards four times, completed more than 20 touchdown passes four times, and ran for more than 500 yards six times as a member of the team, leading the club in rushing on four separate occasions. A three-time Bert Bell Award winner as NFL Player of the Year, Cunningham won the award twice while playing for the Eagles, whom he led to five playoff appearances and one division title. Cunningham also earned three trips to the Pro Bowl, two All-Pro nominations, and two All-NFC selections during his time in Philadelphia, with his stellar play eventually gaining him induction into the Eagles Hall of Fame. Yet, Cunningham likely would have accomplished even more had Buddy Ryan made more of an effort to help him fully develop his quarterback skills.

Born in Santa Barbara, California, on March 27, 1963, Randall W. Cunningham attended Santa Barbara High School, where he competed in track and field in the high jump and starred on the gridiron at quarterback, leading his team to a league title and the CIF Finals in his senior year. Continuing to excel behind center for the University of Nevada, Las Vegas, Cunningham led the Rebels to a record of 11-2 as a senior, while also earning All-America honors as a punter for the second straight year.

Impressed with Cunningham's unique skill set, the Eagles selected him in the second round of the 1985 NFL Draft, with the 37th overall pick. Cunningham subsequently spent most of his first two seasons in

Philadelphia backing up veteran starting quarterback Ron Jaworski, being used primarily in third-and-long situations, where his scrambling ability made him more of a threat to make a big play than the less mobile Jaworski. Cunningham finally became the full-time starter after Jaworski suffered a hand injury in Week 10 of the 1986 campaign, completing just over 53 percent of his passes for 1,391 yards and eight touchdowns the remainder of the year, while also finishing the season with 540 yards rushing and five touchdowns.

Sports Illustrated once called Randall Cunningham "The Ultimate Weapon."
George A. Kitrinos

Looking back at the early stages of Cunningham's career years later, former teammate Eric Allen said, "You knew there was something special about Randall. He was extremely athletic, played with a great sense of self, understood that he was good, understood that he could do a lot of things that other quarterbacks in the game could not do, and he had a great deal of confidence."

Developing into one of the league's top signal-callers during the strike-shortened 1987 season, Cunningham began an outstanding four-year run during which he compiled the following numbers:

YEAR	YD PASSING	TD PASSES	INTS	COMP %	QBR	YD RUSHING
1987	2,786	23	12	54.9	83.0	505
1988	3,808	24	16	53.8	77.6	624
1989	3,400	21	15	54.5	75.5	621
1990	3,466	30	13	58.3	91.6	942

In addition to ranking among the NFL leaders in passing yards twice and touchdown passes three times during that period, Cunningham led the league in rushing average twice, averaging 6 yards per carry in 1989, before posting an average of 8 yards per carry the following year. Cunningham, who led the Eagles in rushing all four years, earned three trips to the Pro Bowl and one All-Pro selection during that time, while also being named NFL Player of the Year in both 1988 and 1990. More importantly, the Eagles made the playoffs in each of the last three seasons, although they failed to advance beyond the first round of the postseason tournament even once.

Cunningham accomplished all he did even though he had virtually no weapons at wide receiver or running back, proving to be essentially a one-man wrecking crew for the Eagles over the course of those four seasons. Capable of creating plays out of nothing with his legs, the 6'4", 212-pound Cunningham often used his mobility to scramble out of the pocket and find receivers downfield for huge gains. In discussing the problems that Cunningham presented to opposing defenses, New York Giants linebacker Carl Banks said, "When they would say he was 'The Ultimate Weapon,' he was truly the ultimate weapon. I don't think there was ever a quarterback who was harder to prepare for, or who gave defensive players individually more problems or more concerns before the game even started."

Banks added, "He was the guy you wanted to play against, but you also hated to play against because you knew he was just an incredible football player. I've played against Doug (Williams), Warren (Moon), and Joe (Montana). I don't think any one of those guys brought to a game the fear that Randall Cunningham put in a defense."

Suggesting that Cunningham represented a new breed of NFL quarterback, Warren Moon stated, "He was a guy who was really successful with his legs, but he also had a cannon for an arm. He really was the first dual-threat quarterback. Some people would say Fran Tarkenton, but he was more of a scrambler . . . Randall could scramble, but he could also run. He also had a very good arm. Then, after him, you had Steve Young, Michael Vick, and the guys who came along later. But Randall really was the first to get that started."

Still, Cunningham never truly reached his full potential during his time in Philadelphia. Spending his first several seasons playing under Buddy Ryan, Cunningham received very little direction from his defensive-minded coach, who typically told him before the start of each contest to make a few big plays and allow the defense to take care of the rest. As a result, Cunningham did a poor job of protecting the football, leading the league in fumbles three times. He also endured far too many sacks, failed to read opposing defenses properly, struggled at times against the league's stronger teams, and suffered numerous injuries due to his tendency to hold onto the football too long.

Nevertheless, Cunningham had nothing but praise for his former coach, stating on one occasion, "Buddy Ryan allowed me to be the player he believed I could be. He saw something in me and gave me an opportunity to flourish as an athlete, and not just a quarterback, but to really take it to a whole other level."

After missing virtually all of 1991 with a torn anterior cruciate ligament he suffered in the regular-season opener, Cunningham returned to the Eagles the following year to lead them to an 11-5 record and their first playoff victory in 12 years, earning in the process Second-Team All-Pro and NFL Comeback Player of the Year honors. However, he experienced much less success the next three seasons, appearing in only four games in 1993 due to injury, posting rather pedestrian numbers for an Eagles team that finished just 7-9 in 1994, and starting only four contests in 1995 after being benched in favor of veteran signal-caller Rodney Peete, who did a better job of grasping new offensive coordinator Jon Gruden's complicated schemes. Unhappy with his role as a backup, Cunningham announced his retirement following the conclusion of the 1995 campaign, ending his 11-year stay in Philadelphia with 22,877 yards passing, 150 touchdown passes, 105 interceptions, a 55.7 pass completion percentage, a 78.7 quarterback rating, 4,482 yards rushing, 32 rushing touchdowns, and a rushing average of 6.6 yards per carry. In his 107 starts as a member of the team, Cunningham led the Eagles to an overall record of 63-43-1.

Cunningham subsequently sat out the 1996 season, before returning to the NFL as a member of the Minnesota Vikings the following year. After assuming a backup role his first year in Minnesota, Cunningham had the greatest season of his career in 1998, when, surrounded by outstanding talent on offense for the first time as a pro, he

Cunningham earned NFL Player of the Year honors twice while playing for the Eagles. Courtesy of George A. Kitrinos led the Vikings to a regular-season record of 15-1 and a berth in the NFC championship game by passing for 3,704 yards, throwing 34 touchdown passes and only 10 interceptions, completing 60.9 percent of his passes, and leading the league with a quarterback rating of 106.0, with his exceptional play earning him NFL Player of the Year honors for the third time. Cunningham spent one more injury-marred year in Minnesota, before being released by the Vikings following the conclusion of the 1999 campaign. He then split his final two seasons between the Dallas Cowboys and the Baltimore Ravens, serving as a backup for both teams, before retiring for good at the end of 2001. Cunningham concluded his playing career with 29,979 yards passing, 207 touchdown passes, 134 interceptions, a completion percentage of 56.6 percent, a quarterback rating of 81.5, 4,928 yards rushing, and 35 rushing touchdowns, retiring as the NFL's all-time leading rusher among quarterbacks.

After announcing that he wished to retire as an Eagle, Cunningham drew the following words of praise from team chairman and CEO Jeffrey Lurie, who said, "Randall brought so much excitement to the city of Philadelphia and to the NFL. Personally, I'm very proud and excited that he wanted to retire as an Eagle. He's meant so much to this city and this franchise."

Eagles head coach Andy Reid added, "Randall was a big part of Eagles history, at least in the modern era of Eagles football. When you think of Eagles football, you think of Randall Cunningham and the great things he did as a quarterback. Really, he kind of changed the position and added flair to it. . . . It's great to have him retire as an Eagle, and it's great to have the former players come back and be part of this organization again."

Following his retirement, Cunningham, a born-again Christian, became an ordained Protestant minister, founded a church in Las Vegas called Remnant Ministries, and became active in the gospel music business, opening a recording studio that produced Christian worship music. He later accepted the position of offensive coordinator for Silverado High School's football team, before being named head coach in December 2014.

Remaining a huge fan of Cunningham to this day, Carl Banks suggests that the Pro Football Hall of Fame should strongly consider opening its doors to the former quarterback, stating, "He has never been appreciated by those people who never played against him. But people who played against him know how great he was. If you combine Cam Newton and Michael Vick, both of their skill sets, you still don't get Randall Cunningham."

EAGLES CAREER HIGHLIGHTS

Best Season

Cunningham played his best ball for the Eagles from 1988 to 1990, earning Pro Bowl honors all three years and being named the winner of the Bert Bell Award as NFL Player of the Year in both 1988 and 1990. In addition to throwing for a career-high 3,808 yards in the first of those campaigns, Cunningham tossed 24 touchdown passes and 16 interceptions, completed 53.8 percent of his passes, posted a quarterback rating of 77.6, and ran for 624 yards and six touchdowns. However, he had his finest all-around season in 1990, throwing for 3,466 yards, finishing second in the league with 30 TD passes, throwing only 13 interceptions, completing 58.3 percent of his passes, posting a QBR of 91.6, and running for a career-high 942 yards and five touchdowns.

Memorable Moments/Greatest Performances

Although the Eagles lost to Dallas by a score of 17–14 on October 19, 1986, Cunningham played well in his first pro start, completing a 15-yard touchdown pass to Mike Quick and scoring the first TD of his career on a 14-yard run.

Cunningham proved to be the difference in a 33–27 overtime win over the Los Angeles Raiders on November 30, 1986, throwing for 298 yards and three touchdowns, all of which went to Mike Quick, and scoring the game-winning TD in OT on a 1-yard run.

Cunningham earned NFC Offensive Player of the Week honors for the first of four times by passing for 291 yards and three touchdowns during a 28–23 victory over the St. Louis Cardinals on November 1, 1987. After hooking up with Kenny Jackson earlier in the game on a 70-yard scoring play, Cunningham gave the Eagles the win when he threw a 9-yard strike to Gregg Garrity in the closing moments.

Cunningham had another big day on November 29, 1987, leading the Eagles to a 34–31 overtime victory over the New England Patriots by passing for 314 yards and two touchdowns, with both of his TD passes, which covered 61 and 29 yards, going to Mike Quick.

Cunningham led the Eagles to a 38–27 win over the New York Jets on December 20, 1987, by throwing for 280 yards and three touchdowns, the longest of which went 45 yards to Quick.

Cunningham used both his arm and his legs to lead the Eagles to a 33–23 victory over the Houston Oilers on October 2, 1988, passing for 289 yards and two touchdowns, and scoring himself on a 33-yard run.

Cunningham leaped into the national spotlight with an exceptional performance against the Giants on *Monday Night Football* on the evening of October 10, 1988, earning NFC Offensive Player of the Week honors by leading the Eagles to a 24–13 win over their Eastern Division rivals. Completing 31 of 41 passes for 369 yards and three touchdowns, the longest of which went 80 yards to Cris Carter, Cunningham made one of the most memorable plays of his career when, after being hit at the New York 10-yard line by linebacker Carl Banks, he used his left hand to stabilize himself, popped up, and threw a touchdown pass to tight end Jimmie Giles. Looking back on Cunningham's extraordinarily athletic effort, Banks said, "It was a pretty damn good tackle, and he was just better. I'd salute that any day of the week. He was just better than I was on that play. It's something you shake your head at and just salute that dude."

Cunningham starred during a 30–24 win over the Los Angeles Rams on November 6, 1988, throwing for 323 yards and three touchdowns, with two of those going to Keith Jackson and the other to Keith Byars.

Cunningham had a huge game against Washington on September 17, 1989, completing 34 of 46 pass attempts for 447 yards and five touchdowns during a 42–37 victory. With his final two TD passes enabling the Eagles to overcome a nine-point fourth-quarter deficit, Cunningham ended up being named NFC Offensive Player of the Week.

Cunningham displayed his tremendous versatility during a 24–17 win over the Giants on December 3, 1989, when he unleashed a franchise-record 91-yard punt that remains the fourth-longest in NFL history.

Cunningham performed brilliantly during a 48–20 win over the Patriots on November 4, 1990, throwing for 240 yards and four touchdowns, and carrying the ball eight times for 124 yards and one touchdown, which came on a career-long 52-yard run.

Cunningham led the Eagles to a convincing 31–13 victory over the previously undefeated New York Giants on November 25, 1990, by passing for two touchdowns and running for another, with his outstanding play gaining him recognition as the NFC Offensive Player of the Week.

Although the Eagles lost to the Buffalo Bills by a score of 30–23 the following week, Cunningham displayed his exceptional athletic ability during the contest when he threw a 95-yard touchdown pass to Fred Barnett while rolling out to his left, with the ball traveling more than 70 yards in the air. In discussing Cunningham's extraordinary effort years later, Barnett said,

"That play didn't surprise me because Randall had the athletic ability to come up with anything."

Cunningham ran for a career-high 121 yards during a 28–17 win over the Minnesota Vikings on December 6, 1992.

Cunningham followed that up with an outstanding effort against Seattle on December 13, running for one score and passing for a season-high 365 yards during a 20–17 overtime win.

Cunningham gave the Eagles a dramatic 34–31 victory over the Washington Redskins on September 19, 1993, when he connected with Calvin Williams on a 10-yard scoring play in the game's closing moments. Cunningham finished the contest with 360 yards passing and three TD passes, all of which went to Williams.

Cunningham threw another two touchdown passes to Williams during a 30–22 win over the Bears on September 12, 1994, finishing the game with 311 yards passing and three TD passes.

Notable Achievements

- Passed for more than 3,000 yards four times, topping 3,800 yards once (3,808 in 1988).
- Threw more than 20 touchdown passes four times, tossing 30 TD passes in 1990.
- Completed more than 60 percent of passes twice.
- Posted touchdown-to-interception ratio of better than 2–1 once.
- Posted quarterback rating above 90.0 once (91.6 in 1990).
- Rushed for more than 500 yards six times, including mark of 942 yards in 1990.
- Rushed for 32 touchdowns.
- Averaged more than 6 yards per carry eight times, posting mark in excess of 8.0 twice.
- Led Eagles in rushing four times.
- Led NFL in average yards per carry twice.
- Led NFL quarterbacks in game-winning drives once and fourth-quarter comebacks once.
- Finished second in NFL with 30 touchdown passes in 1990.
- Finished third in NFL with 3,808 yards passing in 1988.
- Ranks second in NFL history with career rushing average of 6.4 yards per carry.
- Ranks among Eagles career leaders with: 3,362 pass attempts (3rd); 1,874 pass completions (3rd); 22,877 passing yards (3rd); 150

touchdown passes (3rd); 4,482 yards rushing (6th); and 32 rushing touchdowns (5th).
- 1988 division champion.
- Four-time NFC Offensive Player of the Week.
- 1990 NFC Player of the Year.
- Two-time Bert Bell Award winner as NFL Player of the Year (1988 and 1990).
- 1992 NFL Comeback Player of the Year.
- Three-time Pro Bowl selection (1988, 1989, and 1990).
- Two-time Second-Team All-Pro selection (1988 and 1992).
- Two-time First-Team All-Conference selection (1988 and 1990).
- Inducted into Philadelphia Eagles Hall of Fame in 2009.

13

— JASON PETERS —

Acquired from the Buffalo Bills for three draft picks on April 17, 2009, Jason Peters established himself as arguably the preeminent left tackle in all of football during his time in Philadelphia. An excellent pass-protector and superb run-blocker, Peters earned four All-Pro selections and seven trips to the Pro Bowl, before age and injuries began to take their toll on him, with his seven Pro Bowl nominations tying him with Reggie White and Brian Dawkins for the second most in franchise history. In addition to making him one of the most decorated players in team annals, Peters's stellar play helped the Eagles win three division titles, one NFC championship, and one Super Bowl between 2009 and 2018.

Born in Bowie County, Texas, on January 22, 1982, Jason Raynard Peters always appeared older than his age due to his size, once suffering the embarrassment of being removed from a baseball game at the age of nine because the umpire and opposing coach refused to believe that he did not exceed the league's age limit. Recalling the events that transpired that day, Peters said, "I struck out nine batters in the first three innings. My mother had to go home and get my birth certificate before I was allowed back in the game. After I did, I hit a home run."

Starring in football and basketball while attending Queen City High School, Peters earned All-District and All-Area honors in both sports, averaging 18.4 points per game on the hardwood, while also excelling as a defensive end on the gridiron. Subsequently recruited by several colleges as a defensive tackle, Peters accepted a scholarship from the University of Arkansas, where, after redshirting as a freshman, he transitioned to the other side of the ball in his sophomore year. Spending his final three seasons at Arkansas playing tight end for the Razorbacks, Peters recorded a total of 46 receptions, with his run-blocking skills gaining him far more recognition than his abilities as a pass-catcher.

Choosing to leave Arkansas after his junior year, Peters entered the 2004 NFL Draft, where, after being projected as an offensive tackle, he

Jason Peters has anchored the left side of the Eagles' offensive line for 10 seasons.
Courtesy of Keith Allison

went undrafted by all 32 teams. Signed as a free agent by the Buffalo Bills, Peters spent most of his rookie season serving as a member of the team's practice squad, although he eventually earned a promotion to the 53-man roster, seeing action at both tight end and offensive tackle during the final few weeks of the campaign. Inserted at tackle full-time the following year, Peters later credited Bills coach Mike Mularkey with the career-changing move, stating, "Offensive line was one of our weak points, and I remember wanting to get on the field any way I could. Coach Mularkey told me about it, and Mouse (offensive line coach Jim McNally) and I got to work."

After initially struggling somewhat at his new post, Peters gradually developed into Buffalo's best offensive lineman, nearly earning a spot on the *Sports Illustrated* 2006 All-Pro team, with that magazine's Paul Zimmerman writing, "I was rooting for the Bills' Jason Peters, whom I would have loved to pick, but he isn't there yet. Very athletic, but not enough of a roughneck."

Emerging as one of the league's top players at his position the following year, Peters gained Pro Bowl and All-Pro recognition for the first time in his career, with Buffalo line coach Jim McNally saying of his protégé, "His ability is limitless." After being similarly honored in 2008, Peters, unhappy with his contract situation, chose not to attend any of Buffalo's offseason workouts, prompting the Bills to trade him to the Eagles for a first-round draft pick in 2009, a fourth-round draft pick in 2009, and a sixth-round selection in 2010. Upon completing the deal, Eagles head coach Andy Reid proclaimed, "Jason Peters is the best left tackle in football. He is a powerful and athletic tackle, and I have admired his play over the last few years on film." The Eagles immediately signed Peters to a six-year, $60 million contract, voiding in the process the deal he previously inked with the Bills that still had two years remaining.

Although the Eagles paid a steep price for Peters, they never regretted making the move, with the 6'4", 328-pound tackle earning Pro Bowl honors in each of his first three seasons in Philadelphia, while also gaining All-Pro recognition in both 2010 and 2011. After missing the entire 2012 campaign with a ruptured Achilles tendon he injured during an offseason workout, Peters returned to top form the following year, earning Pro Bowl and First-Team All-Pro honors by helping the NFC East champion Eagles amass a franchise-record 6,676 yards of total offense. Continuing his outstanding play in each of the next three seasons, Peters earned three more trips

to the Pro Bowl and another All-Pro selection, prompting the Eagles to extend his contract through the end of 2018. Expressing his appreciation for everything Peters had contributed to the team since his arrival in Philadelphia, Eagles executive VP of football operations Howie Roseman said at the time, "Jason is a future Hall of Famer, a great player, and leader. He has been an anchor for our offensive line for many years, and now we are thrilled about being able to work something out that will allow him to finish his career here in Philadelphia."

Peters has earned seven trips to the Pro Bowl as a member of the Eagles.
Courtesy of Keith Allison

Unfortunately, Peters tore the ACL and MCL in his right knee against Washington on October 23, 2017, bringing his season to a premature end, and preventing him from taking part in Philadelphia's successful run to the NFL championship. After returning to action in 2018, Peters suffered a right biceps injury against the Giants in Week 6 that plagued him for the rest of the year. Nevertheless, he ended up starting all 16 games for the Eagles at his familiar left tackle position, with Philadelphia offensive line coach Jeff Stoutland commenting at one point during the season, "He's still playing at a very high level. I don't get into all the injuries. I'm not a doctor. But that guy is a warrior. He just keeps playing and playing and playing."

Amid speculation that Peters might have played his last game for the Eagles in 2018, the team announced during the subsequent offseason that it had signed the veteran left tackle to a one-year deal that would enable him to return to Philadelphia for his 16th NFL season. In announcing the team's decision to bring back the 37-year-old Peters for one more year, Howie Roseman said, "Jason is not a normal human being. He's freaky. He's a first-ballot Hall of Famer as a player and as a person."

EAGLES CAREER HIGHLIGHTS

Best Season

It could be argued that Peters had the greatest season of his career in 2013, when he earned one of his two First-Team All-Pro nominations by helping the Eagles score 442 points and set a franchise record by amassing a total of 6,686 yards on offense. Furthermore, with LeSean McCoy rushing for a league-leading 1,607 yards, the Eagles gained more yards on the ground than any other NFL team (2,566), averaging a robust 5.1 yards per carry. However, the Eagles proved to be almost as potent on offense in 2011, accumulating a total of 6,386 yards and tallying 396 points, with Philadelphia running backs gaining 2,276 yards on the ground and averaging 5.1 yards per carry. Additionally, while only the Associated Press accorded Peters First-Team All-Pro honors in 2013, he gained consensus First-Team All-Pro recognition in 2011, making that his most dominant season.

Memorable Moments/Greatest Performances

Peters anchored an offensive line that dominated the Washington defense at the point of attack during a lopsided 59–28 victory on November 15, 2010, with the Eagles amassing 592 yards of total offense, 260 of which came on the ground.

Peters and his line-mates once again dominated the opposition on October 30, 2011, with the Eagles accumulating 495 yards on offense and rushing for a season-high 239 yards during a 34–7 mauling of the Dallas Cowboys.

Peters helped Eagles running backs rush for a season-high 299 yards during a 34–20 win over the Detroit Lions on December 8, 2013, with LeSean McCoy gaining 217 of those yards himself.

Notable Achievements

- Three-time division champion (2010, 2013, and 2017).
- 2017 NFC champion.
- Super Bowl LII champion.
- Seven-time Pro Bowl selection (2009, 2010, 2011, 2013, 2014, 2015, and 2016).
- Two-time First-Team All-Pro selection (2011 and 2013).
- Two-time Second-Team All-Pro selection (2010 and 2014).

14

— WILBERT MONTGOMERY —

Despite being plagued by injuries for much of his career, Wilbert Montgomery established himself as one of the finest running backs of his era during his eight seasons in Philadelphia. One of the most impactful offensive players ever to don an Eagles uniform, Montgomery ranks among the franchise's all-time leaders in several statistical categories, with his 6,538 yards rushing and 45 rushing touchdowns placing him second in team annals. Amassing more than 1,000 yards on the ground three times, Montgomery led the Eagles in rushing on six separate occasions, helping them advance to the playoffs four times in the process. An excellent receiver out of the backfield as well, Montgomery surpassed 50 receptions and 500 receiving yards twice each, with his outstanding all-around play earning him two trips to the Pro Bowl, two All-Pro selections, and eventual induction into the Eagles Hall of Fame.

Born in Greenville, Mississippi, on September 16, 1954, Wilbert Montgomery suffered his first serious sports injury as a fourth-grader when he broke his leg while playing football with friends in a nearby schoolyard. Reminiscing years later about his childhood, Montgomery said, "When you're little, you think your leg is like a stick. You break it in half, it's gonna fall in two pieces. I thought, 'Oh-no, I'm gonna have a cast on my leg forever.' I remember the next few years, kids calling me from the schoolyard wanting me to play football with them. I'd always say no."

Having lost his fear of reinjuring himself by the time he entered Greenville High School, Montgomery deeply wished to play for his high school football team. However, since he knew that his mother would not allow him to do so, he convinced a girl in his class to forge her signature on the parental permission slip. Montgomery then spent the next two years trying to hide his after-school activities from his mother, recalling, "After practice, I'd come home, and she would ask where I'd been. I'd say I was at a friend's house. We played our games Friday night, so I'd say, 'Momma, I'm going out for a while. I'll be home by 10:30.' When we played the coast-places like Gulfport and Biloxi, we'd stay overnight and bus back the next day. Those nights, I told my mother not to worry, I was sleeping over at a friend's house. If I came home limping, I'd say we did it fooling around."

However, Montgomery's devious behavior became increasingly difficult to conceal from his mother as he began to make a name for himself as one of the region's top athletes. Starring for Greenville High as both a running back and defensive back, Montgomery earned numerous trophies, which he hid in a closet at his grandmother's house. But, with college scouts beginning to express interest in him by the start of his junior year, Montgomery knew that the time had come to confess his sins to his mom, stating years later, "I finally told her I was playing football, and she wasn't happy. She argued for a long time, but, when I told her it might win me a scholarship to college, she said, 'All right, go ahead, but don't come running to me when you get hurt.' I never did. I still don't."

Montgomery ultimately accepted a scholarship offer from Jackson State University, before transferring to the small Texas college of Abilene Christian shortly after he discovered that Walter Payton headed a group of talented running backs that comprised the Jack-

Wilbert Montgomery ranks second in franchise history in rushing yards and rushing touchdowns.
Courtesy of SportsMemorabilia.com

son State backfield. Performing brilliantly as a freshman at Abilene Christian, Montgomery led the Wildcats to the NAIA Division I National Championship by averaging 6.4 yards per carry and scoring a single-season record 37 touchdowns. Although Montgomery missed playing time in each of the next three seasons due to injuries he sustained to his shoulder and thigh, he continued to perform at an extremely high level, concluding his college career with 3,047 yards rushing, 76 touchdowns, and 14 100-yard games.

Nevertheless, with pro scouts expressing concerns over his ability to remain healthy, Montgomery ended up slipping to the sixth round of the

1977 NFL Draft, where the Eagles selected him with the 154th overall pick. Montgomery subsequently spent his first NFL season playing mostly on special teams, amassing 619 yards returning kickoffs and another 183 yards on the ground, while scoring three touchdowns, one of which came on a 99-yard kickoff return.

Extremely quiet and shy when he first entered the league, Montgomery spoke in a soft, polite whisper, rarely lifting his head when he spoke to reporters. A small-town boy who seemed uncomfortable with the idea of being famous, Montgomery also lacked confidence during the early stages of his career, with Ron Jaworski recalling, "That first year, Wilbert kept a towel under his door so that they couldn't slide the pink slip into his room. He didn't think he'd make the team. He was insecure, like most rookies, but everyone else in camp recognized his talent. He had that great vision, the ability to cut back and make something out of nothing. He ran hard, blocked, caught the ball well. He had everything it takes to make it in the NFL. The only thing he lacked was confidence."

Inserted into the starting lineup his second year in the league, Montgomery had an exceptional 1978 campaign, earning Pro Bowl and Second-Team All-Pro honors by ranking among the league leaders with 1,220 yards rushing, 1,415 yards from scrimmage, 1,569 all-purpose yards, a rushing average of 4.7 yards per carry, and 10 touchdowns, nine of which came on the ground. He followed that up by posting even more impressive numbers in 1979, once again gaining Pro Bowl and Second-Team All-Pro recognition by leading the NFL with 2,006 yards from scrimmage and 2,012 all-purpose yards, making 41 receptions for 494 yards, and placing near the top of the league rankings with 1,512 yards rushing and 14 touchdowns.

One of the NFL's most complete running backs, the 5'10", 196-pound Montgomery possessed speed, strength, vision, intelligence, and toughness, as teammate Mike Quick suggested when he said, "He wasn't real big, but he was as tough as anybody to play that position. He hit guys in the chest. Guys would smash him, and he'd get right up, straighten his helmet, and be ready to play."

Extremely modest as well, Montgomery proved to be a consummate team player who never kept track of his personal statistics and always credited his offensive line for the success he experienced with the ball in his hands. Yet, Montgomery also possessed a fierce competitive spirit, stating on one occasion, "On any given Sunday, no matter who's on the other side of the field, you have to say, and think, and believe 'I'm the best player on this field today.' I just felt that, hey, when it was time for me to touch the field, I had to be the best of the best, and I wanted to prove to them that I could be the best. That was just my mindset . . . I want to win."

Although Montgomery missed four games in 1980 due to injury, he contributed to the Eagles' successful run to the NFC title by rushing for 778 yards and eight touchdowns, while also catching 50 passes for another 407 yards and two touchdowns. Montgomery subsequently had one of his most productive seasons in 1981, gaining 1,402 yards on the ground and another 521 yards on 49 pass receptions, giving him a total of 1,923 yards from scrimmage that placed him third in the league rankings. Limited by injury to just 13 games over the course of the next two seasons, Montgomery rushed for only 654 yards and scored just nine touchdowns, before making something of a comeback in 1984, when his 789 rushing yards and 501 receiving yards gave him more than 1,000 yards from scrimmage for the fifth and final time in his career.

Unfortunately, the 1984 campaign ended up being Montgomery's last in Philadelphia. After engaging in a contract dispute with team management during the following offseason, Montgomery demanded to be traded to another team, with the Eagles subsequently obliging him by dealing him to the Detroit Lions for linebacker Garry Cobb. However, Montgomery later revealed that his desire to leave Philadelphia stemmed from more than just a disagreement over money, telling the *Philadelphia Inquirer*, "It was my knowledge the team was going to use me up in '85. Someone in the organization told me they were going to run me right, run me left, and I was going to take a terrific beating, and, in '86, I wouldn't be able to come back and compete for a job."

Although Eagles head coach Marion Campbell denied that charge, Montgomery remained steadfast in his beliefs, adding that his disagreement with teammate Jerry Robinson further compromised his situation in Philadelphia. In addressing his differences with Robinson, Montgomery stated that the

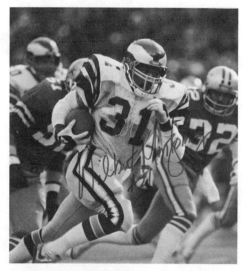

Montgomery amassed more than 1,000 yards from scrimmage five times.
Courtesy of PristineAuction.com

linebacker believed he had said negative things about him to Coach Campbell, claiming, "I hadn't said anything negative about Jerry. Everything I said about Jerry was a plus. But I didn't want to come to camp and get blindsided in practice. I didn't want to worry about one of my teammates taking a blind shot at me."

Montgomery added, "I thought everything over. I thought about all the things, and I just couldn't go back in there. I didn't feel right in my mind. Too many things had been said for me to have a relaxed mind and compete for Philadelphia."

Montgomery spent one season in Detroit, appearing in seven games with the Lions, before announcing his retirement following the conclusion of the 1985 campaign. He ended his career with 6,789 yards rushing, 273 pass receptions, 2,502 receiving yards, 9,291 yards from scrimmage, 10,105 all-purpose yards, and 58 touchdowns, compiling virtually all those numbers as a member of the Eagles.

After remaining away from the game for more than a decade, Montgomery returned to the NFL as running backs coach for the St. Louis Rams in 1997, a position he held until 2008, when he assumed a similar post with the Baltimore Ravens. Montgomery remained in Baltimore until 2014, when he joined the coaching staff of the Cleveland Browns. Montgomery was relieved of his duties following the firing of head coach Mike Pettine on January 3, 2016.

EAGLES CAREER HIGHLIGHTS

Best Season

Montgomery played his best ball for the Eagles from 1978 to 1981, rushing for more than 1,000 yards three times during that period, while amassing more than 1,000 yards from scrimmage and scoring at least 10 touchdowns all four years. It could be argued that Montgomery had his finest season in 1981, when, in addition to scoring 10 touchdowns, he ranked among the league leaders with 1,402 yards rushing, 1,923 yards from scrimmage, and an average of 4.9 yards per carry, which represented the highest mark of his career. However, he made a slightly greater overall impact in 1979, when he rushed for a then franchise-record 1,512 yards, scored 14 touchdowns, and led the NFL with 2,006 yards from scrimmage and 2,012 all-purpose yards.

Memorable Moments/Greatest Performances

Montgomery proved to be a huge factor in his first start as a pro, contributing to a 17–14 win over the Giants on December 11, 1977, by rushing for 59 yards and making the key play of the game when he returned the second-half kickoff 99 yards for a touchdown.

Montgomery followed that up with a strong outing against New York's other team one week later, gaining 103 yards on the ground and scoring two touchdowns during a lopsided 27–0 victory over the Jets.

Although the Eagles lost their September 10, 1978, meeting with the Washington Redskins by a score of 35–30, Montgomery turned in an outstanding all-around effort, gaining 87 yards on the ground, another 48 yards on seven pass receptions, and scoring four touchdowns, the longest of which came on a 34-yard run.

Montgomery put the finishing touches on a memorable fourth-quarter comeback by the Eagles on October 1, 1978, scoring from 14 yards out late in the final period to give them a 17–14 victory over the Baltimore Colts in a game they entered the final period trailing by a score of 14–0. He finished the contest with 144 yards on 25 carries.

Montgomery helped the Eagles clinch a wild card playoff berth in the final game of the 1978 regular season by rushing for 130 yards and two touchdowns during a 20–3 win over the Giants.

Montgomery starred once again against the Giants on September 23, 1979, rushing for 126 yards and collaborating with Ron Jaworski on a career-long 53-yard TD reception during a 17–13 Eagles win.

Montgomery had another huge day two weeks later, rushing for 127 yards and scoring four touchdowns during a 28–17 victory over the Washington Redskins on October 7, 1979.

Although the Eagles suffered a 24–19 defeat at the hands of the Cleveland Browns on November 4, 1979, Montgomery performed brilliantly, gaining 197 yards on the ground and another 40 yards on three pass receptions. Scoring one of Philadelphia's two touchdowns on a 52-yard second-quarter run, Montgomery finished the game with 237 yards from scrimmage.

Montgomery led the Eagles to a 42–7 blowout of the Minnesota Vikings in Week 2 of the 1980 campaign by carrying the ball 20 times for 169 yards and two touchdowns, one of which came on a 72-yard scamper.

Montgomery came up big for the Eagles in the 1980 NFC championship game, when, just four days after twisting his left knee during practice, he rushed for 194 yards and set the tone for their 20–7 win over the Dallas

Cowboys by scoring on a 42-yard run on their first offensive play from scrimmage.

Montgomery proved to be the difference in a 35–14 victory over the Houston Oilers on December 19, 1982, carrying the ball 17 times for a season-high 147 yards and three touchdowns, one of which came on a career-long 90-yard run.

Notable Achievements

- Rushed for more than 1,000 yards three times, topping 1,500 yards once (1,512 in 1979).
- Surpassed 50 receptions and 500 receiving yards twice each.
- Surpassed 1,000 yards from scrimmage five times, topping 1,500 yards twice and 2,000 yards once.
- Scored at least 10 touchdowns four times.
- Averaged at least 4.5 yards per carry five times.
- Led NFL with 2,006 yards from scrimmage and 2,012 all-purpose yards in 1979.
- Finished second in NFL with rushing average of 4.9 yards per carry in 1981.
- Finished third in NFL with 1,923 yards from scrimmage in 1981.
- Led Eagles in rushing six times.
- Ranks among Eagles career leaders with: 6,538 yards rushing (2nd); 8,985 yards from scrimmage (4th); 9,799 all-purpose yards (3rd); 45 rushing touchdowns (2nd); and 58 touchdowns (8th).
- 1980 division champion.
- 1980 NFC champion.
- Two-time Pro Bowl selection (1978 and 1979).
- Two-time Second-Team All-Pro selection (1978 and 1979).
- Two-time Second-Team All-Conference selection (1978 and 1979).
- Inducted into Philadelphia Eagles Hall of Fame in 1987.

15

— SETH JOYNER —

Once called "the glue that holds the Philly defense together" by Paul Zimmerman of *Sports Illustrated*, Seth Joyner did everything the Eagles asked of him during his eight seasons in Philadelphia. Starring at left-outside linebacker for the Eagles from 1986 to 1993, Joyner excelled in all phases of the game, proving to be equally effective against the run, in pass coverage, and applying pressure to opposing quarterbacks. The only player in franchise history to record at least 35 sacks, 20 forced fumbles, and 15 interceptions, Joyner surpassed 100 tackles seven times and five sacks on four separate occasions, earning in the process Pro Bowl, All-Pro, and All-NFC honors twice each. Also named NFL Defensive Player of the Year by *Sports Illustrated* once and Philadelphia's Defensive MVP twice, Joyner helped lead the Eagles to four playoff appearances and one division title, with his exceptional play also gaining him induction into the Eagles Hall of Fame following the conclusion of his playing career. Amazingly, Joyner accomplished all he did after initially being cut by Eagles head coach Buddy Ryan his first year in the league.

Born in Spring Valley, New York, on November 18, 1964, Seth Joyner grew up in a single-parent household, recalling years later, "My mom raised three kids and worked in a state hospital and had another job too . . . I was a quiet and serious kid and had a lot of responsibility at a young age."

In addition to looking after his younger sister, Joyner tended to the needs of his grandmother, Emma Cooper, who lived with the family, telling the *New York Times* in 1992, "My grandmother was partially paralyzed on the left side. She never complained. She took things in stride. She was honest. She never let her disability totally disable her. The thing I learned most from her is patience. Patience has helped me get to this point in my life."

Excelling on the gridiron while attending Spring Valley High School, Joyner recollected, "In junior high, I played offense and defense. Then, at Spring Valley High, my body grew, and I played fullback and linebacker . . . Jimmy Pinkston was my running backs and linebacker coach. He was like a

Seth Joyner recorded more than 100 tackles for the Eagles five times.
Courtesy of Poppel Sports

father figure to me. He poured a lot into me. I would sit in his basement and we would talk football and life till 2 in the morning. He's very important to me to this day."

Despite earning All-State honors while at Spring Valley, Joyner did not draw much attention from college scouts, prompting him to enroll at the University of Texas–El Paso, where he made the football team as a walk-on. Joyner subsequently found himself facing many obstacles over the course of the next four years, recalling, "The head coach, Max Bowman, didn't like me at all. The spring of my freshman year, I started dating a blonde, green-eyed Dutch girl. Bowman really didn't like that, and he did everything he could to keep me from being drafted into the NFL . . . I was a real underdog. It was an uphill battle."

Choosing not to participate in the NFL scouting combine, Joyner fell to the eighth round of the 1986 NFL Draft, where the Eagles finally selected him with the 208th overall pick. Looking back at his late selection, Joyner said, "Drafted 208th in the eighth round. Talk about an underdog. That's why I love Tom Brady." He then added, "Success is sometimes not predicated on how you're positioned. It's what's in your heart. The universe is looking at you to see if you have commitment."

Although Joyner performed well at his first pro training camp, the Eagles cut him just prior to the start of the regular season, with the linebacker remembering years later, "I made it to the last cut, but I knew I was coming back. I think I played well enough to have made the final roster. It was a logistics thing from my conversations with Buddy (Ryan). The team had drafted Keith Byars and was trying to trade Earnest Jackson. That took some time. Someone had to go. It was me. So, for those two weeks, not being on the team was very tough for me. It turned out to be the best thing to ever happen to me. It created something in me. It drove me my entire career."

Joyner continued, "I was pretty miserable for those two weeks. The Eagles played Chicago and then Washington, and I'm sitting at home watching these games feeling I'm missing out. I felt I should be there. Once I re-signed with the team after two weeks, it fueled in me this understanding that there's a balance in the NFL between what you're worth to a team and how a team values you. As a guy who is not a starter, you are dispensable. I resolved that I would never be dispensable again. I had to level that playing field and put myself in a position of power. I had to make it so that the team needed me as much as I needed them."

After rejoining the Eagles in Week 3 of the 1986 campaign, Joyner spent the rest of the year sharing time with Alonzo Johnson at right-outside linebacker, finishing the season with 44 tackles, two sacks, and one interception. Shifted to the left side of Philadelphia's defense the following year, Joyner started all 12 non-strike games for the Eagles, finishing third on the team with 96 tackles, while also recording four sacks, two interceptions, two forced fumbles, two fumble recoveries, and his first career touchdown. Joyner subsequently emerged as one of the NFL's finest all-around linebackers in 1988, helping the Eagles capture the NFC East title by recording a career-high 136 tackles and four interceptions, forcing one fumble, and registering 3½ sacks. Continuing to perform at an extremely high level the next five years, Joyner amassed well over 100 tackles each season, while also recording at least five sacks four times and three interceptions twice, with his brilliant all-around play earning him two trips to the Pro Bowl, two All-Pro nominations, team MVP honors twice, and recognition by *Sports Illustrated* as the NFL Defensive Player of the Year in 1991.

Blessed with good size and outstanding speed, the 6'2", 245-pound Joyner, who anchored the Texas–El Paso 400-meter relay team as a college senior, did an excellent job of defending against the run, chasing down ball-carriers from sideline to sideline, covering tight ends and backs coming out of the backfield, and rushing opposing quarterbacks, prompting Eagles defensive coordinator Bud Carson to state on one occasion, "Seth Joyner can do anything you ask of him. We ask him to do it all. I wouldn't trade him for another linebacker anywhere."

Carson also praised Joyner for all the time he spent watching films of his opponents, claiming, "That's why, week in and week out, he is so consistent. You never see him confused out there. You never see him hesitate. He is so well prepared, he plays with complete confidence."

Gradually establishing himself as one of the Eagles' spiritual leaders during his time in Philadelphia, Joyner became known for the level of intensity he displayed on the playing field, and for the perpetual scowl he wore on his face, which he explained thusly: "I'm an intense person. Sometimes even too intense or too locked in on certain things. Football is supposed to be a fun game, and I try to have fun when I'm playing. But, unfortunately, I only have fun when I'm winning."

Despite the leadership role Joyner assumed as he rose to the upper echelon of NFL linebackers, he rubbed many of his teammates the wrong way with his harsh words and strong criticism, which he extended to team ownership and Rich Kotite, who replaced Buddy Ryan as head coach in 1991. Displeased with Kotite's coaching style and ownership's allocation of resources, Joyner elected to sign with the Arizona Cardinals when he became a free agent in 1994, later saying, "When I left, I couldn't play another year under Kotite. He was full of fake bravado." Over the course of his eight seasons in Philadelphia, Joyner recorded 875 solo tackles, 37 sacks, 17 interceptions, 286 interception-return yards, 21 forced fumbles, eight fumble recoveries, and five touchdowns, with his 875 tackles, 37 sacks, and 21 forced fumbles all placing him among the franchise's all-time leaders. Meanwhile, Joyner's five defensive touchdowns tie him with Eric Allen for the most total in team annals.

Joyner earned Eagles Defensive MVP honors twice.
Courtesy of George A. Kitrinos

Joyner ended up spending three productive seasons in Arizona, earning one Pro Bowl selection and two Second-Team All-NFC nominations while playing for the Cardinals, before splitting his final two seasons between the Green Bay Packers and the Denver Broncos. Announcing his retirement following the conclusion of the 1998 campaign, Joyner ended his career with 1,123 tackles, 52 sacks, 24 interceptions, 26 forced fumbles, 12 fumble recoveries, and those five defensive touchdowns. Joyner, who currently lives in Arizona, embarked on a career in broadcasting following his playing days, spending the last several years serving as an NFL analyst for a variety of TV and radio networks, including NBC Sports Philadelphia, for whom he breaks down Eagles games.

Looking back at his eight years with the Eagles, Joyner now says, "If there's one thing that I wish I could do, I wish that I could go back to those ex-teammates and apologize to them because how I acted was completely wrong and really immature. But, be that as it may, when I see those guys, I do apologize to them. It was what it was. It was the emotions of the moment. But I realize now you've got to be bigger than that. You've got to be a better teammate than I was."

Joyner adds, "I didn't understand, as one of the better players on the team, and as one of the leaders on the team, you can't handle the situation that way. Because, what a leader does, is a leader builds up and raises up guys when things aren't going well. You don't tear them down. Nothing good ever comes of that. A leader looks at those guys that are struggling and tries to find out the positive things to say to try to lift them up and motivate them. Some guys were motivated by it, but there were a lot of guys that didn't like me—at all."

Nevertheless, Eagles chairman and CEO Jeffrey Lurie had nothing but kind words to say about Joyner when he announced that the team intended to induct him into its Hall of Fame in 2018, stating, "Seth Joyner was one of the most talented and fearless outside linebackers of his era, and the way he committed his heart and soul on every play spoke volumes about his love for the game. Seth epitomized the complete defensive player—dominant against the run, extremely skilled in coverage, and relentless in how he blitzed. Seth is one of the all-time greats in our franchise's history, and he set a powerful example for the generations of players that followed him at his position."

EAGLES CAREER HIGHLIGHTS

Best Season

Joyner had a big year for the Eagles in 1988, recording four interceptions, 3½ sacks, and a career-high 136 solo tackles. He also performed extremely well in 1990 and 1992, making 132 tackles, forcing three fumbles, and registering a career-high 7½ sacks in the first of those campaigns, before recording 121 tackles, 6½ sacks, four interceptions, and two touchdowns in the second. However, Joyner had his finest all-around season in 1991, when, in addition to picking off three passes, recovering four fumbles, and scoring two touchdowns, he forced six fumbles and registered 110 solo tackles and 6½ sacks, with *Sports Illustrated* subsequently according him NFL Defensive Player of the Year honors.

Memorable Moments/Greatest Performances

Although the Eagles lost to the Detroit Lions by a score of 13–11 on November 16, 1986, Joyner recorded the first interception of his career during the contest.

Joyner scored the first of his five career touchdowns during a 27–17 win over the Saints on September 20, 1987, when he returned a fumble 18 yards for a TD.

Joyner contributed to a 23–17 overtime victory over the Giants on November 20, 1988, by recording a sack and an interception, which he subsequently returned 30 yards.

Joyner scored the Eagles' only touchdown of a 14–13 loss to Tampa Bay on October 6, 1991, when he recovered a fumble in the end zone.

Joyner lit the scoreboard again during a 34–14 win over the Phoenix Cardinals on November 24, 1991, when he recovered a fumble, which he returned 34 yards for a touchdown.

Joyner turned in a tremendous all-around performance during a 13–6 Monday night win over the Houston Oilers on December 2, 1991, when, despite playing with a 102-degree fever, he sacked Warren Moon twice and recorded eight solo tackles, two forced fumbles, and two fumble recoveries, earning in the process NFC Defensive Player of the Week honors for the first of three times. Observing Joyner's brilliant play from the broadcast booth, ABC-TVs Dan Dierdorf told the national viewing audience, "If there is a better linebacker in the NFL than Seth Joyner, I haven't seen him." Interviewed following the conclusion of the contest, Joyner said, "I've been sick for a week. I got it bad last night. I was throwing up all day. My stomach was bubbling. It was hard to breathe. But you have to play."

Joyner once again gained recognition as the NFC Defensive Player of the Week for his outstanding play during a 7–3 win over the Cardinals on October 25, 1992, punctuating his exceptional performance with an interception.

Joyner made a key play during the Eagles' 47–34 win over the Giants on November 22, 1992, completely shifting the momentum of the contest in the second quarter, when, with New York holding a 20–6 lead, he intercepted a Jeff Hostetler pass and returned the ball 43 yards for a touchdown. The Eagles subsequently went on to score 34 unanswered points.

Joyner again came up big for the Eagles two weeks later, recording a sack and clinching a 28–17 victory over the Minnesota Vikings by intercepting a Sean Salisbury pass in the fourth quarter and returning the ball 24 yards for the last of his five career touchdowns.

Joyner earned NFC Defensive Player of the Week honors for the third and final time by recording a sack and an interception during a 17–13 win over the Redskins on December 20, 1992, that clinched a playoff berth for the Eagles.

Notable Achievements

- Scored five defensive touchdowns.
- Recorded four interceptions twice.
- Forced six fumbles in 1991.
- Recorded more than 100 tackles seven times.
- Recorded more than five sacks four times.
- Led NFL with two non-offensive touchdowns in 1991.
- Finished second in NFL with four fumble recoveries in 1991.
- Led Eagles in interceptions once and tackles twice.
- Ranks among Eagles career leaders with: 21 forced fumbles (2nd); 875 solo tackles (3rd); 37 sacks (10th); and five defensive touchdowns (tied-1st).
- 1988 division champion.
- Three-time NFC Defensive Player of the Week.
- Two-time Eagles Defensive MVP (1991 and 1992).
- 1991 *Sports Illustrated* NFL Defensive Player of the Year.
- Two-time Pro Bowl selection (1991 and 1993).
- Two-time Second-Team All-Pro selection (1991 and 1992).
- Two-time First-Team All-Conference selection (1991 and 1993).
- Named to Eagles 75th Anniversary Team in 2007.
- Inducted into Philadelphia Eagles Hall of Fame in 2018.

16

— LeSEAN MCCOY —

Adynamic runner who amassed more rushing yards than anyone else in franchise history, LeSean McCoy set numerous team records while helping the Eagles win two NFC East titles. In addition to gaining more yards on the ground than any other player in team annals, McCoy holds single-season franchise marks for most yards rushing, yards from scrimmage, rushing touchdowns, and total touchdowns scored. Leading the Eagles in rushing in each of his six seasons in Philadelphia, McCoy gained more than 1,000 yards on the ground four times and accumulated more than 1,600 yards from scrimmage three times, finishing first in the NFL in each category once. An outstanding receiver coming out of the backfield as well, McCoy surpassed 50 receptions three times and 500 receiving yards twice, with his superb all-around play earning him three Pro Bowl selections and two All-Pro nominations.

Born in Harrisburg, Pennsylvania, on July 12, 1988, LeSean Kamel McCoy acquired the nickname "Shady" as a child due to his pronounced mood swings that saw him go from laughing one minute to crying the next. Starring in football while attending Bishop McDevitt High School, McCoy rushed for 406 yards in one game as a sophomore, before earning First-Team Associated Press All-State, Associated Press Class AAAA Player of the Year, and Mid-Penn Commonwealth Conference Offensive MVP honors in his junior year by running for 2,828 yards and scoring 35 touchdowns. Continuing to perform at an elite level as a senior, McCoy again gained First-Team AP All-State recognition, with a 2006 ESPN evaluation describing him as "lightning in a bottle every time he touches the ball."

Rated the nation's number 11 high school prospect by recruiting analyst Tom Lemming, McCoy initially committed to the University of Miami. However, after experiencing difficulties in the classroom and breaking his ankle during his senior year at Bishop McDevitt, McCoy ended up spending one year at Milford Academy, a prep school located in New Berlin, New York. McCoy then chose to enroll at the University of Pittsburgh following a coaching change at Miami, making his decision known on February 16, 2007. Some six months later, in August 2007, Dave Grdnic wrote for Pittsburgh's school newspaper, *Panthers Digest*, "After just one week, LeSean McCoy has been as amazing as advertised. He's been dynamic on the field and off, banging up the middle on runs as hard as he bolts around end, and talking just as good a game to the media."

Excelling in his first year of college ball, McCoy rushed for 1,328 yards, with Rivals .com naming him to its Freshman All-America team, and an article in the *Sporting News*

LeSean McCoy gained more yards on the ground than anyone else in franchise history.
Courtesy of Keith Allison

crediting him with having "one of the best starts by a freshman running back at Pittsburgh since Tony Dorsett." McCoy followed that up with an outstanding sophomore campaign, with his speed and shiftiness prompting Dorsett to tell the Associated Press after watching him in one particular contest, "He reminded me of me. That looked a lot like Number 33 [Dorsett]."

Choosing to leave college after his sophomore year, McCoy entered the 2009 NFL Draft, where the Eagles selected him in the second round, with the 53rd overall pick. McCoy subsequently spent the first part of his rookie campaign backing up Brian Westbrook, before assuming the starting role when Westbrook suffered a concussion in Week 7. Starting four of the season's final nine games, McCoy ended up gaining 637 yards on the ground, making 40 receptions for 308 yards, and scoring four touchdowns, with his strong play convincing the Eagles to release Westbrook at season's end.

Displaying confidence in his team's new featured running back during the early stages of the 2010 regular season, Eagles head coach Andy Reid said of the 5'11", 210-pound McCoy, "He added more strength in the off-season, really bought into the offseason program, worked his tail off, and it's showing up now. He's going out and he's running more physical, he's more deliberate and accurate with his cuts, seeing the daylight and getting North and South, which you have to do in this league."

Despite breaking his rib during a 27–24 win over the San Francisco 49ers on October 10, McCoy missed just one game in his first season as a full-time starter, concluding the 2010 campaign with 1,080 yards rushing, 78 receptions for 592 yards, nine touchdowns, and an average of 5.2 yards per carry that placed him fourth in the league rankings. Posting outstanding numbers once again in 2011, McCoy earned Pro Bowl and First-Team All-Pro honors by gaining 1,309 yards on the ground, making 48 receptions for another 315 yards, and leading the NFL with 17 rushing touchdowns and 20 total touchdowns. After sustaining a concussion that limited him to 12 games, 840 yards rushing, 1,213 yards from scrimmage, and five touchdowns the following year, McCoy gained Pro Bowl and First-Team All-Pro recognition for a second time in 2013 by leading the league with 1,607 yards rushing and 2,146 yards from scrimmage, while also scoring 11 touchdowns and averaging 5.1 yards per carry.

McCoy earned his third trip to the Pro Bowl in 2014 by rushing for 1,319 yards, amassing 1,474 yards from scrimmage, and scoring five touchdowns. Nevertheless, the Eagles traded him to the Buffalo Bills for linebacker Kiko Alonso following the conclusion of the campaign, leaving many people scratching their heads. Expressing his surprise over the deal, McCoy described the trade as a "panic move" by second-year Eagles head coach Chip Kelly, who he went on to say, "got rid of all the good black players" and "doesn't like or respect stars."

Elaborating further on his opinions, McCoy told *ESPN The Magazine*, "The relationship was never really great. I feel like I always respected him as a coach. I think that's the way he runs his team. He wants the full control. You see how fast he got rid of all the good players. Especially all the good black players. He got rid of them the fastest. . . .

McCoy led the Eagles in rushing in each of his six seasons in Philadelphia.
Courtesy of Diana Quinlan

That's the truth. There's a reason. . . . It's hard to explain with him. But there's a reason he got rid of all the black players—the good ones—like that."

However, in all fairness to Kelly, several other factors likely entered into the equation, with the most significant of those being the quality of McCoy's character. Accused multiple times of being involved in violent behavior, McCoy was sued in May 2013 for his alleged actions toward a woman using the alias "Mary Roe" aboard a party bus on the New Jersey Turnpike, with Roe testifying that McCoy humiliated her and 15 other women by spraying them with a beverage before ejecting her from the vehicle. McCoy has also been accused at different times of beating his child and his dog, distributing STDs to teammates' girlfriends, making derogatory comments about women, and publicly insulting the mother of his children.

Leaving the Eagles amid a considerable amount of controversy, McCoy arrived in Buffalo having rushed for 6,792 yards, made 300 receptions for another 2,282 yards, and scored a total of 54 touchdowns during his time in Philadelphia. Continuing his strong play with the Bills from 2015 to 2017, McCoy surpassed 1,000 yards from scrimmage each season, earning in the process three more trips to the Pro Bowl. However, he subsequently suffered through a subpar 2018 campaign during which he rushed for only 514 yards, amassed just 752 yards from scrimmage, and scored only three touchdowns. McCoy will enter the 2019 season with career totals of 10,606 yards rushing, 475 receptions, 3,616 receiving yards, 14,222 yards from scrimmage, 69 rushing touchdowns, and 15 touchdown receptions.

Unfortunately, further aspersions have been cast upon McCoy's character since he left Philadelphia, with his former girlfriend, Delicia Cordon, accusing him on an Instagram post dated July 10, 2018, of battering a woman, beating his son and pet dog, and using illegal steroids. Although McCoy subsequently denied all the allegations made against him, court documents later revealed that he had been trying to evict Cordon from a house he owned in Milton, Georgia, for some time, and that Cordon had been robbed and assaulted at the home by a masked assailant on July 10.

Speaking publicly on the matter for the first time some months later, Cordon stated her belief that McCoy had some involvement in the incident and offered a $40,000 reward for information leading to the arrest of the intruder. She went on to say, "I live my life in fear every day not knowing if I'm walking past the man who savagely attacked me. . . . To be clear, very clear, I believe that LeSean McCoy was involved in the attack. The LeSean McCoy that I know behind closed doors is totally different than the LeSean

McCoy in front of cameras. This attack was about the jewelry that LeSean expressed that he wanted back from me weeks before the attack."

Both the police and the NFL continue to investigate the incident.

EAGLES CAREER HIGHLIGHTS

Best Season

McCoy had a huge year for the Eagles in 2011, gaining 1,309 yards on the ground, amassing 1,624 yards from scrimmage, and leading the NFL with 17 rushing touchdowns and 20 total touchdowns. However, he turned in an even more dominant performance in 2013, when, in addition to scoring 11 touchdowns, he led the league with 1,607 yards rushing and 2,146 yards from scrimmage, setting in the process single-season franchise records in each of the last two categories.

Memorable Moments/Greatest Performances

McCoy scored the first touchdown of his career in his very first game as a pro, running the ball in from 5 yards out during a 34–14 win over Kansas City on September 27, 2009. He finished the contest with 84 yards on 20 carries.

McCoy punctuated a lopsided 40–17 victory over the Giants on November 1, 2009, by closing out the scoring with a season-long 66-yard touchdown run early in the fourth quarter.

McCoy gained more than 100 yards on the ground for the first time in his career during a 35–32 win over the Detroit Lions on September 19, 2010, rushing for 120 yards and three touchdowns, the longest of which covered 46 yards.

McCoy helped lead the Eagles to a 30–27 victory over Dallas on December 12, 2010, by carrying the ball 16 times for 149 yards.

McCoy starred once again against Dallas on October 30, 2011, earning NFC Offensive Player of the Week honors by rushing for 185 yards and two TDs during a lopsided 35–7 Eagles win.

Although the Eagles nearly surrendered a 33–7 third-quarter lead, they ultimately defeated the Redskins by a score of 33–27 in the 2013 regular-season opener, with McCoy leading the way by rushing for 184 yards and one touchdown, which came on a 34-yard run.

McCoy helped lead the Eagles to a 27–13 win over Green Bay on November 10, 2013, by carrying the ball 25 times for 155 yards.

McCoy proved to be the difference in a 34–20 victory over Detroit on December 8, 2013, rushing for a franchise-record 217 yards and two touchdowns, which came on fourth-quarter runs of 40 and 57 yards.

McCoy contributed to a 54–11 thrashing of the Chicago Bears two weeks later by gaining 133 yards on 18 carries, with his outstanding performance earning him NFC Offensive Player of the Week honors.

McCoy went over 100 yards rushing for the last time as a member of the Eagles on Thanksgiving Day 2014, when he rushed for 159 yards and one touchdown during a 33–10 victory over Dallas, with his 38-yard TD run midway through the fourth quarter putting the game out of reach.

Notable Achievements

- Rushed for more than 1,000 yards four times, topping 1,500 yards once (1,607 in 2013).
- Surpassed 50 receptions three times, topping 70 catches once (78 in 2010).
- Surpassed 500 receiving yards twice.
- Amassed more than 1,600 yards from scrimmage three times, topping 2,000 yards once (2,146 in 2013).
- Averaged more than 5 yards per carry twice.
- Led NFL with 17 rushing touchdowns and 20 touchdowns in 2011.
- Led NFL with 1,607 rushing yards and 2,146 yards from scrimmage in 2013.
- Led Eagles in rushing six straight times.
- Holds Eagles single-game record for most rushing yards (217 vs. Detroit on December 8, 2013).
- Holds Eagles single-season records for most: rushing yards (1,607 in 2013); yards from scrimmage (2,146 in 2013); rushing touchdowns (17 in 2011); and total touchdowns (20 in 2011).
- Holds Eagles career record for most rushing yards (6,792).
- Ranks among Eagles career leaders with: 9,074 yards from scrimmage (2nd); 9,074 all-purpose yards (4th); 44 rushing touchdowns (3rd); and 54 total touchdowns (9th).
- Two-time division champion (2010 and 2013).
- Two-time NFC Offensive Player of the Week.
- Three-time Pro Bowl selection (2011, 2013, and 2014).
- Two-time First-Team All-Pro selection (2011 and 2013).

17

— HAROLD CARMICHAEL —

The tallest wide receiver in NFL history, Harold Carmichael stood a towering 6'8", prompting former Atlanta Falcons head coach Norm Van Brocklin to once comment, "That Carmichael is amazing. He could stand flat-footed and eat the apples out of a tree." Possessing much more than just great height, Carmichael proved to be one of the league's top receivers for nearly a decade, surpassing 50 receptions five times and 1,000 receiving yards on three occasions, with his outstanding play earning him four trips to the Pro Bowl, two All-Pro nominations, and six All-Conference selections during his 13 years with the Eagles. The franchise's all-time leader in receptions, receiving yards, TD catches, and touchdowns scored, Carmichael played in 162 consecutive games for the Eagles, which represents the longest such streak in team annals. Meanwhile, Carmichael set a then NFL record by catching at least one pass in 127 straight games during his time in Philadelphia, with his list of accomplishments earning him spots on the NFL 1970s All-Decade Team and the Eagles 75th Anniversary Team, as well as eventual induction into the Eagles Hall of Fame.

Born in Jacksonville, Florida, on September 22, 1949, Lee Harold Carmichael attended William M. Raines High School, where he played quarterback on the school's football team and the clarinet in the school's band. Somewhat unsure of himself as a youngster, Carmichael said during a 1981 interview, "I didn't think I was a good enough athlete to even get a scholarship to college. The first positive sign I got was from this scout who came to our high school to check out (future Houston Oilers star) Kenny Burrough. Kenny was one year ahead of me."

Carmichael continued, "This scout talked to Kenny and me at the same time. When he left, he told me, 'I'll be back to get you next year.' That's when I first started thinking seriously about college ball. I was a late bloomer. It took me awhile to get my feet on the ground at every level, especially the NFL."

Carmichael ended up walking-on at Southern University, where he became a tri-sport athlete, excelling in football as a wide receiver, basketball as a center, and track and field as a javelin and discus thrower. A four-year starter on the gridiron, Carmichael played his best ball for the Jaguars as a senior, when he earned All-Conference honors.

Harold Carmichael's 589 receptions, 8,978 receiving yards, and 79 TD catches all represent franchise records.
Courtesy of SportsMemorabilia.com

Subsequently selected by the Eagles in the seventh round of the 1971 NFL Draft, with the 161st overall pick, Carmichael struggled his first year in the league after being shifted to tight end, making just 20 receptions for 288 yards and no touchdowns, before missing the season's final five games with a knee injury. Although Carmichael returned to his more natural position of wide receiver the following year, he posted similarly unimpressive numbers, concluding the 1972 campaign with 20 catches for 276 yards and two touchdowns.

Carmichael finally began to flourish after Mike McCormack replaced Ed Khayat as head coach and Roman Gabriel took over at quarterback in 1973. Also aided tremendously by new Eagles' receivers coach Boyd Dowler, who smoothed out his stride and improved his footwork, Carmichael earned Pro Bowl and Second-Team All-Pro honors by leading the NFL with 67 receptions and 1,116 receiving yards, while also finishing fourth in the league with nine TD catches.

However, with the Eagles lacking consistent quarterback play and Carmichael struggling with dropped passes in each of the next three seasons, the lanky receiver experienced a precipitous decline in offensive production, making as many as 50 catches just once, and failing to amass more than 649 receiving yards, although he still managed to score a total of 20 touchdowns during that time. Displeased with Carmichael's performance, the Philly fans who earlier cheered his colorful "roll-the-dice" touchdown celebrations in the opposing team's end zone took to booing him, causing the sensitive receiver to lose much of his confidence. In discussing his state of mind at the time, Carmichael revealed, "Nobody likes to be booed. I didn't like it; it hurt me. But I always tried my best. The best thing that could have happened was Dick (Vermeil) came in and built my confidence back up."

Vermeil, who assumed control of the team in 1976, recalled years later, "When I got the job, Harold was beaten down emotionally. He was booed. He was maligned unfairly. What he needed was for someone to believe in him so that he could believe in himself. We talked about the 'hot dog' stigma he had. I said he was a leader on the team, it was important that he show class in everything he did, on and off the field. He said he only did the 'dice roll' thing because he thought people expected it."

Displaying more maturity and increased confidence following the arrival of Vermeil and new Eagles quarterback Ron Jaworski, Carmichael played some of the best ball of his career over the course of the next few seasons, compiling the following numbers from 1978 to 1981:

YEAR	REC	REC YD	TD REC
1978	55	1,072	8
1979	52	872	11
1980	48	815	9
1981	61	1,028	6

In addition to finishing third in the NFL in receiving yards in the first of those campaigns, Carmichael ranked among the league leaders in TD catches in three of the four years, placing as high as second in 1979, when he earned All-Pro honors for the second time in his career. Carmichael also gained Pro Bowl and All-Conference recognition in three of those four seasons, failing to do so only in 1981. More importantly, the Eagles advanced to the playoffs all four years, with Carmichael contributing greatly to the success they experienced during that time.

Although Carmichael lacked great running speed, he proved to be extremely difficult to bring down in the open field, with the Eagles often taking advantage of his ability to run after the catch by getting the ball to him quickly on the outside. The 6'8", 225-pound Carmichael also excelled at making the tough catches over the middle and along the sidelines, making good use of the significant height advantage he had over every defensive back in the league.

In addressing the problems that Carmichael presented to opposing defenses, Ron Jaworski said:

> He's a tremendous physical talent. In the goal-line area, he's almost impossible to stop if you give him single coverage, even by someone as tall as 6'3". That's why we spend a lot of time in our goal-line preparation every week. Harold and I work all the time on the Alley Oop pass over the shorter guy and the quick out or quick slant. Once we see how the cornerback sets up, we instinctively know exactly what we're going to do. We've developed real confidence in each other. He knows where I'm going to throw the ball, and I know what type of route he's going to run.

Jaworski continued, "He's just a super receiver. He's not just a tall guy. He's got flexibility . . . quick feet . . . he can make catches behind him that a quick five-foot-eight guy can't make. He's a real athlete."

For his part, Carmichael tended to downplay his height, stating, "I really don't think that a man's size determines his ability. Pat Fischer was only 5'9", but he was one of the toughest cornerbacks I ever went against. Even when I'm going to be playing a guy 5'9", I don't say I'm going to have a field day. That guy may be able to jump pretty high, and we're not going to throw the ball high all the time. You can't use your height on every pass."

Carmichael added, "I didn't even like those high throws. I might catch it once or twice, but, one of those times, I'm gonna be up in the air and somebody's gonna get a good shot on me. They may not hit me hard, but the way I fall really could do some damage. And I want to play every game."

Carmichael also appeared in a franchise-record 162 straight games.
Courtesy of PristineAuctions.com

Carmichael did indeed appear in every game for the Eagles for 10 straight seasons, before his string of 162 straight games played ended during the latter stages of the 1983 campaign—one in which he made just 38 receptions for 515 yards and three touchdowns. Waived by the Eagles at season's end, Carmichael left Philadelphia with career totals of 589 receptions, 8,978 receiving yards, and 79 TD catches, all of which represent franchise records. He also ranks extremely high in team annals in points scored (474), yards from scrimmage (9,042), all-purpose yards (9,042), and games played (180).

After being released by the Eagles, Carmichael joined the hated Dallas Cowboys, with whom he appeared in two games, before being cut on November 14, 1984, and subsequently announcing his retirement. Although Carmichael has since fallen to a much lower place on the all-time list, he ended his career with the seventh-most touchdown receptions in NFL history.

Following his playing days, Carmichael settled in South Jersey and joined a Philadelphia travel agency as a vice president for sales. He later assumed other various roles in the business world, before returning to the Eagles in 1998 as the team's director of player and community relations, a position in which he served as a "combination mentor, confidant, troubleshooter, and liaison between the players and the authority figures in the organization." Reassigned to the position of fan engagement liaison in 2014, Carmichael spent one year in that post, before retiring to private life in 2015.

Looking back at the career of his former teammate, Ron Jaworski says, "Harold was never given credit for being the great athlete that he was. People would say, 'He's 6-8. Just throw it up there, he gets it.' He did a lot more than that. He ran great patterns. He had good hands. He caught a lot of balls around his ankles. He blocked. I played with some great receivers—Harold Jackson, Lance Rentzel, Jack Snow—but Harold was head and shoulders above them. I mean that in every sense of the word."

EAGLES CAREER HIGHLIGHTS

Best Season

Carmichael performed extremely well for the Eagles in 1979, making 52 receptions for 872 yards and a career-high 11 touchdowns. However, he posted better overall numbers in 1973, 1978, and 1981, surpassing 1,000 receiving yards in each of those three seasons. The 1973 campaign proved to be the finest of Carmichael's career, with the lanky receiver scoring nine touchdowns and leading the NFL with 67 catches and 1,116 receiving yards, earning in the process his first trip to the Pro Bowl, one of his two Second-Team All-Pro nominations, and First-Team All-Conference honors for the first of three times.

Memorable Moments/Greatest Performances

Carmichael scored his first career touchdown during a 23–7 loss to the Super Bowl bound Washington Redskins on December 3, 1972, hooking up with quarterback John Reaves on a 10-yard scoring play.

Carmichael went over 100 receiving yards for the first time as a pro on September 23, 1973, when he made five catches for 103 yards and one touchdown during a 23–23 tie with the Giants.

Carmichael turned in an outstanding performance against St. Louis on October 14, 1973, making 12 receptions for 187 yards and two touchdowns during a hard-fought 27–24 victory over the Cardinals. After Carmichael brought the Eagles to within four points of St. Louis by collaborating with Roman Gabriel on a 27-yard scoring play midway through the fourth quarter, the Eagles won the game a few minutes later when Gabriel hit Don Zimmerman with a 24-yard strike.

Carmichael helped lead the Eagles to a 24–23 victory over the New York Jets on December 9, 1973, by making five receptions for 146 yards and one touchdown, which came on a 62-yard hookup with Gabriel on Philadelphia's opening drive of the second half.

Although the Eagles lost their September 10, 1979, matchup with the Atlanta Falcons by a score of 14–10, Carmichael made a season-high nine receptions during the game, amassing 127 receiving yards in the process.

Carmichael contributed to a 44–7 rout of the Detroit Lions on December 2, 1979, by making five receptions for 96 yards and two touchdowns, which came on connections with Ron Jaworski that covered 20 and 24 yards.

Carmichael and Jaworski hooked up six times during Philadelphia's 27–17 win over the Chicago Bears in the 1979 NFC wild card game, with Carmichael amassing 111 receiving yards and scoring twice on plays that covered 17 and 29 yards.

Carmichael helped the Eagles begin the 1980 campaign on a positive note by making three receptions for 135 yards and one touchdown during their 27–6 win over the Denver Broncos in the regular-season opener.

Carmichael scored Philadelphia's first points of the season when he collaborated with Ron Jaworski on a 56-yard TD pass in the first quarter.

Carmichael made five receptions for 89 yards and three touchdowns during a 34–21 victory over the New Orleans Saints on November 9, 1980.

Although the Eagles suffered a 17–14 defeat at the hands of the archrival Dallas Cowboys on November 1, 1981, Carmichael had a big game, making five catches for 151 yards and one touchdown, which came on a career-long 85-yard connection with Ron Jaworski.

Carmichael recorded the only pass completion of his career during a 22–21 loss to the Baltimore Colts on October 30, 1983, hitting Mike Quick with a 45-yard touchdown pass.

Notable Achievements

- Surpassed 50 receptions five times, topping 60 catches twice.
- Surpassed 1,000 receiving yards three times.
- Led NFL with 67 receptions and 1,116 receiving yards in 1973.
- Finished second in NFL with 11 touchdown receptions in 1979.
- Finished third in NFL in receiving yards once and touchdown receptions once.
- Set new NFL record (since broken) by making at least one reception in 127 consecutive games.
- Holds Eagles record for most consecutive games played (162).
- Hold Eagles career records for most: receptions (589); receiving yards (8,978); touchdown receptions (79); and touchdowns scored (79).
- Ranks among Eagles career leaders with: 474 points scored (4th); 9,042 yards from scrimmage (3rd); 9,042 all-purpose yards (5th); and 180 games played (3rd).
- 1980 division champion.
- 1980 NFC champion.
- 1980 NFL Man of the Year.
- Four-time Pro Bowl selection (1973, 1978, 1979, and 1980).
- Two-time Second-Team All-Pro selection (1973 and 1979).
- Three-time First-Team All-Conference selection (1973, 1978, and 1979).
- Three-time Second-Team All-Conference selection (1974, 1977, and 1980).
- NFL 1970s All-Decade Team.
- Named to Eagles 75th Anniversary Team in 2007.
- Inducted into Philadelphia Eagles Hall of Fame in 1987.

18

— BRIAN WESTBROOK —

One of the most versatile and explosive offensive players in franchise history, Brian Westbrook served as a key member of Eagles teams that appeared in four NFC championship games and one Super Bowl. An exceptional runner, Westbrook gained more than 1,000 yards on the ground twice, establishing himself as the third-leading rusher in team annals during his time in Philadelphia. An outstanding receiver as well, Westbrook recorded the third-most pass receptions in franchise history, with his 9,785 yards from scrimmage representing the highest total amassed by any Eagles player. Westbrook also contributed greatly to the success of the Eagles as a punt returner, with his superb all-around play earning him two trips to the Pro Bowl, one All-Pro selection, and a place in the Eagles Hall of Fame.

Born in Washington, DC, on September 2, 1979, Brian Collins Westbrook attended DeMatha Catholic High School in Hyattsville, Maryland, where, in addition to excelling in the classroom, he lettered in football and basketball. Performing especially well on the gridiron, Westbrook gained First-Team All-League, First-Team All–Prince George's County, and All-State Honorable Mention recognition as a running back in his senior year. Nevertheless, Westbrook received little interest from the nation's larger college programs as graduation neared due to his diminutive 5'8" stature, forcing him to ultimately enroll at Division I-AA Villanova University.

Despite being plagued by injuries during his time at Villanova, Westbrook ended up amassing a total of 9,512 all-purpose yards for the Wildcats, setting in the process a new NCAA record that still stands. Putting up historic numbers over the course of his college career, Westbrook rushed for more than 1,000 yards three times, becoming in 1998 the first collegiate player ever to surpass 1,000 rushing yards and 1,000 receiving yards in the same season. Westbrook, who also became the only player in I-AA history to score at least 160 points in a season twice, tallied a total of 542 points in 46 career games, gained 4,298 yards on the ground, caught 219 passes

Brian Westbrook amassed a franchise-record 9,785 yards from scrimmage.
Courtesy of Kevin Burkett

for 2,582 yards, and accumulated another 2,289 yards on kickoff returns, establishing 41 school and five NCAA records along the way. Particularly dominant in his senior year, Westbrook amassed 2,823 all-purpose yards and scored 29 touchdowns, with his brilliant play earning him consensus All-America and CAA Offensive Player of the Year honors. Westbrook also was named the winner of the Walter Payton Award as the top player in NCAA Division I-AA football.

Yet, once again, Westbrook found himself being largely overlooked after he entered the 2002 NFL Draft. With pro teams concerned over his size, small-college background, and injury history (he missed an entire college season with a knee injury), Westbrook ended up falling to the third round, where the Eagles finally selected him with the 91st overall pick. Assuming a minor role his first year in Philadelphia, Westbrook spent his rookie season backing up Duce Staley and Dorsey Levens, gaining only 193 yards on the ground and another 86 yards through the air. Although Westbrook garnered increased playing time in his second season, he remained a part-time player, sharing running back duties with Staley and Correll Buckhalter. Still, even in somewhat limited duty, Westbrook began to establish himself as a force on offense, rushing for 613 yards and seven touchdowns, making 37 receptions for 332 yards and four TDs, scoring twice on punt returns, amassing 1,738 all-purpose yards, and finishing second in the league with an average of 15.3 yards per punt return. Looking back at his first two years in Philadelphia, Westbrook said, "I think when you go to a smaller school, you're never quite sure until you get out there and do it. Splitting time was great for me because it allowed me to get on-field experience and play special teams. Then, my third year, I got some starts, and that's when I was able to take it to the next level."

Westbrook did indeed take it to the next level in 2004, beginning an exceptional five-year run during which he posted the following numbers:

YEAR	RUSH YD	REC	REC YD	YD FROM SCRIMMAGE	TD
2004	812	73	703	1,515	9
2005	617	61	616	1,233	7
2006	1,217	77	699	1,916	11
2007	1,333	90	771	**2,104**	12
2008	936	54	402	1,338	14

Westbrook compiled those lofty numbers even though injuries forced him to miss playing time each season, with a mid-foot injury sidelining him for the final four games of the 2005 campaign. In addition to leading the Eagles in rushing all five seasons, Westbrook finished first on the team in pass receptions three times, with his 90 catches in 2007 setting a new single-season franchise record (since broken). Westbrook's league-leading 2,104 yards from scrimmage in 2007 also established a new franchise mark that stood until LeSean McCoy eclipsed it six years later. Westbrook earned Pro Bowl honors in 2004 and 2007, and he gained All-Pro recognition for the only time in his career in 2007. Meanwhile, the Eagles advanced to the playoffs in three of those five seasons, winning their second NFC championship in 2004.

Rivaling Donovan McNabb as the Eagles' most valuable player on offense throughout the period, Westbrook created problems for opposing defenses with his speed, quickness, and tremendous versatility. Blessed with soft hands, Westbrook proved to be as capable a receiver coming out of the backfield as anyone in the league. An extremely elusive runner who did most of his damage outside the tackles, the 5'8", 200-pound Westbrook excelled at zigzagging his way around defenders until he found a hole, making him a big-play threat anytime he got his hands on the football. In discussing his team's primary offensive weapon, Eagles head coach Andy Reid said, "He has no weaknesses."

Unfortunately, Westbrook's days as a dominant player ended shortly after he suffered a concussion during a 27–17 win over Washington on October 26, 2009, when his helmet collided with the right knee of Redskins linebacker London Fletcher. Sustaining a similar injury against San Diego three weeks later, Westbrook sat out the final five games of the season, concluding the campaign with only 274 yards rushing, 25 receptions, 181 receiving yards, and two touchdowns. With second-year running back LeSean McCoy waiting in the wings, the Eagles elected to release Westbrook on March 5, 2010. Upon announcing the team's decision, Andy Reid said, "Brian is one of the greatest Eagles of all time, and he is an even better person and leader. In my mind, there has not been a more versatile running back that the NFL has seen."

When asked about leadership on offense, Reid added, "Donovan's obviously here. Leadership is not what I'm worried about. I will tell you that Brian is a tremendous leader. He does it a little different way in that he's quiet and does it by example. But he was never afraid to speak up if he saw something that he knew wasn't about the team."

Westbrook left Philadelphia with career totals of 5,995 yards rushing, 37 rushing touchdowns, 426 receptions, 3,790 receiving yards, 29 TD receptions, 9,785 yards from scrimmage, 10,769 all-purpose yards, 68 touchdowns, and 410 points scored, with most of those figures placing him among the franchise's all-time leaders. He also averaged 4.6 yards per carry over the course of his eight seasons with the Eagles, which ties him for the third-highest average in team annals among players with at least 300 carries.

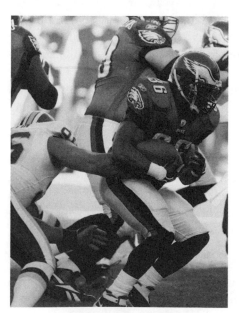

Westbrook helped lead the Eagles to four NFC championship game appearances.
Courtesy of Keith Allison

After being released by the Eagles, Westbrook signed with the San Francisco 49ers, with whom he spent one season serving as a part-time player, before announcing his retirement following the conclusion of the 2010 campaign. Choosing to officially retire as a member of the Eagles, Westbrook signed a one-day contract with the team on August 28, 2012, after which team owner Jeffrey Lurie said in a press release: "I will always remember Brian for the electrifying, game-changing plays he made during his great career in Philadelphia. He was one of those players you knew could score from anywhere on the field and one of the most exciting players I have ever watched. He was a great runner, receiver and returner and was certainly a fan favorite. We are thrilled to have him retire as an Eagle, and we look forward to honoring him at Lincoln Financial Field on December 23 against the Redskins in what should be a very exciting atmosphere." The Eagles later honored Westbrook again by inducting him into their Hall of Fame during halftime of their October 19, 2015, meeting with the New York Giants.

Looking back fondly at the time he spent in Philadelphia, Westbrook now says, "I feel like I grew up in Philly. Before that, I went to Villanova, too, so I feel like I have a special connection with the city. It's the place where I cut my teeth and grew up as a player and a person, and I have a lot of love and admiration for the city, the fans, and how they go about their business."

EAGLES CAREER HIGHLIGHTS

Best Season

Westbrook had a huge year for the Eagles in 2006, scoring 11 touchdowns and ranking among the league leaders with 1,217 yards rushing, 1,916 yards from scrimmage, 1,955 all-purpose yards, and an average of 5.1 yards per carry. However, he posted slightly better overall numbers in 2007, earning his lone First-Team All-Pro nomination by scoring 12 touchdowns and establishing career-high marks with 1,333 yards rushing, 90 receptions, 771 receiving yards, 2,183 all-purpose yards, and a league-leading 2,104 yards from scrimmage.

Memorable Moments/Greatest Performances

Westbrook scored his first career touchdown during a 23–13 win over the Buffalo Bills on September 28, 2003, racing 62 yards for a TD late in the fourth quarter. He finished the game with 96 yards rushing and another 72 yards on special teams.

Westbrook helped lead the Eagles to a 28–10 victory over the Giants on November 16, 2003, by rushing for 48 yards, gaining another 60 yards on five pass receptions, and scoring three touchdowns, the longest of which came on a 29-yard hookup with Donovan McNabb.

Westbrook scored his first touchdown on special teams during a 31–28 overtime loss to the 49ers on December 21, 2003, returning a punt 81 yards for a TD.

Westbrook went over 100 yards rushing for the first time in his career during a 31–17 win over the Giants in the 2004 regular-season opener, gaining 119 yards on 17 carries.

In addition to rushing for 37 yards during a lopsided 47–17 victory over the Packers on December 5, 2004, Westbrook established career-high marks with 11 catches, 156 receiving yards, and three TD receptions.

Westbrook turned in another outstanding all-around effort against Oakland on September 25, 2005, rushing for 68 yards, making six receptions for 140 yards, and scoring a pair of touchdowns during a 23–20 win over the Raiders.

Westbrook contributed to a 19–14 victory over Green Bay on November 27, 2005, by rushing for 120 yards and one touchdown.

Westbrook had a huge game against San Francisco on September 24, 2006, leading the Eagles to a 38–24 win by amassing 164 yards of total offense and scoring three touchdowns, one of which came on a career-long 71-yard run from scrimmage.

Although the Eagles lost to Tampa Bay by a score of 23–21 on October 22, 2006, Westbrook turned in a similarly impressive performance, rushing for 101 yards and amassing another 113 yards on seven pass receptions, one of which went for a 52-yard touchdown.

Westbrook helped the Eagles record a 23–20 victory over the arch-rival New York Giants in the 2006 NFC wild card game by carrying the ball 20 times for 141 yards and one touchdown, which came on a 49-yard run early in the second quarter.

Even though the Eagles ended up losing to New Orleans by a score of 27–24 the following week, Westbrook had another big game, rushing for 116 yards and a pair of touchdowns, the longest of which came on a 62-yard run on Philadelphia's first possession of the second half.

Westbrook earned NFC Offensive Player of the Week honors for the first of two times for his performance during a convincing 56–21 victory over the Detroit Lions on September 23, 2007, when he rushed for 110 yards, made five receptions for 111 yards, and scored three touchdowns.

Westbrook had another tremendous all-around game on November 11, 2007, leading the Eagles to a 33–25 win over the Redskins by rushing for 100 yards, amassing 83 yards on five pass receptions, and scoring three touchdowns, two of which came in the last 3:30 of the final period. Putting the Eagles ahead to stay with 3:16 left in regulation, Westbrook took a short pass over the middle from Donovan McNabb and ran 57 yards for a TD that gave Philadelphia a 26–25 lead. He scored again just 58 seconds later on a 10-yard run.

Westbrook paced the Eagles to a 17–7 victory over Miami on November 18, 2007, by rushing for a season-high 148 yards.

Westbrook topped that performance on October 26, 2008, leading the Eagles to a 27–14 win over Atlanta by catching six passes for 42 yards and rushing for a career-high 167 yards and two touchdowns, with his 39-yard TD run with just under two minutes remaining in the final period sealing the victory.

Westbrook earned NFC Offensive Player of the Week honors for the second time by rushing for 110 yards and scoring four touchdowns during a 48–20 win over Arizona on November 27, 2008.

Westbrook provided much of the offensive firepower during a 20–14 victory over the Giants on December 7, 2008, scoring both Eagles touchdowns on a 30-yard run and a 40-yard pass reception. He finished the game with 131 yards rushing and six catches for 72 yards.

Westbrook experienced the most memorable moment of his career against those same Giants at Giants Stadium on October 19, 2003, when he gave the Eagles a stunning 14–10 win over their Eastern Division rivals by returning a punt 84 yards for a touchdown with just 1:16 left in regulation. Westbrook's brilliant return, which subsequently became known as the "Miracle at the Meadowlands II," enabled the Eagles to emerge victorious even though they gained a total of just 134 yards on offense the entire game. Westbrook, who also scored Philadelphia's first touchdown on a 6-yard pass reception in the first quarter, finished the contest with 67 yards rushing and 223 all-purpose yards, with his extraordinary return gaining him recognition as the NFC Special Teams Player of the Week.

Notable Achievements

- Rushed for more than 1,000 yards twice.
- Surpassed 50 receptions five times, topping 70 catches three times and 90 catches once.
- Surpassed 600 receiving yards four times.
- Amassed more than 1,000 yards from scrimmage five times, topping 1,500 yards three times and 2,000 yards once (2,104 in 2007).
- Accumulated more than 1,000 all-purpose yards six times, topping 1,500 yards four times and 2,000 yards once (2,183 in 2007).
- Scored more than 10 touchdowns four times.
- Averaged more than 5 yards per carry twice.
- Returned two punts for touchdowns.
- Led NFL with 2,104 yards from scrimmage in 2007.

- Finished third in NFL with 1,333 rushing yards and 2,183 all-purpose yards in 2007.
- Led Eagles in rushing six times and receptions three times.
- Holds Eagles career record for most total yards from scrimmage (9,785).
- Ranks among Eagles career leaders with: 5,995 yards rushing (3rd); 10,769 all-purpose yards (2nd); 426 receptions (4th); 37 rushing touchdowns (4th); 68 total touchdowns (3rd); and 410 points scored (7th).
- Four-time division champion (2002, 2003, 2004, and 2006).
- 2004 NFC champion.
- 2003 Week 7 NFC Special Teams Player of the Week.
- Two-Time NFC Offensive Player of the Week.
- Two-time Pro Bowl selection (2004 and 2007).
- 2003 First-Team All-Conference selection.
- 2007 First-Team All-Pro selection.
- Named to Eagles 75th Anniversary Team in 2007.
- Inducted into Philadelphia Eagles Hall of Fame in 2015.

19

— BILL BRADLEY —

The fact that Bill Bradley never experienced a winning season during his time in Philadelphia often prevents him from receiving his just due as one of the finest players in franchise history. Nevertheless, Bradley proved to be invaluable to the Eagles during his eight-year stay in the City of Brotherly Love, with his tremendous versatility enabling him to assume many different roles as a member of the team, including that of punt- and kickoff-returner, punter, and holder on field goal attempts. However, more than anything else, Bradley became known for his exceptional work at free safety, where he became the first player in NFL history to lead the league in interceptions in consecutive seasons. An outstanding ball-hawk, Bradley recorded 34 interceptions over the course of his career, tying him with Eric Allen and Brian Dawkins for the most in team annals. Bradley's superb play earned him three trips to the Pro Bowl, three All-Pro selections, four All-Conference nominations, and eventual induction into the Eagles Hall of Fame, even though the Eagle squads for which he played compiled an overall record of just 35-72-5 between 1969 and 1976.

Born in Palestine, Texas, on January 24, 1947, William Calvin Bradley, as the son of a baseball coach, grew up dreaming of one day playing in the major leagues. An excellent all-around athlete, Bradley starred in multiple sports while attending Palestine High School, excelling as a shortstop in baseball and as a quarterback and defensive back in football. Performing brilliantly on the gridiron in his junior year, Bradley led Palestine to its only Texas 3A State Championship with his exceptional running and passing, earning in the process the nickname "Super Bill." Equally proficient on the diamond, Bradley received a $20,000 offer to sign with the Detroit Tigers after they selected him in the seventh round of the 1965 MLB Draft. However, his desire to go to college prompted him to instead accept a scholarship to play football for the University of Texas.

After initially manning the quarterback position at Texas, Bradley moved to the defensive side of the ball when the Longhorns switched to the

Bill Bradley is tied for first in team annals in career interceptions.
Courtesy of MainlineAutographs.com

Wishbone offense in 1967. Spending his final two years at safety, Bradley co-captained the 1968 Texas squad that finished the season as conference and Cotton Bowl champions, with his four-interception effort against arch-rival Texas A&M in his senior year standing out as the finest performance of his college career.

Subsequently selected by the Eagles in the third round of the 1969 NFL Draft, with the 69th overall pick, Bradley spent his first season in Philadelphia playing mostly on special teams, averaging just under 40 yards per punt, while amassing a total of 648 yards returning kickoffs and punts. Also seeing some action on defense while serving as the primary backup to starting safeties Nate Ramsey and Joe Scarpati, Bradley recorded the first interception of his career, which he returned 56 yards for a touchdown. Hampered by a knee injury the following year, Bradley found himself being limited exclusively to punting duties, averaging 36.8 yards per punt for an Eagles team that finished just 3-10-1.

Fully healthy by the start of the 1971 campaign, Bradley assumed a full-time role on defense, beginning a six-year stint during which he served as the Eagles' starting free safety. Performing brilliantly in his first full season at that post, Bradley earned Pro Bowl, First-Team All-Pro, and First-Team All NFC honors by leading the NFL with 11 interceptions and 248 interception-return yards. He followed that up with another outstanding season, once again gaining Pro Bowl, First-Team All-Pro, and First-Team All-Conference recognition by topping the circuit with nine interceptions, which he returned for a total of 73 yards.

Establishing himself as one of the NFL's most impactful defensive backs even though he lacked superior running speed, the 5'11", 190-pound Bradley relied heavily on his instincts, intellect, and intricate knowledge of defenses, stating years later, "I got to study behind Joe Scarpati at free safety and Nate Ramsey at strong safety, so I had two pretty good mentors. The interceptions just came from studying and, I think, playing quarterback in college helped me a little bit to get inside what I thought was the mind of a quarterback's thinking. I studied and knew the philosophies of the defense."

Bradley continued, "You had to learn the game plan, so I got in on the ground floor of learning the philosophies of defenses and then got to be active as far as calling the coverages according to the formations and what adjustments you had to make. Getting all the interceptions was just basically anticipation and knowing where the quarterback was going, which made up for the lack of speed."

Commenting on Bradley's uncanny instincts, Hall of Fame quarterback Sonny Jurgensen, who competed against him as a member of the Washington Redskins, stated, "He's like a ghost. He's there, but you don't see him until it is too late."

In discussing his longtime teammate, Eagles wide receiver Ben Hawkins said, "Bill was a great free safety. He had a good eye for the ball and always helped everyone else out there. And people forget, he was a great punt returner."

Although Bradley never again recorded more than five interceptions in a season for the Eagles, he continued to perform well for them the next four years, a period during which he earned another trip to the Pro Bowl and All-Conference honors two more times.

One of Philadelphia's most popular citizens for much of the 1970s, Bradley endeared himself to the hometown fans not only with his outstanding on-field play, but, also, with his laid-back and congenial personality, with former teammate Jerry Sisemore saying, "Everywhere we went in South Philly, everyone just smiled and laughed and called out to him, 'Hey, Super Bill!' I was just kind of tagging along and soaking it up. We would

In addition to starring at safety, Bradley punted and returned kickoffs and punts during his time in Philadelphia.
Courtesy of SportsMemorabilia.com

sometimes take excursions down to Amish country. Even the people there in the country loved him. Man alive, it was crazy."

Bradley's friendly demeanor and fondness for the city's nightlife also made him extremely popular with the famed Philadelphia Phillies usherettes, with the longtime bachelor later revealing, "I had many friends that were usherettes. I spent many a night dancing with some of the usherettes. I was called the 'Dance Hall Doctor.'"

A frequent visitor to Philadelphia's Veterans Stadium during the offseason, Bradley spent many a day living out his childhood dream of playing in the big leagues by working out with the Phillies, saying years later, "The most fun I had was in the offseason. I would stay in Philadelphia in the offseason and spent most of my time at 'The Vet.' I would go out there and shag fly balls from all the old Phillies greats, like Mike Schmidt, Greg Luzinski and Pete Rose. I used to tell Mike, 'You can't hit a ball past me, man.' I was like a kid out there with those guys."

Bradley's time in Philadelphia came to an end following the conclusion of the 1976 campaign, when the Eagles traded him to the Minnesota Vikings for a seventh-round draft pick. In addition to recording a franchise-record 34 interceptions in his eight seasons with the Eagles, Bradley amassed 536 interception-return yards, which also represents the highest total in team annals. Meanwhile, Bradley, who continued to return punts for much of his career, ranks eighth in franchise history with 876 punt-return yards.

Subsequently cut by the Vikings during training camp, Bradley briefly worked at his family's restaurant in Palestine, before signing with the St. Louis Cardinals when Mike Sensibaugh broke his leg. After appearing in four games with the Cardinals, Bradley retired for good and returned to Philadelphia, where he spent the next few years investing in a sports management company. Bradley later bought a farm and a gas station in Palestine, before embarking on a lengthy coaching career that saw him spend the next 32 years coaching defensive backs for various teams in college, the USFL, the Canadian Football League, and the NFL. After spending the previous two seasons serving as the defensive coordinator at Lamar University, Bradley retired to private life in 2014, in part to help take care of his stepson, who had suffered brain trauma as the result of a violent attack.

Looking back fondly on his days in Philadelphia, Bradley says, "The fans are fantastic in Philadelphia. They lived and breathed and died the Eagles. We were bad in those days, but we gave it all we had. On defense, we were a blue-collar unit that really got after people. The fans could be brutal, and we heard our share of boos. But I have the distinction of never being booed there. They never booed me, and I gave them everything I had."

Meanwhile, in encapsulating his career, Bradley recalls, "One play sticks out in my mind. We were playing the Cardinals and a receiver named John Gilliam came across the middle. I saw the ball in the air and broke on it. We came together, Gilliam and me, and I just took the ball away. On the films, you could see one guy really wanted the ball and the other guy didn't. That's how I remember my career. I was the guy who wanted the ball."

EAGLES CAREER HIGHLIGHTS

Best Season

Bradley had his finest season for the Eagles in 1971, when he earned Pro Bowl and First-Team All-Pro honors by leading the NFL with 11 interceptions and 248 interception-return yards, setting in the process single-season franchise records in both categories that still stand.

Memorable Moments/Greatest Performances

Although the Eagles lost their October 19, 1969, meeting with the Dallas Cowboys by a score of 49–14, Bradley scored the only touchdown of his career when he picked off a Roger Staubach pass and returned the ball 56 yards for a TD.

Bradley performed brilliantly over a four-game stretch that lasted from October 31 to November 21, 1971, recording two interceptions during a 17–16 win over the Denver Broncos, picking off another two passes in helping the 2-5 Eagles forge a 7–7 tie with the 6-1 Washington Redskins, and intercepting two more passes during a 37–20 win over the St. Louis Cardinals.

Bradley contributed to a 23–20 victory over the Lions on December 5, 1971, when he helped set up an Eagles score by returning an interception 51 yards deep into Detroit territory.

Bradley also proved to be a key figure in Philadelphia's 26–10 upset win over the Redskins on October 5, 1975, intercepting Washington quarterback Billy Kilmer twice.

Notable Achievements

- Scored one touchdown on defense during career.
- Recorded more than 10 interceptions and 200 interception-return yards once each.
- Led NFL in interceptions twice and interception-return yards once.
- Led Eagles in interceptions three times.
- Holds Eagles single-season records for most interceptions (11) and most interception-return yards (248), both in 1971.
- Holds Eagles career records for most interceptions (34) and most interception-return yards (536).
- Ranks eighth in Eagles history with 876 punt-return yards.
- Three-time Pro Bowl selection (1971, 1972, and 1973).
- Two-time First-Team All-Pro selection (1971 and 1972).
- 1973 Second-Team All-Pro selection.
- Two-time First-Team All-Conference selection (1971 and 1972).
- Two-time Second-Team All-Conference selection (1973 and 1974).
- Inducted into Philadelphia Eagles Hall of Fame in 1993.

20

— MIKE QUICK —

An outstanding wide receiver who spent his entire nine-year NFL career with the Eagles, Mike Quick established himself as one of the finest wideouts in franchise history during his time in Philadelphia, amassing the third most receiving yards and touchdown receptions in team annals. Also ranking among the Eagles' all-time leaders in several other statistical categories, Quick finished first on the team in receptions four times and receiving yards five times, setting a single-season franchise record that still stands by accumulating 1,409 receiving yards in 1983. Quick's strong play helped lead the Eagles to three playoff appearances and one division title, earning him in the process five trips to the Pro Bowl, two All-Pro selections, and four All-NFC nominations. And, following the conclusion of his playing career, Quick received the additional honor of being inducted into the Eagles Hall of Fame.

Born in Hamlet, North Carolina, on May 14, 1959, Michael Anthony Quick grew up with his nine siblings in a public housing project, where his mother supported the family by working as a domestic and a nurse's aide. Looking back at his childhood years later, Quick said, "I had a happy childhood. We had a large, close-knit family with a lot of love and respect. Two of the kids smoked, but they

Mike Quick ranks third in franchise history in receptions and TD receptions.
Courtesy of SportsMemorabilia.com

wouldn't touch a cigarette around my mother. And, every time I go home, I go right back to St. Mary's Holiness Church."

Quick then added, "If things come too easy, you don't appreciate them. I learned to work for things. I can remember getting up at 5:30 to take a bus to the fields, where I picked tobacco, cucumbers, and peaches. I can remember collecting garbage for the Job Corps. But the main thing I remember is playing games. All I wanted to do was wear a jockstrap and sweat."

An excellent all-around athlete, Quick excelled in football, basketball, and track while attending Richmond Senior High School in Richmond County, North Carolina, leading his conference in points scored on the basketball court as a senior, while also serving as a member of the state champion 4 x 100 high-hurdle relay team. However, Quick lacked direction and proper motivation in the classroom, making him far less successful as a student. Encouraged by his high school football and track coach, Ron Kroll, to spend one postgraduate year at Fork Union Military Academy before enrolling in college, Quick took his mentor's advice, later revealing that Kroll often told him, "Son, you don't even know how good you are."

Looking back at the time he spent at Fork Union, Quick said, "Fork Union is an all-boys military school out in the woods. We'd be up at 6 a.m., with our outfits on and boots shined, get in formation and march to chow. Get your books, go to class, then formation and a march to lunch. Drill practice twice a week. Strange, different. But it was just what I needed: an excellent school with a lot of decent people. I got my grades up and realized, finally, that football was my sport."

Excelling on the gridiron while at Fork Union, Quick later drew praise from Red Pulliam, the academy's football coach, who said of his former protégé, "I thought he could have played pro ball by the end of his year here. He was one of the finest athletic talents that I've seen in my 25 years of coaching."

Subsequently offered a football scholarship by North Carolina State University, Quick spent his early days at NC State being used primarily as a blocker for running back Ted Brown, before eventually emerging as one of the premier wide receivers in the nation. After being named offensive MVP of the Blue-Gray Game in his senior year, Quick became the 20th overall pick of the 1982 NFL Draft when the Eagles used their first-round selection on him. In explaining the decision to draft Quick, Eagles executive director of player personnel Lynn Stiles stated, "We had a highlight film of him, and most of it was blocking. I liked his toughness and ability to go into a crowd. On the basis of what I'd seen, I called him the most competitive and sure-handed receiver in the draft."

Spending his first NFL season serving as a backup to starting wide-out Ron Smith, Quick saw very little action as a rookie, making just 10 receptions for 156 yards and one touchdown. However, at one point the following year, Quick revealed that he considered his limited amount of playing time during the early stages of his career to be a blessing in disguise, suggesting, "I wasn't ready to start. On the sidelines, I could pick up little things, like how opponents were disguising their defenses on us. This season, I can just react."

Taking note of the advancements made by Quick, Marion Campbell, who succeeded Dick Vermeil as head coach in 1983, said, "I saw his ability in camp this summer. He was flashy, by which I mean he really stood out. I had to see how well he could catch, and the only way to do that was to put him in."

Eagles cornerback Herman Edwards, who often covered the 6'2", 190-pound Quick during practice, also noticed the changes in the young wide receiver, saying, "He's very smooth. And those long strides can lull you to sleep. Suddenly, he's in your face, and it's too late."

After breaking into the starting lineup in 1983, Quick went on to have an outstanding season, beginning an exceptional five-year run during which he posted the following numbers:

YEAR	REC	REC YD	TD REC
1983	69	**1,409**	13
1984	61	1,052	9
1985	73	1,247	11
1986	60	939	9
1987	46	790	11

In addition to leading the NFL with 1,409 receiving yards in 1983, Quick finished second in the league in that category two years later. He also ranked among the league leaders in TD catches all five years, placing as high as second in both 1983 and the strike-shortened campaign of 1987. Quick earned Pro Bowl honors all five years, gained All-NFC recognition in four of those five seasons, and made All-Pro in both 1983 and 1985.

Despite his track background, Quick lacked elite running speed for a wide receiver, posting a time of 4.6 seconds in the 40-yard dash at the NFL

Quick surpassed 1,000 receiving
yards three straight times.
Courtesy of SportsMemorabilia.com

scouting combine. Yet, Quick maintained that he did not require blazing speed to succeed at the professional level, agreeing with Eagles tight end John Spagnola, who stated, "Quickness is one of the most overrated factors in football." In expressing his feelings on the matter, Quick said, "I run with the same motion at full speed as I do when I'm just starting, and guys tell me it's hard to key on me. What's important are good, disciplined routes and a knack for catching the ball. A lot of guys aren't burners, but they can catch in traffic. Look at Fred Biletnikoff."

Doing a superb job of catching the ball in traffic, Quick had outstanding hands, tremendous leaping ability and body control, and the ability to run well with the ball after making the catch, as his league-leading total of 53 touchdown receptions from 1983 to 1987 would seem to indicate. Quick also proved to be an excellent blocker, with Philadelphia's executive director of player personnel, Lynn Stiles, commenting, "Mike's blocking gives us a dimension we didn't have in the past."

Meanwhile, in assessing Quick's overall contributions to the team, Eagles quarterback Ron Jaworski stated, "He stretches the zones with his deep routes. Even when he's not the primary receiver, he helps the others by creating more of an area for them to work in."

Unfortunately, Quick suffered a broken leg in 1988 that brought his days as a premier receiver to an end. Appearing in just eight games, he made only 22 receptions for 508 yards and four touchdowns. Plagued by knee and quadriceps problems in each of the next two seasons, Quick started only nine more contests, totaling just 22 receptions, 363 receiving yards, and three touchdowns during that time, before announcing his retirement following the conclusion of the 1990 campaign. Quick ended his career with 363 receptions, 6,464 receiving yards, 61 TD catches, and an average of 17.8 yards per reception, all of which place him among the franchise's all-time leaders.

Although Quick retired as an active player in 1990, he has remained close to the Eagles throughout most of his post-playing career. After being inducted into the Eagles Hall of Fame in 1995, Quick returned to the team as a broadcaster three years later, since which time he has served as a color commentator on the club's radio broadcasts, working alongside longtime play-by-play announcer Merrill Reese.

CAREER HIGHLIGHTS

Best Season

Quick had a big year in 1985, earning First-Team All-Pro honors by making 73 receptions for 1,247 yards and 11 touchdowns. However, he compiled slightly better overall numbers in 1983, earning his other First-Team All-Pro nomination by making 69 receptions, catching 13 TD passes, and leading the league with 1,409 receiving yards.

Memorable Moments/Greatest Performances

Quick scored the first touchdown of his career when he hauled in a 49-yard TD pass from Ron Jaworski during a 35–14 win over the Houston Oilers on December 19, 1982.

Quick went over 100 receiving yards for the first time during a 23–13 loss to the Washington Redskins on September 11, 1983, finishing the game with four catches for 106 yards and one touchdown, which came on a 27-yard pass from Jaworski.

Quick followed that up with a strong outing against Denver on September 18, making six receptions for 152 yards and one touchdown during a 13–10 win.

Quick gave the Eagles a 28–24 win over the Atlanta Falcons on October 2, 1983, when he collaborated with Ron Jaworski on a 53-yard scoring play late in the fourth quarter. He finished the game with four catches for 122 yards and that one touchdown.

Although the Eagles lost to the St. Louis Cardinals by a score of 34–14 on October 28, 1984, Quick had a huge afternoon, making six receptions for 170 yards and one touchdown, which came on a 90-yard connection with Jaworski.

Almost exactly one year later, on October 27, 1985, Quick gave the Eagles a 21–17 come-from-behind victory over the Buffalo Bills by hauling in a 32-yard TD pass from Jaworski during the latter stages of the fourth quarter. Quick finished the game with eight receptions for 117 yards and that one TD, with his outstanding play helping the Eagles overcome a 17–0 deficit heading into the final period.

Quick starred in defeat on November 3, 1985, catching six passes for 146 yards and one touchdown during a 24–13 loss to the 49ers, with his TD reception covering 82 yards.

After the Eagles blew a 17–0 fourth-quarter lead against Atlanta one week later, Quick gave them a 23–17 win over the Falcons when he hooked up with Ron Jaworski on a franchise-record 99-yard scoring play in overtime.

Quick came up big for the Eagles in another contest that went into overtime on November 30, 1986, making eight receptions for 145 yards and three touchdowns during a 33–27 win over the Los Angeles Raiders, with his TD grabs covering 62, 5, and 10 yards.

Quick contributed to a 38–27 victory over the New York Jets on December 20, 1987, by making six receptions for 148 yards and two touchdowns, which came on 45- and 13-yard connections with Randall Cunningham.

Quick topped 100 receiving yards for the final time in his career in the opening game of the 1989 regular season, making six receptions for 140 yards and one TD during a 31–7 win over Seattle.

Notable Achievements

- Surpassed 60 receptions four times.
- Surpassed 1,000 receiving yards three times.
- Made more than 10 touchdown receptions three times.
- Averaged more than 20 yards per reception twice.
- Led NFL with 1,409 receiving yards in 1983.
- Finished second in NFL in: receiving yards once; TD catches twice; and touchdowns once.
- Holds share of NFL record for longest TD reception (99 yards vs. Atlanta on 11/10/85).
- Led Eagles in receptions four times and receiving yards five times.
- Holds Eagles single-season record for most receiving yards (1,409 in 1983).
- Ranks among Eagles career leaders with: 363 receptions (8th); 6,464 receiving yards (3rd); 6,459 total yards from scrimmage (9th); 61

touchdown receptions (tied-3rd); 61 touchdowns (7th); and average of 17.8 yards per reception (4th).

- 1988 division champion.
- Five-time Pro Bowl selection (1983, 1984, 1985, 1986, and 1987).
- Two-time First-Team All-Pro selection (1983 and 1985).
- Two-time First-Team All-Conference selection (1983 and 1985).
- Two-time Second-Team All-Conference selection (1986 and 1987).
- Inducted into Philadelphia Eagles Hall of Fame in 1995.

21

— ERIC ALLEN —

One of the NFL's finest cover corners for more than a decade, Eric Allen spent the first half of his 14-year pro career with the Eagles, during which time he tied franchise marks for most career interceptions and most defensive touchdowns scored. The only player in NFL history to run back three or more interceptions for TDs in two different seasons, Allen accomplished the feat for the first time in 1993, when he recorded a franchise-record four pick-sixes. Intercepting at least five passes in four of his seven seasons in Philadelphia, Allen appeared in five Pro Bowls, made All-Pro three times, and helped the Eagles advance to the playoffs four times, earning him eventual induction into the team's Hall of Fame.

Born in San Diego, California, on November 22, 1965, Eric Andre Allen attended Point Loma High School, where he starred on the gridiron under highly respected head coach Bennie Edens. After accepting an athletic scholarship from Arizona State University, Allen spent four years starting at cornerback for the Sun Devils, playing his best ball for them as a senior in 1987, when he recorded eight interceptions, two of which he returned for touchdowns.

Eric Allen recorded a franchise-record four pick-sixes in 1993.
Courtesy of MEARSOnlineAuctions.com

Subsequently selected by the Eagles in the second round of the 1988 NFL Draft, with the 30th overall pick, Allen drew high praise from Buddy

Ryan immediately following the draft, with Philadelphia's head coach saying of his prize rookie, "He was my favorite of all the defensive backs. When I first saw him on film, he just stood out. He plays the game all the way to the hilt."

Laying claim to the starting right cornerback job his first year in the league, Allen earned a spot on the 1988 NFL All-Rookie Team by recording 65 tackles and five interceptions, which he returned for a total of 76 yards. Emerging as one of the league's top cover corners the following year, Allen earned Pro Bowl and First-Team All-Pro honors by finishing second in the NFL with eight interceptions. Continuing to perform well in each of the next three seasons, Allen picked off a total of 12 passes from 1990 to 1992, earning in the process two more trips to the Pro Bowl and another All-Pro selection.

Allen's rapid ascent to stardom could be attributed largely to his superior physical gifts, which included outstanding running speed and soft, sure hands. Yet, the 5'10", 184-pound cornerback also possessed several other attributes that helped make him one of the league's most successful players at his position, as legendary Eagles writer Ray Didinger articulated when he wrote, "Allen was that rare athlete who combined great physical ability with a great work ethic. He could have done just fine relying on his natural skills. He ran the 40-yard dash in 4.48 seconds, and he had a thickly muscled upper body and quick hands which allowed him to control receivers at the line of scrimmage. Many players blessed with the same skill set would have just relied on that and done quite well."

Didinger continued, "But what made Allen special was his willingness to work on the mental part of the job. He was a student of the game. He studied film for hours, taking notes on every quarterback and receiver, charting their patterns, their moves, their tendencies. Often, when he intercepted a pass, it was because he saw something in how the quarterback positioned his feet, or how the receiver lined up. He knew where the ball was going before it was snapped. At that point, he said, it was just a matter of making the catch."

For his part, Allen, who worked with a punching bag to develop fast hands and a hard jab that enabled him to jam receivers at the line of scrimmage, said, "I'm not as flashy as Deion Sanders. I'm a blue-collar worker. When I'm on the job, I work hard to get it done."

After earning Pro Bowl honors in each of the previous two seasons, Allen turned in arguably his finest all-around performance in 1993, when he gained Second-Team All-Pro recognition by picking off six passes and leading the league with 201 interception-return yards and four defensive

Allen led the Eagles in interceptions four times.
Courtesy of DynastySports.com

touchdowns. He followed that up with another solid year, earning his fourth straight Pro Bowl selection by recording three interceptions and 57 tackles, before signing with New Orleans as a free agent at season's end. In explaining his decision to leave Philadelphia, Allen said, "I knew I wasn't going to be an Eagle early in the offseason. The whole environment around there has to change, it's so negative, so pessimistic. It just wasn't right, and I knew the best thing for me would be to go elsewhere. Sometimes, you just have to make a change."

Allen later provided further insight into his departure from Philadelphia, claiming that ownership's unsuccessful courting of free agent Deion Sanders helped push him out the door. Revealing how the pursuit of Sanders impacted his decision, Allen said, "I understand it's a business, but to bring people in and treat them better than those who've been here, and just throw money at them, like, 'Here, it's yours'. . . . It was the ultimate disrespect. For them to go chasing Deion Sanders around when they had important people at home to take care of. . . . What was that? And it's happened over and over and over and over."

Allen then added, "People wonder why we always seemed incomplete. That's why. We never could get over that final hurdle because we never felt the people upstairs were committed to win the way you have to be today. It just gets to you."

Allen ended up spending three seasons in New Orleans, earning Pro Bowl honors for the sixth and final time in 1995, before moving on to Oakland, where he spent the last four years of his career. Making history during his time in Oakland, Allen became the only NFL player ever to record as many as three pick-sixes in two different seasons when he returned three interceptions for touchdowns in 2000. Choosing to announce his retirement following the conclusion of the 2001 campaign, Allen ended his career with 54 interceptions, 826 interception-return yards, 789 tackles, six forced fumbles, seven fumble recoveries, three sacks, and nine touchdowns. While playing for the Eagles, he recorded 34 interceptions, 482 interception-return yards, 408 tackles, four forced fumbles, five fumble recoveries, two sacks, and five touchdowns on defense. Extremely durable, Allen missed just seven games his entire career, appearing in 111 out of a possible 112 contests during his time in Philadelphia.

Following his playing days, Allen began a career in broadcasting, joining ESPN as an NFL studio analyst in 2002. Now living in San Diego, Allen currently works as an NFL analyst for Pac-12 Networks, where he frequently appears on the station's flagship show, *Sports Report*.

When asked how he would like to be remembered, Allen says, "I would like to have the respect of the young players. I'd like to have them say, 'Damn, that Eric Allen, he could play today.' To have the respect of the players, that's real important."

EAGLES CAREER HIGHLIGHTS

Best Season

Allen earned First-Team All-Pro honors for the only time in 1989, when he finished second in the NFL with a career-high eight interceptions. Nevertheless, he had his finest all-around season in 1993, when, in addition to recording 64 solo tackles, two sacks, and three forced fumbles, he intercepted six passes, which he returned for a league-leading total of 201 yards and four touchdowns.

Memorable Moments/Greatest Performances

Allen recorded the first interception of his career during a 41–14 victory over Tampa Bay in the 1988 regular-season opener.

Allen contributed to a 17–3 win over the Dallas Cowboys on December 23, 1990, by intercepting two passes, one of which he returned 35 yards for his first career touchdown.

Allen again picked off two passes during a 31–10 victory over the Raiders on November 8, 1992.

Allen proved to be a huge factor in the 1992 NFC wild card game, intercepting two passes and sealing the Eagles' 36–20 win over the Saints in the fourth quarter by returning his second pick 18 yards for a touchdown.

Allen lit the scoreboard for the first of four times in 1993 during a 34–31 win over the Redskins on September 19, when he returned an interception 29 yards for a touchdown.

Allen earned NFC Defensive Player of the Week honors for his performance during a 37–26 win over the Saints on December 26, 1993, when he intercepted two passes, both of which he returned for touchdowns, with one of those covering 33 yards and the other 25 yards.

Allen made the most memorable play of his career during a 35–30 victory over the New York Jets on October 3, 1993, when he scored the game-winning touchdown late in the fourth quarter on a spectacular 94-yard interception return, eluding several would-be tacklers in the process. After scoring his TD, Allen sprinted over to the sideline and handed the ball to an injured Randall Cunningham, as if to say, "This one's for you." Allen's brilliant effort, which Steve Sabol of NFL Films later called the "Greatest Interception Return in NFL History," earned him NFC Defensive Player of the Week honors for the first time in his career.

Notable Achievements

- Recorded at least five interceptions in a season four times.
- Led NFL with 201 interception-return yards and four interception-return TDs in 1993.
- Finished second in NFL in interceptions once and interception-return yards once.
- Led Eagles in interceptions four times.
- Holds NFL single-season record for most interception-return touchdowns (4 in 1993).
- Holds Eagles career records for most interceptions (34) and most interception return TDs (5).
- Ranks third in Eagles history with career total of 482 interception-return yards.
- 1988 division champion.
- Member of 1988 NFL All-Rookie Team.
- Two-time NFC Defensive Player of the Week.
- Five-time Pro Bowl selection (1989, 1991, 1992, 1993, and 1994).
- 1989 First-Team All-Pro selection.
- Two-time Second-Team All-Pro selection (1991 and 1993).
- Three-time First-Team All-Conference selection (1989, 1992, and 1993).
- 1994 Second-Team All-Conference selection.
- Pro Football Reference All-1990s Second Team.
- Named to Eagles 75th Anniversary Team in 2007.
- Inducted into Philadelphia Eagles Hall of Fame in 2011.

22

FRANK "BUCKO" KILROY

A pillar of strength for the Eagles on both sides of the ball for 12 seasons, Frank "Bucko" Kilroy spent his entire playing career in Philadelphia, establishing himself as one of the NFL's finest two-way linemen. Excelling at right guard on offense and middle guard (or nose tackle) on defense during the greatest era in franchise history, Kilroy helped lead the Eagles to three consecutive Eastern Division titles and two NFL championships, earning in the process three Pro Bowl selections, six All-Pro nominations, and a spot on the NFL 1940s All-Decade Team. One of the league's most durable players, Kilroy missed just four games in his first 12 seasons, at one point appearing in 96 consecutive contests. And, following the conclusion of his playing career, Kilroy continued to serve the NFL in one capacity or another for 51 more years, with only former New York Giants owner Wellington Mara logging more consecutive years of service.

Born in the Port Richmond section of Philadelphia, Pennsylvania, on May 30, 1921, Francis Joseph Kilroy attended Northeast Catholic High School, where he starred in football, prompting the University of Notre Dame to offer him an athletic scholarship. Choosing instead to enroll at nearby Temple University, Kilroy subsequently became the first player in that school's history to earn Honorable Mention All-America honors with his exceptional two-way play. After leading the Owls to a 7-2 record and victories over rivals Penn State, Bucknell, and Villanova as a senior in 1941, Kilroy spent most of the next two years serving in the Merchant Marines during World War II, before joining the Eagles as an undrafted free agent during the early stages of the 1943 campaign.

Adapting well to the pro game, Kilroy earned a starting job before long, after which he helped the Eagles usher in the most successful period in team annals. Considered one of the league's best interior linemen by the mid-1940s, Kilroy performed exceptionally well on both sides of the ball for Philadelphia's 1947 Eastern Division championship team, before earning All-Pro honors in six of the next seven years, with the Eagles capturing the NFL title in both 1948 and 1949. In addition to creating gaping holes for Eagles running backs on offense, the 6'2", 243-pound Kilroy proved to be a relentless defender who never stopped playing until the referee blew his whistle.

Frank "Bucko" Kilroy starred on both sides of the ball for the Eagles for 12 seasons. Courtesy of RMYAuctions.com

However, while Kilroy's aggressive and physical style of play earned him the favor of his teammates, it also caused him to develop a reputation as arguably the dirtiest player of his era, with Baltimore Colts Hall of Fame defensive end Gino Marchetti saying during a 1999 interview, "If there's a dirty player in the National Football League, they'd show you a picture of Bucko Kilroy."

Longtime teammate Vic Sears stated, "I don't think that Buck would ever try to be dirty, but . . . well . . . I shouldn't say that."

Eagles legend Chuck Bednarik, who spent his first six years in the league playing alongside Kilroy, claimed, "For a so-called teammate, Bucko Kilroy was the dirtiest football player I ever saw."

Once described by a Chicago sportswriter as "a knuckle-duster in knee pants who gives our fellows that boyish grin while knocking their teeth loose in a pileup," Kilroy took full advantage of the rules in place at that time, explaining years later, "In the '40s and '50s, it was smash-mouth, or mash-mouth, football. The rules were different. First of all, you played two ways up to 1950. Then, you had to put the ball carrier down. Another thing, forearms were legal."

Kilroy continued, "The Eagles then were like the Raiders today. We were tough and intimidated teams. The nature of our offense added to our toughness. Our backs were taught to cut back against the grain. That put the blockers on the other side of the tacklers. We blindsided most of the defensive players. They didn't see us, and we demolished them!"

Revealing that he recorded several knockouts of opposing players over the course of his career, Kilroy stated, "Oh yeah. That happened when you blindsided a guy and he didn't see you coming. It was perfectly legal. But they checked me out pretty good on the films."

Claiming that the players of his era possessed an inner toughness that the modern-day player lacks, Kilroy suggested:

> I think the glory days of the NFL, as far as personnel, were the late '40s and early '50s because all the players were back from World War II. They'd been killing Germans and Japanese, and then later came the Korean War. These kids today were never in a war. . . . When the All-America Football Conference folded, there were only 12 teams, with 35 players on a team. That meant that 60 percent of the players today would not have been playing. . . . It was a survival of the fittest—a different mentality. We were taught to love your God, respect your elders, and fear no son of a bitch that walks.

After earning his first three All-Pro selections primarily for his outstanding play at right guard on offense, Kilroy made All-Pro three straight times from 1952 to 1954 while playing middle guard on defense almost exclusively. Suggesting that the responsibilities associated with his position required that he be extremely mobile, Kilroy said, "The middle guard very seldom crossed the line of scrimmage. Most of the time, he was in pass coverage. Weak side zone, strong side zone, or man-to-man on the fullback." He then added, "I enjoyed playing defense. Offense was drudgery."

After starting every game for the Eagles in each of the previous eight seasons, Kilroy suffered a knee injury that limited him to just one contest in 1955. He subsequently announced his

Kilroy earned a spot on the NFL 1940s All-Decade Team.
Courtesy of RMYAuctions.com

retirement, ending his career with five interceptions and 11 fumble recoveries in 134 regular-season games.

Following his retirement as an active player, Kilroy, who spent his final three seasons in uniform serving the Eagles as a player/coach, became the team's full-time line coach. He remained in that position until 1959, when he transitioned into the role of director of player personnel. Choosing to leave Philadelphia following the conclusion of the 1961 campaign, Kilroy assumed a similar position with the Washington Redskins, with whom he remained until 1966, when he became a "super scout" for the Dallas Cowboys. Remaining in Dallas until 1970, Kilroy subsequently traveled north to New England, where he spent the next 36 years serving the Patriots in various capacities, including personnel director (1971–1978), general manager (1979–1982), vice president (1983–1993), and scouting consultant (1994–2007), giving him 64 years of unbroken NFL service. Sadly, Kilroy's lengthy association with the game he loved ended on July 10, 2007, when he passed away at the age of 86 at his home in Foxboro, Massachusetts.

CAREER HIGHLIGHTS

Best Season

Kilroy had his finest season on offense in 1948, when his outstanding lead-blocking helped the NFL champion Eagles place near the top of the league rankings with 376 points scored (second) and 2,378 yards rushing (third). He performed his best on the other side of the ball in 1954, recording four interceptions and four fumble recoveries for the league's second-ranked defense.

Memorable Moments/Greatest Performances

Kilroy came up big for the Eagles in the 1948 NFL championship game, helping them limit Chicago to 131 yards of total offense and making a key fumble recovery on defense during their 7–0 win over the Cardinals.

Kilroy's strong blocking at the point of attack helped the Eagles amass 519 yards of total offense and gain a season-high 331 yards on the ground during a 49–14 dismantling of the Washington Redskins on October 23, 1949.

Kilroy proved to be a key figure in the Eagles' 14–0 victory over the Los Angeles Rams in the 1949 NFL title game, recovering two fumbles on offense.

Notable Achievements

- Missed just four games in first 12 seasons, at one point appearing in 96 consecutive contests.
- Three-time Eastern Division champion (1947, 1948, and 1949).
- Two-time NFL champion (1948 and 1949).
- Three-time Pro Bowl selection (1952, 1953, and 1954).
- Six-time Second-Team All-Pro selection (1948, 1949, 1950, 1952, 1953, and 1954).
- NFL 1940s All-Decade Team.

23

BOB BROWN

In discussing Bob Brown, Pro Bowl defensive end Joe Robb, who faced him as a member of the St. Louis Cardinals, said, "Bob was the most devastating blocker I ever played against. I played against (Hall of Fame linemen) Jim Parker and Forrest Gregg, but Brown was bigger, stronger, and better than both of them."

One of the most dominant offensive linemen of his era, Bob Brown spent 10 seasons in the NFL, earning six Pro Bowl selections and eight All-Pro nominations during that time. Starring for the Eagles at right tackle his first five years in the league, the massive Brown used his size, strength, quickness, and nasty temperament to intimidate the opposition and create gaping holes through which Philadelphia backs ran, earning in the process his first three trips to the Pro Bowl and first five All-Pro selections. And, following the conclusion of his playing career, Brown earned the additional distinctions of being inducted into both the Eagles Hall of Fame and the Pro Football Hall of Fame.

Born in Cleveland, Ohio, on December 8, 1941, Robert Stanford Brown attended local East Tech High School, before enrolling at the University of Nebraska, where, while majoring in biology, he starred on the gridiron as a guard on offense and a linebacker on defense. After earning unanimous All-America honors and recognition as college football's offensive lineman of the year as a senior in 1963, Brown became the second overall pick of the 1964 NFL Draft when the Eagles selected him right after the San Francisco 49ers used the first pick on wide receiver Dave Parks. But, with the Denver Broncos also tabbing Brown with the fourth overall pick of that year's AFL Draft, the Eagles found themselves in a bidding war for his services, prompting them to offer him a $100,000 signing bonus that made him the team's highest paid lineman.

Moving to right tackle upon his arrival in Philadelphia, Brown, who stood close to 6'4" and weighed nearly 300 pounds, had an outstanding rookie season for the Eagles, gaining Second-Team All-Pro recognition his

Bob Brown spent the first five years of his Hall of Fame career in Philadelphia.
Courtesy of Richard Albersheim of Albersheims .com

first year in the league. He followed that up by earning Pro Bowl and First-Team All-Pro honors in each of the next two seasons, before suffering torn tendons in his right knee that forced him to the sidelines for the final six games of the 1967 campaign. After undergoing surgery and losing more than 30 pounds, Brown regained his weight and earlier form during the subsequent offseason, enabling him to earn Pro Bowl and First-Team All-Pro honors for the third time in 1968, while also being named NFL Offensive Lineman of the Year.

Combining tremendous size and strength with exceptional quickness, Brown proved to be surprisingly light on his feet for a man of his immense proportions, with his unique skill set often prompting Philadelphia's coaching staff to assign him the task of occupying multiple defenders on extra-point and field goal attempts. Typically outweighing his opponent by some 20 or 30 pounds, Brown sported an 18½-inch neck, 20-inch biceps, 33-inch thighs, and a chest that measured 57 inches, with Hugh Brown of the *Philadelphia Bulletin* describing him as "a splendid specimen of young manhood" and adding, "His shoulders, without any pads mind you, are wider than a water buffalo's."

One of the NFL's first serious powerlifters, Brown helped build up his strength by installing a weight room in his house, at one point coming within 10 pounds of the American record in the military press. Meanwhile, he polished his footwork by skipping rope and playing basketball.

In discussing his training regimen, Brown explained, "In college, I got by on my size. I was bigger than most of the other players. But, in the pros, there are a lot of big men who are also very strong, very smart, and very quick. Opposing them, I have to have something more than mere size."

Equally effective in pass protection, creating running room up the middle, or leading backs to the outside on sweeps, Brown excelled in every aspect of offensive line play, with Dick Vermeil, who served as an assistant on the coaching staff of the Rams when Brown joined them in 1969, stating, "Bob was an explosive drive blocker. When he fired out, he catapulted people off the line. Knocked them back five yards. You just don't see that in pro football. Bob was one of a kind."

Revealing the thoughts that crossed his mind whenever he saw Brown coming toward him, Green Bay cornerback Herb Adderley once said, "When Bob Brown pulls out to lead a sweep, there are two things a guy like me can do: Get out of the way or get hurt."

Employing a three-point stance from which he shot forward with awesome force at the snap of the ball, Brown earned the nickname "Boomer" for the sound he made when he contacted the defender at the point of attack. Often delivering a vicious forearm to his opponent's upper body, Brown noted, "I was trying to hit that area that was just below where the shoulder pads stop. There's a lot of real meaty, nice parts in that area; we can get a little bit of the spleen; usually it worked."

Describing how it felt when Brown drove his patented forearm into him, Atlanta linebacker Tommy Nobis stated, "Bob hit me, and it felt like the world turned upside down. I've never been hit like that before."

Feeling very little compassion for his opponent, Brown told Gordon Forbes of the *Philadelphia Inquirer* in 1967, "I dislike every man I play. I may not even know the guy . . . but I dislike him because he is standing between me and All-Pro, between me and my paycheck."

Commenting on Brown's dour disposition, Hall of Fame defensive end Deacon Jones stated, "Bob Brown had a cold-blooded mentality. He'd kill a mosquito with an ax."

In describing the aggressive approach that Brown took to his craft, John Madden, his coach at Oakland, said, "Bob Brown took the game, and he played offense with a defensive guy's personality."

Brown earned All-Pro honors in each of his five seasons with the Eagles.
Courtesy of MEARSOnlineAuctions.com

Madden continued, "Bob was the most aggressive offensive lineman that ever played. Bob used to say that, if he could get the right hit on a defensive end, hit him in the right place, like the solar plexus, that he could take a quarter out of him. And he would do it. He'd hit a guy in the first quarter and say, 'I won't see him again until the third quarter.'"

Providing credence to Madden's contention, Brown stated on one occasion, "I didn't finesse guys. I just tried to beat up on them for 60 minutes."

Unfortunately, Brown's time with the Eagles proved to be far too short. Displeased with the team's poor 2-12 showing in 1968, and unhappy over the subsequent firing of head coach Joe Kuharich, who became like a father figure to him during his time in Philadelphia, Brown asked to be traded following the conclusion of the campaign. Granting the disgruntled offensive lineman's request, the Eagles dealt him and defensive back Jim Nettles to the Los Angeles Rams for three players on May 12, 1969, receiving in return Pro Bowl cornerback Irv Cross, guard Don Chuy, and offensive tackle Joe Carollo. Expressing his glee upon learning of the trade, Brown said, "I am so ecstatic, I can hardly find words to describe my feelings. I just feel great."

Meanwhile, Rams head coach George Allen declared, "Bob Brown is the finest offensive lineman in pro football. With Brown and Charlie Cowan, the Rams will have the finest set of offensive tackles in the game."

Brown performed exceptionally well for the Rams over the course of the next two seasons, continuing his string of consecutive Pro Bowl and First-Team All-Pro selections, while also being named NFL Offensive Lineman of the Year for the second time in 1969. Nevertheless, the Rams elected to trade him to the Oakland Raiders on June 23, 1971. Despite being hampered by knee problems that ended up bringing his career to a premature end, Brown earned one more trip to the Pro Bowl, another All-Pro selection, and a pair of All-Conference nominations during his time in Oakland, before announcing his retirement following the conclusion of the 1973 campaign.

Finally gaining induction into the Pro Football Hall of Fame in 2004, Brown explained his on-field motivation during his acceptance speech, stating, "I could either go out there and be real good and be the beater, or I could go out there and be very mediocre and be the beaten. I liked the role of the beater better."

EAGLES CAREER HIGHLIGHTS

Best Season

Although Brown gained All-Pro recognition in each of his five seasons in Philadelphia, he made his greatest overall impact in 1966, when he helped the Eagles compile a record of 9-5 that represented their only winning mark from 1962 to 1977, with the 1000-Yard Club subsequently naming him the league's Outstanding Blocker of the Year.

Memorable Moments/Greatest Performances

Brown's superb blocking at the point of attack helped the Eagles amass 452 yards of total offense during a 21–7 win over the Pittsburgh Steelers on October 4, 1964. Philadelphia gained 272 of those yards on the ground, with Earl Gros rushing for 129 yards and Timmy Brown running for another 116 yards.

Although the Eagles suffered a 38–34 defeat at the hands of the Cleveland Browns on November 7, 1965, they accumulated a total of 582 yards on offense, with 230 of those coming on the ground. With Brown and his offensive line–mates leading the way, Philadelphia running backs averaged 7.7 yards per carry, with Timmy Brown rushing for a career-high 186 yards.

Notable Achievements

- 1966 1000-Yard Club NFL Outstanding Blocker of the Year Award winner.
- 1968 NFL Offensive Lineman of the Year.
- Three-time Pro Bowl selection (1965, 1966, and 1968).
- Three-time First-Team All-Pro selection (1965, 1966, and 1968).
- Two-time Second-Team All-Pro selection (1964 and 1967).
- Three-time First-Team All-Conference selection (1966, 1967, and 1968).
- NFL 1960s All-Decade Team.
- Inducted into Philadelphia Eagles Hall of Fame in 2004.
- Elected to Pro Football Hall of Fame in 2004.

24

— MAXIE BAUGHAN —

One of the best linebackers not in the Pro Football Hall of Fame, Maxie Baughan earned nine Pro Bowl selections and six All-Pro nominations during his 12-year NFL career, which he began in Philadelphia in 1960. A key member of the Eagles' 1960 NFL championship team, Baughan became a starter immediately upon his arrival in Philadelphia, contributing to the success of the squad with his outstanding play at right-outside linebacker. Continuing to perform well for the Eagles in subsequent seasons, Baughan gained Pro Bowl recognition five times and made All-Pro twice, before being dealt to the Los Angeles Rams following the conclusion of the 1965 campaign due to philosophical differences with Philadelphia's coaching staff. Maintaining a high level of play in Los Angeles, Baughan appeared in four more Pro Bowls and earned All-Pro honors four more times as a member of the Rams, leading to him eventually being named to Pro Football Reference's 1960s All-Decade Team.

Born in Forkland, Alabama, on August 3, 1938, Maxie Calloway Baughan started playing football at a very young age, recalling years later, "Football was a way of life back then. I lived in a steel town in Alabama. You either played football or you were in the band. I couldn't play an instrument, so I played football. We all played football. You lived in a neighborhood where all the steel workers were on strike. You hadn't got anything, but you always had football."

After graduating from Bessemer High School, Baughan enrolled at Georgia Tech, where he spent three seasons starring on the gridiron, excelling as a center on offense and a linebacker on defense. In explaining his choice of colleges, Baughan recollected, "I wanted to go to work and wear a white shirt. I figured if I took Industrial Management and Engineering, that I would be able to go to work. . . . My daddy climbed telephone poles at U.S. Steel. About two or three times a year, he would come home with marks all over his arms and his legs from having to grab the pole as he fell and came down. I didn't want to do that. That is the reason why I went to

Georgia Tech. It was a great football program. I am glad I went there and would do it again."

Exceeding even his own expectations while at Georgia Tech, Baughan earned All-America and Southeastern Conference Lineman of the Year honors as a senior in 1959, when, while serving as team captain, he set a school record by recording 124 tackles. Looking back at his final year at Tech, Baughan stated, "I never thought about playing professional football until my senior year when I started to receive some flyers from various pro teams. Being consensus All-American didn't

Maxie Baughan started at right-outside linebacker for Philadelphia's 1960 NFL championship team.
Courtesy of RMYAuctions.com

hurt, either. When all that stuff started happening, I started thinking about it. I thought I might as well try it. I thought I would probably play two or three years, but, as the years went on, I never thought about quitting."

Selected by Philadelphia in the second round of the 1960 NFL Draft, with the 20th overall pick, Baughan became the only rookie to start every game for the Eagles after making an extremely favorable impression on the coaching staff during the preseason. Recalling his earliest days as an Eagle, Baughan said, "I missed the first couple weeks of Training Camp because I was at the College All-Star Game. We played on a Friday night in Chicago. Next day, I flew to Los Angeles because the Eagles were playing an exhibition game against the Rams. I met the team at the hotel, shook a few hands, and rode the bus to the stadium. I played a little on special teams that night, but that was it."

Baughan continued, "The next week, we played San Francisco and (head coach) Buck Shaw put me in on defense. Early in the game (49ers halfback) Hugh McElhenny kicked (Eagles tackle) Eddie Khayat in the head. It was right in front of me. I went after him, and he took off running. I chased him about 30 yards, but I finally caught him. I knocked him down, and we went at it pretty good."

Praising the rookie linebacker for coming to the aid of his teammate after the game, Buck Shaw gushed, "That Maxie is a real tough kid. I thought McElhenny was pretty rugged himself, but Maxie chased him down, then yanked off his helmet and began letting him have it where it hurts."

Excelling in his first year as a pro, Baughan gained Pro Bowl recognition by recording three interceptions for an Eagles team that went on to win the NFL championship. Taking note of the poise that Baughan displayed in his first NFL season, Eagles safety Don Burroughs commented, "You look at some rookies in the huddle and their eyes are wide open. Maxie was never like that. He looked like a veteran from Day One."

Baughan, who made just $15,000 as a rookie, said years later, "People would laugh at that salary today, but I was in hog heaven. I was only playing half the game compared to playing both ways in college. Plus, I was getting paid for it. I was doing pretty good for a country boy from Alabama."

Baughan continued, "My daddy worked in the steel mills all his life. That's where I would've wound up, too, if it wasn't for football. Only 15 kids from my high school class went to college, and most of us went on athletic scholarships. That was the only way out of town."

He then added, "I was lucky. My rookie year, I started every game. I went to the Pro Bowl. We won the World Championship. We beat Green Bay. I got a ring as a rookie. It was a lot of fun. I thought, 'Well, hey, we will do this every year.' I did go to nine Pro Bowls, but I never went back to that World Championship Game again. I was in the playoffs a lot, but I never won another World Championship. Never got another ring. A lot of players go their entire career and never get one. At least I have one."

Although Baughan never returned to the playoffs as a member of the Eagles, he continued to perform at an elite level his five remaining seasons in Philadelphia, earning four more trips to the Pro Bowl and All-Pro honors twice. Consistently ranking among the league's leading tacklers, the 6'1", 227-pound Baughan possessed great intelligence and keen instincts that enabled him to read plays and locate the football quickly. A constant force on defense, Baughan also had superior leadership ability, assuming the role of team captain on that side of the ball his last three seasons in Philadelphia following the retirement of Chuck Bednarik.

But, with the Eagles struggling on the field and Baughan engaging in a salary dispute with team ownership while also disagreeing with the defensive strategies being employed by the coaching staff, the veteran linebacker requested a trade following the conclusion of the 1965 campaign. Recalling the events that transpired at the time, Baughan said, "I think that it was time for me to move on. There were a few of us that had to move on. We didn't agree with Coach Kuharich. He asked me, 'Do you want to get traded?' I said, 'Yes, sir. I would like to go to New York. That is where the money is, or I would like to go to Atlanta. That is where I live.' So, he traded me to Los Angeles. But, that was the best thing that ever happened to me."

Dealt to the Rams for linebacker Fred Brown and defensive tackle Frank Molden, Baughan spent the next five years starring for his new team at his familiar post of right-outside linebacker, establishing himself during that time as one of head coach George Allen's favorite players. Allen, who later included Baughan among his all-time linebackers in his book, *Pro Football's 100 Greatest Players*, raved about the man who served as his defensive captain for five years in his work, writing, "One thing that all great linebackers have is toughness, and Maxie sure had it. I remember games when he was hurt, and no one thought he could play, but he not only played—he performed as well as ever. Maxie enjoyed the physical game. He had an abundance of ability, and he was smart enough to make the most of it. He never gave up on a play. He hated to lose, and he fired up his teammates game after game. No one loafed when Maxie was around."

Calling his trade to the Rams "a Godsend," Baughan also had high praise for Allen, whom he claimed, "trained me for a career in coaching." In speaking of his former coach, Baughan said, "George Allen was a great football mind. I called the defenses. Back then, you didn't have signaling in like today. I went to his office every morning, early. He and I would look at film. We would go over the practice schedule and prepare with him. Then, all of a sudden, I am thinking like he is. That is what he wanted to happen. In practice, we wound up doing what we talked about earlier that day. I had called the defenses for the Eagles. Now, I am calling them for the Rams."

Baughan earned five trips to the Pro Bowl as a member of the Eagles.
Courtesy of RMYAuctions.com

After earning Pro Bowl and All-Pro honors in each of his first four seasons with the Rams, Baughan suffered through an injury-plagued 1970 campaign that prompted him to announce his retirement at season's end. Although he later served as player/coach under Allen after the latter assumed head coaching duties in Washington, Baughan appeared in only two games in 1974, before retiring for good. In addition to recording 10 fumble recoveries over the course of his career, Baughan intercepted 18 passes, which he returned for a total of 218 yards and one touchdown. During his time in Philadelphia, he picked off seven passes, amassed 114 interception-return yards, recovered five fumbles, and scored his only touchdown.

Following his playing days, Baughan began a lengthy career in coaching that included serving as defensive coordinator for Georgia Tech (1972–1973) and the Baltimore Colts (1975–1979), linebacker coach for the Detroit Lions (1980–1982), Minnesota Vikings (1990–1991), Tampa Bay Buccaneers (1992–1995), and Baltimore Ravens (1996–1998), and head coach for Cornell University (1983–1988).

Baughan, who retired from coaching in 1998 and currently lives in Maryland with his wife, looks back fondly on his career in football, saying, "I had the opportunity to be a football coach. It was my livelihood. I got a degree and didn't have to work a day for the rest of my life. I was doing something I loved, playing and coaching football. I was fortunate enough to be able to do that and feel like I never worked a day in my life."

Baughan also considers himself quite fortunate to have spent six seasons in Philadelphia, stating, "My six years that I played there, I could not want to be treated any better than I was. The fans were always great to me, and I always thought that Philadelphia was very special. I won't knock the L.A. fans, but they were different. It was personal with Philadelphia fans. The Rams fans were supportive, but not as personal."

Returning to Philadelphia in 2010 with 17 other members of the 1960 team to celebrate the 50th anniversary of that championship season, Baughan later expressed surprise that the city's younger fans knew who he and his teammates were, saying, "I was amazed. There were so many young people who knew us and called us by name. I said to one guy, 'You weren't even around in 1960.' He said, 'No, but my father told me all about you.' It says so much about these fans. They really are a special group."

Even though Baughan has yet to be inducted into the Pro Football Hall of Fame, there are those who continue to champion his cause, with *Talk of Fame Network* co-host Ron Borges stating, "These guys all have strong resumes, but it's tough to ignore all that Maxie Baughan accomplished during a long and distinguished career with the Eagles and Rams.

He played well on bad teams, helped make them good, then played well on good teams. What else is there? There's this: he made the Pro Bowl nine times in 11 years, then came out of retirement in 1974 to help out a third team, the Redskins, learn how to play."

Fellow *Talk of Fame* co-host Clark Judge added, "Maxie Baughan was to defense what Johnny Unitas was to offense—a thinking man who made big plays when big plays were demanded. That he's never been discussed by the Hall of Fame's board of selectors is not just perplexing; it's an injustice."

EAGLES CAREER HIGHLIGHTS

Best Season

Baughan made huge contributions to the Eagles as a rookie in 1960, making three interceptions, which he returned for a total of 50 yards. However, he performed even better in 1964, earning his lone First-Team All-Pro selection as a member of the team by excelling against the run and recording an unofficial total of six sacks.

Memorable Moments/Greatest Performances

Baughan recorded the first interception of his career during a 19–13 win over the Washington Redskins on November 13, 1960, subsequently returning the ball 18 yards.

Baughan helped the Eagles make history on December 12, 1965, when he recorded one of the franchise-record nine interceptions they registered during a 47–13 thrashing of the Pittsburgh Steelers. Picking off Tommy Wade seven times and Bill Nelson twice, the Eagles returned three of those interceptions for touchdowns, with Baughan joining in the festivities late in the first quarter, when he returned his interception of a Nelson pass 33 yards for a TD that put the Eagles up by a score of 27–0. The touchdown ended up being the only one of Baughan's career.

Notable Achievements

- Scored one defensive touchdown during career.
- Missed just two games in six seasons.
- 1960 Eastern Division champion.
- 1960 NFL champion.

- Five-time Pro Bowl selection (1960, 1961, 1963, 1964, and 1965).
- 1964 First-Team All-Pro selection.
- 1965 Second-Team All-Pro selection.
- Two-time First-Team All-Conference selection (1964 and 1965).
- Pro Football Reference All-1960s First Team.
- Inducted into Philadelphia Eagles Hall of Fame in 2015.

25
— TIMMY BROWN —

Perhaps the most dynamic and exciting player of his time, Timmy Brown proved to be the NFL's best all-purpose running back and most dangerous kickoff returner for much of the 1960s. A sensational open-field runner with exceptional speed, outstanding quickness, and superb moves, Brown returned five kickoffs and one punt for touchdowns during his time in Philadelphia, while also gaining more than 800 yards on the ground twice. An excellent receiver as well, Brown made more than 50 receptions and amassed more than 600 receiving yards twice each, accumulating in the process more than 1,000 yards from scrimmage on three separate occasions. The fleet-footed Brown also amassed more than 2,000 all-purpose yards twice, leading the NFL in that category both times. The Eagles' career and single-season record holder for most all-purpose yards, Brown also holds the franchise mark for most kickoff-return yards, with his brilliant all-around play earning him three trips to the Pro Bowl, one All-Pro nomination, and eventual induction into the Eagles Hall of Fame.

Born in Richmond, Indiana, on May 24, 1937, Thomas Allan Brown suffered through a lonely childhood that saw his parents separate when he was seven. Raised an orphan at the Soldiers and Sailors Children's Home in Knightstown, Indiana, young Thomas grew up lacking confidence, for which he compensated by excelling in sports. Starring in football and basketball at Morton Memorial High School, Brown performed so well on the hardwood that he received an offer to attend Michigan State University on a basketball scholarship. However, he instead chose to enroll at tiny Ball State Teachers College in Muncie, Indiana, where he made a name for himself on the gridiron. Although Brown had to wait until his senior year to break into the starting lineup, he opened eyes the first time he carried the football by recording a 91-yard touchdown run.

Impressed with Brown's speed and versatility, the Green Bay Packers selected him in the 27th round of the 1959 NFL Draft, with the 313th overall pick. But, after earning a roster spot as a rookie, Brown suffered the

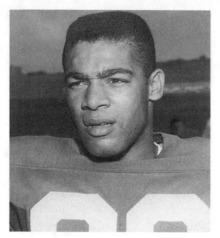

Timmy Brown holds Eagles career and single-season records for most all-purpose yards.
Public domain (photographer unknown)

indignity of being cut by the Packers after he fumbled a punt in his first regular-season game. Subsequently signed by the Eagles, Brown spent the remainder of the 1959 campaign serving as a member of Philadelphia's taxi squad, before making the team as a backup halfback and kickoff returner the following year. Seeing extremely limited duty over the course of his first full season, Brown rushed for only 35 yards, although he scored four touchdowns and made nine receptions for 247 yards, en route to amassing a total of 624 all-purpose yards for the eventual NFL champions.

After returning the opening kickoff of the 1961 season 105 yards for a touchdown, Brown received more significant playing time at running back in subsequent weeks, enabling him to gain 338 yards on the ground and another 264 yards through the air. Yet, he continued to make his greatest impact on special teams, recording a pair of touchdowns, while leading the NFL with 811 kickoff-return yards and ranking among the league leaders with 1,538 all-purpose yards and an average of 28 yards per kickoff return.

After having his playing time limited his first two seasons in Philadelphia due to concerns that his 5'11", 198-pound frame might not hold up to the rigors of being an every-down back, Brown finally became a full-time starter in 1962 when his roommate, Ted Dean, suffered a broken leg. Making the most of his opportunity, Brown began an exceptional five-year run during which he posted the following numbers:

YEAR	RUSH YD	REC YD	YD FROM SCRIMMAGE	ALL-PURPOSE YD	TD
1962	545	849	1,394	**2,306**	13
1963	841	487	1,328	**2,428**	11
1964	356	244	600	1,388	10
1965	861	682	1,543	1,602	9
1966	548	371	919	1,481	8

In addition to leading the NFL in all-purpose yards in two of those five seasons, Brown ranked among the league leaders in that category in each of the other three years. He also led the league in yards per rushing attempt once (5.4 in 1965) and placed near the top of the league rankings in rushing yards twice and yards from scrimmage, touchdowns, kickoff-return yards, and kickoff-return average three times each, with only a thigh injury that forced him to sit out four games in 1964 preventing him from compiling even better numbers that season. After setting an NFL record by amassing 2,306 all-purpose yards in 1962, Brown broke his own mark the following year by accumulating 2,428 yards. Brown's superb all-around play earned him Pro Bowl honors in 1962, 1963, and 1965, Second-Team All-Pro recognition in 1965, and First-Team All-Conference honors in both 1963 and 1965.

One of the league's swiftest players, Brown possessed 9.8 speed in the 100-yard dash and tremendous elusiveness in the open field, making him virtually impossible to contain in one-on-one situations. Blessed with soft hands as well, Brown proved to be an outstanding target coming out of the backfield, posting career-high marks of 52 receptions and 849 receiving yards in 1962. And, even though Brown gained most of his yardage on the outside, he also ran well between the tackles, displaying surprising power against defenses that made stopping him their primary objective. Meanwhile, Brown exhibited his toughness by playing through pain in 1965, missing just one game despite being plagued at various times by a hairline fracture to his ribs, a torn thumb ligament, a bruised thigh, and a sprained ankle.

Yet, even with the many contributions that Brown made to the Eagles during his time in Philadelphia, he often found himself at odds with the team's coaching staff, with his relationship with head coach Joe Kuharich proving to be particularly contentious. Moody and sensitive, Brown did not react well to being yelled at for blowing assignments during practice. He became further incensed when Kuharich and his underlings questioned the commitment of a player who spent his Mondays taking singing lessons in New York, openly stated his preference for achieving success as a singer and an actor, rather than as a football player, and frequently violated team rules by staying up late at night and availing himself of room service the night before games.

Things finally came to a head in 1967, after Kuharich stated during the previous offseason that Brown no longer fit into his plans. Already disheartened by his coach's proclamation, Brown then missed the first half of the season with a hamstring pull, prompting some of his teammates to accuse

Brown amassed more than 2,000 all-purpose yards for the Eagles twice.
Courtesy of BoxingTreasures.com

him of malingering. Brown's woes continued to mount upon his return to the team when Dallas linebacker Lee Roy Jordan struck him in the jaw while running a pass pattern, knocking out nine of his teeth, and forcing him to sip food through a straw for the next several days. Finishing the year with just 381 yards from scrimmage, 682 all-purpose yards, and two touchdowns, Brown demanded to be traded at season's end, with the Eagles obliging him by dealing him to the Baltimore Colts for defensive back/return man Alvin Haymond. Brown left Philadelphia with career totals of 3,703 yards rushing, 231 receptions, 3,346 receiving yards, 7,049 yards from scrimmage, 29 rushing touchdowns, 26 touchdown receptions, 62 total touchdowns, 514 punt-return yards, 4,483 kickoff-return yards, and 12,049 all-purpose yards, with each of the last two figures representing franchise records.

Brown spent just one year in Baltimore, amassing only 212 yards from scrimmage and 635 all-purpose yards for a Colts team that suffered a stunning 16–7 defeat at the hands of the New York Jets in Super Bowl III, before announcing his retirement at season's end. He subsequently embarked on a singing and acting career that failed to bring him the same level of notoriety he attained as a football player, with his most notable roles being bit parts in the movies *M*A*S*H* and *Nashville*. Brown also briefly served as a color analyst for NFL telecasts on CBS, before taking a job as a correctional officer in Los Angeles. After retiring to private life, Brown moved to Palm Springs, California, where he currently resides.

Named to the Eagles All-Time Team as an offensive back in 1965, Brown later received the additional honor of being included on the Eagles 75th Anniversary All-Time Team as a kickoff returner. Yet, Brown continued to maintain years after he retired that he should have accomplished so much more, stating, "I had a great career with the Eagles until Kuharich came. Joe made up his mind that he was going to bend and break my spirit. I was jovial. He didn't like that . . . I feel very unfulfilled in football. My four years with Kuharich were just a waste. He was determined to break me. Hey, Joe never had a winning record except in college at San Francisco. I could never play for him. I hated the guy with a passion."

However, Brown also paid tribute to the fans of Philadelphia and accepted part of the blame for his problems, saying, "I had a great time in Philadelphia. I was never booed, and they're known for booing. I really felt loved there, and I really loved Philadelphia. I was very insecure because of my background. I kept people at arm's length, so I wouldn't hurt anyone."

EAGLES CAREER HIGHLIGHTS

Best Season

Brown excelled for the Eagles as a running back in 1965, establishing career-high marks with 861 yards rushing and 1,543 yards from scrimmage, scoring nine touchdowns, and leading the league with an average of 5.4 yards per carry. However, he had his finest all-around season in 1963, gaining 841 yards on the ground and 1,328 yards from scrimmage, scoring 11 touchdowns, and leading the NFL with 945 kick-return yards and 2,428 all-purpose yards, which remains a single-season franchise record.

Memorable Moments/Greatest Performances

Although the Eagles lost their December 11, 1960, meeting with the Steelers by a score of 27–21, Brown had his breakout game as a pro, making three receptions for 112 yards, amassing a total of 162 all-purpose yards, and scoring a pair of touchdowns, with one of those coming on a 53-yard pass from Sonny Jurgensen and the other on a 7-yard run.

Brown turned in another outstanding all-around effort in the 1960 regular-season finale, helping the Eagles record a 38–28 victory over the Washington Redskins by carrying the ball six times for 25 yards and one touchdown, while also catching five passes for 128 yards and one TD, which came on a 34-yard pass from Jurgensen.

Brown scored his first TD on special teams in the 1961 regular-season opener, when he thrilled the fans at Philadelphia's Franklin Field by returning the opening kickoff 105 yards for a touchdown. The defending NFL champions went on to defeat Cleveland by a score of 27–20.

Brown again displayed his explosiveness on December 3, 1961, when he helped lead the Eagles to a 35–24 victory over the Steelers by returning a punt 66 yards for a touchdown and scoring another TD on a 42-yard run.

Even though the Eagles ended up losing the 1962 regular-season opener to the St. Louis Cardinals by a score of 27–21, Brown once again exhibited his ability to score from anywhere on the field when he returned a missed field goal attempt by Gerry Perry 99 yards for a touchdown.

Brown played an outstanding all-around game against New York the following week, gaining 160 yards on nine pass receptions, scoring one touchdown, and amassing 284 all-purpose yards during a 29–13 loss to the Giants.

Brown once again starred in defeat on October 28, 1962, making five receptions for 174 yards and one touchdown, which came on an 80-yard catch-and-run, and amassing 263 all-purpose yards during a 31–21 loss to the Minnesota Vikings.

Brown helped lead the Eagles to just their second win of the 1962 campaign on November 25, when he carried the ball 17 times for 107 yards and two TDs during a 28–14 victory over Dallas.

Brown followed that up with a strong outing against Washington, scoring twice on short TD runs and scoring a third time on a 99-yard kickoff return, in leading the Eagles to a 37–14 victory.

Although the Eagles lost the 1962 regular-season finale to the St. Louis Cardinals by a score of 45–35, Brown turned in a tremendous all-around performance. In addition to making five receptions for 199 yards and two touchdowns, which came on 60- and 82-yard connections with Sonny Jurgensen, he gained 50 yards on the ground and amassed another 92 yards on kickoff returns, giving him career-high totals of 249 yards from scrimmage and 341 all-purpose yards.

Brown once again excelled against St. Louis on September 22, 1963, scoring one touchdown on a 7-yard run and another on a 100-yard kickoff return during a 28–24 loss to the Cardinals.

Brown led the Eagles to a 24–21 victory over the Cowboys two weeks later by running 91 yards for one touchdown and scoring another TD on an 80-yard catch-and-run.

Brown had a huge day against Pittsburgh on October 4, 1964, leading the Eagles to a 21–7 win by rushing for 116 yards and scoring twice on passes from Norm Snead that covered 23 and 87 yards.

Brown helped pace the Eagles to a 34–27 victory over the Cardinals in the opening game of the 1965 regular season by rushing for 50 yards, gaining another 129 yards on seven pass receptions, and scoring a pair of touchdowns.

Although the Eagles lost to Cleveland by a score of 38–34 on November 7, 1965, Brown rushed for a career-high 186 yards and scored the game's first points on a 54-yard TD run.

Brown nearly matched that total three weeks later, carrying the ball 18 times for 180 yards and one touchdown during a 28–24 victory over the Cardinals.

Brown made history on November 6, 1966, when he became the first player ever to return two kickoffs for touchdowns in the same game, leading the Eagles to a 24–23 win over the Dallas Cowboys. Brown, whose TD returns covered 93 and 90 yards, finished the game with 247 kickoff-return yards and 38 yards rushing, giving him a total of 285 all-purpose yards.

Notable Achievements

- Returned five kickoffs and one punt for touchdowns.
- Rushed for more than 800 yards twice.
- Surpassed 50 receptions twice.
- Amassed more than 600 receiving yards twice, topping 800 yards once (849 in 1962).
- Amassed more than 1,000 yards from scrimmage three times, topping 1,500 yards once (1,543 in 1965).
- Amassed more than 1,000 all-purpose yards six times, topping 1,500 yards four times and 2,000 yards twice.
- Averaged more than 5 yards per carry twice.
- Scored more than 10 touchdowns three times.
- Led NFL in: all-purpose yards twice; kickoff return yards twice; non-offensive touchdowns twice; and rushing average once.
- Finished second in NFL with 1,543 yards from scrimmage in 1965.
- Finished third in NFL in: rushing yards twice; yards from scrimmage twice; all-purpose yards once; kickoff return yards once; and kickoff return average once.
- Led Eagles in rushing four times.
- Holds share of NFL record for most kickoff-return TDs in one game (2 vs. Dallas on 11/6/66).
- Holds Eagles record for longest kickoff return (105 yards vs. Cleveland on 9/17/61).
- Holds Eagles single-season record for most all-purpose yards (2,428 in 1963).

- Holds Eagles career records for most all-purpose yards (12,049) and most kickoff-return yards (4,483).
- Ranks among Eagles career leaders with: 3,703 yards rushing (8th); 7,049 total yards from scrimmage (7th); 29 rushing touchdowns (7th); and 62 total touchdowns (6th).
- Tied for second in NFL history with five kickoff returns for touchdowns.
- 1960 Eastern Division champion.
- 1960 NFL champion.
- Three-time Pro Bowl selection (1962, 1963, and 1965).
- 1965 Second-Team All-Pro selection.
- Two-time First-Team All-Conference selection (1963 and 1965).
- Named to Eagles 75th Anniversary Team in 2007.
- Inducted into Philadelphia Eagles Hall of Fame in 1990.

26

— JEREMIAH TROTTER —

The emotional leader of Eagle teams that won three division titles and one NFC championship, Jeremiah Trotter helped lead a resurgence in Philadelphia that saw the team go from winning a total of just eight games his first two years in the league to making five straight playoff appearances. Starting at middle linebacker for the Eagles for most of his eight seasons in Philly, Trotter did three tours of duty with the club, leading the team in tackles in each of his five seasons as a full-time starter. One of only four linebackers in team annals to earn four or more Pro Bowl invitations, Trotter's four selections enabled him to join Chuck Bednarik, Maxie Baughan, and Bill Bergey on an extremely exclusive list. Trotter also earned All-Pro honors twice while playing for the Eagles, with his outstanding play gaining him induction into the team's Hall of Fame following the conclusion of his playing career.

Born in Texarkana, Texas, on January 20, 1977, Jeremiah Trotter attended Hooks High School, where he starred on the gridiron, earning All-District honors three straight times and being named District MVP in his senior year. Choosing to remain in-state following his graduation from Hooks High, Trotter accepted an athletic scholarship from Stephen F. Austin State University, where he spent three seasons starting at linebacker for the Lumberjacks, recording a total of 300 tackles during that time.

Selected by the Eagles in the third round of the 1998 NFL Draft, with the 72nd overall pick, Trotter had a difficult first season as a pro, playing only on special teams, and being deactivated for part of the year after losing his father. However, things began to turn around for Trotter in his second season after Andy Reid replaced Ray Rhodes as head coach and hired Jim Johnson to be his defensive coordinator. Named the starter at middle linebacker, Trotter blossomed into one of the NFL's finest players at that position under Johnson's tutelage, recording a team-leading 122 tackles (91 solo), intercepting two passes, forcing two fumbles, and registering 2½ sacks for an Eagles team that finished the regular season with a record of just 5-11.

Jeremiah Trotter helped lead the Eagles to three division titles and one NFC championship.
Courtesy of Matt Breese

Recalling the way that Johnson impacted his career, Trotter said, "Jim came in. I didn't really know what to expect. Anytime there's a transition of power, especially with players, you don't know what to expect. Especially if you're not their guy. I was fortunate, that was one of the best things that happened in my career; Andy Reid hiring Jim Johnson and Jim believing in me. Obviously, I had to go out and make the plays."

Trotter continued, "Jim was a guy who built his scheme around his players. He allowed me and Dawkins and Hugh Douglas to go out and make plays and play football. Anytime you have a coordinator who can build his system around what you do best, that's when you know you have one of the great ones, and Jim was one of the great ones."

Trotter followed up his exceptional 1999 campaign with another outstanding year, gaining Pro Bowl and First-Team All-Pro recognition in 2000 by recording a team-high 120 tackles, in helping the Eagles compile a regular-season mark of 11-5 that earned them their first playoff berth in four seasons. Performing extremely well once again in 2001, Trotter earned team MVP, Pro Bowl, and Second-Team All-Pro honors by picking off two passes, scoring one touchdown, and recording 115 tackles and a career-high 3½ sacks.

Possessing good size, excellent quickness, and superb instincts, the 6'1", 262-pound Trotter proved to be extremely effective at shedding blockers and swarming to the ball, with his practice of swinging an imaginary ax in celebration each time he brought down an opposing ball-carrier earning him the nickname "The Axeman" during his time in Philadelphia. An outstanding team leader, Trotter drew praise from teammate Brian Dawkins, who said, "He is a leader. In the huddle, there is a certain way he carries himself. There is a mentality that he plays with, and he tries to let that rub off on the other guys the way he approaches it, and the way that he makes a play."

Unfortunately, Trotter failed to come to terms with the Eagles on a new contract when he became a free agent at the end of 2001, with the two sides engaging in a bitter contract dispute that led to him signing a seven-year, $35 million deal with the rival Washington Redskins. However, Trotter ended up spending just two seasons in Washington, recording 91 tackles during the first 12 weeks of the 2002 campaign, before tearing his right anterior cruciate ligament against the Dallas Cowboys on Thanksgiving Day. Although Trotter started every game for the Redskins the following year, he failed to regain his earlier form, prompting the team to release him at season's end. Looking back at the time he spent in Washington, Trotter said, "It was a real humbling, learning experience. It made me a better player. The more you play, the more you see. You get smarter, you get wiser, you understand the game more."

Following his release by the Redskins, Trotter re-signed with the Eagles, even though they offered him no guarantees of a starting job. But, after assuming a backup role during the first half of the 2004 campaign, Trotter returned to the starting lineup in Week 9, performing so well the rest of the year that he earned a trip to the Pro Bowl.

In discussing the tre-mendous impact that Trot-ter made after he joined the starting unit, Andy Reid said, "Jeremiah brought a presence to the middle of the defense that I thought was needed. He's an emotional player, and I think that can be contagious on a defense."

Jim Johnson noted, "The thing about Trotter is he brings a physical presence to the game. He's always been a good middle line-backer as far as being very physical inside. He's a good tempo-setter, and he's done a great job."

Trotter did three tours of duty in Philadelphia.
Courtesy of PristineAuction.com

Eagles safety Michael Lewis added, "He's had a huge impact. You're talking about our defensive MVP."

With the Eagles capturing their first NFC championship in 24 years, Trotter said of his return to Philadelphia, "I'm just happy and fortunate that things worked out the way they did. I made the decision that I didn't want to make when I left and went to that team up the street, but it's all a growing experience. You learn from your decisions. On one hand, my family was set up for life. On the other hand, I got hurt and my heart was never in it. My heart was always in Philly."

Trotter continued, "My teammates and the fans welcomed me back with open arms. I had to work hard to get back into the starting lineup, but it was a humbling experience. I learned a lot about patience. It worked out for us. We just didn't finish the job down in Jacksonville."

Trotter continued to perform well for the Eagles in each of the next two seasons, earning Pro Bowl honors once again in 2005 by recording a team-leading 119 tackles (101 solo), before making 112 stops the following year. Nevertheless, with rookie linebacker Omar Gaither showing a great deal of promise, the Eagles elected to cut Trotter following the conclusion of the 2006 campaign, leaving him to sign with the Tampa Bay Buccaneers. After sustaining an injury that limited him to just three games in 2007, Trotter sat out the entire 2008 season. But, with starting middle linebacker Stewart Bradley tearing his ACL during 2009 training camp, the Eagles signed Trotter to a one-year contract, after which he went on to register just 32 tackles for them in a part-time role in his final stint with the team. Released by the Eagles at season's end, Trotter subsequently announced his retirement, ending his career with 909 tackles, 12½ sacks, nine interceptions, 163 interception-return yards, nine forced fumbles, three fumble recoveries, and two defensive touchdowns. In his eight years with the Eagles, Trotter recorded 692 tackles (564 solo) and 11 sacks, picked off seven passes, which he returned a total of 140 yards, forced seven fumbles and recovered two others, and scored his only two touchdowns.

Since retiring as an active player, Trotter has been involved in various business ventures, including owning a unisex salon and a car wash in southern New Jersey. He also has a shore house on the famous Ocean City boardwalk between 6th and 7th Streets near the Wonderland Pier.

Welcomed into the Eagles Hall of Fame in 2016, Trotter received the following words of praise from team owner Jeffrey Lurie, who stated prior to the induction ceremonies, "Jeremiah Trotter embodies everything we strive for as an organization. He was an emotional and inspirational player who captured the hearts of our fans. As an anchor of our defense, he led with an immeasurable amount of toughness and a fiery attitude."

EAGLES CAREER HIGHLIGHTS

Best Season

Trotter had an outstanding season for the Eagles in his second tour of duty with them in 2005, recording a career-high 101 solo tackles. But he played his best ball as a member of the team from 1999 to 2001, with the 2000 campaign proving to be his finest all-around season. Earning First-Team All-Pro honors for the only time in his career, Trotter recorded 120 tackles (100 solo), three sacks, and one interception, which he returned for a touchdown.

Memorable Moments/Greatest Performances

Although the Eagles lost to the Giants by a score of 16–15 on October 3, 1999, Trotter performed extremely well during the contest, recording 13 tackles and the first interception of his career.

Trotter scored the first points of his career when he returned an interception 27 yards for a touchdown during a convincing 41–14 win over the Cowboys in the opening game of the 2000 regular season.

Trotter victimized Dallas again on November 18, 2001, scoring the only other touchdown of his career when he returned an interception 50 yards for a TD just before halftime of a 36–3 thrashing of the Cowboys.

Trotter had a big game against the Giants on December 30, 2001, recording a sack and 14 tackles during a 24–21 Eagles win.

Trotter contributed to a 20–17 victory over the San Diego Chargers on October 23, 2005, by recording a sack, an interception, and seven tackles.

Identifying the 2004 NFC championship game victory over the Atlanta Falcons as the most memorable of his career, Trotter claims that he holds that win closest to his heart because of his love for the fans of Philadelphia, stating, "I can't begin to explain how much that game meant to myself, my teammates and especially the fans. I was happier for the fans than I was for myself or any of my teammates. Players come and go. Every year, there's a high turnover ratio. It's the fans that are going through the thick and thin year after year. The disappointments. The ups and downs. I was so excited for them and, seeing them running through the streets, that was more exciting for me than the win itself."

Notable Achievements

- Scored two defensive touchdowns.
- Recorded more than 100 tackles five times.
- Led Eagles in tackles five times.
- Ranks ninth in Eagles history with 692 career tackles (564 solo).
- Three-time division champion (2001, 2004, and 2006).
- 2004 NFC champion.
- 2005 Week 7 NFC Defensive Player of the Week.
- 2001 Eagles Defensive MVP.
- Four-time Pro Bowl selection (2000, 2001, 2004, and 2005).
- 2000 First-Team All-Pro selection.
- 2001 Second-Team All-Pro selection.
- 2000 First-Team All-Conference selection.
- Inducted into Philadelphia Eagles Hall of Fame in 2016.

27

TROY VINCENT

The first big-name defensive player to sign with the Eagles as a free agent, Troy Vincent arrived in Philadelphia in 1996 after spending the previous four seasons with the Miami Dolphins. Excelling at left cornerback for the Eagles for the next eight years, Vincent led the team in interceptions five times, earning in the process five Pro Bowl selections and two All-Pro nominations. Along the way, Vincent, who served as a team captain his entire time in Philadelphia, helped the Eagles earn five playoff berths and capture three division titles, with his outstanding play eventually gaining him induction into the Eagles Hall of Fame.

Born in Trenton, New Jersey, on June 8, 1971, Troy Darnell Vincent grew up in the low-income Wilbur section of that city dreaming of one day playing in the NBA. Raised in a single-parent home that he shared with his mother and grandparents, young Troy competed in basketball games held at a nearby park that rival drug dealers sponsored. Concerned that her son's unsavory surroundings might influence him in a negative way, Alma Vincent did everything possible to place him in a better environment, finally sending him to Pennsbury, Pennsylvania, where he spent his last two years of high school attending Pennsbury High, while living with the parents of his good friend, James Bodley Jr.

Taking up football during his senior year at Pennsbury, Vincent, who also lettered in basketball and track in high school, proved to be a natural on the gridiron, with his exceptional play earning him numerous scholarship offers. Choosing to enroll at the University of Wisconsin, Vincent subsequently embarked on an extremely successful college career that saw him earn First-Team All-America and Big Ten Defensive Player of the Year honors as a senior in 1991. Looking back at the years he spent in Pennsylvania and Wisconsin, Vincent said, "Going to Pennsbury and then living in Madison, with all their diversity and different ways of thinking, meant everything to me. Most of all, it helped me appreciate where I'm from."

Troy Vincent served as a team captain his entire time in Philadelphia.
Courtesy of Scott Miller

Impressed with Vincent's stellar play at the collegiate level, the Miami Dolphins made him the seventh overall pick of the 1992 NFL Draft, after which he spent the next four seasons starting for them at left cornerback, recording 14 interceptions, amassing 284 interception-return yards, and scoring two touchdowns. However, when Vincent became a free agent prior to the start of the 1996 campaign, he elected to sign with the Eagles, with then–Eagles defensive coordinator, Emmitt Thomas, later saying, "I think Cincinnati actually offered him a little bit more money. But he wanted to play for the Eagles."

Making an impact his first year in Philadelphia, Vincent helped the Eagles earn a wild card playoff berth in 1996 by intercepting three passes, amassing 144 interception-return yards, registering 52 tackles, and scoring one touchdown on defense. Although the Eagles compiled a losing record in each of the next three seasons, Vincent continued to perform extremely well, earning Pro Bowl honors for the first of five straight times in 1999 by recording a league-leading seven interceptions and a career-high 82 tackles.

Standing 6'1" and weighing 200 pounds, Vincent possessed excellent size for a cornerback, allowing him to punish opposing wide receivers and defend well against the run. Meanwhile, his 4.3 speed enabled him to run with the league's swiftest wideouts, with Houston Texans offensive coordinator Chris Palmer saying, "He's out on an island in that defense, especially on the left side, where teams throw more often, and he's as good as it gets. It's clear he's done his homework."

An extremely intelligent player who spent hours in the film room each week, Vincent became well versed in the tendencies of his opponents, making him a valuable source of information to his defensive mates, with Brian Dawkins stating, "He'll tell me to make an adjustment, and, sure enough, I'll get a pick." In discussing the exorbitant amount of time that he spent studying film, Vincent said, "It's the little things we do that separate us. Everyone goes to the mandatory meetings, so, what are you going to do above and beyond that? When I'm watching film of a guy that I'm covering that week early in the morning, I feel good because I know he's home sleeping."

Praising Vincent for his football acumen, Tampa Bay wide receiver Keenan McCardell said, "You can tell he studies his opponents. When you face him, you have to be on your game because he's going to know everything you do."

Yet, as much as Vincent contributed to the Eagles on the playing field, he also made a huge impact in the personal lives of his teammates, many of whom sought out his advice on matters not related to football, with Eagles head coach Andy Reid saying, "Troy sets an example without being showy. He's a great listener, and he's helpful with the young guys. He's like a grandfather in the locker room. I feel lucky to have him here."

Revealing that Vincent established himself as one of the Eagles' team leaders almost as soon as he arrived in Philadelphia, Emmitt Thomas stated, "Troy was a natural leader. We had a young secondary. Bobby Taylor was young. Al Harris was young. Then, we drafted Brian Dawkins. Troy just gravitated into a natural leader." Growing especially close to Dawkins, Vincent spent his entire time in Philadelphia playing alongside him in the Eagles' defensive secondary, with Dawkins later choosing his good friend to be his presenter at his Pro Football Hall of Fame induction ceremonies.

Vincent continued his string of consecutive Pro Bowl appearances in 2000, picking off five passes and recording 77 tackles, before earning All-Pro honors in each of the next two seasons. But, after helping the Eagles advance to the NFC title game for the third straight time in 2003, Vincent signed with the Buffalo Bills as a free agent at season's end. Over the course of his eight seasons in Philadelphia, Vincent recorded 28 interceptions, amassed 341 interception-return yards, registered 516 tackles, forced 10 fumbles, recovered six others, recorded 4½ sacks, and scored one touchdown, with his 28 picks representing the seventh-highest total in franchise history.

Moving to free safety after he joined the Bills, Vincent spent two seasons manning that post in Buffalo, before spending one last year with the Washington Redskins. Announcing his retirement following the conclusion of the 2006 campaign, Vincent ended his playing career with 47 interceptions, 711 interception-return yards, 890 tackles (734 solo), 12 forced fumbles, 12 fumble recoveries, 5½ sacks, and three defensive touchdowns.

Since retiring as an active player, Vincent, who received the prestigious Walter Payton Man of the Year award in 2002 for his contributions to several charitable causes, including the Troy Vincent Foundation, which provides educational and counseling services to troubled youth, has garnered many other individual accolades. In addition to being named the winner of the Lifetime of Inspiration Award that the NFL presented during its Super Bowl Gospel Celebration in 2017, Vincent gained recognition as one of the NFL's Most Important People by *USA Today*. Vincent has also been presented with the John Wooten Executive Leadership Award, the Jim Mandich Courage and Commitment Award for his stance on domestic abuse, and the Call to Men Award for Institutional Change for fighting to prevent violence against women.

Vincent led the Eagles in interceptions five times.
Courtesy of SportsMemorabilia.com

Named NFL executive vice president of football operations in 2014, Vincent has since used his position to encourage players around the league to use football as a means of preparing themselves for successful careers once their playing days have ended. In discussing his role, Vincent says, "In this capacity, I have the opportunity to continue to be a contributor.

I can touch the player, touch the coach, and touch the fan. It allows me to still be a positive, active contributor in growing and developing, but, more importantly, preserving the game of football. It has meant so much to me."

Inducted into the Eagles Hall of Fame in 2012, Vincent received high praise at the time from team owner Jeffrey Lurie, who said:

> Troy Vincent was one of the best defensive players to ever put on an Eagles uniform. He was both a great playmaker and a true shutdown corner, but what raised his greatness to another level was the way he approached the game. He was a spokesman for the defense, and his leadership set the tone for both the younger players on the team and the veterans. He has taken that same passion and intensity into the next phase of his life as vice president of player engagement for the NFL, where he continues to help former and current players succeed off the field.

EAGLES CAREER HIGHLIGHTS

Best Season

Vincent earned All-Pro honors for the only two times in his career in 2001 and 2002, recording three interceptions, 67 tackles, and a league-leading 27 pass deflections in the first of those campaigns, before picking off two passes and registering 66 tackles the following year. However, he had his finest all-around season in 1999, when, in addition to recording 82 tackles (62 solo), one sack, and two forced fumbles, he led the NFL with seven interceptions, which he returned for a total of 91 yards.

Memorable Moments/Greatest Performances

Vincent recorded his first interception as a member of the Eagles during a 33–18 win over Atlanta on September 22, 1996.

Vincent's only touchdown during his time in Philadelphia proved to be a big one, since it sealed a 31–21 victory over the Cowboys on November 3, 1996. With the Eagles holding a 24–21 lead over their Eastern Division rivals and Dallas in possession of the ball deep in Philadelphia territory with less than a minute remaining in the final period, James Willis intercepted a Troy Aikman pass 4 yards into the end zone. After returning the ball to the Philadelphia 10-yard line, Willis lateraled it to Vincent, who ran the remaining 90 yards for a 104-yard TD return that tied the record for the longest interception return in franchise history.

Vincent picked off two passes in one game for the only time as a member of the Eagles during a 21–7 win over the New Orleans Saints on September 24, 2000.

Notable Achievements

- Scored one defensive touchdown.
- Recorded at least five interceptions in a season twice.
- Amassed more than 100 interception-return yards once (144 in 1996).
- Led NFL with seven interceptions in 1999.
- Led Eagles in interceptions five times.
- Ranks among Eagles career leaders with 28 interceptions (7th) and 341 interception-return yards (9th).
- Three-time division champion (2001, 2002, and 2003).
- 2002 NFL Walter Payton Man of the Year.
- Five-time Pro Bowl selection (1999, 2000, 2001, 2002, and 2003).
- 2002 First-Team All-Pro selection.
- 2001 Second-Team All-Pro selection.
- Three-time First-Team All-Conference selection (2000, 2001, and 2002).
- Named to Eagles 75th Anniversary Team in 2007.
- Inducted into Philadelphia Eagles Hall of Fame in 2012.

28

— TRENT COLE —

A model of consistency during his time in Philadelphia, Trent Cole missed just five games in his 10 years with the Eagles, bringing down opposing quarterbacks behind the line of scrimmage at least eight times in seven of those seasons. Second in franchise history only to the great Reggie White in career sacks, Cole recorded double-digit sacks four times, leading the Eagles in that category on five separate occasions. Also ranking extremely high in team annals in tackles and forced fumbles, Cole helped lead the Eagles to three division titles and five playoff appearances, earning in the process two trips to the Pro Bowl and one All-Pro selection.

Born in Xenia, Ohio, on October 5, 1982, Trent James Cole Jr. starred in multiple sports while attending Xenia High School, lettering in football, baseball, basketball, and track. Particularly proficient on the gridiron, Cole earned All-State and area Defensive Player of the Year honors as a senior by registering 121 tackles and eight sacks, while also rushing for 1,241 yards and 10 touchdowns on offense.

After accepting a scholarship offer from the University of Cincinnati, Cole spent his first two seasons of college ball manning the nose tackle position for the Bearcats, before eventually moving to defensive end. Performing well at both posts, Cole gained First-Team All-Conference recognition twice by recording 19

Trent Cole ranks second in franchise history to Reggie White with 85½ career sacks.
Courtesy of Andrei Snitko

sacks, 238 tackles, 48 tackles for a loss, four forced fumbles, two fumble recoveries, two blocked kicks, and one safety during his time at Cincinnati. Especially dominant during his senior year, Cole registered 8½ sacks, 68 tackles, and 22 tackles for a loss, prompting the Eagles to select him in the fifth round of the 2005 NFL Draft, with the 146th overall pick.

After initially assuming a backup role in his first season with the Eagles, Cole laid claim to the starting right defensive end job in Week 10, finishing the year with five sacks and 46 combined tackles, with his strong play earning him First-Team All-Rookie honors. Making an extremely favorable impression on Philadelphia's coaching staff over the course of the campaign, Cole drew praise from head coach Andy Reid, who said, "I can't get him out of the game. He's relentless."

Continuing to perform well in his second season, Cole recorded eight sacks and 62 tackles, before emerging as one of the NFL's top pass-rushers in 2007, when, in addition to registering 70 tackles and forcing four fumbles, he finished sixth in the league with 12½ sacks, earning in the process his first Pro Bowl nomination. After recording nine sacks and a career-high 77 tackles the following year, Cole began an outstanding three-year run during which he got to opposing quarterbacks a total of 33½ times, with his 12½ sacks in 2009 gaining him Pro Bowl and Second-Team All-Pro recognition.

A product of legendary defensive coordinator Jim Johnson, the 6'3", 270-pound Cole played with a motor that never quit, proving to be particularly relentless in his pursuit of opposing quarterbacks. In discussing that aspect of his game, Cole stated, "That's the only way I know how to play. I know if there's a way I can get to the quarterback, I'm going to find a way to do it. I don't care what it takes."

Hampered by injuries in 2012, Cole recorded just three sacks and 40 tackles for an Eagles team that finished the season with a disappointing 4-12 record. However, after being moved to outside linebacker in Philadelphia's new 3-4 hybrid defense the following year, Cole helped the Eagles capture the NFC East title by registering 56 tackles, three forced fumbles, and a team-leading eight sacks. Asked to frequently drop into pass coverage to defend against running backs and tight ends after spending his first several years in the league playing exclusively on the line of scrimmage, Cole adapted well to his new role, saying, "I told myself in the beginning of the year that I was going to make it work regardless. Hard work pays off, man. If you work hard, good things will happen."

Cole spent two more years in Philadelphia, recording another 14½ sacks and 108 tackles during that time, before being released by the Eagles in a salary cap–related move on March 4, 2015. Following Cole's release by the team, Eagles head coach Chip Kelly said, "We spoke with Trent and his agent and expressed a desire to have him back. We have been talking for a couple of weeks. However, at this point, we think it's best to let him explore other options around the NFL." Cole left the Eagles with career totals of 85½ sacks, 569 tackles (436 solo), 19 forced fumbles, three fumble recoveries, one interception, and one touchdown.

Following his departure from Philadelphia, Cole signed with the Indianapolis Colts, with whom he spent the next two seasons serving as a part-time player, appearing in only seven games in 2016 after suffering a back injury during the early stages of the campaign. Failing to receive any substantial offers prior to the start of the 2017 season, Cole elected to sign a one-game contract with the Eagles prior to their Christmas Day game against Oakland so that he might officially end his pro career as a member of the team. Making his feelings known to the hometown fans in attendance at the Eagles' Monday night meeting with the Raiders, Cole stated during the halftime festivities, "It was just that time. A lot of people don't get the chance to do this. Some people do. I'm just very thankful to have the opportunity. Thank you, Mr. (Jeffrey) Lurie and the Eagles' organization for allowing me to come back and go out like this. There's no better feeling than to come out here on

Cole led the Eagles in sacks five times.
Courtesy of Mr. Schultz via Wikipedia

Christmas Day and Christmas Night and Monday Night Football, with the Eagles having a great season, and end my career and start a new one."

Looking back at his playing career, Cole added, "I had that drive. I had to do my part as a teammate and make sure I left everything out on the field. Everyone knows that I was going to give everything I had. That's just the way I was. I was going to give 110 percent. I refused to lose. I wanted to win. I had that drive, I just can't explain to you. I had that fire."

Since retiring as an active player, Cole has spent most of his time presiding over the nearly 1,200 acres of land he either owns or leases in South Jersey. An avid hunter and farmer, Cole uses some of the land for hunting and the rest for growing soybeans, corn, and hay. In discussing his new career, Cole says, "I think I work harder now than when I played football. I can really say that. But it's love. I get up every day, every morning, and I have something to look forward to. I'm looking forward to the next day to get up and go to the farm with a cup of coffee and get to work."

EAGLES CAREER HIGHLIGHTS

Best Season

It could be argued that Cole played his best ball for the Eagles in 2009, when he earned one of his two trips to the Pro Bowl and his lone All-Pro nomination by recording 12½ sacks, 57 tackles, and two forced fumbles. However, he posted better overall numbers in 2007, concluding the campaign with 12½ sacks, 70 tackles, and four forced fumbles, earning in the process Pro Bowl honors for the first time.

Memorable Moments/Greatest Performances

Although the Eagles lost to the Redskins by a score of 17–10 on November 6, 2005, Cole recorded the first sack of his career during the contest when he brought down Mark Brunell behind the line of scrimmage.

Cole got off to a tremendous start in 2006, recording five sacks in Philadelphia's first three games, including two during a 24–10 win over the Houston Texans in Week 1 and another pair during a 30–24 loss to the Giants the following week.

Cole sealed a 36–22 victory over the Giants on December 17, 2006, by recording the only interception of his career with under three minutes remaining in the game and subsequently returning the ball 19 yards for his only career touchdown.

Cole contributed to a 56–21 win over the Detroit Lions on September 23, 2007, by recording a career-high 3½ sacks.

Cole earned NFC Defensive Player of the Week honors by recording two sacks, six tackles, and three tackles for a loss during a 23–16 victory over the Vikings on October 28, 2007.

Although the Eagles suffered a 24–20 defeat at the hands of the Chicago Bears on September 28, 2008, Cole turned in an outstanding all-around effort, recording a sack, forcing a fumble, and making eight tackles.

Cole helped the Eagles forge a 13–13 tie with the Cincinnati Bengals on November 16, 2008, by recording two sacks and 10 tackles, five of which were of the solo variety.

Cole proved to be a huge factor in the Eagles' 26–14 win over Minnesota in the 2008 NFC wild card game, making a game-high 13 tackles, including seven solo stops.

Notable Achievements

- Scored one defensive touchdown.
- Finished in double digits in sacks four times.
- Led Eagles in sacks five times.
- Ranks among Eagles career leaders with: 85½ sacks (2nd); 19 forced fumbles (3rd); and 569 tackles (10th).
- Three-time division champion (2006, 2010, and 2013).
- Member of 2005 NFL All-Rookie Team.
- 2007 Week 8 NFC Defensive Player of the Week.
- Two-time Pro Bowl selection (2007 and 2009).
- 2009 Second-Team All-Pro selection.

29

— TRA THOMAS —

Spending most of his 11 seasons in Philadelphia protecting Donovan McNabb's blind side from his left tackle position, Tra Thomas proved to be an invaluable member of Eagles teams that made eight playoff appearances, captured five division titles, and won one NFC championship. Excelling in pass protection, the massive Thomas helped McNabb set numerous club records by manhandling many of the league's top pass-rushing defensive ends. An outstanding run-blocker as well, Thomas helped pave the way for running backs Duce Staley and Brian Westbrook to gain more than 1,000 yards on the ground a total of five times, with his superb blocking at the point of attack earning him three trips to the Pro Bowl, one All-Pro nomination, and a spot on the Eagles 75th Anniversary Team.

Born in DeLand, Florida, on November 20, 1974, William Thomas III attended DeLand High School, where he lettered in football. After enrolling at Florida State University, Thomas took some time to develop into a dominant offensive lineman, spending his first three seasons assuming a backup role, before emerging as a force in his senior year, when he earned Second-Team All-America honors and won the Jacobs Blocking Trophy, presented annually to the ACC's best offensive lineman.

Subsequently selected by the Eagles with the 11th overall pick of the 1998 NFL Draft, Thomas laid claim to the starting left tackle job as a rookie, beginning a string of seven seasons during which he started all but four games at that post for the team. Although the Eagles struggled on both sides of the ball during Thomas's first two years with the club, compiling an overall record of just 8-24 from 1998 to 1999, they soon established themselves as one of the NFC's most formidable teams, earning five straight playoff appearances and four consecutive trips to the conference championship game from 2000 to 2004. Performing extremely well throughout the period, Thomas earned Pro Bowl honors in three of those five seasons, gained First-Team All-NFC recognition twice, and made Second-Team All-Pro once.

Excelling as a run-blocker from the time he first entered the league, Thomas, who stood 6'7" and weighed close to 350 pounds, gradually developed into an elite pass-protector as well, using his long arms and quick feet to ward off the smaller and swifter defensive ends he faced each week. In fact, at one point during his career, Thomas did not commit a single penalty for two straight seasons, allowing just two sacks in one of those campaigns.

Tra Thomas helped Eagles running backs gain more than 1,000 yards on the ground five times.
Courtesy of Kevin Doohan

After missing six games in 2005 due to injury, Thomas started 47 out of a possible 48 contests over the course of the next three seasons, before signing with the Jacksonville Jaguars as a free agent following the conclusion of the 2008 campaign. Paying tribute to Thomas upon learning of his impending departure, Eagles head coach Andy Reid said, "Tra helped this team win a lot of games from a very important position. He's a proven winner and will go down as one of the finest tackles in the history of the Philadelphia Eagles. We wish he and his family all the best in Jacksonville." During his time in Philadelphia, Thomas appeared in a total of 166 regular-season games, 165 of which he started. He also started 17 playoff contests, including five NFC championship games and one Super Bowl.

Thomas ended up spending just one season in Jacksonville, appearing in only eight games for the Jaguars in 2009, before being released by them early in 2010. He subsequently signed with the San Diego Chargers but never appeared in a single game with them after undergoing arthroscopic surgery on his knee during training camp. After sitting out all of 2010 and 2011, Thomas officially announced his retirement on August 16, 2012, doing so after signing a one-day contract with the Eagles. Expressing his satisfaction with Thomas's decision to retire as a member of the team, Eagles owner Jeffrey Lurie stated, "Tra Thomas is one of the best offensive linemen to ever put on an Eagles uniform. He was an anchor at the left

Thomas, seen here with Seattle's
Walter Jones.
Courtesy of Luis Antonio Rodriquez Ochoa

tackle position for many years and played such an integral role in our success, though he probably never got all the credit he deserved. Besides being such a great player, Tra is an even better person and someone I've always had a great relationship with."

Lurie then added, "I'm proud of what he has done with his career after football, as he has remained very successful while keeping his home in this area. We are very happy that he is retiring as an Eagle."

Remaining close to football following his retirement, Thomas spent one year serving as an analyst for Eagles games on Comcast SportsNet Philadelphia, before rejoining the Eagles as an assistant coach in 2013. After fulfilling the roles of assistant offensive line coach in 2013 and outside linebacker coach in 2014, Thomas remained away from the spotlight until October 2018, when he became co-host of the "Farzetta and Tra In the Morning" show that airs from 6:00 a.m. to 10:00 a.m. on 97.5 The Fanatic/WPEN-FM radio in Philadelphia.

EAGLES CAREER HIGHLIGHTS

Best Season

Thomas gained All-Pro recognition for the only time in his career in 2002, when he helped the Eagles finish seventh in the NFL with 2,220 yards rushing, with Philadelphia running backs averaging a robust 4.5 yards per carry over the course of the campaign.

Memorable Moments/Greatest Performances

Thomas and his offensive line–mates dominated the Dallas defense at the point of attack during a 41–14 win over the Cowboys in the 2000 regular-season opener, with the Eagles rushing for a season-high total of 306 yards.

Thomas and the rest of the Philadelphia offensive line turned in a similarly dominant performance during a lopsided 48–17 victory over Minnesota on November 11, 2001, with the Eagles amassing 487 yards of total offense, including 272 on the ground.

Thomas helped pave the way for Eagles running backs to rush for 295 yards during a 17–3 win over the Giants on October 28, 2002.

Notable Achievements

- Five-time division champion (2001, 2002, 2003, 2004, and 2006).
- 2004 NFC champion.
- Three-time Pro Bowl selection (2001, 2002, and 2004).
- 2002 Second-Team All-Pro selection.
- Two-time First-Team All-Conference selection (2002 and 2004).
- Named to Eagles 75th Anniversary Team in 2007.

30

— VIC SEARS —

dentified by Earle "Greasy" Neale as the Eagles' most valuable defensive lineman during his tenure as head coach, Vic Sears spent his entire 12-year NFL career in Philadelphia, logging more on-field minutes than anyone else in franchise history. A true iron man who rarely left the playing field, Sears failed to appear in every game the Eagles played in just two of his 12 seasons. Excelling at left tackle on both offense and defense, Sears gained All-Pro recognition from at least one major news source a total of five times, helping the Eagles win three division titles and two NFL championships in the process. And, following the conclusion of his playing career, Sears earned the additional distinction of being named to the NFL 1940s All-Decade Team.

Born in Ashwood, Oregon, on March 4, 1918, Victor Wilson Sears grew up some 180 miles west, in the city of Eugene, where he starred on the gridiron while attending Eugene High School. Choosing to remain close to home, Sears subsequently accepted a scholarship offer from Oregon State University, where he went on to earn All-America honors as a two-way tackle. Selected by the Pittsburgh Steelers in the fifth round of the 1941 NFL Draft, with the 33rd overall pick, Sears soon found himself headed to Philadelphia when new Steelers owner Alexis Thompson swapped franchises with Eagles owners Bert Bell and Art Rooney. Looking back at his earliest days as an NFL player, Sears recalled years later:

> You want to know how Greasy Neale came to know about me? A newspaper reporter for the *Portland Oregonian* tipped him off that I was a pretty fair country player. So, I got to Pittsburgh—that's who drafted me—and Greasy looked at me. So did that playboy owner they had at the time, Lex Thompson, who had just bought the Steelers. And I think they were both disappointed. They had a different notion of what a tackle should look like. You

see, Greasy was a tough old bird. He had played with Jim Thorpe, and, to Greasy, a tackle was supposed to be a mean-looking cuss. I was baby-faced and rangy.

After assuming a part-time role as a rookie in 1941, the 6'3", 223-pound Sears became a starter in his second season. Establishing himself as one of the NFL's best two-way linemen the following year, Sears earned Second-Team All-Pro honors while serving as a member of the "Steagles," a team that resulted from the temporary merger of the Eagles and Steelers necessitated by the league-wide manpower shortages brought on by World War II. Sears then missed the entire 1944 campaign with a broken leg, before appearing in every game for the Eagles in each of the next two seasons.

An extremely consistent performer, Sears did an outstanding job of blocking for quarterback Tommy Thompson and running backs Steve Van Buren and Josh Pritchard on offense, while also excelling as a run-defender from his left tackle position on defense, where he usually lined up against the opposing team's offensive right tackle. Considered to be the cleanest member of Philadelphia's rough-and-tumble defense, Sears earned the respect of his opponents, who generally viewed him as a skillful athlete who played within the rules of the game.

Despite missing five games in 1947 with stomach ulcers, Sears played well enough whenever he took the field to help the Eagles capture the first of their three straight division titles. He then proved to be a key figure on Philadelphia's NFL championship teams of 1948 and 1949, with Greasy Neale stating during the latter stages of the 1949 campaign that he considered Sears to be the club's most valuable defensive lineman. Speaking with Dick Cresap of the *Philadelphia*

Vic Sears logged more on-field minutes than anyone else in franchise history.
Courtesy of Oregon Sports Hall of Fame

Sears excelled at left tackle for the Eagles on both offense and defense.
Courtesy of MEARSOnlineAuctions.com

Bulletin, Neale suggested, "Sears has done the best job of all the last two years. He's not as spectacular as (Al) Wistert, but then Wistert is an open tackle. That is, he can be handled when the play is run straight at him. He's not as big as Sears. But Sears is just as tough when the play heads directly at him as he is when they're trying to go around. There's never any doubt on plays into our left side. We know Sears will make the tackle."

Sears continued to perform at an extremely high level for three more years, earning All-Pro honors for the second time in 1952, before announcing his retirement at season's end. However, the Eagles eventually convinced him to return for one more year, with second-year head coach Jim Trimble expressing his glee over Sears's decision by saying, "You'll have to pull me down out of the clouds. Vic is one of the all-time greats in my book."

Retiring for good following the conclusion of the 1953 campaign, Sears ended his career having appeared in 131 games, 108 of which he started. In 12 NFL seasons, he recorded two interceptions, 11 fumble recoveries, and two touchdowns on defense. Following his retirement, Sears lived another 53 years, dying peacefully at his home in Winston-Salem, North Carolina, on September 22, 2006, at 88 years of age, with his loving wife of 57 years by his side.

CAREER HIGHLIGHTS

Best Season

Sears earned Second-Team All-Pro honors for the only two times in his career in 1943 and 1952. Since he excelled on both sides of the ball in the first of those campaigns and played defense almost exclusively in the second, we'll identify 1943 as his finest all-around season.

Memorable Moments/Greatest Performances

Playing for a combined Eagles and Steelers team on November 28, 1943, Sears helped open holes that allowed "Steagles" runners to amass a season-high total of 308 yards on the ground during a 27–14 win over the Washington Redskins.

Sears anchored an Eagles defense that surrendered just one first down and 34 yards of total offense during a 7–0 victory over the New York Bulldogs in the 1949 regular-season opener.

Sears scored the first of his two touchdowns on September 20, 1942, when he returned a fumble 33 yards for a TD during a 24–14 loss to the Cleveland Rams.

Sears tallied his only other points a decade later, when he returned an interception 9 yards for a touchdown during a 38–21 win over the Dallas Texans on December 7, 1952.

Sears drew praise from teammate Dusan Maronic for his performance during Philadelphia's 14–0 victory over the Los Angeles Rams in the 1949 NFL championship game, with the Eagles guard commenting afterwards, "Our defense—guys like Vic Sears, (Walt) Piggy Barnes, and Mike Jarmoluk—was outstanding. It was really fun to sit on the bench and watch them when the offense was out. They just shut the Rams' running game off completely." (Los Angeles netted only 21 yards on 24 rushing attempts.) Later identifying the 1949 title tilt as the most memorable game of his career, Sears said:

> I was happy to be going back to warmer weather. I remember that cold weather—the blizzard—in the championship game the year before. And we were going to play in the Coliseum. . . . We got out to that field and it was pouring rain. It was the second year in a row we played a championship game in terrible conditions, and it was the second year in a row that we ended up shutting out the opponent. They tell me no other team has ever done that. Nobody else has ever won two consecutive NFL championships by shutout. Of course, this was a real special trip for me, returning to the West Coast with my new wife for the first time. That made everything extra special.

Sears then added, "After that '49 championship, our fortunes changed, but that championship . . . I'll never forget that day! I was with the woman that I was going to spend the rest of my life with, and I had just earned what turned out to be the last championship check I would ever receive."

Notable Achievements

- Scored two defensive touchdowns during career.
- Three-time Eastern Division champion (1947, 1948, and 1949).
- Two-time NFL champion (1948 and 1949).
- Two-time Second-Team All-Pro selection (1943 and 1952).
- NFL 1940s All-Decade Team.

31

DeSEAN JACKSON

An explosive offensive player who excelled as both a wide receiver and punt returner during his time in Philadelphia, DeSean Jackson amassed more than 1,000 all-purpose yards in five of his six seasons with the Eagles, leading the team in receptions twice and receiving yards five times. Also surpassing 1,000 yards from scrimmage on five separate occasions, Jackson ranks among the franchise's all-time leaders in several offensive categories, with his 1,294 punt-return yards representing the second-highest total in team annals. A member of Eagle teams that won two division championships, Jackson earned three Pro Bowl selections and one All-Pro nomination while playing in the City of Brotherly Love. Nevertheless, the Eagles ultimately decided to part ways with Jackson due to the immaturity and lack of professionalism he often displayed on the playing field and in the locker room.

Born in Long Beach, California, on December 1, 1986, DeSean William Jackson grew up in the rugged Crenshaw section of Los Angeles. Starring in multiple sports while attending Long Beach Polytechnic High School, Jackson excelled in baseball, football, and track, where he posted a personal-best time of 10.5 seconds in the 100 meters. Despite being scouted by MLB's Tampa Bay Rays and Philadelphia Phillies in his senior year, Jackson decided to focus on a career in football after his 60 receptions, 1,075 receiving yards, and 15 TD catches prompted the *Los Angeles Times* to name him the winner of the 2004 Glenn Davis Award as Southern California's player of the year. Considered one of the top wide receiver prospects in the nation, Jackson received numerous scholarship offers, before finally committing to the University of California, Berkeley, where he spent three seasons playing under head coach Jeff Tedford.

Blossoming into a star in his sophomore year at Cal, Jackson earned All–Pac-10 and All-America honors as both a punt returner and wide receiver by amassing 1,060 receiving yards and recording nine touchdown receptions, while also returning four punts for touchdowns. He followed that up by making 65 receptions for 762 yards and six touchdowns as a junior, with his exceptional play on special teams also earning him All-America honors as a return specialist. Choosing to forgo his final year of college eligibility, Jackson declared himself eligible for the 2008 NFL Draft, leaving Cal with the third-most receiving yards (2,423) and receiving touchdowns (22) in school history, while also holding Pac-10 records for most punts returned for a touchdown in a season (four) and in a career (six).

Ranked as one of the best wide receivers coming out of college, Jackson drew praise from Hall of Fame wideout Jerry Rice during the pre-draft period, with the legendary receiver saying, "He has all the talent in the world. There's no reason he can't be everything he wants to be at the next level." Yet, even though Jackson posted an outstanding time of 4.35 seconds in the 40-yard dash at the NFL Combine, his smallish 5'10", 175-pound frame caused him to slip to the middle of the second round, where the Eagles selected him with the 49th overall pick.

DeSean Jackson amassed more than 1,000 all-purpose yards in five of his six seasons with the Eagles.
Courtesy of Matthew Straubmuller

Laying claim to a starting job upon his arrival in Philadelphia, Jackson performed extremely well his first year in the league, earning a spot on the NFL All-Rookie Team by leading the Eagles with 62 receptions and 912 receiving yards, scoring three touchdowns, finishing third in the NFL with 440 punt-return yards, and amassing a total of 1,460 all-purpose yards. After losing his father to pancreatic cancer during the subsequent offseason, Jackson posted even better numbers in 2009, earning Pro Bowl and Second-Team All-Pro honors by recording 62 receptions, 1,156 receiving yards, 1,293 yards from scrimmage, 1,734 all-purpose yards, and 12 touchdowns. Named to the *Sporting News*' All-Pro team as a punt returner, Jackson averaged a league-leading 15.2 yards per punt return, scoring two of his touchdowns in that fashion. Continuing his outstanding play in 2010, Jackson earned his second consecutive trip to the Pro Bowl by catching 47 passes, scoring eight touchdowns, and amassing 1,056 receiving yards and 1,391 all-purpose yards, with his average of 22.5 yards per reception leading the NFL.

Blessed with exceptional athletic ability, Jackson possessed outstanding speed that enabled him to separate himself from most defensive backs, whom he easily outran once he broke into the open field. Meanwhile, his extraordinary quickness, which made him appear even faster than his 4.35-second 40-yard dash time, made him one of the game's most dangerous punt returners.

Although Jackson posted solid numbers once again in 2011, concluding the campaign with 58 receptions, 961 receiving yards, 1,123 all-purpose yards, and four touchdowns, he began to display a level of immaturity and selfishness that eventually bought him a ticket out of Philadelphia. After being deactivated the previous week for missing a special teams meeting, Jackson drew a $10,000 fine from the league office for flipping the ball at New York defensive coordinator Perry Fewell after making a 50-yard reception during a 17–10 victory over the Giants on November 20. The very next week, Eagles head coach Andy Reid benched him for the entire fourth quarter after he dropped two potential touchdown passes earlier in the contest.

Jackson continued to test the patience of his coaches and teammates the following year—one in which he missed the final five games after fracturing his ribs against Carolina in Week 12. Contributing only 45 receptions, 700 receiving yards, and two touchdowns to an Eagles team that finished the season just 4-12, Jackson often conducted himself in a petulant manner on the sidelines, demanding that the ball be thrown to him, and complaining when it wasn't. He also frequently arrived late to position meetings, sometimes even falling asleep at them.

The situation only worsened when Chip Kelly replaced Reid as head coach in 2013. Although Jackson had one of his most productive seasons, earning his third Pro Bowl selection by making 82 receptions for 1,332 yards and nine touchdowns, he grew increasingly hostile, often screaming at Kelly in front of the other players, while also clashing with new wide receiver coach Bob Bicknell. Having grown weary of Jackson's antics, the Eagles chose to release him on March 28, 2014, announcing their decision with a two-sentence statement that read: "After careful consideration this offseason, the Eagles have decided to part ways with DeSean Jackson. The team informed him of his release today."

Responding to initial reports that the Eagles based their decision largely on Jackson's purported connection to gangs, the wide receiver subsequently

Jackson returned four punts for touchdowns during his time in Philadelphia. Wigstruck via Wikipedia

released the following statement: "I would like to address the misleading and unfounded reports that my release has anything to do with any affiliation that has been speculated surrounding the company I keep off the field. I would like to make it very clear that I am not, and never have been, part of any gang. I am not a gang member, and to speculate and assume that I am involved in such activity off the field is reckless and irresponsible."

However, while the media did perhaps help create a somewhat false image of Jackson, who established The DeSean Jackson Foundation, which helps promote literacy, educates youth about bullying, and helps fight pancreatic cancer, several inside sources later revealed that many of Jackson's former teammates disliked him, with some of them accusing him of being insubordinate and immature.

Claiming that Chip Kelly believed that Jackson set a bad example for the team's younger players, one unidentified source said, "You see little kids and how they cry and whine when they don't get their way—that was D-Jax. I don't think he gave Kelly the respect he deserved. Kelly tried to reach him plenty of times, and he tuned him out. Then you look at team functions, when everyone is out together at charity things or social stuff. He was the one missing. It was like he was in 'D-Jax world' and we just happened to be there."

That same source continued, "With Reid, Jackson tried pushing boundaries there, too. But he looked at Reid, I think, much differently than he looked at Kelly. Reid came in with an NFL pedigree. He was the guy that drafted Jackson. He was the one that called him on draft day and laid the law down right then. Reid wouldn't tolerate any outside interference from anyone. Now, you get this college guy (Kelly), and he's not going to tell Jackson what to do."

Another anonymous source stated, "Reid thought he could control Jackson. He could, to a degree. Kelly put up with Jackson behind closed doors. A lot of guys didn't like how he talked to Kelly. And a lot of guys just didn't like him. They thought he was more into his rap label than he was about winning games. The guy performed, there's no questioning that. But you had to keep a constant eye on him. Guys put in extra time. He didn't. It's like he never grew up."

Still another source claimed, "The fact is, Jackson was a 'me-guy' with an attitude problem. . . . Funny how he has this anti-bullying thing, and he thought he could push Kelly around; he found out otherwise. His being cut had nothing to do with the gang stuff. The team knew it. Everyone knew he had 'ties.' Those were his guys. That's okay. What put him out was his selfishness. He can try and spin it all he wants how he's 'a team player.' He's not. I'll put it this way: when it came out last Friday that he was released, more than a few guys were happy it happened. They said, 'good riddance.' He had no real connection with anyone."

After being released by the Eagles, Jackson, who left Philadelphia with career totals of 356 receptions, 6,117 receiving yards, 32 touchdown catches, 6,490 yards from scrimmage, 1,294 punt-return yards, 7,813 all-purpose yards, and 39 touchdowns scored, signed with the Washington Redskins, with whom he spent the next three seasons, topping 50 receptions and 1,000 receiving yards twice each during that time. Choosing to sign with the Buccaneers as a free agent at the end of 2016, Jackson spent the last two seasons in Tampa Bay, recording a total of 91 receptions and 1,442 receiving yards for the Bucs. In a strange twist of fate, the Eagles reacquired Jackson from the Buccaneers on March 11, 2019, sending a sixth-round pick in the 2019 NFL Draft to Tampa Bay for Jackson and a seventh-round selection in the 2020 draft. Still only 32 years of age as of this writing, Jackson returns to Philadelphia boasting career totals of 589 receptions, 10,261 receiving yards, 53 TD catches, 61 touchdowns scored, 10,708 yards from scrimmage, and 12,058 all-purpose yards.

EAGLES CAREER HIGHLIGHTS

Best Season

Jackson posted his best numbers as a receiver for the Eagles in 2013, concluding the campaign with 82 receptions, 1,332 receiving yards, and nine TD catches. However, he had his finest all-around season in 2009, when, in addition to making 62 receptions for 1,156 yards and nine touchdowns, he ran for 137 yards and one touchdown, amassed 441 yards and scored twice on punt returns, accumulated 1,734 all-purpose yards, and led the NFL with an average of 15.2 yards per punt return.

Memorable Moments/Greatest Performances

Jackson excelled in his first game as a pro, making six receptions for 106 yards and amassing 97 yards on eight punt returns during a 38–3 dismantling of the Rams in the 2008 regular-season opener.

Jackson scored the first touchdown of his career when he hauled in a 22-yard TD pass from Donovan McNabb during a 24–20 loss to the Chicago Bears on September 28, 2008. He finished the game with five catches for 71 yards and two carries for another 35 yards.

Jackson scored his first touchdown on special teams the following week, returning a punt 68 yards for a TD during a 23–17 loss to the Washington Redskins.

Although the Eagles ended up losing the 2008 NFC championship game to the Arizona Cardinals by a score of 32–25, Jackson made one of the most memorable plays of his career during the contest when he gave his team a 25–24 lead early in the fourth quarter by making a juggling catch of a 62-yard TD pass thrown by Donovan McNabb. In describing the play, Arizona cornerback Dominique Rodgers-Cromartie, who tipped the ball into the air before it bounced off Jackson's hands five times as he ran toward the end zone, said, "I never thought he'd catch it. I figured it was going to hit the ground. But he showed great concentration and focus. He kept his eye on it and brought it in. It was a great play." Fellow Cardinals cornerback Matt Ware added, "I've seen guys bat a ball up in the air once or maybe twice. But four or five times? It was an amazing play."

Jackson earned NFC Special Teams Player of the Week honors by returning a punt 85 yards for a touchdown during the Eagles' 38–10 win over Carolina in the 2009 regular-season opener.

Jackson had a big day against Kansas City on September 27, 2009, making six catches for 149 yards and one touchdown during a 34–14 victory, with his TD coming on a 64-yard connection with Kevin Kolb.

Jackson earned NFC Offensive Player of the Week honors for the first time by scoring a pair of touchdowns during a 27–17 win over the Redskins on October 26, 2009, with his first TD coming on a 67-yard run and his second on a 57-yard hookup with Donovan McNabb.

Jackson proved to be too much for the Giants to handle on December 13, 2009, helping the Eagles record a 45–38 victory over their Eastern Division rivals by making six catches for 178 yards and one touchdown, while scoring another TD on a 72-yard punt return. Jackson, who finished the game with 261 all-purpose yards, earned NFC Special Teams Player of the Week honors for the second time that season with his outstanding performance.

Jackson contributed to a 28–3 win over the Jacksonville Jaguars on September 26, 2010, by making five catches for 153 yards and one touchdown, which came on a 61-yard connection with Michael Vick.

Jackson helped lead the Eagles to a 30–27 victory over the Dallas Cowboys on December 12, 2010, by making four receptions for 210 yards and one touchdown, which came on a career-long 91-yard hookup with Vick.

Jackson experienced the most surreal moment of his career the following week, when he gave the Eagles a dramatic 38–31 come-from-behind victory over the Giants by returning a punt 65 yards for a touchdown on the game's final play. Jackson's effort, which represents the only game-winning punt return on the final play from scrimmage in NFL history, capped off a tremendous comeback by the Eagles, who trailed their NFC East rivals by a score of 31–10 with less than eight minutes remaining in regulation.

Although the Eagles lost to the San Diego Chargers by a score of 33–30 on a last-second field goal in Week 2 of the 2013 campaign, Jackson had a huge game, making nine catches for 193 yards and one touchdown, which came on a 61-yard connection with Michael Vick during the latter stages of the third quarter.

Jackson earned NFC Offensive Player of the Week honors by making seven receptions for 132 yards and one touchdown during a 36–21 win over the Giants on October 6, 2013.

Jackson had his last big game as a member of the Eagles on December 15, 2013, when he made 10 catches for 195 yards and one touchdown during a 48–30 loss to the Minnesota Vikings.

Notable Achievements

- Made 82 receptions in 2013.
- Surpassed 1,000 receiving yards three times.
- Surpassed 1,000 yards from scrimmage five times.
- Made nine touchdown receptions twice.
- Scored 12 touchdowns in 2009.
- Returned four punts for touchdowns.
- Led NFL with average of 22.5 yards per reception in 2010.
- Led NFL with average of 15.2 yards per punt return in 2009.

- Finished second in NFL with average of 18.6 yards per reception in 2009.
- Finished third in NFL in punt return yards twice.
- Led Eagles in receptions twice and receiving yards five times.
- Holds Eagles single-season record for most yards per reception (22.5 in 2010).
- Ranks among Eagles career leaders with: 356 receptions (9th); 6,117 receiving yards (4th); 32 touchdown receptions (tied-9th); 6,490 total yards from scrimmage (8th); 7,813 all-purpose yards (8th); and 1,294 punt-return yards (2nd).
- Two-time division champion (2010 and 2013).
- Member of 2008 NFL All-Rookie Team.
- Two-time NFC Special Teams Player of the Week.
- Three-time NFC Offensive Player of the Week.
- Three-time Pro Bowl selection (2009, 2010, and 2013).
- 2009 Second-Team All-Pro selection.

32

— RON JAWORSKI —

The offensive leader of Eagle teams that earned four straight playoff berths and one trip to the Super Bowl, Ron Jaworski served as a key figure in the franchise's return to prominence during the late-1970s. Starting at quarterback for the Eagles from 1977 to 1986, Jaworski helped revitalize football in Philadelphia with his strong play behind center, positive outlook, and outstanding leadership ability, guiding the Eagles to four consecutive postseason appearances after they failed to post a winning record in any of the previous 11 seasons. Along the way, "Jaws" or "The Polish Rifle," as he came to be known, threw for more than 3,000 yards four times and tossed more than 20 touchdown passes on three separate occasions, earning in the process one Pro Bowl selection, one All-Conference nomination, and recognition as the NFL Player of the Year in 1980.

Born in the steel mill town of Lackawanna, New York, on March 23, 1951, Ronald Vincent Jaworski attended Lackawanna High School, where he excelled in multiple sports, starring in both baseball and football. Particularly proficient on the gridiron, Jaworski began his high school career at running back before being switched to quarterback after the coaching staff realized that he had the strongest arm on the team. Offered a contract by Major League Baseball's St. Louis Cardinals as graduation neared, Jaworski also found himself being recruited by several major colleges to play football. However, he ultimately chose to enroll at Youngstown State University in Ohio, since doing so allowed his parents to drive to his games.

After spending three years showcasing his passing skills at Youngstown, Jaworski headed for the West Coast when the Los Angeles Rams selected him in the second round of the 1973 NFL Draft, with the 37th overall pick. Jaworski subsequently saw very little action over the course of the next three seasons, serving as a backup at different times to starting signal-callers John Hadl, James Harris, and Pat Haden from 1974 to 1976. Jaworski's NFL career took a sudden turn for the better, though, when the Rams dealt him to the Eagles for tight end Charles Young prior to the

Ron Jaworski led the Eagles to four straight playoff appearances and one trip to the Super Bowl.
Courtesy of Pristineauction

start of the 1977 campaign. Recalling his initial meeting with second-year Eagles head coach Dick Vermeil, Jaworski recounted, "I remember coming to Philadelphia to meet with Dick. The deal with the Rams wasn't even final yet, but I flew in and Dick met me at the airport. We talked for two hours. By the time we finished, I knew this was where I wanted to play. Dick said, 'We're going to turn this thing around. We're going to build a winner here.' I was young and eager. I wanted to be a part of that."

Reflecting back on his conversation with Jaworski, Vermeil recollected, "I told him he was my quarterback. And I said, 'You're going to play on your bad days until they become your good days. It may cost us three bad games in a row, but you're going to start and play, no matter what.'"

Neither Jaworski nor the Eagles performed particularly well his first year behind center, with the team finishing just 5-9 in 1977 and "Jaws" completing just 48 percent of his passes, throwing for 2,183 yards and 18 touchdowns, and tossing 21 interceptions. But, with his confidence buoyed by the faith his coach placed in him, Jaworski soon developed into an efficient and disciplined quarterback who led the Eagles into the playoffs in each of the next four seasons. Describing the metamorphosis he underwent his first few years in Philadelphia, Jaworski stated during a 1980 interview, "I didn't like the 18-hour workdays any better than anybody else, but I soon realized that I'd gotten all the way from high school and into the pros with very little more than a strong arm. I thought I could throw the ball right through defenders. I was just a gunner, a slinger. Dick opened my eyes and taught me how the game should be played. He taught me how to be patient, how to take something off a throw, how to play smart, basically."

After leading the Eagles to a record of 9-7 and a wild card playoff berth in 1978 by completing nearly 52 percent of his passes and throwing for 2,487 yards and 16 touchdowns, Jaworski helped lead them to a mark of 11-5 the following year by passing for 2,669 yards, while also tossing 18 TD passes and only 12 interceptions. He then reached the zenith of his career in 1980, gaining recognition as the NFL Player of the Year by ranking among the league leaders with 3,529 yards passing, 27 touchdown passes, and a 91.0 passer rating, in helping the NFC champion Eagles compile a regular-season record of 12-4.

As Jaworski established himself as one of the league's better quarterbacks, he also emerged as the Eagles' unquestioned leader on offense, with teammate Wilbert Montgomery stating, "We had a lot of good players, but Ron was the one who made things go. He was our leader, on and off the field. He was a guy who would say something crazy to pick everybody up. He'd come up with the big play when we needed it."

Meanwhile, offensive tackle Stan Walters spoke of the impact that Jaworski made on the rest of the team with his infectious personality, saying, "The thing I remember was his enthusiasm. You've gotta realize, the Eagles hadn't won in a long time before he got there. There were a lot of guys in that locker room who didn't know what it felt like to win. They were beaten down emotionally. Jaworski was like a breath of fresh air. He came in and said, 'We're gonna win; we've got what it takes, let's go.' He was so genuine, guys just responded."

A pure pocket-passer, the 6'2", 200-pound Jaworski lacked mobility, three times suffering the most sacks of any NFL quarterback. Yet, he hung in extremely well against the pass rush, earning him the respect of teammates and opponents alike, with New York Giants Hall of Fame linebacker Harry Car-

Jaworski ranks second in franchise history in passing yards and touchdown passes.
Courtesy of SportsMemorabilia.com

son once stating, "Jaworski is from the old school. He takes a licking and keeps on ticking. He battles you for four quarters, regardless of the score. He's a tough guy; I respect that."

Although Jaworski never again reached the heights he attained in 1980, he continued to perform well for the Eagles in each of the next four seasons, a period during which he extended his then-NFL record of 116 straight starts by a quarterback. After missing the final three games of the 1984 campaign with a broken leg, Jaworski returned the following year to throw for 3,450 yards, which represented the second-highest total of his career. He then lost his starting job to Randall Cunningham midway through the 1986 season, prompting the Eagles to release him at the end of the year. Over the course of his 10 seasons in Philadelphia, Jaworski threw for 26,963 yards, completed 53.3 percent of his passes, tossed 175 touchdown passes and 151 interceptions, and posted a quarterback rating of 74.0, with his 26,963 passing yards and 175 TD passes representing the second-highest totals in franchise history. Although the Eagles compiled a rather mediocre record of 69-67-1 with Jaworski as their starting quarterback, they won 42 regular-season games with him behind center from 1978 to 1981, with only Pittsburgh's Terry Bradshaw leading his team to more victories during that time.

After being released by the Eagles, Jaworski signed with the Miami Dolphins, with whom he spent the next two seasons serving as a backup to Dan Marino. He then joined the Kansas City Chiefs prior to the start of the 1989 campaign, appearing in only a handful of games with them, before announcing his retirement at season's end.

Following his playing days, Jaworski began a career in broadcasting, first serving as a sports commentator at various local stations in the Philadelphia area, before eventually replacing Joe Theismann as color commentator for ESPN's *Monday Night Football* telecasts in 2007. After serving in that role for five years, Jaworski accepted an in-studio position in 2012, since which time he has remained with ESPN as an analyst on the station's other football programs. Jaworski also is part owner and team president of the Philadelphia Soul of the Arena Football League, serves as chairman of that league's Executive Committee, and is among the primary investors and advisors for the Elite Football League of India. Additionally, he is the owner/operator of the Valleybrook Country Club in Blackwood, New Jersey, and the Running Deer Golf Club in Pittsgrove, New Jersey.

Looking back at the 10 years he spent with the Eagles, Jaworski now says, "I might not be the most revered athlete in Philadelphia history, but I think I earned the fans' respect. I think they knew I gave it all I had every week. Win or lose, I was out there, busting my butt."

EAGLES CAREER HIGHLIGHTS

Best Season

Jaworski had easily the best season of his career in 1980, when he led the Eagles to the NFC championship by passing for 3,529 yards and 27 touchdowns, throwing only 12 interceptions, completing 57 percent of his passes, and posting a quarterback rating of 91.0 that placed him second in the league rankings. In addition to earning him Pro Bowl and First-Team All-Conference honors, Jaworski's outstanding play gained him recognition as the NFL Player of the Year.

Memorable Moments/Greatest Performances

Jaworski led the Eagles to a 28–7 win over the New Orleans Saints on November 6, 1977, by throwing a pair of touchdown passes to Harold Carmichael and running for two scores himself.

On October 1, 1978, Jaworski led the Eagles on three fourth-quarter scoring drives that gave them a 17–14 win over the Baltimore Colts in a game they trailed by a score of 14–0 heading into the final period.

Jaworski began his banner year of 1980 in fine fashion, passing for 281 yards and three touchdowns during a 27–6 win over Denver in the regular-season opener, with the longest of his TD passes going to Harold Carmichael for 56 yards.

Jaworski followed that up with a strong outing in Week 2, completing 20 of 26 pass attempts, for 234 yards and two touchdowns, in leading the Eagles to a lopsided 42–7 victory over Minnesota.

Jaworski had another big game on November 9, 1980, throwing for 323 yards and three touchdowns during a 34–21 win over New Orleans, with all his TD passes going to Harold Carmichael.

Although the Eagles lost the final game of the 1980 regular season to the Dallas Cowboys by a score of 35–27, they clinched the division title by keeping the game close, with Jaworski helping them cut into an earlier 25-point deficit by leading them on three fourth-quarter scoring drives. He finished the game with a season-high 331 yards passing, which included a 30-yard TD toss to Rodney Parker.

Jaworski threw a career-high four touchdown passes during a 52–10 manhandling of the St. Louis Cardinals on November 8, 1981, with the longest of those coming on a 38-yard connection with Harold Carmichael.

Jaworski performed heroically during a 37–34 overtime loss to Washington in the 1982 regular-season opener, completing 27 of 38 pass attempts for 371 yards and two touchdowns, despite being sacked six times.

Jaworski performed extremely well the following week as well, leading the Eagles on three fourth-quarter touchdown drives that gave them a 24–21 win over the Cleveland Browns. He finished the game with 334 yards passing and two TD passes.

Jaworski earned NFC Offensive Player of the Week honors for his performance during a 16–14 win over the Dallas Cowboys on October 20, 1985, when he led the Eagles on a pair of fourth-quarter scoring drives, the second of which culminated with a 36-yard touchdown pass to Kenny Jackson. He ended the day 22-of-35, for 380 yards and that one TD.

Jaworski experienced arguably the most memorable moment of his career on November 10, 1985, when he gave the Eagles a 23–17 overtime victory over the Atlanta Falcons by hitting Mike Quick with a franchise-record 99-yard touchdown pass.

Notable Achievements

- Passed for more than 3,000 yards four times, topping 3,500 yards once (3,529 in 1980).
- Threw more than 20 touchdown passes three times.
- Posted touchdown-to-interception ratio of better than 2–1 once.
- Posted quarterback rating above 90.0 once (91.0 in 1980).
- Rushed for five touchdowns in 1977.
- Finished second among NFL quarterbacks with passer rating of 91.0 in 1980.
- Finished third among NFL quarterbacks with 18 touchdown passes in 1977.
- Started 116 consecutive games.
- Ranks among Eagles career leaders with: 3,918 pass attempts (2nd); 2,088 pass completions (2nd); 26,963 passing yards (2nd); and 175 touchdown passes (2nd).
- 1980 division champion.
- 1980 NFC champion.
- 1985 Week 7 NFC Offensive Player of the Week.
- 1980 NFC Player of the Year.
- 1980 Bert Bell Award winner as NFL Player of the Year.
- 1980 Pro Bowl selection.
- 1980 First-Team All-Conference selection.
- Inducted into Philadelphia Eagles Hall of Fame in 1992.

33

— WES HOPKINS —

A key member of Philadelphia's vaunted "Gang Green" defense of the late 1980s and early 1990s, Wes Hopkins spent his entire 10-year NFL career with the Eagles, combining with Andre Waters much of that time to form the hardest-hitting safety tandem in the league. Outstanding against the run, Hopkins proved to be a sure tackler who instilled fear into his opponents with his ability to deliver vicious hits. Extremely effective in pass coverage as well, Hopkins recorded at least five interceptions in a season on five separate occasions, with his 30 career picks ranking as the fifth-highest total in franchise history. Hopkins's excellent all-around play earned him team MVP honors once, one trip to the Pro Bowl, one First-Team All-Pro nomination, and two All-Conference selections.

Born in Birmingham, Alabama, on September 26, 1961, Wesley Carl Hopkins attended John Carroll High School, where he received his introduction to organized football. Although Hopkins performed well on the gridiron while at John Carroll, he failed to receive any scholarship offers, causing him to try out for the Southern Methodist University football team as a walk-on. After earning a roster spot, Hopkins went on to gain All–Southwest Conference recognition in each of his last two seasons at SMU, prompting the Eagles to select him in the second round of the 1983 NFL Draft, with the 35th overall pick.

Laying claim to the starting free safety job immediately upon his arrival in Philadelphia, Hopkins had a solid rookie season, before emerging as one of the league's best players at his position the following year, when he earned First-Team All-NFC honors by recording five interceptions, 107 interception-return yards, three fumble recoveries, and 1½ sacks. Performing even better in 1985, Hopkins picked off six passes, recovered two fumbles, recorded two sacks, and scored one touchdown, earning in the process Pro Bowl and First-Team All-Pro honors, while also gaining recognition as the Eagles Defensive MVP.

Wes Hopkins starred at SMU before being drafted by the Eagles in 1983.
Courtesy of Southern Methodist University

Unfortunately, Hopkins subsequently suffered a serious knee injury in Week 4 of the 1986 campaign that forced him to miss the rest of the season and all of 1987. Recalling Hopkins's state of mind during his period of convalescence, former SMU teammate Harvey Armstrong said, "When he got hurt, they weren't even sure he'd be able to walk again, let alone play football. I was with the Colts after he got hurt. I remember him calling me and saying, 'I've got to find a way to get back on the field.'"

Through much hard work and dedication, Hopkins eventually returned to action, reclaiming his starting free safety job in 1988. Picking up right where he left off, Hopkins recorded five interceptions for the NFC East champions, with his teammates honoring him at season's end by naming him the winner of the Ed Block Courage Award.

Hopkins continued to perform at a high level for the Eagles for five more seasons, combining with fellow safety Andre Waters to form an intimidating back-end of an imposing Eagles defense that also included Reggie White, Clyde Simmons, and Seth Joyner. Providing passion and energy to the unit each week, the 6'1", 213-pound Hopkins often launched himself into opposing ball-carriers and receivers, prompting White to state on one occasion, "When other teams watch film of our defense, I know what they're saying. They're saying, 'Watch out for number 48.'"

Yet, even though Hopkins remained a playmaker after he returned from his injury, Seth Joyner revealed that he lacked some of the burst he had during the early stages of his career, stating, "He struggled when he came back to be as explosive as he was before the injury. But he figured out how to play the game the best he could with what he had. But, even with that, he still was one of the top safeties in the game. The guy just would not give up. He went through hamstring injuries and quad injuries and a million other things. And he never gave up."

Discussing his fortitude during a 1990 interview, Hopkins said, "You just learn not to quit. You learn how to overcome it. There is no quit in me. I have the confidence to know I'm one of the best. Whether somebody else knows, that is something else."

Hopkins remained with the Eagles until the end of 1993, when he announced his retirement. In addition to intercepting 30 passes during his career, Hopkins amassed 241 interception-return yards, recovered 16 fumbles, and recorded 12 sacks, with his 16 fumble recoveries representing the second-highest total in franchise history. He is also the only Eagles player ever to record at least five interceptions in a season five or more times.

Sadly, Hopkins did not live a long and fruitful life following his playing days, passing away in a Birmingham, Alabama, hospital on September 28, 2018, just two days after turning 57 years of age. Admitted to the hospital a few weeks earlier, Hopkins, said Harvey Armstrong, had been showing signs of chronic traumatic encephalopathy, the same degenerative brain disease that caused Andre Waters to commit suicide 12 years earlier. In addressing his former college teammate and longtime friend's condition, Armstrong said, "I went to see

Hopkins ranks among the Eagles career leaders in interceptions and fumble recoveries.
Courtesy of SportsMemorabilia.com

him when he was first admitted to the hospital. They didn't think he was going to make it through the week. But I sat there with him for two days, and you could see him getting stronger and trying to speak. A week later, his family sent me pictures of him doing rehab. He had gotten out of ICU. He was moving better. Speaking."

Armstrong continued, "Wes fought his whole life. I thought he would get through this because he's always persevered. He's always beaten the obstacles that he's faced. But it got to a point where he couldn't fight anymore. . . . He just went into a shell, much like Andre did. You could see some of the things he was dealing with, the depression and the anxiety and the other things CTE causes."

Upon learning of Hopkins's passing, Eagles owner Jeffrey Lurie issued a statement that said:

> Wes Hopkins is one of the best safeties in the history of our franchise, and he played a major role in the team's success during his time here in Philadelphia. He was well-respected among his teammates and coaches, not only because of the way he played the game and what he was able to accomplish on the field, but also because of the way he carried himself and the type of leader he was. He had a genuine love of the game and that's one of the reasons he connected so well with the people of Philadelphia. Wes will be forever remembered as an Eagles Legend and somebody who helped build the foundation for our organization's success. Our thoughts are with his family during this time.

Mike Quick, who spent his entire time in Philadelphia playing with Hopkins, said of his former teammate:

> He was a great player and a great intimidator. Being an intimidator at that time was a real valued thing because the game was different then . . . I remember being at the Pro Bowl with [former Cardinals wide receiver] Roy Green the year Wes hurt his knee. Roy was worried about whether Wes was going to be coming back. He kept asking me about him. . . . I thought that was a heck of a compliment. I mean, here's an All-Pro wide receiver out at the Pro Bowl, and he's worried about whether he was going to have to face a guy the next season who had torn up his knee.

Harvey Armstrong also paid tribute to his close friend by stating, "People speak of the big hitters that played the game, but I don't hear Wes' name enough. I was just talking with Eric Dickerson, and he was talking about the big hitter that Wes was. He put him right up there with the top hitters who have ever played the game."

CAREER HIGHLIGHTS

Best Season

Although Hopkins picked off five passes for the Eagles in four different seasons, the 1985 campaign would have to be considered the finest of his career. In addition to recording six interceptions and two sacks, Hopkins recovered two fumbles and scored his only career touchdown, earning in the process his lone Pro Bowl and All-Pro nominations.

Memorable Moments/Greatest Performances

Hopkins recorded the first interception of his career during a 20–0 loss to the Washington Redskins on September 30, 1984.

Hopkins picked off two passes in one game for the first time during a 26–10 loss to the Dallas Cowboys on December 2, 1984, intercepting a pair of Danny White aerials.

Hopkins recorded another two interceptions against the Cowboys on October 20, 1985, in helping the Eagles defeat their Eastern Division rivals by a score of 16–14.

Hopkins provided much of the impetus for the Eagles to mount a 21–17 come-from-behind victory over the Buffalo Bills on October 27, 1985, by returning an interception 24 yards for a touchdown that closed the gap to 17–14 midway through the fourth quarter.

Hopkins came up big for the Eagles in the final game of the 1988 regular season, helping them clinch the NFC East title by recording a pair of interceptions during a 23–7 win over Dallas.

Hopkins again picked off two passes during a 17–10 victory over the Cincinnati Bengals on November 17, 1991.

Yet, when asked what he considered to be his finest individual performance as a member of the Eagles, Hopkins referred to an October 6, 1991, meeting with the Tampa Bay Buccaneers, saying, "There were so many great moments and games during my years there. I remember playing at Tampa Bay in 1991 and having two sacks and an interception, a couple of fumble recoveries, and something like 10 tackles, but we lost the game, 14–13, at the end."

Notable Achievements

- Scored one defensive touchdown.
- Recorded at least five interceptions in a season five times.

- Amassed more than 100 interception-return yards once (107 in 1984).
- Finished third in NFL with 77 fumble-return yards in 1989.
- Led Eagles in interceptions three times.
- Ranks among Eagles career leaders with 30 interceptions (5th) and 16 fumble recoveries (2nd).
- 1988 division champion.
- 1985 Eagles Defensive MVP.
- 1988 Eagles Ed Block Courage Award winner.
- 1985 Week 3 NFC Defensive Player of the Week.
- 1985 Pro Bowl selection.
- 1985 First-Team All-Pro selection.
- Two-time First-Team All-Conference selection (1984 and 1985).

34

BOBBY WALSTON

An extremely versatile and underrated player, Bobby Walston performed well for the Eagles at multiple positions throughout the 1950s, contributing to the team in many ways during his time in Philadelphia. A dependable receiver, Walston ranked among the league leaders in touchdown receptions three times, with his 46 TD catches representing the sixth-highest total in franchise history. A reliable placekicker, Walston annually placed near the top of the league rankings in points scored, field goals made, and field goal percentage, ending his career as the NFL's second-leading all-time scorer. Extremely durable as well, Walston never missed a game in 12 NFL seasons, appearing in 148 consecutive regular-season contests before announcing his retirement following the conclusion of the 1962 campaign. A key member of Philadelphia's 1960 NFL championship team, Walston earned two trips to the Pro Bowl, one All-Pro nomination, and a spot on the NFL 1950s All-Decade Team with his consistently excellent play, making him one of the most overlooked and underappreciated players to ever don an Eagles uniform.

Born in Columbus, Ohio, on October 17, 1928, Robert Harold Walston attended Linden-McKinley High School, before accepting a scholarship offer from the University of Georgia, where he became a collegiate boxing champion. Also starring on the gridiron while at Georgia, Walston excelled for the Bulldogs as a receiver and placekicker, prompting the Eagles to select him in the 14th round of the 1951 NFL Draft, with the 166th overall pick.

Earning a starting job immediately upon his arrival in Philadelphia, Walston performed well his first year in the league, gaining recognition as the NFL Rookie of the Year by making 31 receptions for 512 yards and eight touchdowns, while also successfully converting 6 of 11 field goal attempts and 28 of 31 PATs, with his 94 points scored placing him fourth in the league rankings. After posting solid numbers again in 1952, Walston had his two most productive seasons as a receiver, establishing career-high marks in receptions (41) and receiving yards (750) in 1953, before amassing 581 receiving yards and finishing second in the league with 11 TD catches in 1954.

Spending time at both the left end (wide receiver) and tight end positions during his time in Philadelphia, the 6-foot, 190-pound Walston excelled at both posts, with his superb hands, deceptive speed, and precise route-running making him an outstanding target for Eagle quarterbacks Adrian Burk, Bobby Thomason, Norm Van Brocklin, and Sonny Jurgensen at different times. An effective blocker as well, Walston drew praise from Eagles head coach Buck Shaw for his willingness to engage defenders at the line of scrimmage, with Shaw commenting. "Bobby isn't big enough to be a textbook blocker. But he'll bite, claw, kick, and just plain out-nasty anyone he's up against." And, despite being a chain-smoker, Walston had exceptional stamina, prompting Van Brocklin to once predict, "Bobby will play until he's 60."

Bobby Walston spent his entire 12-year NFL career in Philadelphia.
Courtesy of MEARSOnlineAuctions.com

Although Walston remained a dependable receiver for the rest of his career, surpassing 30 receptions and 500 receiving yards three more times each, he became equally well known for his reliable place-kicking, scoring more than 100 points twice and successfully converting more than 70 percent of his field goal attempts on two separate occasions. In discussing the totality of Walston's game, longtime Eagles general manager Vince McNally stated, "Bobby Walston was the best draft pick I ever made. I remember scouting him at a Georgia-Maryland game. He played halfback and safety and kicked like hell. We drafted him more for his kicking than anything because he could kick the hell out of the ball. The fact that Bobby blossomed into a great receiver was a bonus."

Meanwhile, in addressing his former teammate's athletic ability, Tommy McDonald suggested, "Bobby was the best all-around athlete on our team. He could do anything—basketball, baseball, boxing. If we stayed at a hotel with a pool, he'd put on a diving exhibition. You'd think he was in the Olympics, he was that good. He had unbelievable body control. He was a great pass receiver and a clutch kicker. We never worried about him in a pressure situation."

One of the NFL's toughest players, Walston, who spent his offseasons working as a deputy sheriff in Georgia, chasing down moonshiners in the hills of Tattnall County, played through some extremely painful injuries, returning to action just one week after breaking his jaw during a 1954 contest after being advised by doctors to remain on the sidelines for at least three weeks. Borrowing a pair of pliers, he removed the wires that attached his broken jaw and played the following week with a homemade brace consisting only of gauze and tape. Walston also spent much of the 1962 season serving as the Eagles' placekicker after breaking his arm, taking the field with his arm in a sling.

Choosing to announce his retirement following the conclusion of the 1962 campaign, Walston ended his career with 311 receptions, 5,363 receiving yards, 46 touchdown receptions, 80 field goals made in 157 attempts, 365 extra points made in 384 attempts, and 881 points scored, which, at the time, placed him second only to Lou Groza in NFL history. Walston's 881 points also remained the highest total in franchise history until David Akers surpassed it 40 years later.

After retiring as an active player, Walston spent the next few years working in the Eagles front office, before becoming the special teams coach for the AFL's Miami Dolphins in 1966. After fulfilling that role for two seasons, Walston served as personnel director for the Chicago Bears from 1968 to 1975, a period during which he scouted, oversaw the drafting of college players, and assisted Bears president George Halas Jr. in the overall

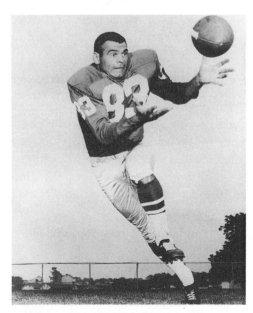

Walston proved to be a dependable receiver and reliable placekicker over the course of his career.
Courtesy of BoxingTreasures.com

operations of the team. He also later served as a scout for the Canadian Football League's Edmonton Eskimos from 1978 to 1980 and the United States Football League from 1983 to 1985. Sadly, Walston's life ended all too soon, as he passed away on October 7, 1987, at Alexian Brothers Medical Center in Elk Grove Village, Illinois, just 10 days before his 59th birthday.

CAREER HIGHLIGHTS

Best Season

Walston compiled his best numbers as a receiver in 1953, when he scored five touchdowns and posted career-high marks in receptions (41) and receiving yards (750). He had his finest season as a kicker in 1960, when, in addition to making 30 receptions for 563 yards and four touchdowns, he successfully converted 14 of 20 field goal attempts and 39 of 40 point-after attempts, en route to finishing second in the league with 105 points scored. However, Walston had his finest all-around season in 1954, when he caught 31 passes for 581 yards, finished second in the NFL with a career-high 11 touchdowns, and topped the circuit with 114 points scored, which remained a single-season Eagles record until 1984.

Memorable Moments/Greatest Performances

Walston proved to be a huge contributor in his first game as a pro, leading the Eagles to a 17–14 victory over the Chicago Cardinals in the opening game of the 1951 regular season by scoring a touchdown on a 22-yard pass reception and kicking a 23-yard field goal.

Walston displayed his versatility during a 26–21 win over the Steelers on October 12, 1952, by kicking a career-high four field goals and making a 40-yard reception.

Walston topped 100 receiving yards for the first time in his career on November 23, 1952, when he made four receptions for 121 yards and one touchdown during a 28–20 win over the Browns.

Walston helped lead the Eagles to a convincing 30–7 victory over the Giants on November 8, 1953, by making eight receptions for a career-high 176 yards and two touchdowns, which came on a pair of connections with quarterback Bobby Thomason that covered 62 and 13 yards.

Walston had a big day against Chicago on October 3, 1954, making five receptions for 110 yards and three touchdowns during a 35–16 win over the Cardinals.

Walston led the Eagles to a 49–21 victory over the Redskins on October 17, 1954, by making six receptions for 90 yards and three touchdowns, while also successfully converting all seven of his extra-point attempts, with his 25 points scored setting a single-game franchise record that still stands.

Walston amassed more than 100 receiving yards for the final time in his career on November 20, 1960, when he caught six passes for 119 yards during a 17–10 win over the Giants.

Walston, though, is remembered most for the game-winning 38-yard field goal he converted against the Cleveland Browns on October 23, 1960, that helped propel the Eagles into the playoffs. Later identified by most Eagles players as the moment their championship vision came into focus, Walston's kick, delivered into a swirling wind at Cleveland's Municipal Stadium on the game's final play, gave the Eagles a 31–29 victory over their Eastern Division rivals, capping off an afternoon in which he also made four receptions for 94 yards and one touchdown. Looking back at Walston's late-game heroics, then-Eagles GM Vince McNally recalled:

> Bobby didn't have the world's strongest leg. He was accurate, but anything outside 35 yards and you held your breath. I didn't think he would make this kick. The field was all torn up, so it was hard to get a decent spot. The wind was blowing in off the lake. Bobby had been running pass patterns all day, so his leg had to be tired. Remember, he was no youngster by then. But he got the strength from somewhere. It barely cleared the crossbar, but it got there. It was the greatest clutch kick I ever saw.

Notable Achievements

- Made 11 touchdown receptions in 1954.
- Scored more than 100 points twice.
- Led NFL with 114 points scored in 1954.
- Led NFL in field goal percentage twice.
- Finished second in NFL in: points scored twice; field goals made once; touchdown receptions once; and touchdowns scored once.

- Finished third in NFL with eight touchdown receptions in 1951.
- Finished sixth in NFL with 750 receiving yards in 1953.
- Never missed a game his entire career, appearing in 148 consecutive contests over 12 seasons.
- Holds Eagles single-game record for most points scored (25 vs. Washington on 10/17/54).
- Ranks among Eagles career leaders with: 881 points scored (2nd); 46 touchdowns (11th); 311 receptions (11th); 5,363 receiving yards (7th); 46 touchdown receptions (6th); and 80 field goals made (tied-5th).
- Retired as NFL's second-leading all-time scorer.
- 1960 Eastern Division champion.
- 1960 NFL champion.
- 1951 NFL Rookie of the Year.
- Two-time Pro Bowl selection (1960 and 1961).
- 1951 Second-Team All-Pro selection.
- NFL 1950s All-Decade Team.

35

— BYRON EVANS —

Easily the most overlooked and underappreciated member of Philadelphia's vaunted "Gang Green Defense" of the late 1980s and early 1990s, Byron Evans spent his entire eight-year NFL career with the Eagles, serving as the centerpiece of one of the most dominant defenses in league history. Starting at middle linebacker for the Eagles from 1989 to 1994, Evans recorded more than 100 tackles five straight times, leading the team in that category twice, despite being surrounded by other notable run-stuffers such as Reggie White, Clyde Simmons, and Jerome Brown. And, although the presence of White, Simmons, Brown, Seth Joyner, and Eric Allen prevented Evans from receiving the recognition he most certainly deserved, he spent his last several seasons in Philadelphia serving as the Eagles' defensive captain.

Born in Phoenix, Arizona, on February 23, 1964, Byron Nelson Evans attended South Mountain High School, before enrolling at the University of Arizona, where he spent four years starring at linebacker for the Wildcats, leading the Pac-10 in tackles in each of his final two seasons. After being named a finalist for the Butkus Award as the nation's top linebacker and earning Pac-10 Defensive Player of the Year honors his senior year, Evans entered the 1987 NFL Draft, where the Eagles selected him in the fourth round, with the 93rd overall pick.

Although the 6'2", 235-pound Evans possessed all the physical attributes necessary to excel in head coach Buddy Ryan's aggressive defensive scheme, it took him two years to establish himself as a full-time starter since he first had to earn Ryan's complete trust. Sharing playing time with the less-athletic, but more experienced, Mike Reichenbach in 1987 and 1988, Evans started only eight games over the course of those two seasons, often being replaced by Reichenbach in passing situations.

Reflecting back on the challenges he faced in fully grasping Ryan's intricate "46" defense, Evans told Jim Gehman of PhiladelphiaEagles.com during a 2008 interview, "It was very complicated, probably one of the most complex defenses of all time, but it wasn't intimidating. I think, more than anything, I was surrounded by a good bunch of guys who were willing to go the extra mile and help me out, and really give me the confidence boost that I needed. If I studied, I could make it happen."

Having earned the trust of his head coach and improved his pass-coverage skills, Evans laid claim to the starting middle linebacker job in his third NFL season, after which he went on to establish himself as a tremendous all-around player. In addition to leading the league with 184 tackles in 1989, Evans recorded two sacks, three interceptions, and three fumble recoveries, prompting Ryan to call him the team's most improved player. Evans followed that up by amassing a total of 223 tackles over the course of the next two seasons, before having arguably his finest all-around year in 1992, when he made a career-high four interceptions and team-leading 175 tackles.

A natural hitter, Evans had good speed, excellent instincts, and long arms, which helped him bring down runners and receivers on the move, with Tommy Lawlor of Fan-demonium recalling years later, "The thing that pops in my mind with Evans is his long arms. I can always see him in his stance with his arms dangling. . . . He was an outstanding wrap-up tackler, but the arms also helped in pass defense."

Combining with Seth Joyner and William Thomas to give Philadelphia arguably the league's finest trio of linebackers, Evans contributed as much to the success the Eagles experienced between 1989 and 1992 as anyone else on their much-heralded defense. Responsible for calling the defensive signals, getting everyone lined up correctly, stuffing the run up the middle, making tackles from sideline to sideline, assisting in pass coverage, and blitzing effectively, Evans made everyone around him better, allowing players such as Reggie White, Clyde Simmons, Jerome Brown, Joyner, and Thomas to thrive as much as they did. Yet, due, at least in part, to his quiet and understated demeanor, Evans played

Byron Evans recorded more than 100 tackles for the Eagles five straight times.
Courtesy of SportsMemorabilia.com

in virtual anonymity, receiving little publicity and consistently being bypassed for Pro Bowl and All-Pro honors.

Nevertheless, Evans remained content with the role of leadership he assumed during his time in Philadelphia, telling PhiladelphiaEagles.com, "To be named one of the captains, you had to trust the person and really believe in what they were doing. They believed that you were a leader, and that made me feel real good."

Evans had one more solid season for the Eagles, recording 109 tackles in 1993, before breaking his leg and tearing his MCL while bringing down Cleveland Browns running

Evans served as the centerpiece of Philadelphia's vaunted "Gang Green Defense."
Courtesy of George A. Kitrinos

back Leroy Hoard in Week 10 of the ensuing campaign. Forced into premature retirement, Evans ended his career with 806 solo tackles, which represents the fourth-highest total in franchise history. He also recorded 13 interceptions, 214 interception-return yards, 3½ sacks, four forced fumbles, 12 fumble recoveries, and two touchdowns. Particularly effective from 1989 to 1993, Evans averaged 138 tackles per season during that five-year period.

After retiring as an active player, Evans moved back to Phoenix, where he began teaching at his old junior high school, before joining the faculty at South Mountain High School, where he currently teaches physical education and serves as head football coach. Evans also is a pastor at his hometown church.

CAREER HIGHLIGHTS

Best Season

Although Evans failed to garner any postseason honors in 1989, it could be argued that he played his best ball for the Eagles that year, concluding the campaign with three interceptions, two sacks, and a career-high 184 solo tackles. But, with Evans being named Second-Team All-Pro by the Newspaper Enterprise Association and First-Team All-NFC by *Pro Football Weekly* in 1992 after recording four interceptions and 175 tackles during the regular season, we'll identify that as his finest season.

Memorable Moments/Greatest Performances

Evans recorded the first interception of his career during a 17–7 win over the Buffalo Bills in the final game of the 1987 regular season.

Evans put the finishing touches on a convincing 31–13 victory over the previously undefeated New York Giants on November 25, 1990, when he picked off a Phil Simms pass and returned the ball 23 yards for the first of his two career touchdowns.

Evans anchored a dominating Eagles defense that surrendered just four first downs and 82 yards of total offense to Denver during a 30–0 manhandling of the Broncos on September 20, 1992.

Evans lit the scoreboard for the second and final time in his career in the 1993 regular-season finale when he returned a fumble 30 yards for a touchdown during a 37–34 overtime victory over the San Francisco 49ers.

Notable Achievements

- Scored two defensive touchdowns.
- Recorded more than 100 tackles five times.
- Led Eagles in tackles twice and interceptions once.
- Ranks fourth in Eagles history with 806 solo tackles.
- 1988 division champion.
- Two-time Newspaper Enterprise Association (NEA) Second-Team All-Pro selection (1990 and 1992).
- 1992 First-Team All-Conference selection.

36

— FLETCHER COX —

The backbone of the Eagles' defense the last several seasons, Fletcher Cox has established himself as one of the NFL's premier defensive tackles during his time in Philadelphia. A tremendous force up front, Cox does an outstanding job of applying pressure to opposing quarterbacks, while also excelling against the run. Versatile enough to play inside or outside, Cox has earned Pro Bowl and All-Pro honors four times each, with his four Pro Bowl selections placing him second only to Reggie White in franchise history among defensive linemen. Cox's exceptional all-around play has also helped lead the Eagles to four playoff appearances, two division titles, and one NFL championship.

Born in Yazoo City, Mississippi, on December 13, 1990, Fletcher Cox attended Yazoo City High School, where he dominated his opponents on the gridiron as a 6'2", 210-pound defensive lineman, later telling *USA Today Sports*, "I'd bully them or just run circles around them and finesse it. Whatever I felt like." Blessed with superior athletic ability, Cox, who bench-pressed 300 pounds and posted a time of 4.47 seconds in the 40-yard dash while in high school, also played for Yazoo City's basketball team and competed in track as a sprinter and high jumper.

After fielding scholarship offers from LSU, Alabama, Auburn, and Ole Miss, Cox elected to enroll at Mississippi State University, where he continued to impose his will on the offensive linemen who opposed him, earning All–Southeastern Conference and All-America honors as a junior in 2011, before declaring himself eligible for the 2012 NFL Draft. Subsequently selected by the Eagles with the 12th overall pick, Cox realized that special things awaited him shortly after he arrived in Philadelphia, later crediting Eagles defensive line coach Jim Washburn for his epiphany when he said, "It really clicked when I was drafted. Coach Washburn always told me, 'God created you to play the Wide 9.' Ever since, I've just had that mindset. I try to go out there and try to be different."

Performing well at right tackle his first year in the league, Cox earned a spot on the NFL All-Rookie Team by recording 5½ sacks, 39 tackles, 10 quarterback hits, and one forced fumble. Continuing to play well after the Eagles moved him to defensive end when they switched to a 3-4 defense the following year, Cox posted similar numbers, before earning Second-Team All-Pro honors in 2014 by registering four sacks, making 61 tackles, recovering three fumbles, and scoring the first touchdown of his career. Emerging as a full-fledged star in 2015, Cox gained Pro Bowl and All-Pro recognition by recording 9½ sacks, 71 tackles, three forced fumbles, and two fumble recoveries.

Although Cox proved to be one of the Eagles' best defenders his first few years in the league, he truly began to establish himself as the focal point of their defense when he moved back inside to defensive tackle prior to the start of the 2016 campaign. Since that time, he has done a tremendous job of using his quickness, athleticism, strength, and sturdy 6'4", 310-pound frame to stuff the run and apply pressure to opposing quarterbacks up the middle.

Fletcher Cox has excelled both inside and outside during his time in Philadelphia.
Courtesy of Jeffrey Beall

Commenting on the totality of Cox's game, Minnesota Vikings head coach Mike Zimmer stated, "He's strong, physical and has great quickness. In the four-down lineman scheme, those inside pass rushers are extremely valuable, and he is an outstanding player. He's good against the run, he's good in the passing game. He's got great quickness, great hands and power, and I think that's what makes him good."

Cox also drew praise from Bill Belichick prior to Super Bowl LII, with the Patriots head coach saying, "Cox is as good as anybody in the league at his position. He's a very disruptive player, hard to block, run, pass, no matter what it is."

Even though Cox represents arguably the best bull-rushing threat in the league, he considers himself to be much more than just a straight-ahead rusher, suggesting, "I'm not a big finesse guy. But I can bend, I can rush, I've got a quick twitch, and the thing about it is, I can move guys. I've got the speed and power, and that's what makes an interior defensive lineman dominant: when you can create that separation to make tackles and all that."

Crediting much of his speed and agility to his offseason workouts with trainer Deon Hodges, who trains the massive lineman much as he would a wide receiver, defensive back, or running back, Cox says, "That's how I make sure I have those quick moves. Hodges always creates stuff to make me uncomfortable, and that's the type of stuff you want, because, if you're not, then you're just going to be where you are, and I'm never where I want to be."

Cox also watches a considerable amount of film, studying the other top players at his position and his opponents, looking for any weaknesses in their game. Explaining his reasoning, Cox says, "Every interior D-lineman is different, and you can't really compare us, but if I'm playing a team they played, you watch to see how they attacked him so I can know how they plan to attack me the same way."

Meanwhile, Cox feels that his contributions to the Eagles cannot be measured merely by statistics, claiming, "I can't always get a sack. So, evaluating my games, I look at pressures, look at the what-ifs, look at the things you affected, and how you helped another player get a sack, how you helped that DB get an interception. It's about helping and things like that, and you take it and grow from it and don't be selfish."

Cox's unselfish attitude prompted his teammates to name him a team captain prior to the start of the 2018 season, with fellow Eagles defensive lineman Chris Long saying, "He's a leader. He's got a 'C' on his chest this year, which is a big thing. I feel like he's been a leader. I'm just excited about him having that 'C' on his

Cox's exceptional play has helped the Eagles win two division titles and one NFL championship.
Courtesy of Keith Allison

chest. Having been one before, I know what that means, and he's respected like that in this locker room. He's somebody that now feels empowered by that, and he can do those things like push us along on bad days. Not just be the best player on the field, he can be one of the best leaders."

Having one of his finest seasons for the Eagles in 2018, Cox earned his fourth consecutive trip to the Pro Bowl and fourth All-Pro selection by recording a career-high 10½ sacks and 34 quarterback hits, while also making 46 tackles, 12 of which resulted in a loss. Subsequently asked if Cox deserves to be ranked among the game's elite interior defensive linemen, Brian Billick stated, "I do. Yeah. I think he should be talked about in the same breath as Aaron Donald. They're in that category."

Entering the 2019 campaign at 28 years of age, Cox has amassed 44½ sacks, 330 tackles, and eight forced fumbles to this point in his career. Since he is currently in the middle of a six-year, $103 million contract he signed with the Eagles on June 13, 2016, he figures to add significantly to those totals before his time in Philadelphia comes to an end.

CAREER HIGHLIGHTS

Best Season

Although Cox gained First-Team All-Pro recognition for the only time in his career in 2018, he had his finest all-around season in 2015, when he earned his first Pro Bowl selection and one of his three Second-Team All-Pro nominations by registering 9½ sacks, 20 quarterback hits, 71 tackles (50 solo), 11 tackles for loss, and three forced fumbles.

Memorable Moments/Greatest Performances

Cox recorded the first sack of his career in his first game as a pro, bringing down Cleveland quarterback Brandon Weeden behind the line of scrimmage during a 17–16 victory in the 2012 regular-season opener.

Cox helped the Eagles begin the 2014 campaign on a positive note, closing out the scoring of a 34–17 win over the Jacksonville Jaguars in the opening game of the regular season when he recovered a fumble and returned the ball 17 yards for a TD late in the fourth quarter.

Cox earned NFC Defensive Player of the Week honors for his performance during a 39–17 win over New Orleans on October 11, 2015. In addition to sacking Saints quarterback Drew Brees three times, Cox recorded six tackles and forced two fumbles, one of which he recovered deep in New Orleans territory to help set up an Eagles touchdown.

Cox contributed to a 23–20 victory over the Buffalo Bills on December 13, 2015, by recording a sack and a season-high eight tackles (seven solo).

Cox helped lead the Eagles to a lopsided 34–3 victory over the Pittsburgh Steelers on September 25, 2016, by registering two sacks, five tackles, and one forced fumble.

Cox proved to be a key figure in the Eagles' 30–17 win over Washington in the 2017 regular-season opener, recording a sack, forcing a fumble, and recovering two others, one of which he returned 20 yards for a fourth-quarter touchdown that sealed the victory.

Cox continued his outstanding play in that year's postseason, recording seven tackles, a sack, and two quarterback hits during the Eagles' 15–10 win over Atlanta in the divisional round of the 2017 playoffs.

Cox once again assumed a prominent role during the Eagles' 34–13 win over the Giants on October 11, 2018, registering one sack, six tackles, and three quarterback hits.

Cox came up big for the Eagles in the final game of the 2018 regular season, leading them to a convincing 24–0 victory over the Washington Redskins that earned them a playoff berth by recording three sacks and four solo tackles, three of which went for a loss.

Notable Achievements

- Has scored two defensive touchdowns.
- Has recorded more than 10 sacks once (10½ in 2018).
- Has led Eagles in sacks four times.
- Ranks seventh in Eagles history with 44½ career sacks.
- Two-time division champion (2013 and 2017).
- 2017 NFC champion.
- Super Bowl LII champion.
- Member of 2012 NFL All-Rookie Team.
- 2015 Eagles Ed Block Courage Award winner.
- 2015 Week 5 NFC Defensive Player of the Week.
- September 2016 NFC Defensive Player of the Month.
- Four-time Pro Bowl selection (2015, 2016, 2017, and 2018).
- Three-time Second-Team All-Pro selection (2014, 2015, and 2017).
- 2018 First-Team All-Pro selection.

37

— DAVID AKERS —

A study in perseverance, David Akers rose to prominence with the Eagles after previously going undrafted by all 30 NFL teams, being cut by three different pro clubs, and spending two years supporting himself by waiting tables and serving as a substitute school teacher. Finally finding a home in Philadelphia in 1999, Akers went on to establish himself as the greatest kicker in franchise history over the course of the next 12 seasons, scoring more points, successfully converting more field goal and extra-point attempts, and appearing in more games than anyone else in team annals. Gaining Pro Bowl and All-Pro recognition five times each during his time in Philadelphia, Akers helped the Eagles win six division titles and one NFC championship, with his outstanding kicking also earning him a spot on the NFL 2000s All-Decade Team and a place in the Eagles Hall of Fame.

Born in Lexington, Kentucky, on December 9, 1974, David Roy Akers attended Tates Creek High School, before enrolling at the University of Louisville, where he set a school record by kicking 36 field goals, en route to scoring a total of 219 points that represents the second-highest figure in Cardinals history. After subsequently being bypassed by all 30 teams in the 1997 NFL Draft, Akers signed with Atlanta as a free agent. Cut by the Falcons shortly thereafter, Akers signed with the Carolina Panthers, only to suffer a similar fate. Picked up by Washington in 1998, Akers appeared in one game with the Redskins, missing a pair of long field goal attempts, before being released at season's end. Discouraged by his early failures, Akers later admitted, "There were times I was ready to give up. My wife said give it one more year."

Contacted by the Eagles early in 1999, Akers traveled to Berlin at the team's behest, after which he spent the next few months competing in NFL Europe. Summoned to Philadelphia prior to the start of training camp later that year, Akers arrived at his eventual home feeling somewhat under the weather, having lost 30 pounds after spending one week in the hospital with food poisoning. After recovering from his illness, Akers earned a roster spot with his strong left leg, replacing regular placekicker Norm Johnson on long field goal attempts and kickoffs.

Having displaced the aging Johnson as the team's full-time kicker by the start of the ensuing campaign, Akers proved to be one of the NFL's biggest surprises, successfully converting 29 of 33 field goal attempts (87.9 percent) and 34 of 36 extra-point attempts (94.4 percent), with his total of 121 points scored setting a new single-season franchise record. Continuing his success in 2001, Akers earned Pro Bowl and First-Team All-Pro honors by ranking among the league leaders with 26 field goals (in 31 attempts), 115 points, and a field goal percentage of 83.9 percent, in helping the Eagles capture the NFC East title for the first of four straight times. Akers followed that up with another outstanding year, gaining Pro Bowl and Second-Team All-Pro recognition in 2002 by placing near the top of the league rankings with 30 field goals (in 34 attempts), 133 points, and a conversion rate of 88.2 percent.

David Akers appeared in more games than anyone else in franchise history. Courtesy of Kevin Burkett

In addition to establishing himself as one of the NFL's most accurate placekickers his first few years in Philadelphia, the 5'10", 200-pound Akers became known for his powerful leg, which enabled him to successfully convert more than half of his field goal attempts from more than 50 yards out over the course of his career. Expressing his confidence in Akers's ability to hit from long range, Eagles head coach Andy Reid stated, "I think he has the strongest leg in the league, and he is just so mentally tough."

Akers, though, took greater pride in being one of the league's more consistent kickers, stating on one occasion, "More important to me would be getting to a point where I almost never miss. I'd much rather be known as an accurate kicker than a long kicker. But those two attributes do kind of intertwine."

Claiming that Akers reached his ultimate objective, Eagles special teams coach John Harbaugh said, "He has become so compact and so consistent with his technique, and that has been developed through really hard work. I think he's the best in the business, and I think he has a chance to be the best kicker in NFL history, I really do."

Agreeing with Harbaugh's assessment, Rich Hofmann of the *Philadelphia Daily News* wrote, "There is no money in betting against Akers, none. You might as well bet against winter. Maybe the day will come when you're not sure anymore, when Akers runs out there for that 42-yarder and you really wonder, but it will almost certainly be because of an injury. Or because he's 50."

Yet, the extremely modest Akers preferred to credit his teammates for most of his success, singling out long snapper Mike Bartrum and holder Koy Detmer when he said, "It really means a lot for the three of us to have that comfort level." Akers then added, "And our line does such a great job of blocking. Sometimes people take all that for granted. . . . It's not like the old mantra where you kick field goals and pick up checks. You need that rapport with your entire special teams unit. Everybody has to be in unison before you even have a chance to do your job."

Akers remained the Eagles' placekicker for eight more years, earning Pro Bowl and All-Pro honors three times each during that time. Performing particularly well from 2008 to 2010, Akers successfully converted 97 of 115 field goal attempts (84.3 percent) over the course of those three seasons, with his point totals of 144, 139, and 143 placing him first in the league once and second the other two times. However, after becoming a free agent following the conclusion of the 2010 campaign, Akers signed with the San Francisco 49ers, leaving Philadelphia with career totals of 1,323 points, 294 field goals made, and 441 extra points made—all of which represent franchise records. Akers successfully converted 82.4 percent of his field goal attempts during his time in Philadelphia and appeared in a franchise-record 188 games. An outstanding clutch performer, Akers established an NFL record by successfully converting 19 consecutive field goal attempts in playoff competition. He also holds the league mark for most points scored in a decade, tallying a total of 1,169 points from 2000 to 2009.

Continuing to perform at an elite level after he joined the 49ers, Akers had arguably the greatest season of his career in 2011, earning Pro Bowl and First-Team All-Pro honors by setting NFL single-season records for most points scored without scoring a TD (166) and most field goals made (44). After Akers experienced less success the following year, converting only 69 percent of his field goal attempts, the 49ers released him, prompting the 38-year-old veteran to sign with the Lions. Akers subsequently spent one year in Detroit, scoring a total of 99 points for the Lions in 2013, before announcing his retirement at season's end with career totals of 1,721 points scored, 386 field goals made, and 563 extra points made. Over the course of 16 NFL seasons, he successfully converted 80.9 percent of his field goal attempts and 98.8 percent of his extra-point attempts. As of this writing, Akers ranks 13th in NFL history in points scored and 11th in field goals made.

Since retiring as an active player, Akers, who formed the David Akers Kicks for Kids Foundation in 2001 with the purpose of providing sick chil-

Akers also holds franchise records for most points scored and most field goals made. Courtesy of Darrin Schieber

dren living in the Greater Philadelphia/Delaware Valley area an opportunity to pursue their dreams, has continued his philanthropic work. Working in conjunction with the Children's Hospital of Philadelphia, the foundation has established programs that provide emotional and financial assistance to sick children and their families. Akers also co-hosted a Monday night radio program for 10 seasons, serves as a spokesperson for Lincoln Financial, BMW of Devon Hill, Pennsylvania, and Jefferson Hospital Heart Health Program, and entertains as an effective corporate speaker.

Welcomed into the Eagles Hall of Fame in 2017, Akers received high praise from team owner Jeffrey Lurie, who stated during the induction ceremonies, "David Akers embodies everything we look for in a player, both on and off the field. He was talented, reliable, tough, and, of course, clutch. He played a major role in the success of this franchise during his time here, but he also loved this city and our fans and made a tremendous impact in the community. We are proud to enshrine him alongside the greatest figures in Eagles history."

EAGLES CAREER HIGHLIGHTS

Best Season

Akers had several outstanding seasons for the Eagles, earning Pro Bowl and All-Pro honors five times each as a member of the team. However, even though he failed to gain such recognition in 2002, Akers proved to be more accurate that season than in any other. Finishing third in the league with 133 points, Akers successfully converted 30 of 34 field goal attempts and all 43 of his extra-point attempts, concluding the campaign with a career-high 88.2 field-goal percentage.

Memorable Moments/Greatest Performances

Akers came up big for the Eagles twice on November 5, 2000, kicking a game-tying 34-yard field goal with only 11 seconds remaining in regulation, before giving them a 16–13 victory over the Dallas Cowboys by splitting the uprights from 32 yards out nearly eight minutes into the overtime session.

Akers again came through in the clutch for the Eagles the following week, kicking two late field goals to give them a 26–23 overtime win over the Pittsburgh Steelers. After successfully converting two earlier field goal attempts, Akers sent the game into overtime by kicking a 42-yarder as time expired in regulation. He subsequently won the game less than five minutes later with another 42-yard field goal, with his late-game heroics earning him NFC Special Teams Player of the Week honors for one of seven times as a member of the Eagles.

Akers kicked five field goals in one game for the first time in his career during a lopsided 36–3 victory over the Cowboys on November 18, 2001, earning in the process NFC Special Teams Player of the Week honors once again.

Akers gave the Eagles a 24–21 win over the Giants on December 30, 2001, by splitting the uprights from 35 yards out with only seven seconds remaining in regulation.

Akers earned NFC Special Teams Player of the Week honors by successfully converting all four of his field goal attempts during a 25–16 victory over the Carolina Panthers on November 30, connecting from 35, 48, 38, and 29 yards out.

Akers once again displayed his ability to perform well under pressure in the divisional round of the 2003 playoffs, giving the Eagles a 20–17 overtime win over Green Bay by kicking a 31-yard field goal nearly five minutes into the overtime session, after earlier tying the game with a 37-yard field goal with just five seconds remaining in regulation.

Akers proved to be the difference in a 19–9 win over the Chicago Bears on October 3, 2004, earning NFC Special Teams Player of the Week honors by successfully converting field goal attempts of 51, 42, 42, and 40 yards.

Akers gave the Eagles a 34–31 victory over the Cleveland Browns three weeks later by kicking a game-winning 50-yard field goal nearly 10 minutes into overtime.

After tearing the hamstring in his non-kicking leg during the opening kickoff of a 23–20 victory over the Oakland Raiders on September 25, 2005, Akers returned to the fray in the second half with his leg heavily taped to make two extra points and deliver the game-winning 28-yard field goal with only nine seconds remaining in regulation. He subsequently collapsed in pain while being mobbed by his teammates.

Akers earned NFC Special Teams Player of the Week honors for the final time as a member of the Eagles by successfully converting field goal attempts of 44, 38, 37, and 33 yards during a 19–14 win over the Packers on November 27, 2005.

Akers delivered one of his biggest kicks for the Eagles in the 2006 NFC wild card game, giving them a 23–20 win over the Giants by driving the ball through the uprights from 38 yards out as time expired in regulation.

Akers came up big for the Eagles once again in the 2008 NFC wild card game, contributing to their 26–14 victory over the Minnesota Vikings by converting all four of his field goal attempts, which came from 43, 51, 31, and 45 yards out.

Akers delivered another clutch kick on December 27, 2009, giving the Eagles a 30–27 win over Denver by splitting the uprights from 28 yards out with only four seconds remaining in regulation.

Notable Achievements

- Scored more than 100 points 10 times, surpassing 120 points six times and 140 points twice.
- Converted more than 85 percent of field goal attempts three times.
- Led NFL in points scored once and field goals made once.
- Finished second in NFL in points scored twice.
- Finished third in NFL in points scored once and field goals made twice.

- Holds NFL records for most points scored in a decade (1,169 from 2000 to 2009) and most consecutive field goals made in playoff competition (19).
- Holds Eagles career records for most: points scored (1,323); field goals made (294); extra points made (441); and games played (188).
- Six-time division champion (2001, 2002, 2003, 2004, 2006, and 2010).
- 2004 NFC champion.
- Seven-time NFC Special Teams Player of the Week.
- Four-time NFC Special Teams Player of the Month.
- Five-time Pro Bowl selection (2001, 2002, 2004, 2009, and 2010).
- 2001 First-Team All-Pro selection.
- Four-time Second-Team All-Pro selection (2002, 2004, 2009, and 2010).
- Three-time First-Team All-Conference selection (2001, 2002, and 2004).
- NFL 2000s All-Decade Team.
- Named to Eagles 75th Anniversary Team in 2007.
- Inducted into Philadelphia Eagles Hall of Fame in 2017.

38

── JEROME BROWN ──

His life tragically cut short by a fatal automobile accident that occurred in the summer of 1992, Jerome Brown spent only five seasons in Philadelphia. Nevertheless, the big defensive lineman left his mark on everyone with whom he came into contact over the course of those five seasons, with his larger-than-life personality making him one of the most beloved members of Eagles teams that advanced to the playoffs three straight times and captured one division title. One of the NFL's best all-around defensive tackles throughout most of his stay in Philadelphia, Brown excelled against both the run and the pass, recording more than 10 sacks once, while also doing a superb job of stuffing the run. A two-time Pro Bowler and two-time First-Team All-Pro, Brown gained induction into the Eagles Hall of Fame posthumously and had his number 99 retired by the team, even though his time in Philadelphia proved to be all too brief. Yet, we are all left to wonder what might have been had he not been taken from us at only 27 years of age.

Born in Brooksville, Florida, on February 4, 1965, William Jerome Brown III attended Hernando High School, where he starred on the gridiron as both an offensive and defensive lineman. Often seen during the offseason running laps around the school's track, Brown received praise for the calm demeanor he displayed while helping to disperse a group of Ku Klux Klan protestors that assembled in his hometown in June 1988.

After graduating from Hernando High, Brown enrolled at the University of Miami, where he spent the next four years helping the Hurricanes compile an overall record of 40-9. Having earned consensus All-America honors as a senior in 1986, Brown entered the 1987 NFL Draft, where the Eagles selected him in the first round, with the ninth overall pick.

Laying claim to the starting right defensive tackle job shortly after he arrived in Philadelphia, Brown performed well his first year in the league, earning a spot on the 1987 NFL All-Rookie Team by recording four sacks and two interceptions. He followed that up with another solid season,

Jerome Brown's colorful personality made him one of the most beloved members of the Eagles teams for which he played.
Courtesy of Richard Albersheim of Albersheims .com

making five sacks, picking off one pass, and helping to limit opposing ball-carriers to an average of 3.5 yards per rush for an Eagles team that won the NFC East title for the first time in seven years. Although Brown subsequently failed to gain either Pro Bowl or All-Pro recognition in 1989, he had his finest season to-date, recovering two fumbles and recording a career-high 10½ sacks, prompting Eagles head coach Buddy Ryan to proclaim, "If you had 45 Jerome Browns, you'd win every game. Nobody could beat you."

Playing immediately next to right end Clyde Simmons when the Eagles lined up on defense, Brown proved to be quite the opposite of his fellow lineman in terms of the way he carried himself, both on and off the playing field. While Simmons said very little, preferring to let his play do his talking for him, Brown described himself as a "big, old kid" who frequently exchanged barbs with his opponents during contests and enjoyed cursing, singing, whistling, and intimidating reporters with his insulting wit in the locker room. Extremely loud and boisterous, Brown brought attention to himself with his playful and colorful demeanor, with former teammate Mike Golic saying, "He was the team's personality. He kept that room loose."

Brown also displayed a great deal of intensity and aggressiveness on the playing field, with Golic stating, "Jerome was like a wild man on the field. Every play was a search-and-destroy mission."

Brown's engaging personality, relentless style of play, and tremendous talent enabled him to gradually emerge as one of the Eagles' team leaders, even though he lacked discipline his first few years in the league. But, after earning Pro Bowl and First-Team All-Pro honors in 1990 by recording five fumble-recoveries, one sack, and numerous tackles for loss, Brown began to display a new level of maturity during the subsequent offseason, shedding

30 pounds from his 6'2", 300-pound frame and dedicating himself more to his profession than ever before. In discussing the transformation he underwent during the offseason, Brown said early in 1991, "It took me four years to get my priorities in place. Now, I realize how important it is to get in good shape and work at things. I don't take stuff for granted the way I used to. I guess I'm maturing. Either that, or I'm just getting old, like Reggie."

Making good use of his increased mobility, quick feet, and powerful arms, Brown turned in the finest all-around performance of his career in 1991, earning Pro Bowl and First-Team All-Pro recognition for the second straight time by recording nine sacks and nearly 150 tackles, including 88 of the solo variety.

Sadly, the 1991 campaign ended up being the last of Brown's career. Nearly six months after the regular season ended, on June 25, 1992, Brown lost his life when, while driving on a rain-soaked road in his hometown of Brooksville, Florida, he lost control of his vehicle, causing it to flip over and strike a utility pole, killing him and his 12-year-old nephew instantly. Informed of his close friend and former teammate's passing moments before going on stage to speak at a Billy Graham Crusade at Philadelphia's Veterans Stadium later that evening, Reggie White broke the news to the stunned crowd, which realized it had lost one of its most beloved players.

Upon learning of Brown's passing, Buddy Ryan said, "He was the best defensive lineman in the league. He wound the defense up on game day."

A tragic automobile accident took Brown from us all too soon.
Courtesy of MEARSOnlineAuctions.com

After revealing that he had many private talks with Brown, Eagles director of player personnel, Joe Woolley, stated, "He had a heart of gold. I helped bring Jerome here in 1987, and that's something I will always remember. With his passing, I feel like a little bit of me is gone, too."

The Eagles subsequently kept Brown's Veterans Stadium locker intact for the 1992 season, preserving it just as he had left it, with his football shoes stacked in the bottom and his shoulder pads and helmet resting on its shelf. They also mounted his number 99 jersey in a silver frame, which they placed inside the stall. After the Eagles retired his jersey number during an emotional pregame ceremony at Veterans Stadium prior to the regular-season opener, Brown's former teammates paid tribute to him by wearing a patch with the initials "J.B." on their jerseys the entire year. Commenting on Brown's absence at one point during the 1992 campaign, Eagles head coach Rich Kotite said, "Jerome might not be here, but his presence is still here. We all feel it in some way every day."

Expressing his love for Brown years later, former Eagles tight end Keith Jackson said, "He did things that people didn't know about. He had a big heart. He was a different person behind the scenes." Jackson then went on to reveal that Brown ran a camp for underprivileged children in the offseason and once helped a Brooksville native pay for hospital bills after his 11-year-old daughter remained in a coma following an auto accident.

In speaking of his former teammate, Seth Joyner stated, "He's the one guy I wish I could have seen play for a full career. He was cat quick and strong as an ox, and he could take on a double team. I shudder to think how good he could have been . . . I told him he needed to take care of his body. His death was a tragedy. He was the heart and soul of our defense."

Meanwhile, Mike Golic waxed philosophical when he said, "He loved to drive fast cars. He lived fast and he drove fast. That was Jerome."

CAREER HIGHLIGHTS

Best Season

Brown established himself as one of the NFL's best defensive tackles in 1989, when he recorded a career-high 10½ sacks. However, he had his finest all-around season in 1991, earning Pro Bowl and First-Team All-Pro honors for the second straight time by leading all NFL tackles with 88 solo tackles, while also registering nine sacks and two fumble recoveries for the league's number one ranked defense.

Memorable Moments/Greatest Performances

Brown recorded the first two sacks of his career during a 28–23 win over the St. Louis Cardinals on November 1, 1987.

Brown starred during a 30–24 win over the Rams on November 6, 1988, intercepting a pass and helping to limit Los Angeles running backs to just 69 yards rushing, with his stellar performance earning him NFC Defensive Player of the Week honors for the first of two times.

Brown earned that distinction again by recording 2½ sacks during the Eagles' 17–5 win over the Phoenix Cardinals on October 15, 1989.

Brown registered 2½ of the 11 sacks the Eagles recorded against Troy Aikman during a 24–0 whitewashing of the Dallas Cowboys on September 15, 1991.

Notable Achievements

- Intercepted two passes in 1987.
- Recorded 10½ sacks in 1989.
- 1988 division champion.
- Two-time NFC Defensive Player of the Week.
- Member of 1987 NFL All-Rookie Team.
- Two-time Pro Bowl selection (1990 and 1991).
- Two-time First-Team All-Pro selection (1990 and 1991).
- Two-time First-Team All-Conference selection (1990 and 1991).
- Named to Eagles 75th Anniversary Team in 2007.
- Inducted into Philadelphia Eagles Hall of Fame in 1996.
- #99 retired by Eagles.

39

— JASON KELCE —

An extremely quick and athletic center who has excelled as a downfield blocker ever since he earned the starting job in Philadelphia as a rookie in 2011, Jason Kelce overcame early doubts about his ability to compete against some of the league's larger defensive tackles to establish himself as one of the NFL's best players at his position. A fundamentally sound blocker who depends largely on his agility, intelligence, and outstanding technique to outmaneuver his opponent, Kelce has helped lead the Eagles to two division titles, one NFC championship, and one NFL title, earning in the process Pro Bowl and All-Pro honors twice each. Yet, it is for the impassioned speech he made at the team's Super Bowl victory parade that Kelce will likely be remembered most once his playing days end.

Born in Cleveland Heights, Ohio, on November 5, 1987, Jason D. Kelce attended Cleveland Heights High School, where he earned All–Lake Erie League honors twice as a running back and linebacker. After making the University of Cincinnati football team as a walk-on, Kelce switched to fullback, before finally settling in at left guard after he gained 40 pounds one summer. Adapting well to his new position, Kelce started every game at that post for the Bearcats in each of the next two seasons, earning Second-Team All–Big East honors as both a sophomore and junior. Continuing to display his versatility after being moved to center prior to the start of his senior year, Kelce gained Second-Team All–Big East and Honorable Mention All-America recognition.

Although the 6'3", 295-pound Kelce ran the fastest 40-yard dash time of any offensive lineman at the 2011 NFL Scouting Combine, posting a mark of 4.89 seconds, his lack of experience at the center position and relatively smallish frame caused him to slip to the sixth round of that year's draft, where the Eagles finally selected him with the 191st overall pick. Likened to a hedgehog by fellow Eagles rookie Danny Watkins due to his quickness and stoutness, Kelce subsequently beat out veteran Jamaal Jackson for the starting center job during training camp, after which he went on to become the first rookie in franchise history to start all 16 games at that position.

The 2012 campaign proved to be far less productive for Kelce, who suffered a partially torn MCL and torn ACL in Week 2 that forced him to miss the rest of the season. Returning to action in 2013, Kelce helped lead the Eagles to the NFC East title, with his superior blocking up front gaining him First-Team All-Pro recognition from *Pro Football Focus*. Despite missing four games the following year after undergoing surgery for a sports hernia, Kelce earned his first Pro Bowl nomination. He then began in 2015 a string of four straight seasons in which he has started every game at center for the Eagles, earning his second trip to the Pro Bowl in 2016 and First-Team All-Pro honors in both 2017 and 2018.

Jason Kelce has established himself as one of the NFL's top centers over the course of the last eight seasons.
Courtesy of Jeffrey Beall

Commenting on the many contributions that Kelce has made to the Eagles the past few seasons, safety Rodney McLeod says, "He's got a lot of responsibility and he handles it well. He can move, he's agile, he's strong, smart. He's the definition of a lineman, man. He has that savviness to him—a little dirty play to him—but you like it. He does go unnoticed at times, but he's always in the right place and always making the right calls."

Yet, even though Kelce made the Pro Bowl in 2016, he struggled at times, particularly during the first half of the season, when he had a difficult time adapting to new head coach Doug Pederson's offense after spending the previous three campaigns operating in Chip Kelly's system. With some fans and football experts beginning to question his ability to continue to compete at a high level, Kelce took note of the criticism, later saying, "I'm naturally a smaller guy. It's not like it's an unwarranted knock—it's a realistic knock."

Reflecting back on the events that transpired over the course of the season, Kelce said, "The start of the year was really, really tough. I was playing

Kelce earned First-Team All-Pro honors in each of the last two seasons.
Courtesy of Keith Allison

with some really bad technique . . . I think I got away with a lot of stuff when I was maybe a little bit younger and a little bit stronger. Once I started getting beat with that, it was a wakeup call. 'All right. We've got to fix this now.'"

However, following a midseason meeting with offensive line coach Jeff Stoutland, Kelce began to correct his mistakes. After the two men watched a considerable amount of film together, Kelce realized that his errors were fundamental in nature, prompting him to reemphasize the importance of leverage and correct his hand and hip placement. With the adjustments Kelce made carrying over to the 2017 campaign, he had arguably his finest season, gaining consensus First-Team All-Pro recognition for the first of two straight times. Looking back at the renaissance he underwent, Kelce says, "It was a pretty big change. I think that it was really great just to be playing better and feeling that I was a productive member of the team rather than somebody that was just taking up a spot. The way the season went, and the way that it ended, with a Super Bowl win, was all just icing on the cake, for sure."

Kelce capped off that unforgettable 2017 season by delivering a memorable speech during the Eagles' Super Bowl parade in which he defended his teammates, coaches, and front office and compared fans of the team to hungry dogs who, "for 57 years have been starved of this championship." Recalling what will likely go down as the signature moment of his career, Kelce later said, "It was a very real moment for myself, and I think that the fans and really everybody watching it picked up on that as well, that it was really coming from the heart. It wasn't some sort of show, even though it might have looked like it with the Mummer outfit and all the spectacle around it. It was something that came from a burning place down inside that had been engrained through a lot of hard work, a lot of failures, a lot of success throughout my entire career, and the same thing with the city and this entire organization."

CAREER HIGHLIGHTS

Best Season

Kelce had an outstanding 2013 season, helping to pave the way for LeSean McCoy to rush for a league-leading and franchise-record 1,607 yards. He also performed extremely well in 2018, gaining First-Team All-Pro recognition for the second straight time. However, Kelce reached the apex of his career in 2017, when he helped lead the Eagles to their first NFL championship since 1960, earning in the process unanimous First-Team All-Pro honors, with *Pro Football Focus* also giving him the highest rating of any NFL offensive lineman and naming him its Run Blocker of the Year.

Memorable Moments/Greatest Performances

Kelce anchored an offensive line that helped the Eagles amass 514 yards of total offense during a 54–11 rout of the Chicago Bears on December 22, 2013, with 289 of those yards coming on the ground.

Kelce helped pave the way for Eagles running backs to gain a season-high 256 yards on the ground during a convincing 33–10 win over the Dallas Cowboys on Thanksgiving Day 2014.

Kelce and his line-mates once again dominated their opponents at the line of scrimmage on November 13, 2016, with the Eagles rushing for a season-high 208 yards during a 24–15 victory over the eventual NFC champion Atlanta Falcons.

Notable Achievements

- Two-time division champion (2013 and 2017).
- 2017 NFC champion.
- Super Bowl LII champion.
- 2013 Eagles Ed Block Courage Award winner.
- 2017 *Pro Football Focus* Run Blocker of the Year.
- Two-time Pro Bowl selection (2014 and 2016).
- Two-time First-Team All-Pro selection (2017 and 2018).

40

— RANDY LOGAN —

A hard-hitting safety who spent his entire 11-year NFL career in Philadelphia, Randy Logan persevered through the dark days of the mid-1970s to take part in the resurgence the Eagles experienced during the latter part of the decade. Extremely consistent and durable, Logan never missed a game as a pro, appearing in 159 consecutive contests for the Eagles, which represents the second-longest streak in franchise history. Meanwhile, even though Logan went about his job quietly, bringing very little attention to himself, he proved to be one of the NFL's better defensive backs throughout his career, recording the 10th-most interceptions in team annals, en route to earning one All-Pro selection and two All-Conference nominations.

Born in Detroit, Michigan, on May 1, 1951, Randolph Logan attended Northern High School, where he excelled on the gridiron as a running back and defensive back to such a degree that he became the first player in that school's history to win a scholarship to a Big Ten Conference college. Enrolling at the University of Michigan in 1969, Logan spent three years playing under legendary head coach Bo Schembechler, establishing himself during that time as one of the nation's finest safeties. After beginning his college career as a backup wingback, Logan transitioned to the defensive side of the ball in his junior year, starting all 12 games at strong safety for a Wolverines team that suffered just one defeat, with that being a heartbreaking 13–12 loss to Stanford in the 1972 Rose Bowl. Continuing his outstanding play his final year at Michigan while manning the "wolfman" position (a linebacker/safety hybrid), Logan helped the Wolverines compile a record of 10-1 by recording 45 tackles, four interceptions, and two fumble recoveries, earning in the process team MVP and consensus First-Team All-America honors.

Subsequently selected by the Eagles in the third round of the 1973 NFL Draft, with the 55th overall pick, Logan drew praise from Philadelphia head coach Mike McCormack, who stated, "I watched every (Michigan) game on tape, and I never saw the kid out of position. And, when he hit, he made their heads snap."

Logan later revealed that former USC tight end Charle Young, who the Eagles tabbed two rounds earlier in that year's draft, also had a significant amount of input into the coaching staff's decision, saying, "They asked Charle who he felt was the best strong safety that he played against in college. Charle gave them my name because I had played against him in the East-West Shrine Game and the Hula Bowl. I was excited just to get

Randy Logan never missed a game in his 11 years with the Eagles.
Public domain (photographer unknown)

an opportunity to get into the National Football League. I was somewhat surprised that it was the Eagles because all the contact that I had during my senior year came from teams in the southwest, especially the Dallas Cowboys."

Logan continued, "But it didn't matter. I just wanted the opportunity to play. To get that call was very exciting. Here was a team in the National Football League that was calling me and saying that they were picking me, and would I like the opportunity to come and play with them? And it was just a resounding yes! Yes, I would love to do it!"

Earning the starting strong safety job as a rookie, Logan had an outstanding first season, recording a team-leading five interceptions, which he returned for a total of 38 yards. Remaining one of the Eagles' best defenders in each of the next four seasons, Logan performed especially well in 1977, when, in addition to picking off another five passes, he amassed a career-high 124 interception-return yards.

Yet, despite his consistently strong play, Logan often found it difficult to maintain a positive outlook his first five years in Philadelphia due to the poor performance of the team as a whole. Having tasted defeat just twice in three varsity seasons at Michigan, Logan had a hard time accepting the fact that the Eagles compiled an overall mark of just 25-44-1 from 1973 to 1977, stating on one occasion, "It hurts to lose, but I'll never just give up and go through the motions. I approach every game with the attitude that this will be the one we win, this will be the one that turns it around. I remember what it was like at Michigan. We didn't know what losing was. Every time we went on the field, we knew we were going to win. It was the greatest feeling in the world. I want to be here when the Eagles are in the same position."

Fortunately, things began to improve shortly after Dick Vermeil took over as head coach in 1976. Gradually purging the roster of those players with a losing attitude, Vermeil chose to retain the services of Logan, with Ray Didinger writing in *The Eagles Encyclopedia*, "Logan was part of the nucleus Vermeil built around as he changed the Eagles from sad sacks to winners."

Expressing his admiration for Logan following his arrival in Philadelphia, Vermeil said, "Randy has two key ingredients. One, he's a damn good athlete. Two, he's a character individual. Playing well and giving 100 percent effort is important to him. Everybody knows what kind of hitter he is. He hits so hard, he scares me. He's only 190 pounds. The way he takes on those 260-pound blockers, I'm afraid he's going to get hurt."

Logan ended up helping the Eagles earn four consecutive playoff appearances from 1978 to 1981, starting all 64 regular-season games at strong safety during that time, and gaining All-Pro recognition for the only time in his career during the NFC championship campaign of 1980. He remained with the Eagles until the end of 1983, when the team cut him after he assumed a backup role during the latter stages of the campaign. In explaining the decision to release Logan, head coach Marion Campbell said, "I made the decision based on the emergence of Ray Ellis at strong safety. We contacted every team trying to make a deal for Randy, but there were no takers. Randy told me he'd rather be placed on waivers than retire."

After nearly signing with the Michigan Panthers of the USFL, Logan elected to announce his retirement, ending his career with 23 interceptions, 293 interception-return yards, and five fumble recoveries. His string of 159 consecutive games played ranks second in team annals only to the 162 straight contests in which Harold Carmichael appeared from 1972 to 1983. In addressing his tremendous durability, Logan stated, "I have to attribute it to the goodness of the Lord. To do all that in 11 years, the constant hitting and playing and everything, it had to have been His mercy to watch over me because a lot of players that I've seen definitely didn't last that long . . . I had the aches and the pains and the dislocated fingers and that sort of thing, but nothing really major to keep me out. It could have happened to me, but, through the grace of the Lord, it didn't."

Looking back on Logan's playing career, former Eagles center Guy Morriss said, "He was a quiet, low-key kind of guy. Randy was a tremendous football player who didn't say a whole lot. A good, solid player week in and week out who had a great attitude."

Jerry Sisemore, another former teammate of Logan, added, "Randy was a real quiet individual. A very solid individual who was very firm in his religious life. On the football field, he would knock you out. He would come up and really force the play. What a fierce competitor. But all you ever got out of him was a smile."

Logan's streak of 159 consecutive games played ranks as the second longest in team annals.
Courtesy of Philadelphia Connection

After retiring as an active player, Logan spent 11 years working in the accounts payable department at Electronic Data Systems in the Detroit area, before returning to Philadelphia with his wife. He subsequently became the assistant dean of student affairs at Saint Gabriel's Hall, a reform school in Audubon, Pennsylvania, dedicated to the rehabilitation of boys between the ages of 11 and 18. Logan remained in that post for 13 years, before semi-retiring to become an agent with iMerchant Direct, whose card processing service he helps sell.

CAREER HIGHLIGHTS

Best Season

Although the success the Eagles experienced as a team in 1980 enabled Logan to earn his lone All-Pro nomination, he had his finest statistical season in 1977, when he established career-high marks in interceptions (5) and interception-return yards (124).

Memorable Moments/Greatest Performances

Even though the Eagles lost the 1973 regular-season opener to the St. Louis Cardinals by a score of 34–23, Logan performed well in his first game as a pro, intercepting a Jim Hart pass, which he subsequently returned 30 yards.

Logan recorded two interceptions in one game for the first time in his career on December 4, 1977, picking off Roger Staubach twice during a 24–14 loss to the Dallas Cowboys.

Logan accomplished the feat again during a 24–20 win over the Cardinals on October 14, 1979, returning his two picks a total of 47 yards.

Notable Achievements

- Recorded five interceptions in a season twice.
- Amassed more than 100 interception-return yards once (124 in 1977).
- Never missed a game in 11 seasons, appearing in 159 consecutive contests.
- Holds second-longest consecutive games played streak in Eagles history.
- Led Eagles with five interceptions in 1973.
- Ranks among Eagles career leaders with 23 interceptions (tied-10th).
- 1980 division champion.
- 1980 NFC champion.
- 1980 Second-Team All-Pro selection.
- Two-time Second-Team All-Conference selection (1980 and 1981).

41

ZACH ERTZ

Well on his way to becoming the most prolific pass-receiving tight end in Eagles history, Zach Ertz has established himself as one of the NFL's finest players at his position over the course of the past few seasons. A two-time Pro Bowl selection, Ertz has surpassed 70 receptions and 800 receiving yards in each of the last four seasons, with his 116 catches in 2018 setting a new single-season NFL record for tight ends. Currently third in franchise history in pass receptions, Ertz has led the Eagles in receptions and receiving yards in each of the last three seasons, with his stellar play during that time helping them make two playoff appearances and win one Super Bowl.

Born in Orange, California, on November 10, 1990, Zachary Adam Ertz moved with his family to Northern California at the age of seven, after which he spent the remainder of his youth competing in several sports while growing up in Danville. Developing a love for the game of basketball at an early age, Ertz recalled, "It's the first sport that I truly excelled at and enjoyed. I never got tired of playing it or watching it. I think those traits of being a good basketball player, going up for a rebound, catching a ball, truly translated to my success on the football field as well."

Hoping to one day play in the NBA, Ertz entered high school planning to focus

Zach Ertz's 116 receptions in 2018 established a new NFL record for tight ends.
Courtesy of Keith Allison

exclusively on basketball, later saying, "Throughout my entire childhood and early adulthood, I thought I would become a basketball player. Everything I did in life was geared toward being as good as I possibly could be at basketball and getting a scholarship to play basketball. I probably could have played in the Ivy Leagues or maybe a small D1 school."

But, while Ertz grew up loving basketball, he loathed the sport of football, remembering, "Since I was the biggest kid on the team, they made me play offensive line, and I hated that. There was also a weight limit for peewee football, so, just to play, I had to lose like 15 pounds, and it was miserable. I hated it, and I never wanted to play again."

Encouraged by his mother, Ertz decided to give football one more try, joining the freshman team at Monte Vista High School in Danville. Discovering a newfound love for the game after being employed as a quarterback, receiver, and safety on the MVHS freshman squad, Ertz ended up having an extremely successful high school career, blossoming under the tutelage of coach Brent Jones, a former All-Pro tight end with the San Francisco 49ers.

Speaking of his onetime protégé, Jones told CSN Philadelphia in 2013, "I instantly saw some phenomenal things in Zach. The first thing that stood out was his size and his unbelievable hands. He was a basketball player, and he was very good at using his body and getting the ball up high. Here's a kid who had never played varsity, was going into his junior year, and I looked at him and told him, 'Zach, you're going to play in the NFL.'"

Crediting Jones with much of his success, Ertz said, "Brent came out and kind of opened my eyes to how good I could be. He would always say when I was a junior in high school that I'd be playing in the pros one day, and I just kind of laughed at him. I was 16 years old, how am I supposed to know how good I'm supposed to be. But, at that point, I had already grown and was probably about the same size that I am now. I just didn't have the passion for football. Brent showed me how to really enjoy it and be a dominant football player. And that's kind of when everything opened up to me. So, I think everything that I turned out to be as a football player was because of how he initially showed me the path."

Ertz continued, "After Brent came out and coached me, my game picked up, the level of enjoyment skyrocketed, and the recruiting picked up almost immediately. I received the first scholarship offer like 4–6 weeks into my junior year, and, before my junior year started, I wouldn't even have thought about scholarships. I just felt very fortunate to be in the situation, as a 17-year-old kid, to have college coaches calling me. That time in my life was a lot of fun and something that I'll never really forget."

After earning First-Team All-State honors as a senior at Monte Vista High by catching 56 passes for 756 yards and 14 touchdowns, Ertz enrolled at Stanford University, where he spent the next three seasons playing under head coach Jim Harbaugh. Appearing in a total of 38 games during his time at Stanford, Ertz recorded 112 receptions, amassed 1,434 receiving yards, and scored 15 touchdowns, with his 69 catches, 898 receiving yards, and six TDs as a junior earning him First-Team All–Pac-12 and consensus All-America honors.

Choosing to forgo his senior year at Stanford, Ertz declared himself eligible for the 2013 NFL Draft, where the Eagles selected him in the second round, with the 35th overall pick. He subsequently spent his first three seasons in Philadelphia sharing playing time with Brent Celek, with Celek serving as the primary blocking tight end and Ertz being used more as a receiver in passing situations. Yet, even though Ertz did not take the field on every down, he managed to post some extremely impressive numbers his first three years in the league, totaling 169 receptions, 2,019 receiving yards, and nine touchdowns during that time, with his 75 catches and 853 receiving yards in 2015 placing him near the top of the league rankings for tight ends.

Still, Ertz remained somewhat dissatisfied with the fact that he had yet to establish himself as a complete player. Considered to be a below-average blocker despite his hulking 6'5", 250-pound frame, Ertz lacked the physicality of many NFL tight ends, prompting him to reach out to former Dallas Cowboys offensive line coach Hudson Houck following the conclusion of the 2014 campaign. Discussing his decision at the time, Ertz explained, "Hudson is basically the guru of blocking, so I headed down to San Diego a couple months back to train with him. We worked on everything from coordinating where my hand placement should go to how to use my hips in blocking. We focused on being the perfect blocker. Obviously, I'm not perfect yet, but that's something I'm going to strive to be. With everything I've learned, I'm expecting to have that much more impact on the field every play, whether I'm blocking or making catches."

Commenting on Ertz's desire to improve that particular aspect of his game, Eagles tight ends coach Justin Peele said, "That's always been something that's not his strength. He takes pride in it, he wants to be better. He doesn't want it to be a weakness, but it was not a natural thing for him. We worked a lot on his technique, his hands, his understanding of the game. You have to consistently work on it, and, to his credit, he's embraced it and hasn't shied away from it."

Having developed into a more effective blocker, Ertz assumed the full-time starting role in 2016, when, despite missing two games due to injury, he recorded 78 receptions, amassed 816 receiving yards, and scored four touchdowns. Compiling extremely similar numbers in 2017, Ertz earned his first trip to the Pro Bowl by making 74 receptions for 824 yards and eight touchdowns during the regular season, before scoring the

game-winning touchdown of Super Bowl LII. Ertz followed that up with a banner year in 2018, earning his second straight Pro Bowl selection and being named First-Team All-Pro by the *Sporting News* after breaking Jason Witten's single-season NFL record for tight ends by finishing second in the league with 116 receptions, while also amassing 1,163 receiving yards and scoring eight touchdowns.

Still only 28 years old as of this writing, Ertz will enter the 2019 season with career totals of 437 receptions, 4,827 receiving yards, and 29 touch-

Ertz currently ranks third in franchise history in pass receptions.
Courtesy of PristineAuction.com

downs. Hoping to add significantly to those numbers in the years ahead, Ertz says, "When people think of great tight ends in Philly, I want to be the guy that they think of. I look at (Brian) Dawkins, I look at Donovan (McNabb), I look at (Brian) Westbrook. These guys left lasting legacies in the city. Those are the guys I want to be mentioned with."

CAREER HIGHLIGHTS

Best Season

Was there ever any doubt? Ertz had easily the greatest season of his career in 2018, when, in addition to amassing 1,163 receiving yards and scoring eight touchdowns, he established a new NFL record for tight ends by making 116 receptions.

Memorable Moments/Greatest Performances

Ertz contributed to a convincing 49–20 victory over the Oakland Raiders on November 3, 2013, by scoring his first career touchdown on a 15-yard hookup with Nick Foles late in the first half. He finished the game with five receptions for 42 yards and that one TD.

Although the Eagles suffered a heartbreaking 27–24 defeat at the hands of the Washington Redskins on December 20, 2014, losing the game on a last-second field goal, Ertz turned in a tremendous effort, setting an Eagles single-game record by making 15 receptions for 115 yards.

Ertz once again starred in defeat on December 26, 2015, making 13 receptions for 122 yards during a 38–24 loss to the Redskins.

Ertz had another huge game the following week, helping the Eagles record a 35–30 win over the Giants in the 2015 regular-season finale by making nine receptions for 152 yards.

Ertz performed extremely well in the final game of the regular season once again in 2016, catching 13 passes for 139 yards and two touchdowns during a 27–13 win over Dallas.

Although the Eagles lost to the Carolina Panthers by a score of 21–17 on October 21, 2018, Ertz had a big game, making nine receptions for 138 yards.

Ertz turned in another outstanding effort during a 27–20 loss to the Dallas Cowboys on November 11, 2018, making 14 receptions for 145 yards and two touchdowns.

Ertz helped lead the Eagles to a 32–30 victory over the Houston Texans on December 23, 2018, by making 12 receptions for 110 yards and two touchdowns, breaking in the process Jason Witten's NFL single-season record for most catches by a tight end.

Ertz experienced the most memorable moment of his career in Super Bowl LII, when he put the Eagles ahead to stay by collaborating with Nick Foles on an 11-yard scoring play with just 2:21 left in regulation. The touchdown, which concluded with Ertz diving across the New England goal line, gave the Eagles a 38–33 lead in a game they ended up winning by a score of 41–33.

Notable Achievements

- Has surpassed 70 receptions four times, topping 100 catches once (116 in 2018).

- Has surpassed 800 receiving yards four times, topping 1,000 yards once (1,163 in 2018).
- Has made eight touchdown receptions twice.
- Has led Eagles in receptions and receiving yards three times each.
- Holds NFL single-season record for most receptions by a tight end (116 in 2018).
- Holds Eagles single-game record for most receptions (15 vs. Washington on December 20, 2014).
- Holds Eagles single-season record for most receptions (116 in 2018).
- Ranks among Eagles career leaders in: pass receptions (3rd); pass receiving yardage (9th); and touchdown receptions (tied-13th).
- Two-time division champion (2013 and 2017).
- 2017 NFC champion.
- Super Bowl LII champion.
- Two-time Pro Bowl selection (2017 and 2018).

42

NORM VAN BROCKLIN

Stubborn, dictatorial, short-tempered, and abrasive are all words that could be used to describe Hall of Fame quarterback Norm Van Brocklin. "The Dutchman," as he came to be known, treated the media with disdain, argued with officials, and berated his own teammates, many of whom grew to despise him. Yet, despite his shortcomings, Van Brocklin proved to be one of the greatest leaders and finest signal-callers of his time, helping his teams win six division titles and two NFL championships over the course of his career. Already a star by the time he arrived in Philadelphia in 1958, Van Brocklin previously helped the Los Angeles Rams win five division titles and one league championship, earning in the process six trips to the Pro Bowl and two All-Pro nominations. Continuing to perform at an elite level after he arrived in the City of Brotherly Love, Van Brocklin earned three more trips to the Pro Bowl, one All-Pro selection, and NFL MVP honors in 1960, when he led the Eagles to their first league championship in more than a decade. Thus, even though he played for the Eagles for just three seasons, Van Brocklin earned a spot on this list due to the tremendous overall impact he made during his relatively brief stay in Philadelphia.

Born in Parade, South Dakota, on March 15, 1926, Norman Mack Van Brocklin moved with his parents and eight siblings at an early age to Northern California, where he grew up in Walnut Creek, just east of Oakland. After starring at quarterback for two years at Acalanes High School in nearby Lafayette, Van Brocklin chose to forgo his senior year of high school and enlist in the US Navy, where he spent the next three years serving his country during World War II. Enrolling at the University of Oregon in Eugene following his discharge from the military in 1946, Van Brocklin spent two years starting at quarterback for the Ducks, leading them to an overall record of 16-5 during that time. Particularly effective as a junior in 1948, Van Brocklin earned All-America honors and finished sixth in the Heisman Trophy voting.

Permitted to leave college after only three years due to his time spent in the Navy during World War II, Van Brocklin subsequently declared himself eligible for the 1949 NFL Draft, where the Los Angeles Rams selected him in the fourth round, with the 37th overall pick. He then spent his first few seasons in Los Angeles being platooned with fellow Hall of Fame quarterback Bob Waterfield, annually ranking among the league leaders in passing yards, touchdown passes, and passer rating despite his somewhat limited playing time. Performing particularly well for the Rams in 1950, Van Brocklin earned Pro Bowl honors for the first of six straight times by throwing for 2,061 yards, finishing second in the league with 18 TD passes and a 54.5 pass completion percentage, and topping the circuit with an 85.1 passer rating. The following year, Van Brocklin turned in one of the greatest single-game performances in league history in the regular-season opener, when he led the championship-bound Rams to a 54–14 victory over the New York Yanks by passing for five touchdowns and a still-NFL record 554 yards.

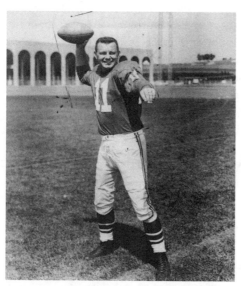

Norm Van Brocklin led the Eagles to the NFL title in 1960.
Courtesy of MEARSOnlineAuctions.com

With Waterfield retiring following the conclusion of the 1952 campaign, Van Brocklin took over behind center full-time for the next five seasons, during which time he led the Rams to one more division title and earned three more trips to the Pro Bowl. But, while still at the top of his game, "The Dutchman" surprised everyone by announcing his retirement at only 31 years of age in January 1958, with his tempestuous relationship with Rams head coach Sid Gillman greatly influencing his decision. However, Van Brocklin chose to unretire less than five months later, after which he requested a trade to "anywhere but Pittsburgh or Philadelphia." Failing to heed the disgruntled quarterback's wishes, the Rams subsequently dealt him to the Eagles for two players (offensive lineman Buck Lansford and defensive end Jimmy Harris) and a first-round draft pick. Displaying his dissatisfaction with the move, Van Brocklin initially threatened to remain retired, before changing his mind after, according to him, Eagles ownership promised to name him the successor to Buck Shaw when the latter eventually stepped down as head coach.

Given total control of the offense upon his arrival in Philadelphia, Van Brocklin, a classic pocket-passer with a strong, accurate arm and a quick release, gradually turned the Eagles' stagnant attack into one of the league's best. Although "The Dutchman" posted solid numbers in 1958, earning Pro Bowl honors for the first of three straight times by finishing among the league leaders with 2,409 yards passing and 15 TD passes, the Eagles continued to struggle with him behind center, winning just two games and finishing toward the bottom of the league rankings in points scored and yards gained. However, with Van Brocklin ranking among the league leaders with 2,617 yards passing, 16 touchdown passes, a 56.2 completion percentage, and a 79.5 passer rating the following year, the Eagles finished 7-5 and scored the fourth-most points in the NFL.

Building upon their strong showing the previous season, the Eagles came together as a team in 1960, compiling a regular-season record of 10-2, before laying claim to the league championship with a 17–13 victory over the Green Bay Packers in the NFL title game. While several players contributed significantly to Philadelphia's successful title run, no one made as big an impact as Van Brocklin, who earned Bert Bell NFL Player of the Year and league MVP honors with his outstanding play and superb leadership. In addition to finishing second among NFL quarterbacks with 2,471 passing yards, 24 touchdown passes, and a passer rating of 86.5, Van Brocklin instilled confidence in his teammates, whom he pushed to the very limit of their abilities.

In discussing Van Brocklin's influence on the rest of the team, defensive tackle Eddie Khayat stated, "One thing people fail to see is that a quarterback has to be the toughest guy on the team. He doesn't need to be a fighter, like a Bednarik or J.D. Smith, with fisticuffs. But he has to be tough. Dutch was so smart and so tough, and he brought out the best in everybody. He taught everybody how to win. He was a great leader, the first one to practice every day."

Receiver Pete Retzlaff added, "He had authority. When Buck Shaw gave us something new to use, he'd turn to Van Brocklin and say, 'That okay with you, Dutch?' When that happened, the message came through about who the authority was on the team."

Revealing the level of responsibility that Shaw placed on Van Brocklin's shoulders, linebacker Maxie Baughan, in his first NFL season at the time, recalled, "Van Brocklin was like a coach. He ran the practices, not Buck. . . . Practice would end when Dutch said so. He'd yell out, 'OK, that's it.' Buck was fine with it, and so were the other players. It was an unusual setup. It was different than anything I saw in college playing for (coach) Bobby Dodd, but it worked because of the chemistry of that team. There was a closeness among those players that was unique."

Acknowledging the degree to which Van Brocklin impacted the fortunes of the Eagles that year, New York Giants linebacker Sam Huff said that, without him, they "would have been lucky to break even."

Aside from all the other contributions Van Brocklin made to the Eagles over the course of the campaign, the 34-year-old quarterback helped develop the pass-receiving skills of Pete Retzlaff and Tommy McDonald, both of whom emerged as stars under his guidance. Van Brocklin, who spent most of his career serving as his team's punter, also did an outstanding job in fulfilling that role for the Eagles, averaging more than 41 yards per punt in each of his three seasons in Philadelphia, including an average of 43.1 yards in 1960 that ranked as the fifth-best in the league.

Yet, even though Van Brocklin inspired a resurgence in Philadelphia with his outstanding play and exceptional leadership, he proved to be a polarizing figure to everyone he encountered. While some of his teammates loved him, others found his abrasive personality, volatile disposition, and short temper intolerable. Van Brocklin's gruff demeanor also made him unpopular with the members of the media, whom he treated contemptuously. But even those who hated him greatly appreciated his ability, which allowed him to be a strong leader. And, despite his infamous foul temper, Van Brocklin could be incredibly gentle and generous toward others when he chose to be. Especially fond of children, Van Brocklin raised money for the widow of a local sportswriter during his

Van Brocklin earned league MVP honors during the championship campaign of 1960.
Courtesy of Richard Albersheim of Albersheims .com

time in Philadelphia, and he also became a surrogate father for the children of Eagles trainer Tim Dowd after the latter passed away in 1959.

Feeling that he had nothing left to give to the game as a player, Van Brocklin announced his retirement after the Eagles won the NFL championship, saying he "never wanted to see his damn jersey again." Over 12 seasons, he passed for 23,611 yards and 173 touchdowns, threw 178 interceptions, completed 53.6 percent of his passes, posted a quarterback rating of 75.1, and compiled a record of 61-36-4 as a starter. During his time in Philadelphia, Van Brocklin threw for 7,497 yards, tossed 55 TD passes and 51 interceptions, completed 54.3 percent of his passes, posted a quarterback rating of 75.7, and led the Eagles to an overall record of 19-16-1.

Expecting to be named new Eagles head coach when Buck Shaw also retired shortly thereafter, Van Brocklin became livid when the team instead gave the job to Shaw's assistant, Nick Skorich. Leaving Philadelphia acrimoniously, Van Brocklin subsequently spent most of the next 14 years coaching a pair of expansion teams to losing records. After becoming the Minnesota Vikings' first head coach in 1961, Van Brocklin piloted them to an overall mark of 29-51-4 over the course of the next six seasons, before being relieved of his duties following the conclusion of the 1966 campaign. He then directed the Atlanta Falcons to a record of 37-49-3 from 1968 to 1974, before being fired during his seventh season as head coach. Unable to inspire the men who played under him, Van Brocklin found himself being hated by virtually all his players, who came to view him as a tyrant and a bully.

Following his stint in Atlanta, Van Brocklin briefly served as an assistant coach at Georgia Tech and as a college football analyst on "Superstation" WTBS in Atlanta, before health problems forced him to retire to private life. A heavy cigarette smoker, Van Brocklin suffered from numerous health issues in his later years, including a brain tumor, which doctors successfully removed. Displaying his contempt for the media following the operation, Van Brocklin told reporters, "It was a brain transplant. They gave me a sportswriter's brain to make sure I got one that hadn't been used." Van Brocklin lived just a short time longer, dying of complications from a stroke at the age of 57, on May 2, 1983, just five weeks after former teammate Bob Waterfield passed away.

In discussing Van Brocklin's legacy, Chuck Bednarik stated, "I'd put him in the Triple-A category as one of the best quarterbacks who ever lived. Van Brocklin, Bobby Layne, Y.A. Tittle, Otto Graham, and Johnny Unitas—they're Triple-A."

Expressing similar sentiments, Tommy McDonald said, "I'd put him in the class with Unitas. But Unitas had Alan Ameche and Lenny Moore to run. Everybody knew we were going to pass. But, could they stop him? Oh, no. We knew we were never out of a game as long as we had Dutch. He always came up with the big play."

EAGLES CAREER HIGHLIGHTS

Best Season

Although Van Brocklin performed well in each of his three seasons in Philadelphia, he clearly played his best ball as a member of the Eagles in 1960. En route to leading them to the NFL title, "The Dutchman" finished second in the league in passing yards (2,471), touchdown passes (24), and passer rating (86.5), earning in the process First-Team All-Pro and NFL MVP honors. Furthermore, Van Brocklin led all NFL quarterbacks with five fourth-quarter comebacks and four game-winning drives, with longtime Philadelphia sports columnist Larry Merchant writing, "If ever a single player lifted a team that was average into winning a championship, it was him, and he did it by the sheer force of his personality, his will, and his skill."

Memorable Moments/Greatest Performances

Van Brocklin led the Eagles to a convincing 49–21 victory over the Chicago Cardinals on November 16, 1958, by completing 19 of 29 pass attempts, for 318 yards and two touchdowns, with one of those being a 33-yard connection with Clarence Peaks and the other a 47-yard hookup with Tommy McDonald.

On October 25, 1959, Van Brocklin gave an indication of what lay ahead in 1960 by leading the Eagles on a furious second-half comeback that saw them score 28 unanswered points, to defeat the Cardinals by a score of 28–24. Van Brocklin, who completed the comeback with a 22-yard touchdown pass to Tommy McDonald late in the fourth quarter, finished the game with 254 yards passing and two TDs.

The combination of Van Brocklin and McDonald proved to be too much for Washington to overcome on December 6, 1959, with "The Dutchman" tossing three touchdown passes to the diminutive receiver during a 38–14 victory over the Redskins. Van Brocklin finished the game with 275 yards through the air and those three TD passes.

Van Brocklin delivered his first fourth-quarter comeback win to the fans of Philadelphia in 1960 when he gave the Eagles a 31–27 victory over the St. Louis Cardinals on October 9 by hitting Tommy McDonald with an 11-yard scoring strike late in the final period. He finished the contest with 17 completions on only 23 attempts, for 199 yards and three touchdowns.

Van Brocklin continued his late-game magic two weeks later, bringing the Eagles back from a 22–7 third-quarter deficit to defeat the Browns by a score of 31–29 on October 23, 1960. He finished the game with 292 yards passing and three TD passes, connecting with Billy Ray Barnes from 8 yards out, hooking up with Bobby Walston on a 49-yard scoring play, and hitting Tommy McDonald with a 57-yard touchdown pass.

Van Brocklin led the Eagles to a lopsided 34–7 victory over the Steelers on November 6, 1960, by throwing for 295 yards and three touchdowns, all of which went to Tommy McDonald.

Notable Achievements

- Passed for more than 2,400 yards three times.
- Threw more than 20 touchdown passes once (24 in 1960).
- Led NFL quarterbacks in: pass completions once; fourth-quarter comebacks once; and game-winning drives twice.
- Finished second among NFL quarterbacks in: pass completions twice; passing yards twice; touchdown passes once; and passer rating once.
- 1960 Eastern Division champion.
- 1960 NFL champion.
- 1960 NFL Most Valuable Player.
- 1960 Bert Bell Award winner as NFL Player of the Year.
- Three-time Pro Bowl selection (1958, 1959, and 1960).
- 1960 First-Team All-Pro selection.
- 1960 First-Team All-Conference selection.
- NFL 1950s All-Decade Team.
- Pro Football Reference All-1950s First Team.
- Inducted into Philadelphia Eagles Hall of Fame in 1987.
- Number 83 on the NFL Network's 2010 list of the NFL's 100 Greatest Players.
- Elected to Pro Football Hall of Fame in 1971.

43

— JERRY SISEMORE —

An anchor on the right side of the Eagles' offensive line for 11 seasons, Jerry Sisemore spent his entire NFL career in Philadelphia, making a positive impact on the team both on and off the playing field during that time with his outstanding play and quiet leadership. A model of consistency, Sisemore missed just one game his first nine years in the league, at one point starting 127 consecutive contests. A member of Eagle teams that made four playoff appearances and captured one NFC championship, Sisemore earned two trips to the Pro Bowl and two All-Conference selections, with his consistently excellent play also gaining him induction into the Eagles Hall of Fame following the conclusion of his playing career.

Born in Olton, Texas, on July 16, 1951, Jerald Grant Sisemore attended Plainview High School, where he performed well enough on the gridiron to earn a scholarship to the University of Texas. After helping the Longhorns extend their unbeaten streak to 31 games as a sophomore in 1970, Sisemore blossomed into one of the nation's top offensive linemen the following year, earning All-Conference and All-America honors for the first of two straight times.

Sisemore subsequently experienced great surprise when he received an early morning telephone call informing him that the Eagles planned to make him the third overall pick of the 1973 NFL Draft, recalling years later, "I thought it was a joke. I hung up and they called right back and said, 'You've got 15 minutes. We're fixing to draft you with the No. 3 pick. Do you want to go to Philadelphia?' I said, 'Yeah!' So, they said, 'Okay, stand by.' And about five minutes later it was over with."

Sisemore continued, "It was a tremendous blessing. I was excited about going to Philly. I didn't know much about the city, but I knew (fellow Texas alumnus and Eagles safety Bill) Bradley was there. And that the new head coach was Mike McCormack and the new offensive line coach was John Sandusky. The fact that they wanted me in the first round with their first pick was exciting. So, I was all over it."

Jerry Sisemore started 127 consecutive games for the Eagles.
Courtesy of SportsMemorabilia.com

Although Sisemore established himself as the starting right tackle almost as soon as he arrived in Philadelphia, he remained somewhat starstruck for much of his first season, particularly since he found himself blocking for Roman Gabriel, the recently acquired veteran quarterback whom he had spent much of his youth watching on television. Reflecting back on his feelings at the time, Sisemore said, "It's like, here it is. And, man, he's really a great guy. Calm, collected, been there, done all of that. He didn't care about stats or anything. He just wanted the team to go together. We were all fresh, brand-new, and welcome to Philadelphia. . . . And then, you line up on the same field with Bob Lilly and Deacon Jones, Carl Eller and Claude Humphrey, I mean, it's just like, 'Wow, I'm here. I better get my mind right or I could be gone.'"

Acquitting himself extremely well at right tackle his first three years in the league, Sisemore started all but one game during that time, with his outstanding play making him one of the few bright spots on Eagle teams that compiled an overall record of just 16-25-1. Moved to right guard after

Dick Vermeil assumed head coaching duties in 1976, Sisemore continued to perform well at that post for the next two seasons, before returning to his more natural position in 1978. In addressing the change in positions, Sisemore recalled, "The thought was that we needed a guard, and there was a guy that they'd got from Baltimore, Ed George, and that he probably could play right tackle. So, Coach Vermeil moved me. There were so many places that we needed to improve, but at least we got a Band-Aid over that one."

With the Eagles continuing to struggle during Vermeil's first two years in charge, Sisemore recollected, "There were times when I don't know if there would be many people left at the game, but I do know the Philly fans had surrounded the Eagles' entrance and exit from the field, and man, they were cussing and fussing and booing. They were not happy." However, Vermeil eventually helped turn things around in Philadelphia, with the Eagles making the playoffs four straight times from 1978 to 1981, a period during which Sisemore earned Pro Bowl and Second-Team All-NFC honors twice each.

One of the league's most consistent players, Sisemore regularly graded higher than any other Eagles lineman when the team's coaches reviewed game films, with Vermeil once claiming that he did not allow a sack for two full seasons. A superb technician, Sisemore, who stood 6'4" and weighed 265 pounds, typically established inside position against the league's bigger defensive ends, whom he then controlled with his arms and shoulders. In speaking of his protégé, Jerry Wampfler, who served as Sisemore's line coach in Philadelphia for five years, said, "He was the best technician I ever had. He was the best technically sound player I ever coached. Jerry was tough. But his toughness was not a demonstrative toughness. He never cheap-shotted anybody. When somebody put a little cheap-shot on him, he wouldn't say a word. But he had a calculating mind. He'd wait and then kick the shit out of the guy."

Called "the best blocker I've ever seen" by Eagles tight end Keith Krepfle, Sisemore also made a strong impression on Oakland Raiders defensive end John Matuszak, who played with him in the 1973 College All-Star Game. In speaking of Sisemore, Matuszak said, "The first time I ever saw Jerry, I was watching film of a Texas-Miami game. There was a 70-yard run and Sisemore was right downfield next to the guy carrying the ball. That's why he's the kind of player I like, because he never gives up."

Yet, as well as he performed on the field, Sisemore received just two Pro Bowl nominations since his reluctance to speak to the press garnered him little publicity. In explaining his reticence to address the media, Sisemore told Stan Hochman of the *Philadelphia Daily News* in 1980, "I just feel nothing can be gained from opening your mouth in my position. Sometimes the other team will use the stories against you. . . . But, mostly, I've never seen where publicity would help a situation. Not even at contract time. I honestly believe you get paid strictly on your performance."

And, as for his lack of Pro Bowl selections, Sisemore said, "I don't care about the Pro Bowl or individual awards. If my teammates think I did a good job, that gives me all the satisfaction I need. If the coaches approved of my work,

Sisemore earned Pro Bowl and All-Conference honors twice each.
Courtesy of SportsMemorabilia.com

I'll probably keep my job and get paid. And, if we win, I'm a happy man."

Meanwhile, even though Sisemore said very little, he proved to be a solid leader and positive influence on his teammates in the locker room, with fellow offensive lineman Stan Walters crediting him with helping to ease his transition to Philadelphia after the Eagles acquired him from Cincinnati in 1975. Recalling his earliest days in Philadelphia, Walters revealed:

> I had a hard time when I got there. I actually went into a form of depression. It took me a long time to get over the trade. I walked out of training camp my first year. I went home to New York. It wasn't just that I didn't like Philadelphia. I was just still very upset about the trade. . . . Keep in mind, I had made the playoffs twice in three years with the Bengals.
>
> There were guys on the Eagles at that time I don't know if they cared about winning at all. It was a bad situation. Sisemore and Bill Lueck took me aside, I started hanging out with them, and it made it a little better. Then Lueck got traded the next year and it was just me and Sise. We started rooming together and we got closer. Sise was very quiet, but, every once in a while, he would come out with a crazy statement that would have me rolling

and laughing. He was a stabilizing force for me. He really was. . . . He was the rock that kept me under control, especially in those early years.

In discussing the bond that developed between the two men, longtime Eagles broadcaster Merrill Reese stated, "They were totally opposite kind of guys. Stan was outgoing, funny . . . Jerry was quiet, reserved. He didn't really say a lot. But, together, they formed a great pair of tackles."

Sisemore continued to perform at a high level for the Eagles until 1984, when he lost his starting job to Leonard Mitchell, prompting him to announce his retirement at season's end. Over the course of 12 NFL seasons, Sisemore appeared in 156 games, which represents the sixth-highest total in franchise history.

Following his playing days, Sisemore returned to Texas, where he became a real estate salesman and spent several years serving on the Lago Vista ISD School Board, before retiring to private life. Inducted into the Eagles Hall of Fame in 1991, Sisemore expressed his appreciation for that honor by saying, "That's the highest honor that the organization can place on a player, to single a player out. But the real blessing was that Stan Walters and I went in together."

CAREER HIGHLIGHTS

Best Season

Sisemore earned Pro Bowl and All-Conference honors for the only two times in his career in 1979 and 1981. Since the Eagles scored more points, gained more yards on the ground, and averaged more yards per carry in 1981, we'll identify that as his finest season.

Memorable Moments/Greatest Performances

Sisemore helped lead the way for Eagles running backs to gain a season-high 270 yards on the ground during a 27–10 victory over the Seattle Seahawks in the final game of the 1976 campaign, with Tom Sullivan and Mike Hogan rushing for 121 and 104 yards, respectively.

Sisemore's excellent blocking helped the Eagles rush for 229 yards during a 21–10 win over the Packers on November 25, 1979, with Leroy Harris gaining 137 yards on only nine carries.

Notable Achievements

- Missed just one game first nine seasons, starting 127 consecutive games at one point.
- Ranks among Eagles all-time leaders with 12 seasons played (5th) and 156 games played (6th).
- 1980 division champion.
- 1980 NFC champion.
- Two-time Pro Bowl selection (1979 and 1981).
- Two-time Second-Team All-Conference selection (1979 and 1981).
- Inducted into Philadelphia Eagles Hall of Fame in 1991.

44

— BRENT CELEK —

Extremely consistent and reliable, Brent Celek proved to be one of the Eagles' steadiest players for the better part of a decade. Spending his entire 11-year NFL career in Philadelphia, Celek started at tight end for the Eagles for seven seasons, ending his time in Philly with the fifth-most pass receptions and eighth-most receiving yards in franchise history. Recording more than 50 receptions three times and 800 receiving yards twice, Celek helped lead the Eagles to five playoff appearances, three division titles, and one NFL championship, all the while displaying a level of professionalism that prompted the organization to hold him up as an example of what it wanted its players and team to represent.

Born in Cincinnati, Ohio, on January 25, 1985, Brent Steven Celek attended La Salle High School, where he starred in football, earning First-Team All-District honors in both his junior and senior years. An excellent all-around athlete, Celek also lettered in track and field at La Salle, spending his final two seasons there competing in the shotput and discus throw. Choosing to remain close to home following his graduation, Celek accepted a scholarship from the University of Cincinnati, where he continued to excel on the gridiron, earning team MVP and Second-Team All–Big East Conference honors as a senior.

Although Celek did not receive an invitation to the 2007 NFL Scouting Combine, the Eagles made him the 162nd overall pick of that year's draft when they selected him in the fifth round. Celek subsequently spent his first two seasons in Philadelphia sharing playing time with veteran tight end L. J. Smith, recording 43 receptions, 496 receiving yards, and two touchdowns, before laying claim to the starting job when Smith signed with the Baltimore Ravens as a free agent at the end of 2008.

Developing tremendous chemistry with quarterback Donovan McNabb his first year as a full-time starter, Celek recorded 76 receptions, 971 receiving yards, and eight TD catches in 2009, with his outstanding play helping the Eagles compile a record of 11-5 that earned them a wild card playoff berth. Although Celek never again posted such lofty numbers after Philadelphia traded away McNabb following the conclusion of the campaign, he remained a favorite target of Eagle quarterbacks for several more years, amassing more than 500 receiving yards in each of the next four seasons, while also surpassing 40 receptions three times. Having one of his finest seasons in 2011, Celek finished second on the team with 62 receptions, accumulated 811 receiving yards, and tied for the team lead with five TD catches.

Brent Celek spent his entire 11-year NFL career in Philadelphia.
Courtesy of Keith Lovett

An integral part of Philadelphia's passing attack throughout the period, Celek served as a security blanket to Eagle quarterbacks, who knew they could count on him to find an open spot in the defense in third-down situations. Blessed with sure hands, the 6'4", 261-pound Celek also possessed surprising athletic ability for a man his size, often using his speed and agility to separate himself from opposing defenders. And, once he gained possession of the football, Celek used everything at his disposal to break away from would-be tacklers, giving defenders the forearm, the high knee kick, or anything else he could think of. In discussing his running style, Celek said, "When I have the ball, I try to be like Jerome Bettis. The first guy never took him down. He was a beast." An exceptional blocker as well, Celek made significant contributions in the running game, establishing himself in the process as one of the NFL's better all-around tight ends. One of the league's most durable players, Celek also missed just one game his entire career, sitting out one contest in 2012 with a concussion.

Going about his job in an extremely understated manner, Celek never drew attention to himself, with his consistently strong play and workmanlike approach to his craft making him a fan favorite in Philadelphia. Meanwhile, his toughness, humility, and willingness to embrace the city only added to his popularity, allowing him to eventually become one of the most beloved players in franchise history.

Although Celek began to share playing time with rookie tight end Zach Ertz in 2013, he remained the starter at that position until 2016, when he assumed a backup role. Celek spent two more years in Philadelphia, before being released by the Eagles on March 13, 2018, a little over one month after they defeated the New England Patriots in Super Bowl LII. Upon announcing that they had decided to part ways with Celek, the Eagles released a statement that read:

> Brent Celek defines what it means to be a Philadelphia Eagle. His dedication to his profession and this organization is unmatched, and he will go down as one of the best tight ends in franchise history. Brent embodied the City of Philadelphia's temperament and character with his toughness and grit. He has been a huge part of everything we have been building over the last decade, and it is only fitting that he was able to help us win our first Super Bowl last season. Unfortunately, in this business we are forced to make difficult decisions, especially this time of the year. This one is as tough as they come, but, in our eyes, Brent will always be an Eagle.

Two days later, Celek, who ended his time in Philadelphia with 398 receptions, 4,998 receiving yards, and 31 touchdown catches, told TMZ Sports, "One day, I'll be back with the Eagles in some capacity; when—who knows? But I love that organization . . . I owe it to them."

After briefly considering playing for another team, Celek officially announced his retirement on August 31, 2018, writing on the Eagles' website:

> It has been an amazing journey—a journey that is now coming to an end. It's a big decision, but it's not a tough one. Though I know I'm still capable of playing football at a high level, and, though I had offers to continue my NFL career, my heart told me that this was the time. . . . The bottom line was this: When I thought long and hard about the prospect of putting on another uniform, it just seemed wrong. In the end, I couldn't do it. My career began and ended with the Philadelphia Eagles—and, man, did we go out in style.

Celek helped lead the Eagles to three division titles and one NFL championship.
Courtesy of Keith Allison

Following Celek's announcement, Eagles chairman and CEO Jeffrey
Lurie released a statement that read:

> Brent Celek embodies everything it means to be a Phila-
> delphia Eagle. He will obviously be remembered as one of
> the most accomplished tight ends in Eagles history, but his
> impact on our franchise goes far beyond the statistics he

compiled over the course of his career. Brent was one of the toughest, smartest, and most selfless players who has ever stepped on the field for us. He led by example, not just in the way he played the game, but, also, in how he prepared and the way he carried himself around the building and in the community. He was genuine, honest and accountable, and he always represented the organization with class. He gave everything he had to the team. No matter what he was asked to do, Brent always embraced his role in a way that set a wonderful example for his teammates and young athletes everywhere. It was a pleasure watching him grow into the player and man that he became. There is nobody more deserving to finish his career as a Super Bowl Champion. We are excited for him and his family as they embark on the next stage of their lives. Our doors are always open to Brent, and he will be an Eagle forever.

CAREER HIGHLIGHTS

Best Season

Celek had easily his most productive season in 2009, when he led the Eagles with 76 receptions and finished second on the team with 971 receiving yards and eight TD catches.

Memorable Moments/Greatest Performances

Celek scored the first touchdown of his career when he caught a short pass from Donovan McNabb during a 19–7 win over the Buffalo Bills in the final game of the 2007 regular season, finishing the contest with three catches for 18 yards.

Celek went over 100 receiving yards for the first time in his career when he made six receptions for 131 yards during a 26–7 victory over the Seattle Seahawks on November 2, 2008.

Although the Eagles lost the 2008 NFC title game to Arizona by a score of 32–25, Celek had a big day, catching 10 passes for 83 yards and two TDs, the longest of which covered 31 yards.

Celek contributed to a 30–27 victory over Denver on December 27, 2009, by making four receptions for 121 yards and one TD, which came on a 47-yard hookup with Donovan McNabb.

Celek performed well during a 45–19 rout of the New York Jets on December 18, 2011, making five catches for 156 yards and one touchdown, which covered 26 yards. Meanwhile, the 73-yard catch-and-run that Celek recorded during the contest represented the longest play of his career.

Celek had a huge game against Baltimore on September 16, 2012, making eight receptions for a career-high 157 yards during a 24–23 win over the Ravens.

Celek turned in another outstanding effort on November 10, 2014, making five catches for 116 yards during a 45–21 Monday night victory over the Carolina Panthers.

Celek topped 100 receiving yards for the final time in his career on November 15, 2015, when he made four receptions for 134 yards during a 20–19 loss to the Miami Dolphins.

Notable Achievements

- Surpassed 50 receptions three times, making career-high 76 catches in 2009.
- Surpassed 800 receiving yards twice, amassing 971 yards through the air in 2009.
- Made eight touchdown receptions in 2009.
- Led Eagles with 76 receptions in 2009.
- Missed just one game in 11 seasons with Eagles.
- Ranks among Eagles career leaders with: 398 receptions (5th); 4,998 receiving yards (8th); 31 touchdown receptions (tied-11th); and 175 games played (4th).
- Three-time division champion (2010, 2013, and 2017).
- 2017 NFC champion.
- Super Bowl LII champion.

45

— CARSON WENTZ —

One of the NFL's best young quarterbacks, Carson Wentz has excelled for the Eagles behind center ever since he arrived in Philadelphia in 2016. Named the winner of the Bert Bell Award as NFL Player of the Year in just his second season, Wentz led the Eagles to the NFC East title and an eventual berth in Super Bowl LII, establishing in the process a single-season franchise record for most touchdown passes thrown. And, despite being plagued by injuries in two of his three years in the league, Wentz has displayed all the inherent qualities of any franchise quarterback, drawing praise from teammates and opponents alike for his strong arm, good mobility, outstanding pocket presence, and superior leadership skills.

Born in Raleigh, North Carolina, on December 30, 1992, Carson James Wentz moved with his family to Bismarck, North Dakota, at the age of three. An excellent all-around athlete, Wentz played baseball, basketball, and football while attending Bismarck Century High School, starring on the gridiron at quarterback and defensive back. Experiencing a growth spurt while in high school, Wentz grew from 5'8" as a freshman to his current height of 6'5" by the time he graduated in 2011.

Continuing his football career at North Dakota State University, Wentz became the school's starting quarterback in his junior year, leading the Bison to a record of 15-1 and the third of their five straight NCAA Division I FCS National Championships by throwing for 3,111 yards and completing 25 touchdown passes. Although a wrist injury sidelined Wentz for eight games the following year, he returned to the lineup in time to lead North Dakota State to a 37–10 victory over Jacksonville State in the FCS National Championship Game, solidifying his place as one of the top prospects heading into the 2016 NFL Draft.

In desperate need of a franchise quarterback, the Eagles elected to trade three top-100 picks in 2016, a first-round pick in 2017, and a second-round pick in 2018 for the second overall pick of the 2016 Draft, which they subsequently used to select Wentz. Extolling the virtues of Wentz following his sel ection by the Eagles, former NFL Network analyst and current Oakland Raiders general manager Mike Mayock gushed, "He's got everything you want in a franchise quarterback physically, but what has really sold me is the kid himself. He'll be the first guy in every morning and the last guy to leave. He'll be a great teammate. I think the City of Philadelphia will like him because he's a blue-collar kid."

Fellow NFL Network analyst Daniel Jeremiah added, "He can expand the playbook because of what he can do with his arm, as well as being able to move around a little

Carson Wentz earned NFL Player of the Year honors in just his second NFL season. Courtesy of Keith Allison

bit. The toughness, the clutch moments—when there were big plays to be made, he made them. I think he fits in great with Coach Pederson."

New Eagles head coach Doug Pederson agreed, saying, "This kid is determined. He's eager. He studies his craft, and he hones his craft. He's an exciting guy. He's a perfect fit for what we're going to do, and his demeanor fits everything about the Philadelphia Eagles."

Meanwhile, Wentz eagerly anticipated his arrival in Philadelphia, stating, "They're passionate here. They hate losing. I'm like, 'Heck, I fit right in.' I hate losing. I'm real passionate about the game, as well. I think that's the general consensus that I keep getting from this Philadelphia area."

After making an extremely favorable impression on Philadelphia's coaching staff during training camp, Wentz laid claim to the starting quarterback job when the Eagles traded Sam Bradford to the Minnesota Vikings on September 3, 2016. Wentz subsequently went on to start all 16 games behind center, posting solid numbers for an Eagles team that finished the regular season with a record of 7-9. In addition to throwing for 3,782 yards his first year in the league, Wentz tossed 16 touchdown passes and 14 interceptions, completed 62.4 percent of his passes, compiled a passer rating of 79.3, ran for 150 yards and two touchdowns, and set single-season franchise records for most pass attempts (607) and pass completions (379).

Emerging as one of the league's top quarterbacks the following year, Wentz led the Eagles to a record of 11-2 over the first 13 weeks of the 2017 campaign, before tearing the ACL in his left knee during a 43–35 victory over the Los Angeles Rams in Week 14, thereby bringing his season to a premature end. Prior to that, though, Wentz established himself as a viable MVP candidate by passing for 3,296 yards, throwing 33 touchdown passes and only seven interceptions, rushing for 299 yards, compiling a passer rating of 101.9, and leading the league with a QBR of 77.2. Although Wentz ended up finishing third to Tom Brady and Todd Gurley II in the NFL MVP voting, Eagles wide receiver Torrey Smith proclaimed his teammate to be his personal MVP, stating on Twitter: "Carson was able to make plays athletically that Tom (Brady) can't physically do, even though he's the greatest quarterback ever . . . when he's scrambling, the crazy plays he's made . . . it was huge for us."

Arizona defensive backs Tyrann Mathieu and Patrick Peterson also had high praise for Wentz after the Eagles' QB passed for 304 yards and four

Wentz's 33 touchdown passes in 2017 established a new single-season franchise record.
Courtesy of Keith Allison

touchdowns during a 34–7 win over the Cardinals in Week 5, with Mathieu saying, "Obviously, he's one of those emerging superstar quarterbacks. He finds so many different ways to extend series or extend plays for their offense. He's very smart at the line of scrimmage."

Meanwhile, Peterson told *NJ Advance Media,* "He's very mobile and athletic. He has great pocket presence and does a good job of putting his guys in position. He managed the game today very well. He's a soon-to-be top-tier quarterback as he continues to grow. . . . We sent pressure at him a couple of times, and he was able to escape a little bit, especially in the second half. . . . He's a guy that has great pocket presence, and he understands where the pressure and blitzes are coming from. He knows where the outlets are, and he moved very well."

Having undergone successful surgery on his ACL on December 13, 2017, Wentz could only watch as Nick Foles led the Eagles on a successful playoff run that culminated with a 41–33 victory over the New England Patriots in Super Bowl LII. Yet, despite Foles's heroics, Wentz reclaimed his starting job when he returned to the Eagles in 2018, with center Jason Kelce showing his support for his teammate when he told Bruce Murray and Brady Quinn on the *SiriusXM Blitz*:

> Carson, he's a special player, man. I haven't been through an ACL rehab myself, I can't imagine what he went through. I think, obviously, he's happy for everybody with last year winning the Super Bowl, happy that we were able to get that done. But having to sit on the sidelines for that . . . a guy that's as competitive as he is, and then obviously having the grueling rehab to go through every single day trying to get back, trying to hit certain checkpoints to make sure that you're ready to go, I was really, really happy for him to be back out on that field. . . . He's such a hard worker, he's such a dynamic personality that has been felt the moment he was drafted to Philadelphia.

After missing the first two games of the 2018 campaign, Wentz returned to action in Week 3, amassing 3,074 passing yards, throwing 21 touchdown passes and seven interceptions, completing 69.6 percent of his passes, and compiling a passer rating of 102.2, before fracturing the vertebrae in his back during a 29–23 overtime loss to the Dallas Cowboys on December 9. Forced to sit out the remainder of the season, Wentz once again watched as Foles performed well down the stretch, leading the Eagles to wins in their final three regular-season games and a victory over Chicago in the opening round of the playoffs, before finally tasting defeat at the hands of the New Orleans Saints in the divisional round of the postseason tournament.

Expected to assume the role of starting quarterback in Philadelphia once again in 2019, Wentz will enter his fourth year in the league with career totals of 10,152 yards passing, 70 touchdown passes and only 28 interceptions, a pass-completion percentage of 63.7, a passer rating of 92.5, and many fine seasons presumably still ahead of him.

CAREER HIGHLIGHTS

Best Season

Although Wentz threw for a career-high 3,782 yards as a rookie in 2016 and completed a career-best 69.6 percent of his passes in 2018, he had his finest all-around season in 2017, when his exceptional play gained him recognition as the NFL Player of the Year. En route to leading the Eagles to a record of 11-2 in his 13 starts behind center, Wentz passed for 3,296 yards, threw 33 touchdown passes and only seven interceptions, and led all NFL signal-callers with a total quarterback rating of 77.2.

Memorable Moments/Greatest Performances

Wentz excelled in his first game as a pro, leading the Eagles to a 29–10 victory over the Cleveland Browns in the 2016 regular-season opener by completing 22 of 37 pass attempts for 278 yards and two touchdowns, which came on connections of 19 yards with Jordan Matthews and 35 yards with Nelson Agholor.

Wentz earned NFC Offensive Player of the Week honors for his performance during the Eagles' 34–3 win over Pittsburgh on September 25, 2016, finishing the game 23-of-31 for 301 yards and two touchdowns, the longest of which went 73 yards to Darren Sproles.

Wentz began the 2017 campaign in style, leading the Eagles to a 30–17 victory over Washington in the regular-season opener by passing for 307 yards and two TDs, one of which went 58 yards to Nelson Agholor on Philadelphia's first offensive possession of the season.

Wentz threw for 304 yards and four touchdowns during a 34–7 win over the Cardinals on October 8, 2017, with one of his TD tosses going to Torrey Smith for 59 yards and another to Nelson Agholor for 72 yards.

Wentz earned NFC Offensive Player of the Week honors for the second time by rushing for 63 yards and passing for 268 yards and four touchdowns during a 34–24 victory over the Redskins on October 23, 2017, with his longest TD pass of the day being a 64-yard connection with Mack Hollins.

Wentz again threw four touchdown passes during a 51–23 manhandling of the Denver Broncos on November 5, 2017, with the longest of his TD tosses going 32 yards to Alshon Jeffery.

Although Wentz sustained an injury that sidelined him for the rest of the season during a 43–35 win over the Los Angeles Rams on December 10,

2017, he finished the game with 291 yards passing and four TD passes, hitting Brent Celek once, Alshon Jeffery once, and Trey Burton twice.

Wentz led the Eagles to a 34–13 rout of the New York Giants on October 11, 2018, by completing 26 of 36 pass attempts for 278 yards and three touchdowns, posting in the process a season-high passer rating of 122.2.

Wentz performed exceptionally well during a 27–20 loss to Dallas on November 11, 2018, completing 32 of 44 pass attempts for 360 yards and two touchdowns, both of which went to Zach Ertz.

Notable Achievements

- Has passed for more than 3,000 yards three times.
- Has thrown more than 30 touchdown passes once (33 in 2017).
- Has posted touchdown-to-interception ratio of better than 4–1 once.
- Has completed more than 60 percent of his passes three times.
- Has posted passer rating above 100.0 twice.
- Led NFL with total quarterback rating of 77.20 in 2017.
- Finished second in NFL with 33 touchdown passes in 2017.
- Finished third in NFL with 69.6 percent pass-completion percentage in 2018.
- Holds Eagles single-season records for most: pass attempts (607 in 2016); pass completions (379 in 2016); and touchdown passes (33 in 2017).
- 2017 division champion.
- 2017 NFC champion.
- Super Bowl LII champion.
- Two-time NFC Offensive Player of the Week.
- September 2016 NFL Offensive Rookie of the Month.
- October 2017 NFC Offensive Player of the Month.
- 2017 Bert Bell Award winner as NFL Player of the Year.
- 2017 Pro Bowl selection.
- 2017 Second-Team All-Pro selection.

46

— HUGH DOUGLAS —

An outstanding pass-rusher who had two tours of duty with the Eagles, Hugh Douglas spent six of his 10 NFL seasons in Philadelphia, recording the fifth most sacks in franchise history during that time. Compiling double-digit sack totals three times as a member of the team, Douglas led the Eagles in that category on four separate occasions, helping them capture three division titles and one NFC championship in the process. Gradually developing into a solid run-defender as well during his time in Philadelphia, Douglas earned three trips to the Pro Bowl, two All-Pro nominations, and two All-NFC selections with his strong all-around play.

Born in Mansfield, Ohio, on August 23, 1971, Hugh Lamont Douglas attended Mansfield Senior High School, where he starred on the gridiron as a two-way lineman. After accepting a scholarship offer from Central State University, a historically black college also located in Ohio, Douglas spent his freshman year at defensive end practicing against future NFL All-Pro offensive lineman Erik Williams, revealing years later, "Erik almost drove me out of football. He was a senior, getting ready for the NFL. I was a kid just out of high school. I'd never seen the game played the way Erik played it. It was like he wanted to kill me. . . . He'd pick me up and head-butt me. He'd drive-block me down the field, then put me on my back. This was every day. Finally, I couldn't take it anymore, so I left. I packed up and went home. I left like a thief in the night."

After doing some soul-searching back home in Mansfield, Douglas returned to Central State just a few days later, recalling, "It's like the saying, 'Whatever doesn't kill you makes you stronger.' That's what Erik did for me. I made up my mind I'd never allow myself to be intimidated like that again.'"

Douglas went on to record 42 sacks in three seasons of varsity play at Central State, earning in the process NAIA Division I All-America honors twice, and being named Defensive Player of the Year by The Pigskin Club of Washington, DC, after registering 15½ sacks as a senior.

Subsequently selected by the New York Jets in the first round of the 1995 NFL Draft, with the 16th overall pick, Douglas performed extremely well his first year in the league, earning NFL Defensive Rookie of the Year honors by recording a team-leading 10 sacks. He had another solid season for the Jets in 1996, registering eight sacks, forcing two fumbles, and recovering three others. However, after struggling somewhat in the 3-4 defense that new head coach Bill Parcells installed in New York the following year, Douglas found himself headed to Philadelphia when the Jets traded him to the Eagles for a pair of draft picks on March 13, 1998.

Hugh Douglas ranks fifth in franchise history in career sacks.
Courtesy of SportsMemorabilia.com

Far more comfortable in Philadelphia's 4-3 defensive scheme, Douglas had a big year for the Eagles in 1998, ranking among the league leaders with 12½ sacks. Limited by injuries to only four games the following year, Douglas recorded just two sacks for an Eagles team that finished 5-11 in Andy Reid's first year as head coach. Healthy again by the start of the 2000 campaign, Douglas earned Pro Bowl and First-Team All-Pro honors by establishing career-high marks with 15 sacks and 56 tackles. He followed that up with two more outstanding seasons, totaling 22 sacks and 97 tackles from 2001 to 2002, en route to earning two more trips to the Pro Bowl and another All-Pro selection.

After being viewed almost exclusively as a pass-rusher his first few years in the league, Douglas significantly improved his defense against the run during his time in Philadelphia. Revealing his disdain for his earlier reputation, the 6'2" Douglas, who entered the NFL at 250 pounds but gradually bulked up to 280, said, "What good are you if you're a one-dimensional player? All you ever heard was, 'Hugh Douglas, pass rusher.' I got sick of that."

Suggesting that Douglas eventually created a different image of himself in the minds of his peers, Dallas Cowboys Hall of Fame offensive lineman Larry Allen called him "the all-around package."

Douglas also drew praise from another Hall of Fame offensive lineman, Orlando Pace, who stated, "Hugh is an effort guy. He's a smaller guy, but he plays with a lot of power."

Meanwhile, Washington Redskins perennial Pro Bowl tackle Chris Samuels said of his frequent foe, "He's built so low to the ground and so strong that he gets great leverage. That's what separates him from the rest."

Choosing to sign with the Jacksonville Jaguars as a free agent following the conclusion of the 2002 campaign, Douglas spent one season in Jacksonville, before returning to Philadelphia for one final season. Cut by the Eagles after he recorded just three sacks and 15 tackles for them in a part-time role in 2004, Douglas moved into the team's front office shortly thereafter, assuming the role of "Good-Will Ambassador." Douglas ended his playing career with 80 sacks, 356 tackles, 13 forced fumbles, five fumble recoveries, one interception, and one touchdown, recording 54½ sacks, 222 tackles, six forced fumbles, and his lone interception while playing for the Eagles.

Douglas led the Eagles in sacks four times.
Courtesy of SportsMemorabilia.com

Since retiring as an active player, Douglas has been involved in a number of controversial incidents, the first of which took place on November 5, 2005, when he nearly came to blows with former teammate Terrell Owens in the Philadelphia locker room over remarks made by Owens about the organization and, specifically, Eagles quarterback Donovan McNabb. After later embarking on a career in broadcasting, Douglas joined ESPN as an NFL studio analyst. While serving in that capacity, an inebriated Douglas threatened to beat up colleague Michael Smith at the National Association of Black Journalists Convention and Career Fair held in Orlando, Florida, in August 2013. In addition to threatening Smith with bodily harm, Douglas called the *Numbers Never*

Lie co-host an "Uncle Tom" and a "House n*gger," prompting ESPN to relieve him of his duties. Some six months later, Douglas found himself being accused of assaulting his girlfriend at a Hartford, Connecticut, hotel, with court records stating that he "grabbed the victim by the neck and slammed her into the walls several times." Claiming that the incident took place during "rough sex," Douglas pleaded no contest to the charges and avoided jail time, with a prosecuting attorney stating that the case proved to be a difficult one to judge since it came down to Douglas's word against his girlfriend's.

EAGLES CAREER HIGHLIGHTS

Best Season

Douglas had the finest season of his career in 2000, earning consensus First-Team All-Pro honors by finishing fourth in the league with 15 sacks, while also recording 56 tackles (44 solo), two forced fumbles, and one interception.

Memorable Moments/Greatest Performances

Although the Eagles lost to the San Diego Chargers by a score of 13–10 on October 18, 1998, Douglas had a huge game, tying Clyde Simmons's single-game franchise record by registering 4½ sacks.

Douglas turned in another strong performance three weeks later, helping the Eagles defeat Detroit by a score of 10–9 on November 8, 1998, by recording 2½ sacks.

Douglas again registered 2½ sacks during a 6–3 loss to the Green Bay Packers and Brett Favre on September 17, 2000.

Douglas recorded the only interception of his career during a 38–10 win over the Atlanta Falcons on October 1, 2000.

Douglas helped lead the Eagles to a 21–3 victory over Tampa Bay in the 2000 NFC wild card game by getting to Buccaneers quarterback Shaun King twice.

Douglas contributed to a resounding 48–17 victory over the Minnesota Vikings on November 11, 2001, by recording 2½ of the six sacks the Eagles registered against Daunte Culpepper.

Notable Achievements

- Finished in double digits in sacks three times.
- Finished fourth in NFL in sacks twice.
- Led Eagles in sacks four times.
- Ranks fifth in Eagles history with 54½ career sacks.
- Three-time division champion (2001, 2002, and 2004).
- 2004 NFC champion.
- Three-time Pro Bowl selection (2000, 2001, and 2002).
- 2000 First-Team All-Pro selection.
- 2002 Second-Team All-Pro selection.
- Two-time First-Team All-Conference selection (2000 and 2002).

47

— JACK FERRANTE —

A sure-handed receiver who spent his entire eight-year NFL career in Philadelphia, Jack Ferrante combined with Pete Pihos to give the Eagles arguably the finest pass-receiving tandem in the league during the latter half of the 1940s. Excelling at wideout during an era in which teams typically gained most of their yardage on the ground, Ferrante nevertheless managed to surpass 30 receptions and 500 receiving yards twice each, while also recording seven touchdown receptions on two separate occasions. A key member of Philadelphia's NFL championship teams of 1948 and 1949, Ferrante earned All-Pro honors once and gained further recognition following the conclusion of his playing career by being named to the NFL 1940s All-Decade Team. Ferrante accomplished all he did without having the benefit of going to college or playing a single down of college football.

Born in Camden, New Jersey, on March 9, 1916, Jack Anthony Ferrante moved with his family to South Philadelphia at the age of six, before eventually settling with them in the Overbrook section of West Philadelphia as a teenager. Dropping out of high school during his sophomore year, Ferrante began working in local supermarkets to help support his family. In explaining his decision years later, Ferrante stated, "It was the middle of the depression, and I was old enough and big enough to help the family by working. I tried to work and continue school at the same time—I was in my sophomore year of trade school—but a situation came up where the principal wouldn't approve my working. So, I quit school and went to work full time . . . I was going to go back to school after a year, but, after being out that long, it seemed more difficult. I always regretted not finishing."

Instead of returning to school, Ferrante began playing sandlot football in local leagues, signing with Seymour of the Eastern Pennsylvania Football Conference, for whom he played end from 1934 to 1938. Describing his earliest days on the gridiron, Ferrante recalled, "Sports always were important to me, and I began playing for Seymour soon after quitting school. It

Jack Ferrante's outstanding pass-catching earned him a spot on the NFL 1940s All-Decade Team.
Courtesy of MEARSOnlineAuctions.com

was good football. . . . With the depression, a lot of guys hadn't gone to college, so we had some pretty good ballplayers. I was doing pretty good myself. I could always catch the ball."

Revealing many years later that his father had other options as well, Ferrante's son, Joe, said, "He could play every sport. He was offered contracts by the Yankees in baseball and the Celtics in basketball."

But, with football remaining his first love, Ferrante elected to continue pursuing his dream of playing in the National Football League, eventually earning a tryout with the Eagles in 1939. Recalling his first exposure to the pro game, Ferrante stated, "After Jim Lewro talked Bert Bell into giving me a tryout in '39, I went to camp with the Eagles. Right away, I felt that my sandlot background wasn't good enough for the NFL. It wasn't so much my ability as it was experience, but I gave it my best shot."

Although the Eagles did not offer Ferrante a spot on their roster, their farm team, the Wilmington Clippers, signed him to a contract. Ferrante then spent most of the next five years playing at the minor-league level, although he also appeared in three games with the Eagles in 1941. Looking back at his brief stint in Philadelphia, Ferrante said, "After a couple of decent years in the American Association, I took another shot at the Eagles in 1941. This time I made the team, but I really didn't play that much. I caught only two passes that year. . . . Then it was back to Wilmington for more 'seasoning' during '42 and '43, but I was back in Philly to stay in 1944."

Joining the Eagles for good at the rather advanced age of 28 in 1944, Ferrante recalled, "Once I made the team, I never gave not going to college a lot of thought. The other guys on the club didn't say much, either. . . . Even though I didn't go to college, one thing they used to do at the Eagles' home games really made me feel good. When the players were introduced before the game, as we'd run through the goal posts, the P.A. announcer would give their name and college. With me, it was, 'From the sandlots of South Philadelphia, left end, Jack Ferrante.' They'd cheer like crazy for me; I got a special feeling from that."

Establishing himself as a starter midway through the 1944 campaign, Ferrante made just three receptions for 66 yards and one touchdown. However, he proved to be far more productive the following year, when, in addition to recording the only interception of his career on defense, he caught 21 passes and ranked among the league leaders with 464 receiving yards, seven TD catches, and an average of 22.1 yards per reception, earning in the process Second-Team All-Pro recognition. After having another solid all-around year in 1946, Ferrante played exclusively on offense the remainder of his career, contributing significantly to Eagle teams that won three division titles and two league championships. Performing especially well for Philadelphia's NFL championship teams of 1948 and 1949, Ferrante placed near the top of the league rankings with seven TD catches in the first of those campaigns, before making 34 receptions for 508 yards and five touchdowns the following year.

Blessed with good size and speed, the 6'1", 205-pound Ferrante possessed outstanding athletic ability, with his size and strength often allowing him to run over would-be tacklers, and his quickness enabling him to run away from them. In addressing Ferrante's skill set, Eagles head coach Greasy Neale proclaimed, "Not one out of five million boys could play in this league without college or high school experience. Jack is the exception. He can catch the football as well as any receiver in the league, and he knows what to do with the ball once he has it."

Ferrante continued his outstanding play in 1950, establishing career-high marks in receptions (35) and receiving yards (588). However, when the Eagles refused to meet his salary demands at season's end, they sold his contract to the Detroit Lions, prompting Ferrante to announce his retirement. Recounting the events that took place at the time, Ferrante said, "I had a decent year. I caught 35 passes, one more than in '49 and the most I ever caught in a season, but I knew the end of the line was near. They let me go in camp the next year. Detroit claimed me. I think I was in pretty good shape. I was still 6'1", 205 pounds, which I was when I first came up, but I was 34 years old and wanted $10,000 for the season. That was $2,500 more than I had made in '50. The Lions wouldn't do it, so I went to work full time with a brewery. I don't regret it. It's been a pretty good life for me."

Ferrante ended his career with 169 receptions, 2,884 receiving yards, 31 touchdowns, and an average of 17.1 yards per reception that ranks as the seventh-highest mark in franchise history among players with at least 100 catches. He is also tied with Brent Celek for the 11th most TD receptions in team annals.

Following his playing days, Ferrante spent 27 years working as a salesman for a brewing company, while also serving as a volunteer coach at Monsignor Bonner High School, which he led to two Philadelphia city championships, and, later, as head coach of the Wilmington (Delaware) Comets, who competed in the North American Football League during the 1960s. After retiring to private life in 1977, Ferrante lived another 29 years, passing away at the age of 90 on November 23, 2006, while residing in a nursing home in Yardley, Pennsylvania.

CAREER HIGHLIGHTS

Best Season

Ferrante performed extremely well in his final season with the Eagles, reaching career-high marks in receptions (35) and receiving yards (588), while also scoring three touchdowns. Nevertheless, he made his greatest overall impact in 1945, earning his lone All-Pro nomination by making 21 receptions, ranking among the league leaders with 464 receiving yards, seven TD catches, and an average of 22.1 yards per reception, and recording the only interception of his career.

Memorable Moments/Greatest Performances

Ferrante helped the Eagles forge a 31–31 tie with the Washington Redskins on October 8, 1944, by scoring his first career touchdown on a 45-yard pass from Roy Zimmerman.

Ferrante hooked up with Zimmerman again for a career-long 74-yard TD reception during a 28–14 victory over the Cleveland Rams on October 28, 1945.

Ferrante collaborated with Zimmerman twice on scoring plays that covered 26 and 65 yards during a 45–3 thrashing of the Pittsburgh Steelers on November 4, 1945.

Ferrante followed that up with another strong performance, recording touchdown receptions of 64 and 24 yards during a 38–17 Eagles win over the Giants on November 11, 1945.

Ferrante put the finishing touches on a 28–24 come-from-behind victory over the Redskins on October 27, 1946, by hauling in a 30-yard TD pass from Tommy Thompson in the fourth quarter of a contest the Eagles once trailed by a score of 24–0.

Ferrante helped lead the Eagles to a lopsided 32–0 victory over the Boston Yanks on November 16, 1947, by hooking up with Thompson on scoring plays that covered 54 and 14 yards.

Ferrante came up big for the Eagles in the 1947 division championship game, making five catches for 73 yards and one touchdown during a 21–0 win over the Pittsburgh Steelers.

Although the Eagles subsequently suffered a 28–21 defeat at the hands of the Chicago Cardinals in the 1947 NFL title game, Ferrante once again performed extremely well, amassing 73 yards on eight pass receptions.

Ferrante had the biggest day of his career in the 1948 regular-season finale, leading the Eagles to a 45–21 victory over the Detroit Lions by making seven receptions for 184 yards and three touchdowns, which came on plays that covered 66, 15, and 23 yards.

Nevertheless, Ferrante considered the Eagles' 7–0 win over the Chicago Cardinals in the 1948 NFL championship game to be the most memorable contest of his career, stating years later:

> I don't think I'll ever forget that game. Hell, they won't let me. Tommy Thompson and Greasy (Neale) always liked to give the opposition something to think about right away, so we worked all week on a pass play for our first play from scrimmage. It was called the "Ferrante Special." . . . I was to get as deep as fast as I could. They'd call it a fly pattern today. I broke from the line of scrimmage—our 35—and Tommy just let it fly. I grabbed it at their 20, went down, got up again, and ran in. . . . There was only one problem. The play was called back because of an offside penalty. I was really steaming about that. I went up to the ref and said, "Who the hell was offside?" You know, I was really going to line out the guy that cost us the six points. The ref said, "You." That shut me up!

Notable Achievements

- Surpassed 30 receptions and 500 receiving yards twice each.
- Made seven touchdown receptions twice.
- Averaged 22.1 yards per reception in 1945.
- Finished third in NFL in average yards per reception twice.
- Finished fourth in NFL in: receptions once; receiving yards once; and touchdown receptions twice.
- Three-time Eastern Division champion (1947, 1948, and 1949).
- Two-time NFL champion (1948 and 1949).
- 1945 Second-Team All-Pro selection.
- NFL 1940s All-Decade Team.

48

ANDRE WATERS

A hard-hitting safety who acquired the nickname "Dirty Waters" for the overly aggressive style of play he exhibited at times, Andre Waters spent 10 of his 12 NFL seasons in Philadelphia, starting at strong safety for the Eagles in eight of those. Considered by many to be the dirtiest player in the league, Waters earned that reputation by engaging in fisticuffs with the opposition, delivering late hits, and throwing his body at his opponents' knees. Yet, Waters also became known as one of the NFL's better safeties during his time in Philadelphia, making significant contributions to Eagle teams that captured one division title and made four playoff appearances. Recording more than 100 tackles in six straight seasons, Waters led the Eagles in that category four times, concluding his career with the second most stops in franchise history, with his consistently strong play earning him a spot on the franchise's 75th Anniversary Team. Nevertheless, Waters is largely remembered today for tragically taking his own life nearly 11 years after his playing career ended.

Born in the rural city of Belle Glade, Florida, on March 10, 1962, Andre Maurice Waters attended Pahokee High School, where he starred on the gridiron, earning him a scholarship to Cheyney University of Pennsylvania. Although Waters continued to excel on the football field while at Cheyney, gaining All-PSAC recognition as a senior in 1983, his small-college background caused all 28 pro teams to bypass him in the 1984 NFL Draft. Subsequently signed by the Eagles as an undrafted free agent, Waters spent his first two seasons in Philadelphia playing almost exclusively on special teams, making an extremely favorable impression on the coaching staff during that time with his willingness to sacrifice his body for the betterment of the team. Meanwhile, Waters preferred not to draw attention to himself off the playing field, revealing years later, "As a rookie, I was shy and introverted. I had a stammer, and I was too self-conscious about my speech impediment to do interviews. I took classes to lose the stammer and, eventually, I got over being so shy."

Inserted into the starting lineup in 1986 by new Eagles head coach Buddy Ryan, who very much appreciated his ferocious style of play, Waters blossomed under the tutelage of defensive coordinator Bud Carson, leading the team with six interceptions and 129 tackles. Performing well once again during the strike-shortened 1987 campaign, Waters picked off three

Andre Waters's 910 solo tackles rank as the second-highest total in franchise history.
Courtesy of George A. Kitrinos

passes and registered 112 tackles, before helping the Eagles win the NFC East title the following year by recording another three interceptions and finishing second in the league with 154 solo tackles. Waters surpassed 100 tackles in each of the next three seasons as well, with his team-leading 156 stops in 1991 gaining him First-Team All-NFC recognition for the only time in his career.

A fierce tackler and vicious hitter, Waters endeared himself to the hometown fans with his physical style of play, while simultaneously creating fear in his opponents. In discussing how he used his aggressiveness to his advantage, Waters said, "I have it built in me, and it doesn't take much to get me going. All I need is a little push . . . I'm an animal, a beast, and I admit it. But you know what? I've learned to use it to my advantage. I now have people who are afraid of me. I'm intimidating. If you can intimidate your opponent, half the job is already done."

At the same time, though, Waters's extreme physicality and practice of going after his opponents' knees, which often led to penalties and fines from the league office, caused him to develop a reputation as a dirty player that he addressed by saying, "I have a reputation as a dirty player, and it's something I have to live with. The reputation hurts a little bit, but I don't let it get to me. When I get on the field, I'm angry. I have to get fired up. It makes me more aggressive, and that's the edge I have."

However, Waters denied that he played outside the rules, stating, "I've been tackling low like this since I was playing JV in high school. It's kind of like smoking. You can't quit doing it in one day. If I was as big as a linebacker, I wouldn't have to go low. But I'm only 5-11 and 200 pounds. I'm not a big guy . . . I'm not a dirty player, either. I play by the rules. I believe that what goes around, comes around, and nobody has come around after me."

Waters added, "Off the field, I'm quiet, I stay home a lot, and I reach out to God. On the field, I'm a different person. I'm wild and crazy, but I play within the rules."

Former All-Pro lineman-turned-NFL-analyst Dan Dierdorf strongly disagreed with Waters's comments, though, saying, "He's one of the best safeties in the league, but he steps over the line. He's got a track record of going for the knees. Can there be any other intention than to injure when you go for someone's knees?"

Indeed, Waters's tackle of Los Angeles Rams quarterback Jim Everett in 1988 led to the creation of a new rule that prohibited defenders from hitting quarterbacks below the waist while they stood in the pocket. Unofficially termed the "Andre Waters Rule," the law put into place stipulated that a defensive player could not hit a quarterback below the waist after he released the ball in the pocket, and that the defender could not be more than one step away from the QB when he released the ball if he wished to make contact with him.

Although injuries limited Waters to just 15 games from 1992 to 1993, he remained a thorn in the side of offensive players whenever he took the field, recording a total of 111 tackles during that time. However, when Waters became a free agent following the conclusion of the 1993 campaign, the Eagles made little effort to re-sign him, prompting him to accept a two-year offer from the Arizona Cardinals. Waters left Philadelphia with career totals of 15 interceptions, 164 interception-return yards, 3½ sacks, three forced fumbles, 10 fumble recoveries, two touchdowns, and 910 solo tackles, with the last figure representing the second-highest total in team annals.

After assuming a part-time role in Arizona for two seasons, Waters announced his retirement at the end of 1995. He subsequently spent most of the next 10 years coaching at the collegiate level, serving at different times as a defensive backs coach and a defensive coordinator. Waters also did two tours of duty in the NFL as a coaching intern.

Sadly, while serving as defensive coordinator at Fort Valley State, Waters committed suicide on November 20, 2006, dying of a gunshot wound to the head at only 44 years of age. Although family and friends remained uncertain as to why Waters took his own life, neuropathologist Dr. Bennet Omalu, who subsequently studied his brain, stated that he suffered from chronic traumatic encephalopathy (CTE) likely brought on by the numerous concussions he sustained on the football field, which caused his brain tissue to degenerate into that of an 80-year-old man with Alzheimer's disease. Adding that the many blows delivered to Waters's head injured the part of his brain that regulates mood, Dr. Omalu said, "Football killed him."

EAGLES CAREER HIGHLIGHTS

Best Season

Waters performed extremely well for the Eagles in both 1988 and 1991, recording 154 solo tackles and three interceptions in the first of those campaigns, before earning First-Team All-NFC honors in the second by intercepting one pass and making a career-high 156 solo stops. However, he had his finest all-around season in 1986, when, in addition to leading the Eagles with 129 solo tackles, he recorded two sacks, a career-high six interceptions, and two fumble recoveries, which he returned for a total of 81 yards.

Memorable Moments/Greatest Performances

Waters scored what proved to be the game-winning touchdown of a 16–10 victory over the Washington Redskins on November 18, 1984, when he returned a Mark Moseley kickoff 89 yards for a TD late in the third quarter.

Although the Eagles lost to the Chicago Bears in overtime by a score of 13–10 on September 14, 1986, Waters recorded the first two interceptions and first sack of his career during the contest.

Waters earned NFC Defensive Player of the Week honors for his outstanding all-around play during a 33–27 overtime victory over the Los Angeles Raiders on November 30, 1986, finishing the contest with one interception, several tackles, and an 81-yard fumble return during the overtime session that led to the game-winning touchdown moments later. Looking back at his exceptional performance, Waters said, "I had a good game personally. I knocked some passes down and had a lot of tackles. I liked to lock up with the Raiders. You know, I was accused of playing the game rough, and that's the brand of football the Raiders have been famous for forever, so to come up with a big game against these guys was personally satisfying."

Waters contributed to a 28–23 win over the St. Louis Cardinals on November 1, 1987, by setting up an Eagles' touchdown with a 63-yard return of an intercepted pass.

Waters scored the only defensive touchdown of his career during a 24–17 victory over the Giants on December 3, 1989, when he took a lateral from William Frizzell after Reggie White caused a fumble by New York quarterback Phil Simms and ran the ball in from 3 yards out.

Notable Achievements

- Scored two touchdowns during career—one on fumble return and one on kickoff return.
- Intercepted six passes in 1986.
- Recorded more than 100 tackles six times.
- Finished second in NFL in solo tackles once and fumble-return yards once.
- Led Eagles in tackles four times.

- Ranks second in Eagles history with 910 solo tackles.
- 1988 division champion.
- 1986 Week 13 NFC Defensive Player of the Week.
- 1991 First-Team All-Conference selection.
- Named to Eagles 75th Anniversary Team in 2007.

49

— HERM EDWARDS —

Although Herman Edwards is remembered mostly by Philadelphia fans for one startling play he made that helped propel the Eagles into the playoffs in 1978, the team's longtime right cornerback accomplished a good deal more during his nine-year stay in the City of Brotherly Love. Leading the Eagles in interceptions three times, Edwards picked off a total of 33 passes over the course of his career, the fourth-highest figure in team annals. An extremely consistent performer, Edwards helped the Eagles advance to the playoffs four straight times, earning in the process All-NFC honors on two separate occasions. And, following the conclusion of his playing career, the colorful and charismatic Edwards became better known to football fans around the country for his contributions to the game as a coach and television network analyst.

Born in Fort Monmouth, New Jersey, on April 27, 1954, Herman Lee Edwards learned a great deal about life at a very young age from the obstacles his parents faced. The son of an African American father and a white German mother who met at an American Army base in Germany toward the end of World War II, young Herman learned that his parents had to send paperwork to Washington for permission to get married. And, once they received that permission, they had to sign a piece of paper acknowledging that their marriage would not be legal in the South. Looking back at how the relationship between his parents helped shape the man he eventually became, Edwards said, "They taught me a lot about people, about how to communicate. Don't go by what people look like, or where they came from. My whole upbringing was like that."

Growing up in Seaside, California, Edwards attended Monterey High School, where he earned a scholarship to the University of California with his outstanding play on the gridiron. Developing a bad reputation while at Cal, Edwards twice left the university due to problems he experienced with the coaching staff, forcing him to transfer to Peninsula Junior College for one year, before spending his senior year at San Diego State, whose head football coach, Claude Gilbert, later recalled the first time he saw the highly touted cornerback perform during practice: "We have him run the 40 (yard sprint), and he runs a 4.8. . . . We're thinking, 'There's something wrong; that can't be right.' So, we have him run it again. Another 4.8. So, we tried it one more time. He runs a 4.9. We're thinking, 'Oh, shoot, somebody sold us a bill of goods here.' Anyway, we started spring practice, and Herman couldn't run fast, but, boy, could he play."

Nevertheless, Edwards's lack of speed and somewhat questionable reputation caused all 28 teams to bypass him in the 1977 NFL Draft, with Edwards recalling years later, "I had a label as un-coachable and undisciplined. I had long hair, too, which didn't help. Then the scouts timed me and decided I was too slow. But what they couldn't measure was how competitive I was."

Edwards then added, "When you say I can't do something, that's fine. I like hearing that because it motivates me. This goes all the way back to when I was eight years old. I told the other kids in the neighborhood, 'You're gonna see me on TV someday. I'm gonna play in the NFL.' They laughed. I said, 'Okay, just wait and see.'"

Herm Edwards originally signed with the Eagles as an undrafted free agent.
Courtesy of Autographsmadeasy

After signing with the Eagles as an undrafted free agent, Edwards faced the daunting task of making the team, remembering, "My whole goal at that point was to make sure that every day in practice, I made a play. Some kind of play where the coach would go, 'Hmmm. That guy's making another play.'"

Edwards not only earned a roster spot, but he laid claim to the starting right cornerback job his first year in the league, after which he went on to tie for the team lead with six interceptions. Edwards followed that up with an exceptional sophomore season, concluding the 1978 campaign with a team-high seven picks, while also scoring the first of his two career touchdowns in the final minute of a game against the Giants on a 26-yard fumble return that turned an apparent 17–12 defeat into a 19–17 victory for the Eagles.

Recalling the success he experienced during the early stages of his career, Edwards, who stood 6 feet tall and weighed 194 pounds, said, "When you're a young player, people come at you. The thing I think I could do probably the best, and it was just a talent that the good Lord blessed me with, was being able to catch. I mean, I could catch a football. So, most of the time, if the ball was in my vicinity, if I could get my hands on it, I was going to catch it . . . I never went to knock a ball down. I always went to catch it. That was something that I always prided myself on as a player."

Maintaining a high level of play in subsequent seasons, Edwards helped the Eagles make four consecutive playoff appearances, with his consistently excellent play earning him All-Conference honors in both 1980 and 1982. Performing especially well during the strike-shortened 1982 campaign, Edwards finished second in the league with five interceptions in only nine games.

Edwards remained with the Eagles until incoming head coach Buddy Ryan cut him prior to the start of the 1986 season. In addition to picking off 33 passes during his time in Philadelphia, Edwards amassed 98 interception-return yards, recovered six fumbles, and scored two touchdowns. Extremely durable, Edwards started 135 consecutive games at right cornerback for the Eagles, never missing a game during his nine years with the club.

Looking back at Edwards's playing career, Dick Vermeil, who served as his head coach his first six years in the league, said, "When I think of Herman Edwards, I think of a guy who was a student of fundamentals, who understood and perfected technique. He was a 4.85 guy, but what the stop-watch didn't tell you was what a great athlete he was. Smooth turns, no

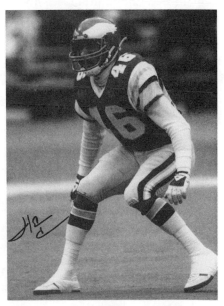

Edwards's last minute touchdown against the Giants in 1978 helped propel the Eagles into the playoffs.
Courtesy of Autographsmadeeasy

wasted motion. He could run with a much faster receiver because he didn't make fundamental mistakes. He was always in great position."

After leaving the Eagles, Edwards spent one more year in the league, splitting the 1986 campaign between the Atlanta Falcons and Los Angeles Rams, before announcing his retirement at season's end. Since retiring as an active player, Edwards has remained close to the game, serving on the coaching staffs of San Jose State University (1987–1989), the Kansas City Chiefs (1990–1995), and the Tampa Bay Buccaneers (1996–2000), before becoming head coach of the New York Jets in 2001. During his time in New York, Edwards became known for his motivational speeches and quotable statements made at press conferences, the most famous of which came after a Jets loss when he told the assembled media in no uncertain terms, "You play to win the game!"

After coaching the Jets for five seasons, Edwards assumed the mantle of leadership in Kansas City, where he remained head coach of the Chiefs for three years, before being relieved of his duties on January 23, 2009. He subsequently became an analyst at ESPN, serving as a member of that station's *NFL Live* program for the next nine years, informing and entertaining viewers with his knowledge of the sport and engaging personality. Edwards remained at ESPN until December 2017, when he accepted the position of head football coach at Arizona State University.

EAGLES CAREER HIGHLIGHTS

Best Season

Although Edwards earned Second-Team All-NFC honors in both 1980 and 1982, he had his best season for the Eagles in 1978, when he recorded a career-high seven interceptions and scored one of his two career touchdowns.

Memorable Moments/Greatest Performances

The seminal moment of Edwards's career occurred in Week 12 of the 1978 season, when he made a play that helped propel the Eagles into the playoffs for the first time in 18 years. With the Eagles trailing the Giants in the Meadowlands by a score of 17–12 on November 19, 1978, and only seconds remaining on the clock, New York quarterback Joe Pisarcik inexplicably attempted to hand the ball off to running back Larry Csonka instead of simply taking the snap from center and going to one knee. With the exchange between Pisarcik and Csonka resulting in a fumble, Edwards scooped up the loose football and returned it 26 yards for a touchdown that gave the Eagles a stunning 19–17 victory that helped keep their playoff hopes alive. The play, which subsequently became known as "The Miracle at the Meadowlands," resulted in New York's coaching staff being fired. Meanwhile, the Eagles went on to make the playoffs as a wild card with a record of 9-7.

Edwards also played a key role in the Eagles' 20–3 win over the Giants in that year's regular-season finale, helping them clinch a playoff berth by intercepting a pair of Pisarcik passes.

Edwards continued to torment the Giants on September 22, 1980, intercepting Phil Simms twice during a lopsided 35–3 Eagles victory.

Edwards had another big game against Minnesota in the divisional round of the 1980 playoffs, recording two of the five interceptions the Eagles registered against Tommy Kramer during a 31–16 win over the Vikings.

Although the Eagles lost to the Giants in overtime by a score of 16–10 on September 29, 1985, Edwards scored the only other points of his career when he returned an interception 3 yards for a touchdown.

Notable Achievements

- Scored two defensive touchdowns during career.
- Recorded at least five interceptions in a season three times.
- Finished second in NFL with five interceptions in 1982.
- Led Eagles in interceptions three times.
- Ranks fourth in Eagles history with 33 career interceptions.
- 1980 division champion.
- 1980 NFC champion.
- Two-time Second-Team All-Conference selection (1980 and 1982).

50

— FRED BARNETT —

A big-play receiver who had the ability to score from anywhere on the field, Fred Barnett used his speed and athleticism to establish himself as one of the NFL's most dangerous wideouts during his time in Philadelphia. One of the league's top deep threats from 1990 to 1995, Barnett surpassed 60 receptions three times and 1,000 receiving yards twice for the Eagles, leading them in each of those categories on three separate occasions. Barnett, who averaged 20 yards per reception as a rookie in 1990, recorded the NFL's longest touchdown that year when he collaborated with Randall Cunningham on a 95-yard scoring play. And, two years later, Barnett earned his lone Pro Bowl selection by ranking among the league leaders with 1,083 receiving yards.

Born in Shelby, Mississippi, on June 17, 1966, Fred Lee Barnett Jr. grew up in nearby Gunnison, Mississippi, a small town with a population of just 702 people. Despite being blessed with outstanding athletic ability, Barnett did not play football until his senior year at Rosedale High School out of respect for his mother's concerns for his health and safety. As a result, even though Barnett displayed a considerable amount of talent in his one year of high school ball, he failed to receive a full scholarship offer from any major colleges, prompting him to eventually enroll at Arkansas State University.

A four-year starter at Arkansas State, Barnett compiled relatively modest numbers in the Red Wolves' run-oriented offense, concluding his college career with only 95 receptions, 1,571 receiving yards, and 11 touchdowns. Yet, Barnett's college coach, Larry Lacewell, had high praise for his former protégé, saying, "It's a funny thing with Fred. He runs on his heels, so it's kind of ugly looking, but he can fly. We ran the wishbone, so we hardly ever threw the ball, which hurt his stock, too. No one knew how good he was."

Nevertheless, after Barnett posted a time of 4.42 seconds in the 40-yard dash at the NFL Scouting Combine, he didn't fall too far in the 1990 NFL Draft, with the Eagles selecting him in the third round, with the 77th overall pick. Although fearful of the big city when he first arrived in Philadelphia, Barnett performed well his first year in the league, earning a spot on the NFL All-Rookie Team by making 36 receptions for 721 yards and eight touchdowns, with his average of 20 yards per reception placing him third in the league rankings. Improving upon his overall numbers the following year, Barnett led the Eagles with 62 catches and 948 receiving yards, while also finishing second on the team with four touchdown receptions.

Becoming something of a man-about-town by his second season in Philadelphia, Barnett moved to the middle of the

Fred Barnett amassed more than 1,000 receiving yards for the Eagles twice. Courtesy of George A. Kitrinos

city, where he often attended the theater in his stylish Italian-cut suits, later saying, "I liked the atmosphere in the city, I liked the energy. When I got to know the people, they were really nice. I felt at home. I bought a bike and rode it everywhere. I rode it to and from the stadium rather than take my car."

Barnett also began to take ballet lessons, stating, "I saw a lot of parallels between football and dance. The two are related in a number of ways; the dedication, the physical discipline. Both require athletes. Dancers have a lot of injuries just like we do. I was more tired in a dance class than I've ever been in a football game."

Barnett's experience with ballet, combined with his speed and exceptional leaping ability, helped transform him into one of the NFL's most exciting receivers, enabling him to make an inordinate number of acrobatic catches, particularly along the sidelines, where he excelled at out-leaping defenders. The 6-foot, 204-pound Barnett also possessed good strength and outstanding vision, making him a superb open-field runner.

Taking his game up a notch in 1992, Barnett helped the Eagles earn a wild card playoff berth by making 67 receptions for 1,083 yards and six touchdowns, with his 1,083 receiving yards placing him fifth in the league rankings. After missing most of the ensuing campaign with a knee injury, Barnett returned to top form in 1994, establishing career-high marks in receptions (78) and receiving yards (1,127), while also making five TD catches.

Barnett spent just one more year in Philadelphia, making 48 receptions for 585 yards and five touchdowns in 1995, before signing with the Miami Dolphins as a free agent at season's end. He subsequently suffered through two injury-marred years in Miami, totaling just 53 receptions for 728 yards and four touchdowns for the Dolphins, before announcing his retirement when they released him following the conclusion of the 1997 campaign. Barnett ended his career with 361 receptions, 5,362 receiving yards, and 32 touchdowns, making 308 catches for 4,634 yards and 28 touchdowns in his six seasons with the Eagles.

Following his playing days, Barnett briefly served as tight ends coach for the Memphis Maniax of the short-lived XFL in 2001, before returning to Philadelphia, where he currently lives with his wife, Lindsay, and their four children. In addition to working as a project manager for Lindsay's corporate event-planning company, Planning Factory International, Barnett devotes much of his time to philanthropic causes in the Philadelphia area.

Barnett led the Eagles in receptions and receiving yards three times each.
Courtesy of George A. Kitrinos

Looking back fondly at his years with the Eagles, Barnett says, "If you play in Philly, you better produce and make plays . . . if we lost, I would be in tears . . . I know what this sport means to the City of Philadelphia . . . that's why I feel I had a great relationship with the fans, because I played Eagles football with a passion."

Unfortunately, several years after he retired as an active player, Barnett began experiencing physical problems likely related to the time he spent on the gridiron, stating during a 2012 interview with 94WIP's Anthony Gargano and Glen Macnow, "One thing that I've been experiencing is headaches, every other day. It's just a headache, that no matter what you take, it doesn't go away. For me to experience that, and for me to see that, it's very scary. . . . This is real. There have been times when I'm walking down the street, and everything that's supposed to be steel starts to move. So, for me to lose that control, it's very, very scary. And it's very, very real to me."

Barnett continued, "I'm not stressed about anything, I eat right, I exercise. And, for me to experience the certain things that I experience, it's really scary. What if 15–20 years from now this just gets worse, and worse, and worse?"

EAGLES CAREER HIGHLIGHTS

Best Season

Barnett had an outstanding season for the Eagles in 1994, posting career-high marks in receptions (78) and receiving yards (1,127), while also scoring five touchdowns. However, he earned his lone trip to the Pro Bowl two years earlier, concluding the 1992 campaign with 67 receptions, 1,083 receiving yards, and six touchdowns, making that the most impressive season of his career.

Memorable Moments/Greatest Performances

Although the Eagles lost their September 30, 1990, meeting with the Indianapolis Colts by a score of 24–23, Barnett made the first touchdown reception of his career during the contest when he collaborated with Randall Cunningham on a 21-yard scoring play in the second quarter.

Barnett topped 100 receiving yards for the first time in his career during a 32–24 victory over the Minnesota Vikings on October 15, 1990, finishing the game with four catches for 114 yards and one touchdown, which came on a 40-yard connection with Cunningham in the fourth quarter.

Barnett helped lead the Eagles to a 32–30 win over the Cleveland Browns on November 10, 1991, by making eight receptions for 146 yards and one touchdown, which came on a 70-yard hookup with Jim McMahon in the second quarter.

Barnett starred during a 31–14 victory over the Phoenix Cardinals on September 13, 1992, catching eight passes for 193 yards and two touchdowns, which came on connections of 17 and 71 yards with Randall Cunningham.

Barnett had another big day on December 13, 1992, making nine receptions for 161 yards during a 20–17 overtime win over the Seattle Seahawks.

Barnett excelled during the Eagles' 36–20 win over New Orleans in the 1992 NFC wild card game, making four catches for 102 yards and two touchdowns, which came on 57- and 35-yard connections with Randall Cunningham.

Barnett contributed to a 21–6 victory over the Houston Oilers on October 24, 1994, by making five receptions for 187 yards and one touchdown, which covered 53 yards.

Barnett proved to be a huge factor in the 1995 NFC wild card game, catching eight passes for 109 yards and one touchdown during the Eagles' 58–37 win over the Detroit Lions.

Although the Eagles lost to the Buffalo Bills by a score of 30–23 on December 2, 1990, Barnett experienced the most memorable moment of his career during the contest when he hooked up with Randall Cunningham on a career-long 95-yard touchdown reception. Recalling the play years later, Barnett said, "The play called for me to run a clear route, or a 'go route' to clear the middle of the field. I ran 60 yards and actually stopped. When I saw Randall come out of a pile, he started pointing to me. So, I kept running and literally saw the ball appear from out of the sky. When I jumped to get it, my defender fell down and I scored."

Yet, Barnett claims that he experienced his greatest joy as a pro during a TV timeout in a game played during his rookie season, stating, "I can remember actually being on the field in my fourth game ever playing against the Indianapolis Colts. From the time that I was in college and went through the four years there and then went through the Combine and all the things to prepare myself to be in the NFL, it seemed like there was this time-lapse . . . I remember there was a television timeout and I kind of stood there and looked around, and it was almost as if reality had hit me. It was just me accepting the fact that I had made it to where I wanted to be. I had accomplished being in the pros. It took this timeout for me to stand there and start to look around. It was like, 'Oh, my gosh, I really made it. I'm here.'"

Notable Achievements

- Surpassed 60 receptions three times, topping 70 catches once (78 in 1994).
- Surpassed 1,000 receiving yards twice.

- Made eight touchdown receptions in 1990.
- Made longest reception in NFL in 1990 (95 yards).
- Finished third in NFL with average of 20 yards per reception in 1990.
- Finished fifth in NFL with 1,083 receiving yards in 1992.
- Led Eagles in receptions and receiving yards three times each.
- Member of 1990 NFL All-Rookie Team.
- 1992 Pro Bowl selection.

SUMMARY
AND HONORABLE MENTIONS
(THE NEXT 25)

Having identified the 50 greatest players in Philadelphia Eagles history, the time has come to select the best of the best. Based on the rankings contained in this book, the members of the Eagles' all-time offensive and defensive teams are listed below. Our squads include the top player at each position, with the offense featuring the three best wide receivers and the two best running backs, tackles, and guards. Even though Jerry Sisemore spent most of his career playing right tackle, I inserted him at guard because he started at that post for two seasons. A third-down back has been included as well. Meanwhile, the defense features two ends, two tackles, two outside linebackers, one middle linebacker, two cornerbacks, and a pair of safeties. Special teams have been accounted for as well, with a place-kicker, punter, kickoff returner, and punt returner also being included. The punter was taken from the list of honorable mentions that will soon follow.

OFFENSE		DEFENSE	
Player	Position	Player	Position
Donovan McNabb	QB	Reggie White	LE
Steve Van Buren	RB	Vic Sears	LT
Wilbert Montgomery	RB	Al Wistert	RT
LeSean McCoy	3rd-Down RB	Clyde Simmons	RE
Pete Retzlaff	TE	Chuck Bednarik	LOLB
Pete Pihos	WR	Bill Bergey	MLB
Tommy McDonald	WR	Maxie Baughan	ROLB
Harold Carmichael	WR	Troy Vincent	LCB
Jason Peters	LT	Brian Dawkins	S
Jerry Sisemore	LG	Bill Bradley	S

OFFENSE		DEFENSE	
Player	Position	Player	Position
Chuck Bednarik	C	Eric Allen	RCB
Bucko Kilroy	RG	Adrian Burk	P
Bob Brown	RT	Brian Westbrook	PR
David Akers	PK		
Timmy Brown	KR		

Although I limited my earlier rankings to the top 50 players in Eagles history, many other fine players have worn a Philadelphia uniform over the years, some of whom narrowly missed making the final cut. Following is a list of those players deserving of an honorable mention. These are the men I deemed worthy of being slotted into positions 51 to 75 in the overall rankings. Where applicable and available, the statistics they compiled during their time in Philadelphia are included, along with their most notable achievements while playing for the Eagles.

51—STAN WALTERS (OT: 1975–1983)

Courtesy of SportsMemorabilia.com

Notable Achievements

- Missed just four games in nine seasons, at one point starting 122 consecutive contests.
- 1980 division champion.
- 1980 NFC champion.
- Two-time Pro Bowl selection (1978 and 1979).
- 1979 Second-Team All-Pro selection.
- Two-time First-Team All-Conference selection (1978 and 1979).
- 1977 Second-Team All-Conference selection.
- Inducted into Philadelphia Eagles Hall of Fame in 1991.

52—TOM BROOKSHIER (DB; 1953, 1956–1961)

Courtesy of MEARSOnlineAuctions.com

Career Numbers

20 Interceptions, 193 Interception-Return Yards, 8 Fumble Recoveries.

Notable Achievements

- Intercepted eight passes in 1953.
- Led Eagles in interceptions twice.
- 1960 Eastern Division champion.
- 1960 NFL champion.
- Two-time Pro Bowl selection (1959 and 1960).
- 1960 First-Team All-Pro selection.
- 1959 Second-Team All-Pro selection.
- Two-time First-Team All-Conference selection (1959 and 1960).
- Inducted into Philadelphia Eagles Hall of Fame in 1989.
- #40 retired by Eagles.

53—DUCE STALEY (RB; 1997–2003)

Courtesy of PristineAuction.com

Eagle Numbers

4,807 Yards Rushing, 275 Receptions, 2,498 Receiving Yards, 7,305 Yards from Scrimmage, 8,451 All-Purpose Yards, 22 Rushing Touchdowns, 32 Touchdowns, 4.0 Rushing Average.

Notable Achievements

- Rushed for more than 1,000 yards three times.
- Surpassed 50 receptions three times.
- Surpassed 500 receiving yards twice.
- Amassed more than 1,000 yards from scrimmage four times.
- Amassed more than 1,000 all-purpose yards five times.
- Led Eagles in rushing four times.
- Ranks among Eagles career leaders in: rushing yardage (5th); rushing TDs (9th); yards from scrimmage (6th); and all-purpose yards (7th).
- Three-time division champion (2001, 2002, and 2003).
- 2000 Week 1 NFC Offensive Player of the Week.

54—FLOYD PETERS (DT; 1964–1969)

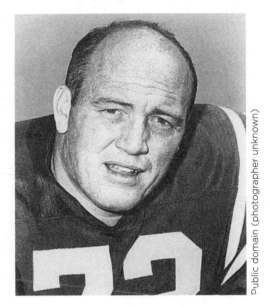

Public domain (photographer unknown)

Notable Achievements

- Recorded 8½ sacks in 1966.
- Named Most Outstanding Lineman at 1967 Pro Bowl.
- Three-time Pro Bowl selection (1964, 1966, and 1967).
- Three-time First-Team All-Conference selection (1964, 1966, and 1967).

55—NORM WILLEY (DE; 1950–1957)

Public domain (photographer unknown)

Notable Achievements

- Scored two defensive touchdowns during career.
- Recorded two interceptions during career.
- Recovered nine fumbles during career.
- Recorded "unofficial" total of eight sacks vs. Giants on October 26, 1952.
- Two-time Pro Bowl selection (1954 and 1955).
- Two-time First-Team All-Pro selection (1953 and 1954).
- 1955 Second-Team All-Pro selection.

56—JEREMY MACLIN (WR; 2009–2012, 2014)

Courtesy of PristineAuction.com

Eagle Numbers

343 Receptions, 4,771 Receiving Yards, 36 Touchdown Receptions, 5,048 All-Purpose Yards.

Notable Achievements

- Surpassed 50 receptions five times, topping 70 catches twice and 80 catches once.
- Surpassed 1,000 receiving yards once (1,318 in 2014).
- Surpassed 1,000 all-purpose yards twice.
- Recorded 10 touchdown receptions twice.
- Led Eagles in receptions three times and receiving yards twice.
- Ranks among Eagles career leaders in: pass receptions (10th); pass receiving yardage (10th); and touchdown receptions (7th).
- 2010 division champion.
- 2014 Week 9 NFC Offensive Player of the Week.
- 2014 Pro Bowl alternate.

57—CARL HAIRSTON (DE; 1976–1983)

Courtesy of SportsMemorabilia.com

Notable Achievements

- Recorded more than 10 sacks once.
- Recorded more than 100 tackles twice.
- Led NFC with 15 sacks in 1979.
- Led Eagles in sacks twice.
- Ranks fourth in Eagles history with 55½ career sacks.
- Missed just one game in eight seasons.
- 1980 division champion.
- 1980 NFC champion.
- Three-time Second-Team All-NFC selection (1979, 1980, and 1981).

58—DON BURROUGHS (DB; 1960–1964)

Public domain (William Jacobellis)

Eagle Numbers

29 Interceptions, 351 Interception-Return Yards, 7 Fumble Recoveries.

Notable Achievements

- Recorded at least seven interceptions three times.
- Amassed more than 100 interception-return yards once (124 in 1960).
- Finished third in NFL in interceptions twice.
- Led Eagles in interceptions four times.
- Ranks among Eagles career leaders in interceptions (6th) and interception-return yards (8th).
- 1960 Eastern Division champion.
- 1960 NFL champion.
- Three-time Second-Team All-Pro selection (1960, 1961, and 1962).

59—RICKY WATTERS (RB; 1995–1997)

Courtesy of George A. Kitrinos

Eagle Numbers

3,794 Yards Rushing, 161 Receptions, 1,318 Receiving Yards, 31 Rushing Touchdowns, 32 Touchdowns, 3.9 Rushing Average.

Notable Achievements

- Surpassed 1,000 yards rushing three straight times.
- Surpassed 1,500 yards from scrimmage three straight times.
- Topped 50 receptions twice and 400 receiving yards three times.
- Scored more than 10 touchdowns twice.
- Led NFL with 1,855 yards from scrimmage in 1996.
- Finished third in NFL with 13 rushing touchdowns in 1996.
- Ranks among Eagles career leaders in: rushing yardage (7th); rushing touchdowns (6th); and rushing attempts (6th).
- Two-time NFC Offensive Player of the Week.
- Two-time Pro Bowl selection (1995 and 1996).
- Two-time Second-Team All-Conference selection (1995 and 1996).
- Pro Football Reference All-1990s Second Team.

60—DENNIS HARRISON (DE; 1978–1984)

Courtesy of SportsMemorabilia.com

Eagle Numbers

34 "Official" Sacks, 6 Fumble Recoveries.

Notable Achievements

- Recorded more than 10 sacks three times.
- Finished second in NFL with 10½ sacks in 1982.
- Led Eagles in sacks three times.
- 1980 division champion.
- 1980 NFC champion.
- 1982 Pro Bowl selection.
- 1982 Second-Team All-Conference selection.

61—BEN HAWKINS (WR: 1966–1973)

Public domain (photographer unknown)

Career Numbers

261 Receptions, 4,764 Receiving Yards, 32 Touchdown Receptions, 33 Touchdowns, 5,356 All-Purpose Yards.

Notable Achievements

- Surpassed 50 receptions once (59 in 1967).
- Surpassed 1,000 receiving yards once (1,265 in 1967).
- Made 10 touchdown receptions in 1967.
- Averaged more than 20 yards per reception twice.
- Led NFL with 1,265 receiving yards in 1967.
- Finished third in NFL with 10 TD receptions and 1,515 all-purpose yards in 1967.
- Led Eagles in receptions twice and receiving yards twice.
- Ranks among Eagles career leaders in: pass receiving yardage (11th); touchdown receptions (tied-9th); and average yards per catch (2nd).
- Made 92-yard TD reception vs. Giants on September 22, 1968.
- Made four TD receptions vs. Steelers on September 28, 1969.

62—JIM RINGO (C; 1964–1967)

Public domain (photographer unknown)

Notable Achievements

- Started 56 straight games at center.
- Three-time Pro Bowl selection (1964, 1965, and 1967).
- Two-time Second-Team All-Pro selection (1964 and 1966).
- NFL 1960s All-Decade Team.
- Pro Football Reference All-1960s First Team.
- Inducted into Philadelphia Eagles Hall of Fame in 1987.

63—KEITH BYARS (RB; 1986–1992)

Courtesy of SportsMemorabilia.com

Eagle Numbers

2,672 Yards Rushing, 371 Receptions, 3,532 Receiving Yards, 17 Rushing Touchdowns, 13 Touchdown Receptions, 5 Touchdown Passes, 3.6 Rushing Average.

Notable Achievements

- Surpassed 1,000 yards from scrimmage twice.
- Surpassed 50 receptions five times, topping 70 catches twice.
- Surpassed 500 receiving yards five times, topping 700 yards three times.
- Scored 10 touchdowns in 1988.
- Finished third in NFL with 81 receptions in 1990.
- Led Eagles in receptions three times and receiving yards twice.
- Ranks seventh in Eagles history in pass receptions.
- 1988 division champion.
- 1990 Second-Team All-Conference selection.

64—WILLIAM THOMAS (LB; 1991–1999)

Courtesy of George A. Kitrinos

Eagle Numbers

720 Tackles (595 solo), 33 Sacks, 18 Interceptions, 233 Interception-Return Yards, 8 Forced Fumbles, 10 Fumble Recoveries, 3 Touchdowns.

Notable Achievements

- Recorded more than 100 tackles twice.
- Recorded at least five sacks four times.
- Surpassed 100 interception-return yards once (104 in 1995).
- Finished third in NFL with seven interceptions in 1995.
- Led Eagles in tackles twice, interceptions once, and interception-return yards once.
- Ranks eighth in Eagles history in tackles.
- Two-time NFC Defensive Player of the Week.
- Two-time Pro Bowl selection (1995 and 1996).
- 1995 Second-Team All-Pro selection.
- 1995 Second-Team All-Conference selection.

65—ASANTE SAMUEL (DB; 2008–2011)

Courtesy of Donna T. Jeffries via Wikipedia

Eagle Numbers

23 Interceptions, 304 Interception-Return Yards, 135 Tackles, 2 Forced Fumbles, 3 Fumble Recoveries, 2 Touchdowns.

Notable Achievements

- Recorded at least seven interceptions twice.
- Amassed more than 100 interception-return yards once (117 in 2009).
- Led NFL with nine interceptions in 2009.
- Finished second in NFL with seven interceptions in 2010.
- Led Eagles in interceptions three times.
- Tied for 10th all-time on Eagles in interceptions.
- 2010 division champion.
- Three-time Pro Bowl selection (2008, 2009, and 2010).
- 2009 Second-Team All-Pro selection.

66—HAROLD JACKSON (WR; 1969–1972)

Courtesy of Sportsmemorabilia.com

Eagle Numbers

215 Receptions, 3,493 Receiving Yards, 21 Touchdown Receptions.

Notable Achievements

- Surpassed 60 receptions twice.
- Surpassed 1,000 receiving yards twice.
- Made nine touchdown receptions in 1969.
- Led NFL in receptions once and receiving yards twice.
- Led Eagles in receptions three times and receiving yards four times.
- Two-time Pro Bowl selection (1969 and 1972).
- 1972 Second-Team All-Pro selection.
- 1972 First-Team All-Conference selection.

67—LITO SHEPPARD (DB; 2002–2008)

Courtesy of DynastySports.com

Eagle Numbers

18 Interceptions, 460 Interception-Return Yards, 253 Tackles, 2 Sacks, 3 Forced Fumbles, 1 Fumble Recovery, 3 Touchdowns.

Notable Achievements

- Recorded at least five interceptions twice.
- Amassed more than 100 interception-return yards twice.
- Led NFL with two interception-return touchdowns in 2004.
- Finished second in NFL with 157 interception-return yards in 2006.
- Finished third in NFL with 172 interception-return yards in 2004.
- Led Eagles in interceptions twice.
- Ranks among Eagles career leaders in interception-return yards (4th) and touchdown interceptions (tied-3rd).
- Four-time division champion (2002, 2003, 2004, and 2006).
- 2004 NFC champion.
- Three-time NFC Defensive Player of the Week.
- October 2004 NFC Defensive Player of the Month.
- Two-time Pro Bowl selection (2004 and 2006).
- 2004 First-Team All-Pro selection.
- 2004 First-Team All-NFC selection.

68—KEITH JACKSON (TE; 1988–1991)

Courtesy of MainlineAutographs.com

Eagle Numbers

242 Receptions, 2,756 Receiving Yards, 20 Touchdown Receptions.

Notable Achievements

- Surpassed 50 receptions three times, topping 80 catches once (81 in 1988).
- Surpassed 800 receiving yards once (869 in 1988).
- Led Eagles in receptions once and receiving yards once.
- 1988 division champion.
- Member of 1988 NFL All-Rookie Team.
- Three-time Pro Bowl selection (1988, 1989, and 1990).
- Three-time First-Team All-Pro selection (1988, 1989, and 1990).
- Three-time First-Team All-NFC selection (1988, 1989, and 1990).

69–MARION CAMPBELL (DE, DT; 1956–1961)

Courtesy of BoxingTreasures.com

Notable Achievements

- Recorded two interceptions and five fumble recoveries.
- 1960 Eastern Division champion.
- 1960 NFL champion.
- Two-time Pro Bowl selection (1959 and 1960).
- 1960 First-Team All-Conference selection.

70—ADRIAN BURK (QB, P; 1951–1956)

Courtesy of RMYAuctions.com

Eagle Numbers

6,203 Yards Passing, 55 Touchdown Passes, 77 Interceptions, 47.6 Completion Percentage, 54.4 QBR, 305 Yards Rushing, 6 Rushing TDs, 16,122 Yards Punting, 41.0 Yards Per Punt Average, Career Long—75 Yards.

Notable Achievements

- Passed for more than 1,000 yards three times.
- Threw more than 20 touchdown passes once.
- Posted QBR above 80.0 once.
- Averaged more than 42 yards per punt twice.
- Led NFL quarterbacks with 23 TD passes and QBR of 80.4 in 1954.
- Led NFL with 2,843 yards punting in 1956.
- Finished third in NFL in average yards per punt twice.
- Ranks among Eagles career leaders in touchdown passes (tied-10th) and total punt yardage (2nd).
- Two-time Pro Bowl selection (1954 and 1955).

71—IRV CROSS (DB; 1961–1965)

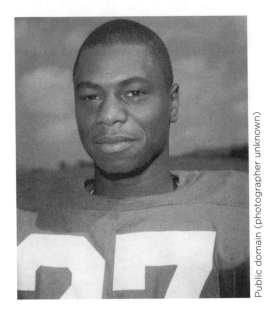

Public domain (photographer unknown)

Eagle Numbers

16 Interceptions, 198 Interception-Return Yards, 9 Fumble Recoveries, 1 Touchdown, 158 Punt-Return Yards, 745 Kickoff-Return Yards, 1,112 All-Purpose Yards.

Notable Achievements

- Amassed more than 100 interception-return yards once (109 in 1964).
- Two-time Pro Bowl selection (1964 and 1965).

72—LANE JOHNSON (OT; 2013–2018)

Courtesy of Keith Allison

Notable Achievements

- Two-time division champion (2013 and 2017).
- 2017 NFC champion.
- Super Bowl LII champion.
- 2017 Pro Bowl selection.
- 2017 First-Team All-Pro selection.

73—SAM BAKER (PK, P; 1964–1969)

Public domain (photographer unknown)

Eagle Numbers

90 Field Goals Made, 153 Field Goal Attempts, 58.8 percent Field Goal Percentage, 475 Points Scored, 9,933 Yards Punting, Averaged 40.7 Yards Per Punt.

Notable Achievements

- Posted field goal percentage above 70 percent once (72.0 in 1966).
- Averaged more than 42 yards per punt once (42.3 in 1964).
- Led NFL in field goal percentage once.
- Finished second in NFL in field goals made once.
- Finished third in NFL in field goal percentage once.
- Ranks among Eagles career leaders in: field goals made (3rd); points scored (3rd); and total punt yardage (11th).
- Two-time Pro Bowl selection (1964 and 1968).
- 1966 First-Team All-Conference selection.

74—MALCOLM JENKINS (DB: 2014–2018)

Courtesy of Keith Allison

Eagle Numbers

11 Interceptions, 289 Interception-Return Yards, 418 Tackles, 3 Sacks, 8 Forced Fumbles, 5 Fumble Recoveries, 4 Touchdowns.

Notable Achievements

- Has recorded more than 100 tackles once (104 in 2015).
- Led NFL with two interception-return touchdowns in 2016.
- Has led Eagles in tackles twice.
- Ranks second in Eagles history with four touchdown interceptions.
- 2017 division champion.
- 2017 NFC champion.
- Super Bowl LII champion.
- Two-time NFC Defensive Player of the Week.
- Three-time Pro Bowl selection (2015, 2017, and 2018).

75—NICK FOLES (QB: 2012–2014, 2017–2018)

Courtesy of Matthew Straubmuller

Eagle Numbers

8,703 Yards Passing, 58 Touchdown Passes, 23 Interceptions, 62.9 Completion Percentage, 93.2 Passer Rating, 351 Yards Rushing, 4 Rushing TDs.

Notable Achievements

- Passed for 2,891 yards in 2013.
- Threw 27 touchdown passes and only two interceptions in 2013.
- Completed more than 60 percent of passes three times, topping 70 percent once.
- Led NFL quarterbacks with passer rating of 119.2 in 2013.
- Holds Eagles single-season record for highest passer rating (119.2 in 2013).
- Holds Eagles career record for highest passer rating (minimum 200 attempts).
- Ranks among Eagles career leaders in: pass attempts (8th); pass completions (7th); pass completion percentage (2nd—minimum 1,000 attempts); passing yards (9th); and touchdown passes (8th).

- Two-time division champion (2013 and 2017).
- 2017 NFC champion.
- Super Bowl LII champion.
- November 2013 NFC Offensive Player of the Month.
- Three-time NFC Offensive Player of the Week.
- Super Bowl LII MVP.
- 2013 Pro Bowl selection.

GLOSSARY

ABBREVIATIONS AND STATISTICAL TERMS

ALL-PURPOSE YD: All-purpose yards.

C: Center.

COMP %: Completion percentage. The number of successfully completed passes divided by the number of passes attempted.

FS: Free Safety.

INTS: Interceptions. Passes thrown by the quarterback that are caught by a member of the opposing team's defense.

KR: Kickoff returner.

LCB: Left cornerback.

LE: Left end.

LG: Left guard.

LOLB: Left-outside linebacker.

LT: Left tackle.

MLB: Middle linebacker.

NT: Nose tackle.

P: Punter.

PK: Placekicker.

PR: Punt returner.

QB: Quarterback.

QBR: Quarterback rating.

RB: Running back.

RCB: Right cornerback.

RE: Right end.

REC: Receptions.

REC YD: Reception yards.

RG: Right guard.

ROLB: Right-outside linebacker.

RT: Right tackle.

RUSH YD: Rushing yards.

SS: Strong Safety.

ST: Special teams.

TD PASSES: Touchdown passes.

TD RECS: Touchdown receptions.

TDS: Touchdowns.

TE: Tight end.

WR: Wide receiver.

YD from SCRIMMAGE: Yards from scrimmage.

YD PASSING: Yards passing.

YD RUSHING: Yards rushing.

— BIBLIOGRAPHY —

BOOKS

Bowen, Les. *Philadelphia Eagles: The Complete Illustrated History*. Minneapolis: MVP Books, 2011.

Carlson, Chuck. *100 Things Eagles Fans Should Know & Do Before They Die*. Chicago: Triumph Books, 2011.

Didinger, Ray, and Robert S. Lyons. *The Eagles Encyclopedia*. Philadelphia: Temple University Press, 2005.

Eckel, Mark. *The Men and Moments That Made the Philadelphia Eagles: The Big 50*. Chicago: Triumph Books, 2016.

Forbes, Gordon. *Tales from the Philadelphia Eagles Sideline*. New York: Sports Publishing, 2002.

Jones, Danny. *More Distant Memories: Pro Football's Best Ever Players of the 50's, 60's, and 70's*. Bloomington, IN: AuthorHouse, 2006.

Zimniuch, Fran. *Eagles: Where Have You Gone?* New York: Sports Publishing, 2004.

VIDEOS

Greatest Ever: NFL Dream Team. Polygram Video, 1996.
SportsCentury—Chuck Bednarik. ESPN, 2000.

WEBSITES

Biographies, online at Hickoksports.com
(hickoksports.com/hickoksports/biograph)

Biography from Answers.com
(answers.com)

Biography from Jockbio.com
(jockbio.com)

CapitalNewYork.com
(capitalnewyork.com)

CBSNews.com
(cbsnews.com)

ESPN.com
(sports.espn.go.com)

Hall of Famers, online at profootballhof.com
(profootballhof.com/hof/member)

Inductees from LASportsHall.com
(lasportshall.com)

LATimes.com
(articles.latimes.com)

Newsday.com
(newsday.com)

NYDailyNews.com
(nydailynews.com/new-york)

NYTimes.com
(nytimes.com)

PhiladelphiaEagles.com
(philadelphiaeagles.com)

Pro Football Talk from nbcsports.com
(profootballtalk.nbcsports.com)

SpTimes.com
(sptimes.com)

StarLedger.com
(starledger.com)

SunSentinel.com
(articles.sun-sentinel.com)

The Players, online at Profootballreference.com
(pro-football-reference.com/players)